SPARKNOTES
101

Psychology

SPARK NOTES

A DIVISION OF BARNES & NOBLE PUBLISHING

SPARKNOTES is a registered trademark of SparkNotes LLC

Spark Publishing
A Division of Barnes & Noble Publishing
120 Fifth Avenue
New York, NY 10011
www.sparknotes.com

ISBN 13: 978-1-4114-0332-1
ISBN 10: 1-4114-0332-0

Please submit changes or report errors to
www.sparknotes.com/errors

Printed and bound in the United States.

Library of Congress Cataloging-in-Publication Data

SparkNotes 101 psychology.-- 1st ed.
      p. cm.
  Includes bibliographical references and index.
  ISBN 1-4114-0332-0
  1. Psychology--Textbooks. I. Title: SparkNotes one hundred one
psychology. II. Title: SparkNotes one hundred and one psychology. III.
Title: One hundred one psychology. IV. Title: One hundred and one
psychology. V. SparkNotes LLC.
  BF121.S63 2005
  150--dc22
                                    2005009728

Contents

Acknowledgments

SparkNotes would like to thank the following writers and contributors:

Ruvanee Vilhauer, Ph.D.
Clinical Psychologist

Terry E. Christenson, Ph.D.
Associate Professor of Psychology, Tulane University

Ruth Wienclaw, Ph.D.
Textbook Developer, Adjunct Professor of Psychology, Old Dominion University

Flannery G. Stevens
I/O Psychology Doctoral Student, Tulane University

Shinah K. Chang, A.B., Harvard University

Joel Grossbard
Child Psychology Doctoral Student, Washington University

Anaxos, Inc.

A Note from SparkNotes

Welcome to the SparkNotes 101 series! This book will help you succeed in your introductory college course for Psychology.

Every component of this study guide has been designed to help you process the material more quickly and score higher on your exams. You'll see lots of headings, lists, charts, and, most important, no long blocks of text. This format will allow you to quickly situate yourself and easily get to the crux of your course.

We've included these features to help you get the most out of this book:

Introduction: Before diving in to the major chapters, you may want to get a broader view of the field of psychology. The Introduction will discuss five major psychological perspectives and describe several types of psychologists, as well as the sort of work they do.

Chapters 1–17: Each chapter provides a clarification of material included in your textbook. Key features include:

- **Sidebars:** Throughout the text, these call out main points and provide related information.

- **Examples:** These clarify main points and show you how psychological concepts are played out in the real world.

- **Key Terms:** Key terms are bolded throughout each chapter for quick scanning and reviewing. Definitions for these terms are compiled in the Glossary at the back of the book.

- **Summary:** This end-of-chapter summary provides an at-a-glance recap of major topics and ideas.

- **Sample Test Questions:** Fifteen study questions, both short answer and multiple choice, show you the kinds of questions you are most likely to encounter on a test and give you the chance to practice what you've learned. Answers are provided.

Major Figures: This section provides a summary of the major figures presented in the chapters, along with their significance. Names of major figures are bolded in each chapter the first time they appear.

Glossary: Review key terms and refresh your memory at exam time with the Glossary at the end of the book.

Index: Use the index to make navigation easier or to look up specific concepts, terms, and people.

We hope *SparkNotes 101: Psychology* helps you, gives you confidence, and occasionally saves your butt! Your input makes us better. Let us know what you think or how we can improve this book at *www.sparknotes.com/comments*.

Introduction

Psychology is essentially the study of behavior. Behavior is rooted in many cognitive and physiological processes, and psychologists aim to understand these processes in order to solve real-world problems and make sense of our feelings and actions. Almost every aspect of the humanities and the sciences influences psychology in some way, and an understanding of psychology can be valuable in virtually any field, including business, medicine, law, education, and the arts.

A study of psychology begins with an understanding of several major ideas, each of which is covered in a chapter of this book. These major ideas include:

- Genetics
- Development
- Consciousness
- Memory
- Intelligence
- Motivation
- Stress
- Treatment

- The Brain
- Perception
- Learning
- Cognition
- Emotion
- Personality
- Psychological Disorders
- Social Psychology

Five Main Perspectives

All psychologists share a foundation of knowledge that is rooted in the work of early psychologists, such as Freud, Piaget, and Erikson. They also share a commitment to upholding ethical standards in their reserach as well as a belief in the scientific approach. However, psychologists may differ from one another in the kinds of questions they ask and how they view the data they find. Therefore, psychology can be divided into roughly five main perspectives: biological, learning, cognitive, sociocultural, and psychodynamic.

BIOLOGICAL PSYCHOLOGY

Biological psychologists are interested in the relationship between the body and the mind. They study the structure of the brain and the central nervous system, the parts of the brain and their specific functions, and the links between physical and emotional reactions to events. Biological psychology also focuses on biological processes such as hunger, thirst, and fatigue.

LEARNING PSYCHOLOGY

Learning is generally defined as a long-lasting change in the way a person or an animal acts or thinks that is attributable to experience. One of the most important concepts in learning psychology is conditioning, which is the way people associate events and outcomes. Learning psychologists study stimuli, reinforcement, and the connections between learning and behavior.

COGNITIVE PSYCHOLOGY

Cognitive psychology is the study of memory, perception, thought, and other mental processes. Cognitive psychologists are concerned with people's emotions, intelligence, motivations, and problem-solving skills. Any subject connected to knowledge, intellect, or the mind in general can fall into the realm of cognitive psychology.

SOCIOCULTURAL PSYCHOLOGY

Sociocultural psychology concerns the ways that social environment and cultural beliefs shape our lives. Other people, cultural norms, and societal expectations all play a large role in how we act and think and what we consider "normal." Sociocultural psychologists study all aspects of society and culture, including authority, group dynamics, religious beliefs, gender roles and stereotypes, and the day-to-day things, such as food and work, that make up our lives.

PSYCHODYNAMIC PSYCHOLOGY

Psychodynamic psychology is the study of unconscious desires and motives, those ideas and feelings that seem to motivate our actions without our being aware of it, including inner conflicts, instincts, and early memories. Psychodynamic psychology stems from psychoanalysis, a field of study that has its roots in the work of Sigmund Freud.

Psychologists who adhere to each of these schools of thought might not always answer questions the same way—their different approaches to psychology will often lead them to find different causes and explanations for behavior. Most psychologists rely on more than one perspective, but these core belief systems influence the way psychologists create, ask, and investigate questions about behavior and the brain.

Types of Psychologists

Psychologists practice and study psychology in many different ways, though all psychologists generally focus on research, practice, teaching, or a combination of the three. A Ph.D. is not required for many psychology careers, though many psychologists obtain one.

CLINICAL AND COUNSELING PSYCHOLOGISTS

Clinical and counseling psychologists work with adults or children either individually or in groups to help them deal with problems such as depression, anxiety, relationship troubles, or major mental illnesses. They may also be psychology professors or social workers.

COGNITIVE PSYCHOLOGISTS

Cognitive psychologists are mostly interested in learning about perception, language, learning, and decision-making. Conducting research is often their primary work.

DEVELOPMENTAL PSYCHOLOGISTS

Developmental psychologists are sometimes described as studying people "womb to tomb." They are interested in how people develop, grow, or change throughout the entire life span, from prenatal development to death. Developmental psychologists often specialize in one life stage, such as adolescence, or on changes that occur during life, such as changes in memory.

EXPERIMENTAL PSYCHOLOGISTS

Experimental psychologists are deeply involved in scientific investigation and spend their careers gathering data about different psychological phenomena. Many experimental psychologists specialize in one particular area of research.

INDUSTRIAL-ORGANIZATIONAL (I/O) PSYCHOLOGISTS

Industrial-organizational psychologists usually practice in the workplace and are concerned with employee productivity, management, hiring, and quality-of-life issues at work.

NEUROPSYCHOLOGISTS

Neuropsychologists study brain function. They are concerned with brain/behavior relationships, normal brain functioning, and the effects of accident or illness on the brain.

QUANTITATIVE PSYCHOLOGISTS

Quantitative psychologists are experts in all of the methods and statistics of psychological research. They design and evaluate tests, experiments, and other psychological data.

*　　*　　*　　*　　*　　*　　*　　*

This is by no means a comprehensive list of psychology occupations. Psychologists are employed in virtually every industry, and the study of psychology is not only the application of the scientific method to the investigation of problems but also a philosophy for understanding life itself.

Research Methods in Psychology

- Psychological Research
- The Scientific Method
- Research Methods
- Ethical Considerations
- Interpreting Data

1

Psychologists do more than just wonder about human behavior: they conduct research to understand exactly why people think, feel, and behave the way they do. Like other scientists, psychologists use the scientific method, a standardized way to conduct research. A scientific approach is used in order to avoid bias or distortion of information. After collecting data, psychologists organize and analyze their observations, make inferences about the reliability and significance of their data, and develop testable hypotheses and theories.

Psychological research has an enormous impact on all facets of our lives, from how parents choose to discipline their children to how companies package and advertise their products to how governments choose to punish or rehabilitate criminals. Understanding how psychologists do research is vital to understanding psychology itself.

Psychological Research

Psychologists study a wide range of topics, such as language development in children and the effects of sensory deprivation on behavior. They use scientifically testable models and methods to conduct their research.

DESCRIBING RESEARCH

Scientists use the following terms to describe their research:

- **Variables:** the events, characteristics, behaviors, or conditions that researchers measure and study.
- **Subject** or **participant:** an individual person or animal a researcher studies.
- **Sample:** a collection of subjects researchers study. Researchers use samples because they cannot study the entire population.
- **Population:** the collection of people or animals from which researchers draw a sample. Researchers study the sample and generalize their results to the population.

THE PURPOSE OF RESEARCH

Psychologists have three main goals when doing research:

- To find ways to measure and describe behavior
- To understand why, when, and how events occur
- To apply this knowledge to solving real-world problems

The Scientific Method

Psychologists use the scientific method to conduct their research. The **scientific method** is a standardized way of making observations, gathering data, forming theories, testing predictions, and interpreting results.

Researchers make observations in order to describe and measure behavior. After observing certain events repeatedly, researchers come up with a theory that explains these observations. A **theory** is an explanation that organizes separate pieces of information in a coherent way. Researchers generally develop a theory only after they have collected a lot of evidence and made sure their research results can be reproduced by others.

> *EXAMPLE: A psychologist observes that some college sopho-*
> *mores date a lot, while others do not. He observes that some*
> *sophomores have blond hair, while others have brown hair.*
> *He also observes that in most sophomore couples at least one*
> *person has brown hair. In addition, he notices that most of*
> *his brown-haired friends date regularly, but his blond friends*
> *don't date much at all. He explains these observations by the-*
> *orizing that brown-haired sophomores are more likely to*
> *date than those who have blond hair. Based on this theory,*
> *he develops a hypothesis that more brown-haired sopho-*
> *mores than blond sophomores will make dates with people*
> *they meet at a party.*
> *   He then conducts an experiment to test his hypothesis. In*
> *his experiment, he has twenty people go to a party, ten with*
> *blond hair and ten with brown hair. He makes observations*
> *and gathers data by watching what happens at the party and*
> *counting how many people of each hair color actually make*
> *dates. If, contrary to his hypothesis, the blond-haired people*
> *make more dates, he'll have to think about why this occurred*
> *and revise his theory and hypothesis. If the data he collects*
> *from further experiments still do not support the hypothesis,*
> *he'll have to reject his theory.*

MAKING RESEARCH SCIENTIFIC

Psychological research, like research in other fields, must meet certain criteria in order to be considered scientific. Research must be:

- Replicable
- Falsifiable
- Precise
- Parsimonious

Research Must Be Replicable

Research is **replicable** when others can repeat it and get the same results. When psychologists report what they have found through their research, they also describe in detail how they made their discoveries. This way, other psychologists can repeat the research to see if they can replicate the findings.

After psychologists do their research and make sure it's replicable, they develop a theory and translate the theory into a precise hypothesis. A **hypothesis** is a testable prediction of what will happen given a certain set of conditions. Psychologists test a hypothesis by using a specific research method, such as **naturalistic observation**, a **case study**, a **survey**, or an **experiment**. If the test does not confirm the hypothesis, the psychologist revises or rejects the original theory.

How Psychologists Do Scientific Research

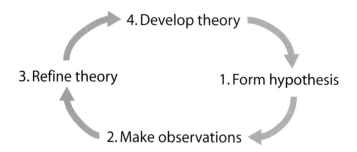

4. Develop theory

3. Refine theory

1. Form hypothesis

2. Make observations

A Good Theory A good theory must do two things: organize many observations in a logical way and allow researchers to come up with clear predictions to check the theory.

Research Must Be Falsifiable

A good theory or hypothesis also must be **falsifiable**, which means that it must be stated in a way that makes it possible to reject it. In other words, we have to be able to prove a theory or hypothesis wrong. Theories and hypotheses need to be falsifiable because all researchers can succumb to the confirmation bias. Researchers who display **confirmation bias** look for and accept evidence that supports what they want to believe and ignore or reject evidence that refutes their beliefs.

> *EXAMPLE: Some people theorize that the Loch Ness Monster not only exists but has become intelligent enough to elude detection by hiding in undiscovered, undetectable, underwater caves. This theory is not falsifiable. Researchers can never find these undiscovered caves or the monster that supposedly hides in them, and they have no way to prove this theory wrong.*

Research Must Be Precise

By stating hypotheses precisely, psychologists ensure that they can replicate their own and others' research. To make hypotheses more precise, psychologists use operational definitions to define the variables they study. **Operational definitions** state exactly how a variable will be measured.

> *EXAMPLE: A psychologist conducts an experiment to find out whether toddlers are happier in warm weather or cool weather. She needs to have an operational definition of happiness so that she can measure precisely how happy the toddlers are. She might operationally define happiness as "the number of smiles per hour."*

Research Must Be Parsimonious

The **principle of parsimony**, also called **Occam's razor**, maintains that researchers should apply the simplest explanation possible to any set of observations. For instance, psychologists try to explain results by using well-accepted theories instead of elaborate new hypotheses. Parsimony prevents psychologists from inventing and pursuing outlandish theories.

> **Parsimony** Parsimonious means "being thrifty or stingy." A person who values parsimony will apply the thriftiest or most logically economical explanation for a set of phenomena.

EXAMPLE: Suppose a student consistently falls asleep in her statistics class. She theorizes that before each class, her statistics professor secretly sprays her seat with a nerve gas that makes her very drowsy. If she had applied the principle of parsimony, she would not have come up with this theory. She can account for her sleepiness with a much simpler and more likely explanation: she finds statistics boring.

Research Methods

Psychologists use many different methods for conducting research. Each method has advantages and disadvantages that make it suitable for certain situations and unsuitable for others.

DESCRIPTIVE OR CORRELATIONAL RESEARCH METHODS

Case studies, surveys, naturalistic observation, and laboratory observation are examples of **descriptive** or **correlational research methods**. Using these methods, researchers can describe different events, experiences, or behaviors and look for links between them. However, these methods do not enable researchers to determine causes of behavior.

Remember: **correlation is *not* the same as causation.** Two factors may be related without one *causing* the other to occur. Often, a third factor explains the correlation.

EXAMPLE: A psychologist uses the survey method to study the relationship between balding and length of marriage. He finds that length of marriage correlates with baldness. However, he can't infer from this that being bald causes people to stay married longer. Instead, a third factor explains the correlation: both balding and long marriages are associated with old age.

Measuring Correlation

A **correlation coefficient** measures the strength of the relationship between two variables. A correlation coefficient is always a number between –1 and +1. The sign (+ or –) of a correlation coefficient indicates the nature of the relationship between the variables.

A **positive correlation** (+) means that as one variable increases, the other does too.

> *EXAMPLE: The more years of education a person receives, the higher his or her yearly income is.*

A **negative correlation** (–) means that when one variable increases, the other one decreases.

> *EXAMPLE: The more hours a high school student works during the week, the fewer A's he or she gets in class.*

The higher the correlation coefficient, the stronger the correlation. A +0.9 or a –0.9 indicates a very strong correlation; a +0.1 or a –0.1 indicates a very weak correlation. A correlation of 0 means that no relationship exists between two variables.

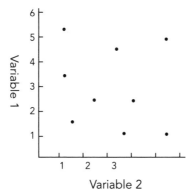

No correlation
Correlation coefficient = 0

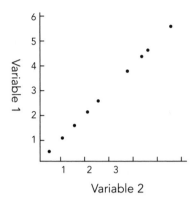

Perfect positive correlation
Correlation coefficient = +1

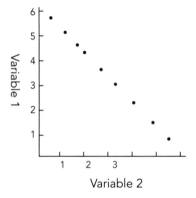

Perfect negative correlation
Correlation coefficient = −1

Common correlational research methods include case studies, surveys, naturalistic observation, and laboratory observation.

Case Studies

In a **case study**, a researcher studies a subject in depth. The researcher collects data about the subject through interviews, direct observation, psychological testing, or examination of documents and records about the subject.

Surveys

A **survey** is a way of getting information about a specific type of behavior, experience, or event. When using this method, researchers give people questionnaires or interview them to obtain information.

When subjects fill out surveys about themselves, the data is called **self-report data**. Self-report data can be misleading because subjects may do any of the following:

- Lie intentionally

- Give answers based on wishful thinking rather than the truth

- Fail to understand the questions the survey asks

- Forget parts of the experience they need to describe

Naturalistic Observation

When using naturalistic observation, researchers collect information about subjects by observing them unobtrusively, without interfering with them in any way. Researchers create a record of events and note relationships among those events. With naturalistic observation, researchers face the challenge of getting a clear view of events without becoming noticeable to the subjects.

Laboratory Observation

As the name implies, researchers perform **laboratory observation** in a laboratory rather than in a natural setting. In laboratory observation, researchers can use sophisticated equipment to measure and record subjects' behavior. They can use one-way mirrors or hidden recording devices to observe subjects more freely while remaining hidden themselves. Unlike observation in a natural setting, laboratory observation offers researchers some degree of control over the environment.

PSYCHOLOGICAL TESTS

Researchers use **psychological tests** to collect information about personality traits, emotional states, aptitudes, interests, abilities, values, or behaviors. Researchers usually **standardize** these tests, which means they create uniform procedures for giving and scoring them. When scoring a test, researchers often compare subjects' scores to **norms**, which are established standards of performance on a test. A well-constructed standardized test can evaluate subjects better than self-report data.

Reliability

A test has good **reliability** if it produces the same result when researchers administer it to the same group of people at different times. Researchers determine a test's **test-retest reliability** by giving the test to a group of people and then giving the test again to the same group of people at a later time. A reliable test will produce approximately the same results on both occasions.

Psychologists also use **alternate-forms reliability** to determine a test's reliability. They measure alternate-forms reliability by giving one version of a test to a group of people and then giving another version of the same test to the same group of people. A reliable test will produce roughly the same results no matter which version of the test is used.

Validity

A test is **valid** if it actually measures the quality it claims to measure. There are two types of validity:

- **Content validity** is a test's ability to measure all the important aspects of the characteristic being measured. An intelligence test wouldn't have good content validity if it measured only verbal intelligence, since nonverbal intelligence is an important part of overall intelligence.

- **Criterion validity** is fulfilled when a test not only measures a trait but also predicts another criterion of that trait. For example, one criterion of scholastic aptitude is academic performance in college. A scholastic aptitude test would have good criterion validity if it could predict college grade point averages.

Overview of Research Methods

Research method	Advantages	Disadvantages
Survey	• Yields a lot of information • Provides a good way to generate hypotheses • Can provide information about many people since it's cheap and easy to do	• Provides information about behavior that can't be observed directly • Relies on self-report data, which can be misleading • Doesn't allow conclusions about cause-and-effect relationships
Case study	• Provides a good way to generate hypotheses • Yields data that other methods can't provide	• Sometimes gives incomplete information • Sometimes relies only on self-report data, which can be misleading • Can be subjective and thus may yield biased results • Doesn't allow conclusions about cause-and-effect relationships
Naturalistic observation	• Can be useful for generating hypotheses • Provides information about behavior in the natural environment	• Sometimes yields biased results • May be difficult to do unobtrusively • Doesn't allow conclusions about cause-and-effect relationships
Laboratory observation	• Enables use of sophisticated equipment for measuring and recording behavior • Can be useful for generating hypotheses	• Sometimes yields biased results • Carries the risk that observed behavior is different from natural behavior • Doesn't allow conclusions about cause-and-effect relationships
Test	• Gives information about characteristics such as personality traits, emotional states, aptitudes, interests, abilities, values, and behaviors	• Requires good reliability and validity before it can be used • Doesn't allow conclusions about cause-and-effect relationships
Experiment	• Identifies cause-and-effect relationships • Distinguishes between placebo effects and real effects of a treatment or drug	• Can be artificial, so results may not generalize to real-world situations

EXPERIMENTS

Unlike correlational research methods or psychological tests, **experiments** can provide information about cause-and-effect relationships between variables. In an experiment, a researcher manipulates or changes a particular variable under controlled conditions while observing resulting changes in another variable or variables. The researcher manipulates the **independent variable** and observes the **dependent variable**. The dependent variable may be affected by changes in the independent variable. In other words, the dependent variable depends (or is thought to depend) on the independent variable.

Independent
variable

Dependent
variable

Experimental and Control Groups

Typically, a researcher conducting an experiment divides subjects into an experimental group and a control group. The subjects in both groups receive the same treatment, with one important difference: the researcher manipulates one part of the treatment in the experimental group but does *not* manipulate it in the control group. The variable that is manipulated is the independent variable. The researcher can then compare the experimental group to the control group to find out whether the manipulation of the independent variable affected the dependent variable.

Often, subjects in the control group receive a placebo drug or treatment, while subjects in the experimental group receive the real drug or treatment. This helps researchers to figure out what causes the observed effect: the real drug or treatment, or the subjects' expectation that they will be affected.

> EXAMPLE: *Suppose a researcher wants to study the effect of drug A on subjects' alertness. He divides 100 subjects into two groups of 50, an experimental group and a control group. He dissolves drug A in saline solution and injects it into all the subjects in the experimental group. He then gives all the control group subjects an injection of only saline solution. The independent variable in this case is drug A, which he administers only to the experimental group. The control group receives a placebo: the injection of saline solution. The dependent variable is alertness, as measured by performance on a timed test. Any effect on alertness that appears only in the experimental group is caused by the drug. Any effect on alertness that appears in both the experimental and control groups could be due to the subjects' expectations or to extraneous variables, such as pain from the injection.*

Extraneous Variables

Ideally, subjects in the experimental and control groups would be identical in every way except for the variables being studied. In practice, however, this would be possible only if researchers could clone people. So researchers try to make groups with subjects that are similar in all respects that could potentially influence the dependent variable. Variables other than the independent variable that could affect the dependent variable are called **extraneous variables**.

One way to control extraneous variables is to use random assignment. When researchers use **random assignment**, they create experimental and control groups in a way that gives subjects an equal chance of being placed in either group. This guarantees the two groups' similarity.

Disadvantages of Experiments

The main disadvantage of experiments is that they usually don't fully reflect the real world. In an experiment, researchers try to control variables in order to show clear causal links. However, to exert control in this way, researchers must simplify an event or a situation, which often makes the situation artificial.

Another disadvantage of experiments is that they can't be used to study everything. Sometimes researchers can't control variables enough to use an experiment, or they find that doing an experiment would be unethical—that is, it would be painful or harmful in some way to the subjects being studied.

BIAS IN RESEARCH

Bias is the distortion of results by a variable. Common types of bias include sampling bias, subject bias, and experimenter bias.

Sampling Bias

Sampling bias occurs when the sample studied in an experiment does not correctly represent the population the researcher wants to draw conclusions about.

EXAMPLE: A psychologist wants to study the eating habits of a population of New Yorkers who have freckles and are between the ages of eighteen and forty-five. She can't possibly study all people with freckles in that age group, so she must study a sample of people with freckles. However, she can generalize her results to the whole population of people with freckles only if her sample is representative of the population. If her sample includes only white, dark-haired males who are college juniors, her results won't generalize well to the entire population she's studying. Her sample will reflect sampling bias.

Subject Bias

Research subjects' expectations can affect and change the subjects' behavior, resulting in **subject bias**. Such a bias can manifest itself in two ways:

- A **placebo effect** is the effect on a subject receiving a fake drug or treatment. Placebo effects occur when subjects believe they are getting a real drug or treatment even though they are not. A **single-blind** experiment is an experiment in which the subjects don't know whether they are receiving a real or fake drug or treatment. Single-blind experiments help to reduce placebo effects.

- The **social desirability bias** is the tendency of some research subjects to describe themselves in socially approved ways. It can affect self-report data or information people give about themselves in surveys.

Experimenter Bias

Experimenter bias occurs when researchers' preferences or expectations influence the outcome of their research. In these cases, researchers see what they want to see rather than what is actually there.

A method called the **double-blind** procedure can help experimenters prevent this bias from occurring. In a double-blind procedure, neither the experimenter nor the subject knows which subjects come from the experimental group and which come from the control group.

Ethical Considerations

In the past, researchers performed all kinds of questionable experiments in the name of science. For example, in one famous experiment, psychologist Stanley Milgram led his subjects to believe that they were giving painful electric shocks to other people. Many people consider this experiment unethical because it caused the subjects emotional discomfort. Today, researchers must abide by basic ethical norms when conducting research. Most important, they must consider whether they might harm their human or animal subjects while doing research.

Ethics Ethics refers to a system of moral values or the way people distinguish right from wrong. The American Psychological Association (APA) requires all its members to adhere to its code of ethics, which applies to the treatment of both humans and animals.

RESEARCH WITH HUMAN SUBJECTS

Researchers must get informed consent from their subjects before beginning research. **Informed consent** means that subjects must know enough about the research to decide whether to participate, and they must agree to participate voluntarily. Furthermore, researchers have an ethical obligation to prevent physical and mental harm to their subjects. If there is any risk of harm, they must warn subjects in advance. Researchers also must allow subjects to withdraw from a study at any time if they wish to stop participating. Finally, researchers have an obligation to protect the anonymity of their subjects.

Some psychological research cannot be done when subjects are fully informed about the purpose of the research, because people sometimes behave differently when under observation. To study people's normal behavior, researchers sometimes have to deceive subjects. Deception is considered ethical only if:

- The study will give researchers some valuable insight
- It would be impossible to do the study without deception
- Subjects can learn the truth about the study's purpose and methods afterward

RESEARCH WITH ANIMAL SUBJECTS

Although most psychological research involves human subjects, some psychologists study animal subjects instead of or in addition to humans. Research with animal subjects has helped psychologists do the following:

- Learn facts about animal species

- Find ways to solve human problems

- Study issues that can't be studied using human subjects for practical or ethical reasons

- Refine theories about human behavior

- Improve human welfare

Many people question the ethics of animal research because it can involve procedures such as deprivation, pain, surgery, and euthanasia. Psychologists have ethical obligations to treat animal subjects humanely and to do research on animals only when the benefits of the research are clear.

People who are against animal research maintain three arguments:

- Animals should have the same rights as humans.

- Society should enact safeguards to protect the safety and welfare of animals.

- Researchers should not put the well-being of humans above the well-being of animals.

Interpreting Data

After psychologists develop a theory, form a hypothesis, make observations, and collect data, they end up with a lot of information, usually in the form of numerical data. The term **statistics** refers to the analysis and interpretation of this numerical data. Psychologists use statistics to organize, summarize, and interpret the information they collect.

DESCRIPTIVE STATISTICS

To organize and summarize their data, researchers need numbers to describe what happened. These numbers are called **descriptive statistics**. Researchers may use **histograms** or **bar graphs** to show the way data are distributed. Presenting data this way makes it easy to compare results, see trends in data, and evaluate results quickly.

> *EXAMPLE: Suppose a researcher wants to find out how many hours students study for three different courses. Each course has 100 students. The researcher does a survey of ten students in each of the courses. On the survey, he asks the students to write down the number of hours per week they spend studying for that course. The data look like this:*

Hours of Study per Week

Course A		Course B		Course C	
Student	Hours per week	Student	Hours per week	Student	Hours per week
Joe	9	Hannah	5	Meena	6
Peter	7	Ben	6	Sonia	6
Zoey	8	Iggy	6	Kim	7
Ana	8	Louis	6	Mike	5
Jose	7	Keesha	7	Jamie	6
Lee	9	Lisa	6	Ilana	6
Joshua	8	Mark	5	Lars	5
Ravi	9	Ahmed	5	Nick	20
Kristen	8	Jenny	6	Liz	5
Loren	1	Erin	6	Kevin	6

To get a better sense of what these data mean, the researcher can plot them on a bar graph. Histograms or bar graphs for the three courses might look like this:

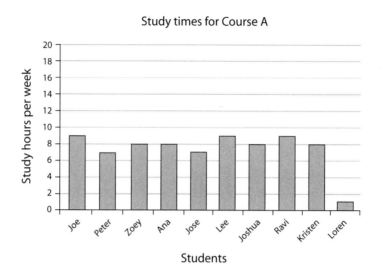

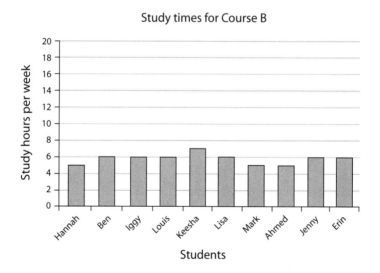

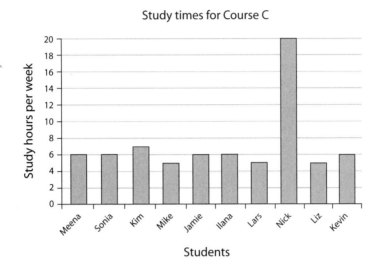

Study times for Course C

Measuring Central Tendency

Researchers summarize their data by calculating **measures of central tendency**, such as the mean, the median, and the mode. The most commonly used measure of central tendency is the **mean**, which is the arithmetic average of the scores. The mean is calculated by adding up all the scores and dividing the sum by the number of scores.

However, the mean is not a good summary method to use when the data include a few extremely high or extremely low scores. A distribution with a few very high scores is called a **positively skewed distribution**. A distribution with a few very low scores is called a **negatively skewed distribution**. The mean of a positively skewed distribution will be deceptively high, and the mean of a negatively skewed distribution will be deceptively low. When working with a skewed distribution, the median is a better measure of central tendency. The **median** is the middle score when all the scores are arranged in order from lowest to highest.

Another measure of central tendency is the mode. The **mode** is the most frequently occurring score in a distribution.

Statistics Statistics is a branch of mathematics. Psychologists need a solid foundation in math to describe, analyze, and summarize the results of their research.

Measuring Variation

Measures of variation tell researchers how much the scores in a distribution differ. Examples of measures of variation include the range and the standard deviation. The **range** is the difference between the highest and the lowest scores in the distribution. Researchers calculate the range by subtracting the lowest score from the highest score. The **standard deviation** provides more information about the amount of variation in scores. It tells a researcher the degree to which scores vary around the mean of the data.

INFERENTIAL STATISTICS

After analyzing statistics, researchers make inferences about how reliable and significant their data are.

> EXAMPLE: *The researcher's survey of the students in three classes showed differences in how long the students studied for each course. The mean number of hours for students in Course A was about eight hours, and for students in Courses B and C, the average was about six hours. Does this mean Course A requires the most hours of study? Were the differences the researcher observed in study time real or just due to chance? In other words, can he generalize from the samples of students he surveyed to the whole population of students? He needs to determine the reliability and significance of his statistics.*

If researchers want to generalize confidently from a sample, the sample must fulfill two criteria:

* It must be large and varied enough to be representative.

* It must not have much variation in scores.

Researchers can use **inferential statistics** to figure out the likelihood that an observed difference was just due to chance. If it's unlikely that the difference was due to chance, then the observed difference could be considered statistically significant. Psychologists usually consider a result to be **statistically significant** if such a result occurs just by chance 5 or fewer times out of every 100 times a study is done. They call this statistical significance at the p ≤ .05 level (p less than or equal to point oh-five).

However, statistical significance alone does not make a finding important. Statistical significance simply means that a result is probably not due to chance.

Summary

Psychological Research

- Researchers use the terms **variable, subject, sample,** and **population** when describing their research.
- Psychologists do research to measure and describe behavior; to understand when, why, and how events occur; and to apply knowledge to real-world problems.

The Scientific Method

- Psychologists use the **scientific method**, which is a standardized way of making observations, gathering data, forming theories, testing predictions, and interpreting results.
- Research must be **replicable, falsifiable, precise,** and **parsimonious.**

Research Methods

- Psychologists use descriptive or **correlational methods** such as **case studies, surveys, naturalistic observation,** and **laboratory observation** to describe events, experiences, or behaviors and to look for links between them.
- Researchers use **tests** to collect information about personality traits, emotional states, aptitudes, interests, abilities, values, or behaviors.
- Tests must be reliable and valid.
- Researchers use **experiments** to collect information about causal relationships between variables.
- In experiments, researchers include **experimental** and **control groups.**
- **Bias** is the distortion of results by a **variable.**
- Types of bias include **sampling bias, subject bias,** and **experimenter bias.**

Ethical Considerations

- Psychologists must consider **ethical norms** when doing research involving humans or animals.

Interpreting Data

- Researchers analyze and interpret the data they've collected by using **descriptive statistics** and organizing their information in **histograms** or **bar graphs**.

- Researchers use **inferential statistics** to determine the likelihood that a result is due simply to chance.

- **Statistical significance** means that a result is probably not due to chance.

Sample Test Questions

1. What are some features of good scientific research?

2. What is sampling bias?

3. Why might it be problematic to rely only on self-report data when doing research?

4. Why is it problematic to draw cause-and-effect conclusions based on correlative data?

5. What does it mean if a researcher claims that a particular result is statistically significant?

6. Which of the following describes single-blind experiments?
    - A.   They are experiments in which the subjects don't know whether they are receiving a real or fake drug or treatment
    - B.   They help reduce placebo effects
    - C.   They help reduce bias in research
    - D.   All of the above

7. What does it mean if two variables have a positive correlation?
    - A.   As one variable increases, so does the other
    - B.   As one variable increases, the other decreases
    - C.   The correlation between the two variables is 0
    - D.   The correlation between the two variables is greater than 1.0

8. In what type of study does a researcher study an individual subject in depth?
    - A.   Naturalistic observation
    - B.   Laboratory observation
    - C.   Case study
    - D.   Survey

9. How can we determine if a test has good validity?
    - A.   It produces the same result when it is given at different times to the same group of people
    - B.   It produces the same result no matter which version of the test is used
    - C.   It measures what it is supposed to measure
    - D.   All of the questions on it can be answered accurately by the subject

10. What is the variable called that a researcher manipulates in an experiment?
  A. Dependent variable
  B. Independent variable
  C. Extraneous variable
  D. None of the above

11. What is the difference between the highest and lowest scores in a data distribution called?
  A. Mode
  B. Standard deviation
  C. Range
  D. Median

12. The social desirability bias can affect which of the following?
  A. The validity of a test
  B. The reliability of a test
  C. Self-report data
  D. None of the above

13. Which of the following is a research method that allows a researcher to get information about a large number of subjects relatively inexpensively and easily?
  A. Naturalistic observation
  B. Case study
  C. Laboratory observation
  D. Survey

14. What is a common way of controlling extraneous variables in an experiment?
  A. Random assignment
  B. Double-blind procedure
  C. Single-blind procedure
  D. Using animal subjects

15. When doing research involving deception with human subjects, researchers have an obligation to do which of the following?
  A. Tell subjects the truth about the study's purpose and methods after the study is completed
  B. Prevent mental and physical harm to subjects
  C. Let subjects withdraw from the study at any time if they don't want to keep participating
  D. All of the above

ANSWERS

1. Good scientific research must have precise hypotheses, replicability, falsifiable theories and hypotheses, and parsimonious explanations.

2. Sampling bias is a type of error that occurs when a sample isn't representative of the population from which it is drawn.

3. Self-report data can be misleading. People sometimes intentionally lie, give answers based on wishful thinking, don't understand the questions asked, or don't remember information.

4. We cannot draw cause-and-effect conclusions about correlative data because one factor can be related to another factor without causing it.

5. If a result is statistically significant, it is probably not due to chance.

6. **D**	11. **C**
7. **A**	12. **C**
8. **C**	13. **D**
9. **C**	14. **A**
10. **B**	15. **D**

Evolution and Genes

- Principles of Genetics
- Types of Genetic Studies
- Evolution and Natural Selection
- Evolutionary Psychology

2

Which has the greater effect on human behavior: nature or nurture? Hair color, height, and many other physical characteristics depend on genes, or nature, but the origin of behavior, intelligence, and personality is not so clear. Most scientists agree that both genes and the environment play a role in behavioral development, but disputes still rage over the degree of influence exerted by each.

A branch of psychology known as behavior genetics examines the genetic base of behavioral and personality differences among people. Behavior genetics is a controversial field, since misuse of psychological research into the genetic roots of behavior can have horrifying results. Several generations ago, psychologists and other scientists used arguments about the genetic influence on behavior and intelligence to support racist theories about the superiority of Anglo Americans. Moreover, these theories often became the foundation of public policies that discriminated against African Americans and Native Americans. Today, behavior geneticists carefully consider the potential political repercussions of their work.

Principles of Genetics

Behavior genetics is a branch of psychology that examines the genetic base of behavior and personality differences among people. An understanding of genetics begins with the following basic concepts:

- A vast number of cells make up the human body. Each cell has forty-six chromosomes, which come in twenty-three pairs. The only exceptions are sex cells.

- Sex cells are sperm in males and eggs in females. Each sex cell has only twenty-three chromosomes.

- **Chromosomes** are made up of thin strands of deoxyribonucleic acid (DNA). Each chromosome pair contains thousands of genes.

- **Genes** are segments of DNA that function as hereditary units. Genes are carried on chromosomes.

- DNA is made up of units called **nucleotides**. There are only four different nucleotides, labeled A, C, G, and T. Long strings of nucleotides make up genes.

- Genes get translated into proteins, which carry out various functions in our bodies. For instance, some proteins serve as the building blocks of cells. Other proteins function as enzymes or hormones.

WHO SHARES GENES?

No two people share the exact combination of genes unless they are identical twins. However, all family members share some genes with one another. The closer the biological relationship between individuals, the more genes they share. The chart below shows the percentage of genes any person shares with his or her close relatives:

Percentage of Shared Genes

Identical twin	100 percent
Parent	50 percent
Brother or sister	50 percent
Nonidentical twin	50 percent
Grandparent	25 percent

MONOGENIC AND POLYGENIC TRAITS

Some characteristics or traits are controlled by a single gene, which means they are **monogenic**. A single gene, for example, can be part of what brings about alcoholism or schizophrenia.

Most traits are controlled by the actions of several genes, which means they are **polygenic**. For example, a person's intelligence is linked to the combination of several genes.

The environment also shapes traits, and later in this chapter we will discuss how genes interact with the environment to produce psychological traits.

HERITABILITY

In a group of people, a particular psychological trait, such as intelligence, usually varies a lot. Differences in groups may be due to genes or the environment, and researchers use a statistic called heritability to see which has the largest influence. **Heritability** is a mathematical estimate that indicates how much of a trait's variation can be attributed to genes. There are three important principles of heritability:

- Heritability estimates don't reveal anything about how much genes influence a person's traits. These figures tell us only to what extent trait differences between people can be attributed to genes.

- Heritability depends on the similarity of the environment for a group of people. In a group of people who share similar environments, heritability of a particular trait may be high. However, that same trait may have low heritability in a group of people who operate in different environments.

- Even if a trait is highly heritable, it can still be influenced by environmental factors.

EXAMPLE: Imagine that ten people live in identical environments. Somehow, they experienced identical prenatal environments while in their mothers' wombs, were raised in identical homes by parents who were identical in every way, and had all the same childhood and adulthood experiences. Suppose that these ten people turn out to be different with respect to one trait, such as the rate at which they can wiggle their ears. Since both genes and environment can influence traits, these differences would have to be genetic, since they could not be due to differences in environment. In such a case, heritability of the ear-wiggling trait would be close to 100 percent.

Now suppose some of these ten people enter different ear-wiggle training camps. The camps vary in effectiveness, so the subjects in some camps increase their ear-wiggling rates, while other subjects remain the same. After the camp training, environment would account for some of the differences among the ten people in ear-wiggling ability. A smaller proportion of the differences would be due to genes alone. Therefore, heritability would be lower.

Types of Genetic Studies

Researchers do different kinds of studies to see whether and to what extent a characteristic might be genetically transmitted.

FAMILY STUDIES

In **family studies**, researchers look at similarities among members of a family with respect to a particular trait. If the trait is genetically inherited, it should be similar in blood relatives. The closer the blood relationship, the more similar people should be.

Family studies alone don't reveal whether a trait is genetically inherited. A family shares genes, but they also share similar environments. When researchers find trait similarity in a family study, their findings may suggest that the trait is genetically inherited, but the study can't prove it.

TWIN STUDIES

Compared to family studies, **twin studies** give researchers more solid evidence about whether a trait is inherited. In twin studies, researchers compare pairs of identical twins to fraternal, or non-identical, twins. When doing these studies, researchers assume that identical twin pairs share the same environment, just as fraternal twin pairs do. However, identical twins share all of their genes with each other, while fraternal twins share only half of their genes. When a trait shows more similarity between identical twins than between fraternal twins, the greater similarity probably comes from shared genes, not shared environment.

One problem with this type of study is that identical twins may not in fact share an identical environment while fraternal twins do. People tend to treat identical twins in unusual ways. For example, people may treat identical twins as if they are similar in every respect, or they might focus intensely on differences between them.

Studies of Separated Twins

In order to avoid uncertain environmental factors, researchers sometimes study separated twins. Twins who are separated when they are very young and brought up in different families have different environmental influences but identical genes. Trait similarities between separated twins result mostly from genes.

However, separated twin studies can also be problematic. The environments of separated twins may not actually be that different from each other for the following reasons:

- The twins shared a similar prenatal environment before they were born.

- Adoption agencies may tend to place twins in similar households.

- Since they are similar in appearance and in genetically inherited abilities, the twins may evoke similar responses from people around them.

As in other types of studies, trait similarities in separated twins may be due to both similar genes and similar environments.

Experiences and Behavior Experiences affect behavior partly because environmental stimulation forms and maintains neural connections. For example, psychological research shows that babies need consistent, loving contact with a caregiver in order to achieve optimal brain development. Neglected babies, lacking attention and physical contact, experience unpleasant emotions that are not simply transitory. Their experiences determine the development of their neural connections. Similarly, soldiers on active combat duty can suffer mental damage from the continuously stressful environment, even if they never experience physical injury.

ADOPTION STUDIES

In **adoption studies**, researchers compare adopted children to their biological parents and to their adoptive parents. Adopted children share more genes with their biological parents. The children's living environments, however, more closely resemble the environments of their adoptive parents. When adoptive children resemble their biological parents more than their adoptive parents with respect to a certain trait, researchers can hypothesize that the trait has a genetic basis.

INTERACTION OF GENES AND ENVIRONMENT

In conducting all these types of studies, researchers have found that while genes influence psychological traits, they don't act alone. Highly influential environmental factors also play a major role. These factors include:

- Prenatal influences

- Child-rearing and other parental influences

- Nutrition

- Experiences throughout life

- Peer influences

- Culture

Genes and environment interact in complex ways. People usually inherit a vulnerability or predisposition to having a particular psychological trait, and the environment in which those people live shapes the development of that trait. The opposite is also

Cultural Norms *Cultural norms are sets of societal expectations that influence behavior. Norms tell us what kinds of behavior are appropriate. For example, in the United States, one cultural norm mandates that children be potty-trained by their third birthday. Parents of children who aren't potty-trained by that point may start to feel worry, shame, and social pressure as their child's third birthday passes.*

true: people's psychological traits influence their environments. People don't just live in environments—they also shape their worlds by exerting their traits.

> EXAMPLE: *Suppose there are two nonidentical twins, Ben and Tom. Ben is calm by nature, while Tom has always been fussy. Mom and Dad will be more taxed by Tom, so they may be less responsive and patient with him than they are with Ben. Therefore, Tom and Ben experience different parental influences, which may make Tom less trusting than Ben as they grow up. Genes and environment influence Tom's personality, but the interaction between genes and environment also plays a role.*

Evolution and Natural Selection

Evolution is a change in the frequency of genes in a population over time. Evolutionary psychologists try to explain universal behaviors. They study how natural selection has encouraged certain behavior patterns to develop.

THE THEORY OF NATURAL SELECTION

Charles Darwin (1809–1882) was a British naturalist who is best known for his contributions to evolutionary theory. Although others had noted that species evolved over time, Darwin first put forward the **theory of natural selection** to explain the process of evolution.

According to this theory, certain inherited characteristics give an organism a survival or reproductive advantage. Organisms pass on these characteristics more often than they pass on other inherited traits.

> EXAMPLE: *The species of primates called mandrills have evolved to have bright blue rear ends, because brightly colored rumps help them attract mates and give them a reproductive advantage. Porcupines evolved to have quills, because quills help them to avoid predators and reproduce. This gives porcupines a survival advantage.*

On the Origin of Species In 1831, Darwin joined a naval expedition on a ship called the HMS Beagle as the unofficial naturalist onboard. Darwin collected many specimens during the ship's five-year expedition around the world. After returning to England, he began developing his ideas about evolution. In 1859, Darwin published his great work, On the Origin of Species.

A characteristic that gives a **reproductive advantage** helps an organism to mate successfully and pass on its genes to the next generation. A characteristic that gives a **survival advantage** helps an organism to live long enough to reproduce and pass on its genes.

REPRODUCTION OF THE FITTEST

People often use the phrase "survival of the fittest" instead of "reproduction of the fittest," but according to evolutionary theory, survival alone isn't enough. Creatures need to survive long enough to reproduce. Reproductive success is measured by how many offspring a creature produces.

INCLUSIVE FITNESS

Another concept related to reproductive success is inclusive fitness, described by W. D. Hamilton in the 1960s. **Inclusive fitness** is the reproductive fitness of an individual organism plus any effect the organism has on increasing reproductive fitness in related organisms. Some researchers believe that the concept of inclusive fitness explains why certain organisms sacrifice themselves to save others in the species. According to this theory, people might risk their lives to save their children or close relatives, but not to save distant relatives or unrelated people. Because people share more genes with close relatives, saving them has more payoff in terms of passing on genes to the next generation.

ADAPTATIONS

An **adaptation** is an inherited characteristic that becomes prevalent in a population because it provides a survival or reproductive advantage. Because evolution occurs over a long period, an adaptation can remain in a population even after it has stopped being useful.

> *EXAMPLE:* *Human beings have a genetic preference for fatty foods, which explains why fried chicken, french fries, and buttery popcorn are so popular. Evolutionary psychologists say that the preference for fatty foods derives from the days when people hunted and gathered and food was scarce. Eating high-fat foods was important because fat gave people the calories they needed. In other words, the preference for fat was adaptive. Today, in wealthy countries with abundant food and sedentary lifestyles, the preference for fat remains, despite the fact that it no longer has beneficial effects. In fact, consuming fatty foods can lead to health problems.*

MUTATIONS

Evolution relies on **mutations**, or small changes in genes. Mutations happen because of two events that can occur during the formation of egg and sperm cells:

- An error during copying of DNA
- Random rearrangement of small pieces of DNA in a chromosome pair

Sometimes, a mutation results in a new trait. If the individual with the mutation reproduces successfully, the mutation will be passed on. If the new trait proves advantageous, the mutated gene that caused the trait will increase in the population over a long period and thus propel evolution.

Evolutionary Psychology

Evolutionary psychology uses evolutionary theory to explain similarities in psychological characteristics. According to evolutionary psychologists, patterns of behavior have evolved through natural selection, in the same way that physical characteristics have evolved. Because of natural selection, **adaptive behaviors**, or behaviors that increase reproductive success, are kept and passed on from one generation to the next.

MATING BEHAVIOR

Because reproductive success is such a hot topic in evolutionary theory, evolutionary psychologists often choose to study mating behavior. Researchers such as Robert Trivers have proposed that mating strategies depend on the amount of parental investment made by males and females of a species. **Parental investment** refers to all the resources spent to produce and raise offspring. In many species, males and females don't make equal parental investments. The sex that invests less competes with others of its sex to mate with the sex that invests more. The sex that invests more in parenting tends to discriminate more when selecting a mate.

Sexual Selection

Usually, the female of the species invests more in parenting. Females of many species choose their mates based on certain characteristics, such as large canine teeth in a male baboon or flashy tail feathers on a peacock, which in turn means those traits will be passed on to their male offspring. Biologists call this process **sexual selection**, which is related to natural selection. Whereas natural selection results in adaptations that make organisms more likely to survive, sexual selection just makes them more likely to mate. Sometimes the adaptations that are a result of sexual selection, such as flashy tail feathers, are not actually much help in terms of survival.

Polygyny

A situation called **polygyny** arises when a single male mates with many different females. Polygyny tends to occur in certain animal species, notably those in which females invest more in parenting than males. In a polygynous mating system, males compete with other males in order to get access to females. Females tend to pick the winners of such competitions. Picking winners helps to ensure that their offspring will have good genes.

> *EXAMPLE: Mountain gorillas are polygynous. The females and children live in groups defended by a mature male, with whom they mate. If they choose, however, females may select a stronger, more desirable mate. In such a case, the hopeful suitor would challenge the dominant male and the females would choose the winner.*

PROBLEMS WITH EVOLUTIONARY EXPLANATIONS

Scientists have used evolutionary theory to explain human behavior patterns, such as a female tendency toward monogamy and a male tendency toward promiscuity. However, other researchers argue that such explanations don't apply well to humans, because the theories stem from stereotypes. Humans behave in complex and variable ways, and factors such as culture strongly influence this behavior. Furthermore, it is difficult to tie variation in behavior to variation in reproductive success. Evolutionary explanations also raise controversy because people can use them to support various social and political agendas.

Some researchers criticize evolutionary explanations because anyone can work backward from an observation to develop an evolutionary explanation. These psychologists point out that the fact that a trait exists does not necessarily mean that trait is adaptive. The trait may have been helpful earlier in our human history but did not remain adaptive, or the trait could be a side effect of another adaptive trait.

Summary

Principles of Genetics

- **Behavior geneticists** study the genetic basis of behavior and personality differences among people.
- The more closely people are biologically related, the more genes they share.
- Traits can be **monogenic** (determined by one gene) or **polygenic** (determined by several genes).
- Researchers use **heritability** to determine how much of a trait's variation within a population is due to genes.

Types of Genetic Studies

- Psychologists use **family studies, twin studies**, and **adoption studies** to see whether, and to what extent, characteristics are genetic.
- Heredity interacts with environment to influence psychological traits.

Evolution and Natural Selection

- **Evolution** is the change in the frequency of genes in a population.
- **Charles Darwin** proposed the **theory of natural selection**, which states that inherited characteristics that give an organism a **survival or reproductive advantage** are passed on more often to future generations than other inherited characteristics.
- An **adaptation** is an inherited characteristic that increases in a population because it provides a survival or reproductive advantage.
- **Inclusive fitness** is the reproductive fitness of an individual organism plus any effect that the organism has on increasing reproductive fitness in related organisms.
- Evolution relies on **mutations**, or small changes in genes.

Evolutionary Psychology

- Evolutionary psychologists use **evolutionary theory** to explain patterns in psychological characteristics.
- Researchers study **mating behavior** to investigate aspects of evolutionary psychology.
- **Parental inverstment** refers to all the resources spent to produce and raise offspring.
- **Sexual selection** refers to the tendancy of females to choose mates pased on certain characteristics, which are then passed on to their male offspring.

Sample Test Questions

1. Why can't family studies alone tell us whether a trait is genetically transmitted?

2. What is the theory of natural selection?

3. Is a trait that allows a person to survive until the age of six likely to be more adaptive, in the long run, than a trait that allows a person to survive until the age of four?

4. How do mutations occur?

5. How can adoption studies give us information about whether a trait is genetically transmitted?

6. What are polygenic traits?
   A.   Psychological traits
   B.   Physical traits
   C.   Traits that result in the transmission of many genes
   D.   Traits that arise from the action of several genes

7. Which of the following cannot affect psychological traits?
   A.   Nutrition
   B.   Child-rearing practices
   C.   Prenatal environment
   D.   None of the above

8. Which of the following statements is false?
   A.   Heritability estimates tell us the degree to which genes influence an individual's traits
   B.   Heritability depends on how similar the environment is for a group of people
   C.   A highly heritable trait can be influenced by environmental factors
   D.   A and C

9. Researchers have proposed that mating strategies depend on which of the following?
   A.   The number of genes coded for mating behavior in males and females
   B.   The heritability of the mating strategy in males and females
   C.   The amount of parental investment made by males and females
   D.   All of the above

10. *Which of the following statements accurately describes genes?*
    A.   They are segments of DNA
    B.   They function as hereditary units
    C.   They are translated into proteins
    D.   All of the above

11. *Which of the following statements accurately describes chromosomes?*
    A.   They are made up of DNA
    B.   They are the building blocks of cells
    C.   They are translated into nucleotides
    D.   All of the above

12. *When doing twin studies, what do researchers assume?*
    A.   Identical twins share the same genes
    B.   Identical twins share the same environment
    C.   A and B
    D.   None of the above

13. *Trait similarities between twins separated at birth may be due not only to genes. Why?*
    A.   Such twins shared a similar prenatal environment before they were born
    B.   Adoption agencies may place twins in similar households
    C.   Similarities in appearance and genetically inherited abilities may evoke similar responses from people
    D.   All of the above

14. *What is one characteristic feature of a polygynous mating system?*
    A.   Females compete with other females to gain access to males
    B.   Males compete with other males to gain access to females
    C.   Males compete with females to gain access to territory
    D.   Males compete with females to gain access to food

15. *What concept explains the tendency of certain organisms to sacrifice themselves to save others in the species?*
    A.   Mutation
    B.   Heritability
    C.   Inclusive fitness
    D.   Reproductive adaptation

ANSWERS

1. Family studies alone cannot tell us whether a trait is genetically transmitted because families share not only genes but also similar living environments.

2. The theory of natural selection explains the process of evolution. It maintains that inherited characteristics that give an organism a survival or reproductive advantage are passed on more often to future generations than other inherited characteristics.

3. This trait is not likely to be more adaptive. As far as natural selection is concerned, survival alone isn't enough. What matters is that a person survives long enough to reproduce and pass on the trait. A person would be unable to pass on the trait regardless of whether he or she died at six or at four.

4. Mutations occur during the formation of egg and sperm cells, when an error occurs as DNA is being copied or when small pieces of DNA exchange places in a chromosome pair.

5. Adoption studies compare adopted children to their biological and adoptive parents. If the children are more similar in a trait to their biological parents than to their adoptive parents, the trait may be genetically transmitted.

6. **D**	11. **A**
7. **D**	12. **C**
8. **A**	13. **D**
9. **C**	14. **B**
10. **D**	15. **C**

Neurons, Hormones, and the Brain

3

The brain is an essential part of the nervous system, a complex, highly coordinated network of tissues that communicate via electrochemical signals. We use our brains in virtually everything we do, from keeping our heart beating to deducing the existence of black holes. Within our brains lie our deepest secrets, our earliest memories, our most amazing capabilities, and the keys to the mystery of consciousness itself.

Hippocrates (460–377 B.C.), the most famous physician of the ancient world, first theorized that our thoughts, feelings, and ideas came from the brain, while others at the time thought the heart and stomach were the seats of emotion. Today, researchers are paying more attention to the roles played by the brain and the hormones that affect it in experiences such as mother-infant bonding, religious ecstasy and prayer, extreme stress, and meditation. Researchers now realize that though our minds and brains may not be exactly the same thing, they are intimately connected.

The Nervous System

The **nervous system** is a complex, highly coordinated network of tissues that communicate via electro chemical signals. It is responsible for receiving and processing information in the body and is divided into two main branches: the central nervous system and the peripheral nervous system.

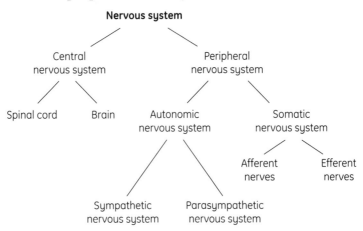

THE CENTRAL NERVOUS SYSTEM

The **central nervous system** receives and processes information from the senses. The brain and the spinal cord make up the central nervous system. Both organs lie in a fluid called the **cerebrospinal fluid**, which cushions and nourishes the brain. The **blood-brain barrier** protects the cerebrospinal fluid by blocking many drugs and toxins. This barrier is a membrane that lets some substances from the blood into the brain but keeps out others.

The **spinal cord** connects the brain to the rest of the body. It runs from the brain down to the small of the back and is responsible for **spinal reflexes**, which are automatic behaviors that require no input from the brain. The spinal cord also sends messages from the brain to the other parts of the body and from those parts back to the brain.

The **brain** is the main organ in the nervous system. It integrates information from the senses and coordinates the body's activities. It allows people to remember their childhoods, plan the future, create term papers and works of art, talk to friends, and have bizarre dreams. Different parts of the brain do different things.

> **Damage to the Spinal Cord** *The spinal cord is what connects the brain and body, and it is protected by the bones in the spinal column. Injuries to the spinal cord can cause serious problems, such as paralysis. Even relatively minor damage to the spinal cord can cause loss of feeling in parts of the body, impaired organ function, and loss of muscular control. Though spinal cord injuries are usually permanent, current research into regenerated axons and stem cells offers hope that one day these injuries may be treated successfully.*

THE PERIPHERAL NERVOUS SYSTEM

All the parts of the nervous system except the brain and the spinal cord belong to the **peripheral nervous system**. The peripheral nervous system has two parts: the somatic nervous system and the autonomic nervous system.

The Somatic Nervous System

The **somatic nervous system** consists of nerves that connect the central nervous system to voluntary skeletal muscles and sense organs. Voluntary skeletal muscles are muscles that help us to move around. There are two types of nerves in the somatic nervous system:

- **Afferent nerves** carry information from the muscles and sense organs to the central nervous system.

- **Efferent nerves** carry information from the central nervous system to the muscles and sense organs.

The Autonomic Nervous System

The **autonomic nervous system** consists of nerves that connect the central nervous system to the heart, blood vessels, glands, and smooth muscles. **Smooth muscles** are involuntary muscles that help organs such as the stomach and bladder carry out their functions. The autonomic nervous system controls all the automatic functions in the body, including breathing, digestion, sweating, and heartbeat. The autonomic nervous system is divided into the sympathetic and parasympathetic nervous systems.

- The **sympathetic nervous system** gets the body ready for emergency action. It is involved in the fight-or-flight response, which is the sudden reaction to stressful or threatening situations. The sympathetic nervous system prepares the body to meet a challenge. It slows down digestive processes, draws blood away from the skin to the skeletal muscles, and activates the release of hormones so the body can act quickly.

- The **parasympathetic nervous system** becomes active during states of relaxation. It helps the body to conserve and store energy. It slows heartbeat, decreases blood pressure, and promotes the digestive process.

Crisis Mode The sympathetic nervous system's activation may manifest as a rapidly thumping heart, sweaty palms, pale skin, or panting breath—the kinds of things we experience during a crisis. We may experience these kinds of symptoms during a panic attack, for example.

Neurons: Cells of the Nervous System

There are two kinds of cells in the nervous system: glial cells and neurons. **Glial cells**, which make up the support structure of the nervous system, perform four functions:

- Provide structural support to the neurons

- Insulate neurons

- Nourish neurons

- Remove waste products

The other cells, **neurons**, act as the communicators of the nervous system. Neurons receive information, integrate it, and pass it along. They communicate with one another, with cells in the sensory organs, and with muscles and glands.

Each neuron has the same structure:

- Each neuron has a **soma**, or cell body, which is the central area of the neuron. It contains the nucleus and other structures common to all cells in the body, such as mitochondria.

- The highly branched fibers that reach out from the neuron are called **dendritic trees**. Each branch is called a **dendrite**. Dendrites receive information from other neurons or from sense organs.

- The single long fiber that extends from the neuron is called an axon. **Axons** send information to other neurons, to muscle cells, or to gland cells. What we call **nerves** are bundles of axons coming from many neurons.

- Some of these axons have a coating called the **myelin sheath**. Glial cells produce myelin, which is a fatty substance that protects the nerves. When an axon has a myelin sheath, nerve impulses travel faster down the axon. Nerve transmission can be impaired when myelin sheaths disintegrate.

- At the end of each axon lie bumps called terminal buttons. **Terminal buttons** release **neurotransmitters**, which are chemicals that can cross over to neighboring neurons and activate them. The junction between an axon of one neuron and the cell body or dendrite of a neighboring neuron is called a **synapse**.

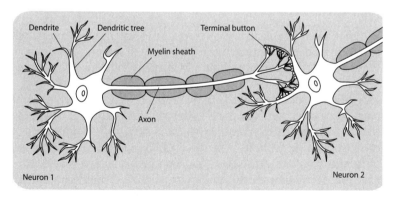

Neuron Structure

**CHAPTER 3
THE BRAIN**

Role of Myelin   People with multiple sclerosis have difficulty with muscle control because the myelin around their axons has disintegrated. Another disease, poliomyelitis, commonly called "polio," also damages myelin and can lead to paralysis.

COMMUNICATION BETWEEN NEURONS

In 1952, physiologists **Alan Hodgkin** and **Andrew Huxley** made some important discoveries about how neurons transmit information. They studied giant squid, whose neurons have giant axons. By putting tiny electrodes inside these axons, Hodgkin and Huxley found that nerve impulses are really electrochemical reactions.

The Resting Potential

Nerves are specially built to transmit electrochemical signals. Fluids exist both inside and outside neurons. These fluids contain positively and negatively charged atoms and molecules called **ions**. Positively charged sodium and potassium ions and negatively charged chloride ions constantly cross into and out of neurons, across cell membranes. An inactive neuron is in the **resting state**. In the resting state, the inside of a neuron has a slightly higher concentration of negatively charged ions than the outside does. This situation creates a slight negative charge inside the neuron, which acts as a store of potential energy called the **resting potential**. The resting potential of a neuron is about –70 millivolts.

The Action Potential

When something stimulates a neuron, gates, or channels, in the cell membrane open up, letting in positively charged sodium ions. For a limited time, there are more positively charged ions inside than in the resting state. This creates an **action potential**, which is a short-lived change in electric charge inside the neuron. The action potential zooms quickly down an axon. Channels in the membrane close, and no more sodium ions can enter. After they open and close, the channels remain closed for a while. During the period when the channels remain closed, the neuron can't send impulses. This short period of time is called the **absolute refractory period**, and it lasts about 1–2 milliseconds. The absolute refractory period is the period during which a neuron lies dormant after an action potential has been completed.

The All-or-None Law

Neural impulses conform to the **all-or-none law**, which means that a neuron either fires and generates an action potential, or it doesn't. Neural impulses are always the same strength—weak stimuli don't produce weak impulses. If stimulation reaches a certain threshold, or minimum level, the neuron fires and sends an impulse. If stimulation doesn't reach that threshold, the neuron simply doesn't fire. Stronger stimuli do not send stronger impulses, but they do send impulses at a faster rate.

The Synapse

The gap between two cells at a synapse is called the **synaptic cleft**. The signal-sending cell is called the **presynaptic neuron**, and the signal-receiving cell is called the **postsynaptic neuron**.

Neurotransmitters are the chemicals that allow neurons to communicate with each other. These chemicals are kept in **synaptic vesicles**, which are small sacs inside the terminal buttons. When an action potential reaches the terminal buttons, which are at the ends of axons, neurotransmitter-filled synaptic vesicles fuse with the presynaptic cell membrane. As a result, neurotransmitter molecules pour into the synaptic cleft. When they reach the postsynaptic cell, neurotransmitter molecules attach to matching receptor sites. Neurotransmitters work in much the same way as keys. They attach only to specific receptors, just as certain keys fit only certain locks.

When a neurotransmitter molecule links up with a receptor molecule, there's a voltage change, called a **postsynaptic potential (PSP)**, at the receptor site. Receptor sites on the postsynaptic cell can be excitatory or inhibitory:

- The binding of a neurotransmitter to an excitatory receptor site results in a positive change in voltage, called an **excitatory postsynaptic potential** or **excitatory PSP**. This increases the chances that an action potential will be generated in the postsynaptic cell.

- Conversely, the binding of a neurotransmitter to an inhibitory receptor site results in an **inhibitory PSP**, or a negative change in voltage. In this case, it's less likely that an action potential will be generated in the postsynaptic cell.

CHAPTER 3
THE BRAIN

Unlike an action potential, a PSP doesn't conform to the all-or-none law. At any one time, a single neuron can receive a huge number of excitatory PSPs and inhibitory PSPs because its dendrites are influenced by axons from many other neurons. Whether or not an action potential is generated in the neuron depends on the balance of excitation and inhibition. If, on balance, the voltage changes enough to reach the threshold level, the neuron will fire.

Neurotransmitter effects at a synapse do not last long. Neurotransmitter molecules soon detach from receptors and are usually returned to the presynaptic cell for reuse in a process called **reuptake.**

Neurotransmitters

So far, researchers have discovered about 15–20 different neurotransmitters, and new ones are still being identified. The nervous system communicates accurately because there are so many neurotransmitters and because neurotransmitters work only at matching receptor sites. Different neurotransmitters do different things.

Neurotransmitter	Major functions	Excess is associated with	Deficiency is associated with
Acetylcholine	Muscle movement, attention, arousal, memory, emotion		Alzheimer's disease
Dopamine	Voluntary movement, learning, memory, emotion	Schizophrenia	Parkinsonism
Serotonin	Sleep, wakefulness, appetite, mood, aggression, impulsivity, sensory perception, temperature regulation, pain suppression		Depression

Neurotransmitter	Major functions	Excess is associated with	Deficiency is associated with
Endorphins	Pain relief, pleasure		
Norepinephrine	Learning, memory, dreaming, awakening, emotion, stress-related increase in heart rate, stress-related slowing of digestive processes		Depression
GABA	Main inhibitory neurotransmitter in the brain		
Glutamate	Main excitatory neurotransmitter in the brain	Multiple sclerosis	

AGONISTS AND ANTAGONISTS

Agonists are chemicals that mimic the action of a particular neurotransmitter. They bind to receptors and generate postsynaptic potentials.

> **Nicotine and Receptors** *Nicotine is an acetylcholine agonist, which means that it mimics acetylcholine closely enough to compete for acetylcholine receptors. When both nicotine and acetylcholine attach to a receptor site, the nerve fibers become highly stimulated, producing a feeling of alertness and elation.*

Antagonists are chemicals that block the action of a particular neurotransmitter. They bind to receptors but can't produce postsynaptic potentials. Because they occupy the receptor site, they prevent neurotransmitters from acting.

> **Paralysis and Poison Arrows** *Curare is a drug that causes paralysis. As an acetylcholine antagonist, it binds to acetylcholine receptors at nerve-muscle junctions, preventing communication between nerves and muscles. Doctors sometimes use curare to immobilize patients during extremely delicate surgery. South American tribes have long used curare as an arrow poison.*

CHAPTER 3
THE BRAIN

Studying the Brain

To examine the brain's functions, researchers have to study a working brain, which means they can't use cadavers. Invasive studies, in which researchers actually put instruments into the brain, can't be done in humans, though they can be done occasionally during medically necessary brain surgery. Researchers usually use invasive techniques in animal studies. There are two main types of invasive animal studies:

- **Lesioning studies:** Researchers use an electrode and an electric current to burn a specific, small area of the brain.

- **Electric stimulation of the brain:** Researchers activate a particular brain structure by using a weak electric current sent along an implanted electrode.

Because they cannot use such invasive techniques on humans, researchers study human brains in two ways:

- They examine people with brain injuries or diseases and see what they can and can't do.

- They use **electroencephalographs (EEGs)**, which can record the overall electrical activity in the brain via electrodes placed on the scalp.

Recently, high-tech innovations have made studying human brains easier. Researchers use three types of imaging equipment to study the brain:

- **Computerized tomography (CT):** In CT, a number of x-rays are taken of the brain from different angles. A computer then combines the x-rays to produce a picture of a horizontal slice through the brain.

- **Magnetic resonance imaging (MRI):** Both brain structure and function can be visualized through MRI scans, which are computer-enhanced pictures produced by magnetic fields and radio waves.

- **Positron emission tomography (PET):** For PET scans, researchers inject people with a harmless radioactive chemical, which collects in active brain areas. The researchers then look at the pattern of radioactivity in the brain, using a scanner and a computer, and figure out which parts of the brain activate during specific tasks, such as lifting an arm or feeling a particular emotion.

Structure and Functions of the Brain

The brain is divided into three main parts: the hindbrain, the midbrain, and the forebrain.

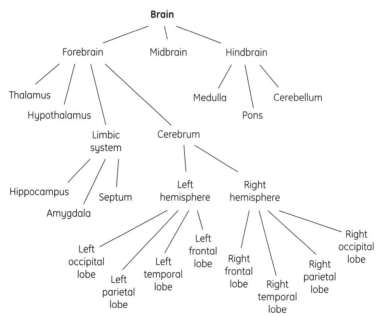

THE HINDBRAIN

The **hindbrain** is composed of the medulla, the pons, and the cerebellum. The **medulla** lies next to the spinal cord and controls functions outside conscious control, such as breathing and blood flow. In other words, the medulla controls essential functions. The **pons** affects activities such as sleeping, waking, and dreaming. The **cerebellum** controls balance and coordination of movement. Damage to the cerebellum impairs fine motor skills, so a person with an injury in this area would have trouble playing the guitar or typing a term paper.

THE MIDBRAIN

The **midbrain** is the part of the brain that lies between the hindbrain and the forebrain. The midbrain helps us to locate events in space. It also contains a system of neurons that releases the neurotransmitter dopamine. The **reticular formation** runs through the hindbrain and the midbrain and is involved in sleep and wakefulness, pain perception, breathing, and muscle reflexes.

THE FOREBRAIN

The biggest and most complex part of the brain is the **forebrain**, which includes the thalamus, the hypothalamus, the limbic system, and the cerebrum.

Thalamus

The **thalamus** is a sensory way station. All sensory information except smell-related data must go through the thalamus on the way to the cerebrum.

Hypothalamus

The **hypothalamus** lies under the thalamus and helps to control the pituitary gland and the autonomic nervous system. The hypothalamus plays an important role in regulating body temperature and biological drives such as hunger, thirst, sex, and aggression.

Limbic System

The **limbic system** includes the **hippocampus**, the **amygdala**, and the septum. Parts of the limbic system also lie in the thalamus and the hypothalamus. The limbic system processes emotional experience. The amygdala plays a role in aggression and fear, while the hippocampus plays a role in memory.

Cerebrum

The **cerebrum**, the biggest part of the brain, controls complex processes such as abstract thought and learning. The wrinkled, highly folded outer layer of the cerebrum is called the cerebral cortex. The **corpus callosum** is a band of fibers that runs along the cerebrum from the front of the skull to the back. It divides the cerebrum into two halves, or hemispheres. Each hemisphere is divided into four lobes or segments: the occipital lobe, the parietal lobe, the temporal lobe, and the frontal lobe:

- The occipital lobe contains the primary visual cortex, which handles visual information.

- The parietal lobe contains the primary somatosensory cortex, which handles information related to the sense of touch. The parietal lobe also plays a part in sensing body position and integrating visual information.

- The temporal lobe contains the primary auditory cortex, which is involved in processing auditory information. The left temporal lobe also contains **Wernicke's area**, a part of the brain involved in language comprehension.

- The frontal lobe contains the primary motor cortex, which controls muscle movement. The left frontal lobe contains **Broca's area**, which influences speech production. The frontal lobe also processes memory, planning, goal-setting, creativity, rational decision making, and social judgment.

BRAIN HEMISPHERES

Lateralization refers to the fact that the right and left hemispheres of the brain regulate different functions. The left hemisphere specializes in verbal processing tasks such as writing, reading, and talking. The right hemisphere specializes in nonverbal processing tasks such as playing music, drawing, and recognizing childhood friends.

Roger Sperry, Michael Gazzaniga, and their colleagues conducted some of the early research in lateralization. They examined people who had gone through **split-brain surgery**, an operation done to cut the corpus callosum and separate the two brain hemispheres. Doctors sometimes use split-brain surgery as a treatment for epileptic seizures.

Control of the Body

Because of the organization of the nervous system, the left hemisphere of the brain controls the functioning of the right side of the body. Likewise, the right hemisphere controls the functioning of the left side of the body.

Vision and hearing operate a bit differently. What the left eye and right eye see goes to the entire brain. However, images in the left visual field stimulate receptors on the right side of each eye, and information goes from those points to the right hemisphere. Information perceived by the right visual field ends up in the left hemisphere.

In the case of auditory information, both hemispheres receive input about what each ear hears. However, information first goes to the opposite hemisphere. If the left ear hears a sound, the right hemisphere registers the sound first.

The fact that the brain's hemispheres communicate with opposite sides of the body does not affect most people's day-to-day functioning because the two hemispheres constantly share information via the corpus callosum. However, severing the corpus callosum and separating the hemispheres causes impaired perception.

Split-Brain Studies

If a researcher presented a picture of a Frisbee to a split-brain patient's right visual field, information about the Frisbee would go to his left hemisphere. Because language functions reside in the left hemisphere, he'd be able to say that he saw a Frisbee and describe it. However, if the researcher presented the Frisbee to the patient's left visual field, information about it would go to his right hemisphere. Because his right hemisphere can't communicate with his left hemisphere when the corpus callosum is cut, the patient would not be able to name or describe the Frisbee.

The same phenomenon occurs if the Frisbee is hidden from sight and placed in the patient's left hand, which communicates with the right hemisphere. When the Frisbee is in the patient's left visual field or in his left hand, the patient may not be able to say what it is, although he would be able to point to a picture of what he saw. Picture recognition requires no verbal language and is also a visual-spatial task, which the right hemisphere controls.

The Endocrine System

The **endocrine system,** made up of hormone-secreting glands, also affects communication inside the body. **Hormones** are chemicals that help to regulate bodily functions. The glands produce hormones and dump them into the bloodstream, through which the hormones travel to various parts of the body. Hormones act more slowly than neurotransmitters, but their effects tend to be longer lasting.

The **pituitary gland,** which lies close to the hypothalamus of the brain, is often called the master gland of the endocrine system. When stimulated by the hypothalamus, the pituitary gland releases various hormones that control other glands in the body. The chart below summarizes the better known hormones along with some of their functions.

Hormone	Produced by	Involved in regulating
Thyroxine	Thyroid gland	Metabolic rate
Insulin	Pancreas	Level of blood sugar
Melatonin	Pineal gland	Biological rhythms, sleep
Cortisol, Norepinephrine, Epinephrine, Adrenaline	Adrenal glands	Bodily functions during stressful and emotional states
Androgens	Testes (and ovaries and adrenal glands to a lesser extent)	Male secondary sex characteristics, sexual arousal in males and females
Estrogens	Ovaries (and testes and adrenal glands to a lesser extent)	Breast development and menarche in females
Progesterone	Ovaries (and testes and adrenal glands to a lesser extent)	Preparation of uterus for implantation of fertilized egg

Summary

The Nervous System

- The **nervous system** comprises the **central nervous system** and the **peripheral nervous system**.

- The central nervous system consists of the **brain** and the **spinal cord**. The spinal cord connects the brain to the rest of the body.

- The peripheral nervous system consists of the **somatic nervous system** and the **autonomic nervous system**. The somatic nervous system affects voluntary muscles and organs. The autonomic nervous system affects the heart, blood vessels, glands, and smooth or involuntary muscles.

- The autonomic nervous system contains the **sympathetic nervous system**, which prepares the body for emergency action, and the **parasympathetic nervous system**, which helps the body conserve energy and relax.

Neurons: Cells of the Nervous System

- **Glial cells** support neuron function.

- **Neurons**, the other type of cell in the nervous system, receive, integrate, and pass along information.

- A neuron contains the **soma, dendrites, axon,** and **myelin sheath**.

- **Terminal buttons** at the ends of axons release **neurotransmitters** or chemicals that cross over to neighboring neurons.

- The space between neurons is the **synapse**.

- The **resting potential** of a neuron is the stable negative charge inside the neuron when it is inactive.

- The **action potential** is a temporary change in electric charge inside a neuron.

- Neural impulses conform to the **all-or-none law**, which means that neurons fire to generate an action potential only if stimulation reaches a minimum threshold.

- In neural communication, receptor sites on postsynaptic cells can be **excitatory** or **inhibitory**.

Neurotransmitters

- **Neurotransmitters** are chemicals that enable neurons to communicate with each other.

- Major neurotransmitters include **acetylcholine, dopamine, serotonin, endorphins, norepinephrine, GABA,** and **glutamate**.

- **Agonists** are chemicals that mimic the action of neurotransmitters.

- **Antagonists** are chemicals that block the action of neurotransmitters.

Studying the Brain

- Researchers use **lesioning** and **electric stimulation of the brain** to study animals.

- To study human brains, researchers use **electroencephalographs,
computerized tomography, magnetic resonance imaging,** and **positron
emission tomography**. Researchers also study the impact of brain injuries
and diseases.

Structure and Functions of the Brain

- The brain consists of the **hindbrain, midbrain,** and **forebrain**. Each section
of the brain contains subsections, which control different functions.

- The hindbrain contains the **medulla,** the **pons,** and the **cerebellum**.

- The midbrain contains a dopamine-releasing system and helps us to locate
events in space.

- The forebrain is the largest part of the brain and includes the **thalamus,** the
hypothalamus, the **limbic system,** and the **cerebrum**.

- **Lateralization** refers to how the right and left sides of the brain specialize in
different functions. The left hemisphere processes verbal skills, while the right
side processes nonverbal tasks.

- The left side of the brain affects the functioning of the right side of the body.
Conversely, the right side of the brain affects the functioning of the left side of
the body.

The Endocrine System

- The **endocrine system,** which consists of glands that release hormones, also
helps communication within the body.

- **Hormones** are chemicals that regulate body functions.

- The **pituitary gland** is the master gland of the endocrine system.

- Major hormones include **thyroxine, insulin, melatonin, adrenal
hormones, androgens, estrogens,** and **progesterone**.

Sample Test Questions

1. What does the all-or-none law refer to?

2. How are neural impulses transmitted from one neuron to another?

3. What are some noninvasive ways of studying the brain?

4. If a baseball is placed in a split-brain patient's right visual field, would she be able to name what she sees?

5. Why is the pituitary sometimes called the master gland?

6. The sensations we experience when we think we'll hit another car on the freeway are due to activation of which system?
   A.   Sympathetic nervous system
   B.   Parasympathetic nervous system
   C.   Somatic nervous system
   D.   Central nervous system

7. Which type of sensory information does not pass through the thalamus?
   A.   Visual
   B.   Tactile
   C.   Olfactory
   D.   Auditory

8. What is damage to the hippocampus likely to affect?
   A.   Hearing
   B.   Vision
   C.   Balance
   D.   Memory

9. In which lobe of the brain is Wernicke's area, the part of the brain involved in understanding language?
   A.   The right parietal lobe
   B.   The left occipital lobe
   C.   The right frontal lobe
   D.   The left temporal lobe

10. Which group of hormones is responsible for the development of male secondary sex characteristics?
   A.   Estrogens
   B.   Androgens
   C.   Adrenal hormones
   D.   Thyroid hormones

11. *Which of the following is a function of the myelin sheath?*
   A.   Increases the speed at which nerve impulses travel along an axon
   B.   Receives information from other neurons or from sense organs
   C.   Releases neurotransmitters that can cross over to neighboring neurons
   D.   All of the above

12. *Why does the resting potential occur?*
   A.   The inside of a neuron has a higher concentration of positive ions than the outside
   B.   The inside of a neuron has a higher concentration of negative ions than the outside
   C.   The inside and outside of a neuron have an equal charge
   D.   None of the above

13. *What is the interval called during which a neuron is dormant after an action potential has been completed?*
   A.   Postaction potential
   B.   Resting potential
   C.   Absolute refractory period
   D.   Postsynaptic potential

14. *What is a function of antagonists?*
   A.   Block the action of a neurotransmitter
   B.   Mimic the action of a neurotransmitter
   C.   Reverse the action of a neurotransmitter
   D.   Speed up the action of a neurotransmitter

15. *What is the main inhibitory neurotransmitter in the brain?*
   A.   Glutamate
   B.   Serotonin
   C.   Dopamine
   D.   GABA

ANSWERS

1.   Neural impulses conform to the all-or-none law, which means that a neuron generates an action potential only if a threshold level of stimulation is reached. If the threshold is not reached, the neuron doesn't fire.

2.   Neural impulses are transmitted from one neuron to another via neurotransmitters. When an action potential reaches the terminal buttons of a neuron, neurotransmitter-filled synaptic vesicles fuse with the cell membrane, releasing neurotransmitter molecules into the synaptic cleft. These molecules link up with receptors on neighboring neurons and generate a voltage change or postsynaptic potential at the receptor site.

3.   There are five noninvasive ways of studying the brain: (1) studying people with brain injuries or diseases, (2) electroencephalograms, (3) computerized tomography, (4) positron emission tomography, and (5) magnetic resonance imaging.

4.   Yes, she could name what she sees. Information about the baseball goes to the left hemisphere, which controls language function.

5.   The pituitary gland is sometimes called the master gland because it releases hormones that control other glands.

6. **D**	11. **A**
7. **C**	12. **B**
8. **D**	13. **C**
9. **D**	14. **A**
10. **B**	15. **D**

Development

- Theories of Development
- Prenatal Development
- Infancy and Childhood
- Adolescence
- Adulthood

4

Life is a series of changes. Beginning as tiny, two-celled organisms, people eventually become babies, children, teenagers, and adults. Countless new skills, both simple and complicated, accompany each new stage. Babies learn how to smile and laugh, children learn how to count and spell, and college students learn how to set their own schedules and wash their own clothes.

All the changes that mark our lives make up a process called development, which is the series of age-related changes that happen over the course of a life span. Many factors influence development, including genes, parental upbringing, parents' educational and economic backgrounds, and life experiences. Even historical events over which we have no control can influence our development.

Theories of Development

Development is the series of age-related changes that happen over the course of a life span. Several famous psychologists, including **Sigmund Freud, Erik Erikson, Jean Piaget**, and **Lawrence Kohlberg**, describe development as a series of stages. A **stage** is a period in development in which people exhibit typical behavior patterns and establish particular capacities. The various stage theories share three assumptions:

1. People pass through stages in a specific order, with each stage building on capacities developed in the previous stage.
2. Stages are related to age.
3. Development is discontinuous, with qualitatively different capacities emerging in each stage.

SIGMUND FREUD'S THEORY OF PERSONALITY

The Austrian psychiatrist Sigmund Freud first described personality development as a series of stages. Of these stages, Freud believed that early childhood was the most important. He believed that personality developed by about the age of five.

Freud's theory of personality development is described in more detail on pages 268–273 of Chapter 13, "Personality."

ERIK ERIKSON'S THEORY OF PSYCHOSOCIAL DEVELOPMENT

Like Freud, Erik Erikson believed in the importance of early childhood. However, Erikson believed that personality development happens over the entire course of a person's life. In the early 1960s, Erikson proposed a theory that describes eight distinct stages of development. According to Erikson, in each stage people face new challenges, and the stage's outcome depends on how people handle these challenges. Erikson named the stages according to these possible outcomes:

STAGE 1: TRUST VS. MISTRUST In the first year after birth, babies depend completely on adults for basic needs such as food, comfort, and warmth. If the caretakers meet these needs reliably, the babies become attached and develop a sense of security. Otherwise, they may develop a mistrustful, insecure attitude.

STAGE 2: *AUTONOMY VS. SHAME AND DOUBT* Between the ages of one and three, toddlers start to gain independence and learn skills such as toilet training, feeding themselves, and dressing themselves. Depending on how they face these challenges, toddlers can develop a sense of autonomy or a sense of doubt and shame about themselves.

STAGE 3: *INITIATIVE VS. GUILT* Between the ages of three and six, children must learn to control their impulses and act in a socially responsible way. If they can do this effectively, children become more self-confident. If not, they may develop a strong sense of guilt.

STAGE 4: *INDUSTRY VS. INFERIORITY* Between the ages of six and twelve, children compete with peers in school and prepare to take on adult roles. They end this stage with either a sense of competence or a sense of inferiority.

STAGE 5: *IDENTITY VS. ROLE CONFUSION* During adolescence, which is the period between puberty and adulthood, children try to determine their identity and their direction in life. Depending on their success, they either acquire a sense of identity or remain uncertain about their roles in life.

STAGE 6: *INTIMACY VS. ISOLATION* In young adulthood, people face the challenge of developing intimate relationships with others. If they do not succeed, they may become isolated and lonely.

STAGE 7: *GENERATIVITY VS. SELF-ABSORPTION* As people reach middle adulthood, they work to become productive members of society, either through parenting or through their jobs. If they fail, they become overly self-absorbed.

STAGE 8: *INTEGRITY VS. DESPAIR* In old age, people examine their lives. They may either have a sense of contentment or be disappointed about their lives and fearful of the future.

Erikson's theory is useful because it addresses both personality stability and personality change. To some degree, personality is stable, because childhood experiences influence people even as adults. However, personality also changes and develops over the life span as people face new challenges. The problem with Erikson's theory, as with many stage theories of development, is that he describes only a typical pattern. The theory doesn't acknowledge the many differences among individuals.

CHAPTER 4
DEVELOPMENT

Erikson's Theory of Psychosocial Development

Stage	Conflict Faced	Typical Age Range	Major Challenge(s)
1	Trust vs. mistrust	First year of life	Having basic needs met, attaching to people
2	Autonomy vs. shame and doubt	1–3 years	Gaining independence
3	Initiative vs. guilt	3–6 years	Acting in a socially responsible way
4	Industry vs. inferiority	6–12 years	Competing with peers, preparing for adult roles
5	Identity vs. role confusion	Adolescence	Determining one's identity
6	Intimacy vs. isolation	Early adulthood	Developing intimate relationships
7	Generativity vs. self-absorption	Middle adulthood	Being productive
8	Integrity vs. despair	Old age	Evaluating one's life

PIAGET'S THEORY OF COGNITIVE DEVELOPMENT

While conducting intelligence tests on children, Swiss psychologist Jean Piaget began to investigate how children think. According to Piaget, children's thought processes change as they mature physically and interact with the world around them. Piaget believed children develop **schema**, or mental models, to represent the world. As children learn, they expand and modify their schema through the processes of assimilation and accommodation. **Assimilation** is the broadening of an existing schema to include new information. **Accommodation** is the modification of a schema as new information is incorporated.

> EXAMPLE: *Suppose a young boy knows his pet parrot is a bird. When he sees a robin outside and calls it a bird too, he exhibits assimilation, since he broadened his bird schema to include characteristics of both parrots and robins. His bird schema might be "all things that fly." Now suppose a bat flaps out at him one night and he shrieks, "Bird!" If he learns it was a bat that startled him, he'll have to modify his bird schema to "things that fly and have feathers." In modifying his definition, he enacts accommodation.*

Piaget proposed that children go through four stages of cognitive development:

STAGE 1: SENSORIMOTOR PERIOD In this stage, which lasts from birth to roughly two years, children learn by using their senses and moving around. By the end of the sensorimotor period, children become capable of **symbolic thought**, which means they can represent objects in terms of mental symbols. More important, children achieve object permanence in this stage. **Object permanence** is the ability to recognize that an object can exist even when it's no longer perceived or in one's sight.

> EXAMPLE: *If a three-month-old baby sees a ball, she'll probably be fascinated by it. But if someone hides the ball, the baby won't show any interest in looking for it. For a very young child, out of sight is literally out of mind. When the baby is older and has acquired object permanence, she will start to look for things that are hidden because she will know that things can exist even when they can't be seen.*

STAGE 2: PREOPERATIONAL PERIOD This stage lasts from about two to seven years of age. During this stage, children get better at symbolic thought, but they can't yet reason. According to Piaget, children aren't capable of conservation during this stage. **Conservation** is the ability to recognize that measurable physical features of objects, such as length, area, and volume, can be the same even when objects appear different.

> EXAMPLE: *Suppose a researcher gives a three-year-old girl two full bottles of juice. The girl will agree that they both contain the same amount of juice. But if the researcher pours the contents of one bottle into a short, fat tumbler, the girl will then say that the bottle has more. She doesn't realize that the same volume of juice is conserved in the tumbler.*

Piaget argued that children are not capable of conservation during the preoperational stage because of three weaknesses in the way they think. He called these weaknesses **centration, irreversibility**, and **egocentrism**:

- **Centration** is the tendency to focus on one aspect of a problem and ignore other key aspects. In the example above, the three-year-old looks only at the higher juice level in the bottle and ignores the fact that the bottle is narrower than the tumbler. Because of centration, children in the preoperational stage cannot carry out **hierarchical classification**, which means they can't classify things according to more than one level.

• **Irreversibility** is the inability to mentally reverse an operation. In the example, the three-year-old can't imagine pouring the juice from the tumbler back into the bottle. If she poured the juice back, she'd understand that the tumbler holds the same amount of liquid as the bottle.

• **Egocentrism** is the inability to take someone else's point of view. **Animism**, or the belief that even inanimate objects are living, results from egocentrism. Children assume that since they are alive, all other things must be too.

Talking Tables and Dancing Dishwashers Animism explains the popularity of children's movies featuring characters such as talking vegetables or singing candlesticks. Young children can readily believe that objects around them are alive, which means they can be entertained by stories involving living objects. Children and adolescents past the age of seven generally lose interest in heroic toasters and prefer stories about people.

STAGE 3: CONCRETE OPERATIONAL PERIOD From the age of seven to about eleven, children become capable of performing mental operations or working through problems and ideas in their minds. However, they can perform operations only on tangible objects and real events. Children also achieve conservation, reversibility, and decentration during this stage:

• **Reversibility** is the ability to mentally reverse actions.

• **Decentration** is the ability to focus simultaneously on several aspects of a problem.

Furthermore, children become less egocentric during this stage as they start to consider simultaneously different ways of looking at a problem.

STAGE 4: FORMAL OPERATIONAL PERIOD In this stage, which begins around eleven years of age and continues through adulthood, children become capable of applying mental operations to abstract concepts. They can imagine and reason about hypothetical situations. From this point on, people start to think in abstract, systematic, and logical ways.

Critiques of Piaget's Theories

Although Piaget made important contributions to the research on cognitive development, his theory has come under attack for several reasons:

- Recent research has shown that he greatly underestimated children's capabilities. For example, researchers have shown that babies achieve object permanence much sooner than Piaget said they do.

- Children sometimes simultaneously develop skills that are characteristic of more than one stage, which makes the idea of stages seem less viable.

- Piaget ignored cultural influences. Research has shown that children from different cultures tend to go through Piaget's stages in the same order, but the timing and length of stages vary from culture to culture.

- Some people never develop the capacity for formal reasoning, even as adults.

Piaget's Theory of Cognitive Development

	Stage	Age	Important Features
1	Sensorimotor	First two years of life	Object permanence, symbolic thought
2	Preoperational	2–7 years	Centration, irreversibility, egocentrism, and animism
3	Concrete operational	7–11 years	Reversibility, decentration, decrease in egocentrism, conservation
4	Formal operational	11 through adulthood	Abstract thought

KOHLBERG'S THEORY OF MORAL DEVELOPMENT

Lawrence Kohlberg focused on **moral reasoning**, or why people think the way they do about right and wrong. Influenced by Piaget, who believed that moral reasoning depends on the level of cognitive development, Kohlberg proposed that people pass through three levels of moral development. He divided each level into two stages.

LEVEL 1: THE PRECONVENTIONAL LEVEL At this level, children ascribe great importance to the authority of adults. For children in the first stage of this level, an action is wrong if it's punished, whereas in the second stage, an action is right if it's rewarded.

LEVEL 2: THE CONVENTIONAL LEVEL In the next level, children value rules, which they follow in order to get approval from others. In the first stage of this level, children want the approval only of people who are close to them. In the second stage, children become more concerned with the rules of the broader society.

LEVEL 3: THE POSTCONVENTIONAL LEVEL In the final level, people become more flexible and consider what's personally important to them. In the first stage of this level, people still want to follow society's rules, but they don't see those rules as absolute. In the second stage, people figure out right and wrong for themselves, based on abstract ethical principles. Only a small proportion of people reach this last stage of moral reasoning.

Critiques of Kohlberg's Theories

Research supports key parts of Kohlberg's theory. People do tend to progress in order through Kohlberg's stages, and cognitive and moral development do affect each other. However, critics of Kohlberg's theory have two main concerns:

- People often show the reasoning characteristic of several different levels simultaneously. For instance, in one situation, a person might reason as if he is at a conventional stage, and in another situation, he might use reasoning typical of a postconventional stage.

- Kohlberg's theory of moral development favors cultures that value individualism. In other cultures, highly moral people may base their reasoning on communal values rather than abstract ethical principles.

Kohlberg's Theory of Moral Development

	Level	Stage	What Determines Right and Wrong
1.	Preconventional	1	Punishment by adults
		2	Reward by adults
2.	Conventional	3	Rules set by close people
		4	Rules set by society
3.	Postconventional	5	Rules set by society, judged by what's personally important
		6	Rules based on abstract ethical principles

Prenatal Development

Development happens quickly during the **prenatal period**, which is the time between conception and birth. This period is generally divided into three stages: the germinal stage, the embryonic stage, and the fetal stage.

STAGE 1: THE GERMINAL STAGE The two-week period after conception is called the **germinal stage**. Conception occurs when a sperm cell combines with an egg cell to form a **zygote**. About thirty-six hours after conception, the zygote begins to divide quickly. The resulting ball of cells moves along the mother's fallopian tube to the uterus.

Around seven days after conception, the ball of cells starts to become embedded in the wall of the uterus. This process is called **implantation** and takes about a week to complete. If implantation fails, as is quite common, the pregnancy terminates. One key feature of the germinal stage is the formation of a tissue called the **placenta**. The placenta has two important functions:

- Passing oxygen and nutrients from the mother's blood into the embryo or fetus
- Removing waste materials from the embryo or fetus

STAGE 2: THE EMBRYONIC STAGE The **embryonic stage** lasts from the end of the germinal stage to two months after conception. The developing ball of cells is now called an **embryo**. In this stage, all the major organs form, and the embryo becomes very fragile. The biggest dangers are teratogens, which are agents such as viruses, drugs, or radiation that can cause deformities in an embryo or fetus. At the end of the embryonic period, the embryo is only about an inch long.

STAGE 3: THE FETAL STAGE The last stage of prenatal development is the **fetal stage**, which lasts from two months after conception until birth. About one month into this stage, the sex organs of the fetus begin to form. The fetus quickly grows as bones and muscles form, and it begins to move inside the uterus. Organ systems develop further and start to function. During the last three months, the brain increases rapidly in size, an insulating layer of fat forms under the skin, and the respiratory and digestive systems start to work independently.

Fetal Viability Around twenty-two to twenty-six weeks after conception, the fetus reaches the age of viability, after which it has some chance of surviving outside the womb if it is born prematurely. The chances of a premature baby's survival increase significantly with each additional week it remains in the mother's uterus.

Adverse Factors Affecting Fetal Development

Although the womb provides protection, the fetus remains indirectly connected to the outside world through its mother. Several factors that are linked to the mother can harm the fetus:

- Poor nutrition
- Use of alcohol
- Smoking
- Use of certain prescription or over-the-counter drugs
- Use of recreational drugs such as cocaine, sedatives, and narcotics
- X-rays and other kinds of radiation
- Ingested toxins, such as lead
- Illnesses such as AIDS, German measles, syphilis, cholera, smallpox, mumps, or severe flu

Fetal Alcohol Syndrome *Mothers who drink heavily during pregnancy may have babies with fetal alcohol syndrome. Babies with this syndrome may have problems such as small head size, heart defects, irritability, hyperactivity, mental retardation, or slowed motor development. Fetal alcohol syndrome is incurable.*

Infancy and Childhood

Babies come into the world with many **innate abilities**, or abilities that are present from birth. At birth, they possess motor reflexes such as the sucking reflex and the grasping reflex. Newborns can also hear, smell, touch, taste, and see, and these sensory abilities develop quickly.

MOTOR DEVELOPMENT

Motor development also progresses quickly. **Motor development** is the increasing coordination of muscles that makes physical movements possible. **Developmental norms** tell us the median age at which babies develop specific behaviors and abilities. Babies often deviate a fair amount from these norms.

Researchers used to think motor skill development could be explained mostly by **maturation**, genetically programmed growth and development. According to this view, babies learn to sit up, pull themselves to a standing position, and walk at particular ages because they are hard-wired that way. However, recent research suggests that motor development isn't just a passive process. Although maturation plays a large role, babies also actively develop motor skills by moving around and exploring their environments. Both maturation and experience influence motor development.

It's Not All Maturation *Maturation plays a much greater role in the development of early motor skills, such as crawling and walking, than in development of later motor skills, such as juggling or playing basketball. The development of later motor skills depends on genetic predisposition, exposure to good teachers, and social factors.*

CHAPTER 4
DEVELOPMENT

Cultural differences also affect how quickly motor skills develop, although the timing and sequence of early motor skill development remains similar across all cultures.

> EXAMPLE: *In cultures where babies receive early training in sitting up, standing, and walking, they develop these skills earlier. Conversely, in other cultures, mothers carry babies most of the time, and babies develop these skills later.*

TEMPERAMENT

Some babies have fussy personalities, while others have chirpy or quiet natures. These differences result from **temperament**, the kind of personality features babies are born with. Researchers generally agree that temperament depends more on biological factors than on environment. In the 1970s, **Alexander Thomas** and **Stella Chess**, two researchers who study temperament, described three basic types of temperament: easy, slow to warm up, and difficult. In their research, 40 percent of the children were easy, 15 percent were slow to warm up, and 10 percent were difficult. The remaining 35 percent of the children displayed a mixture of these temperaments:

- **Easy** children tend to be happy and adapt easily to change. They have regular sleeping and eating patterns and don't upset easily.

- **Slow-to-warm-up** children tend to be less cheerful and less adaptable than easy children. They are cautious about new experiences. Their sleeping and eating patterns are less regular than those of easy children.

- **Difficult** children tend to be glum and irritable, and they dislike change. Their eating and sleeping patterns are irregular.

ATTACHMENT

Attachment is the close bond between infants and their caregivers. Researchers used to think that infants attach to people who feed them and keep them warm. However, researchers Margaret and Harry Harlow showed that attachment could not occur without contact comfort. **Contact comfort** is comfort derived from physical closeness with a caregiver.

The Harlows' Baby Monkeys

The Harlows raised orphaned baby rhesus monkeys and studied their behavior. In place of its real mother, each baby monkey had two substitute or surrogate mothers. One "mother" had a head attached to a wire frame, warming lights, and a feeding bottle. The other "mother" had the same construction except that foam rubber and terry cloth covered its wire frame. The Harlows found that although both mothers provided milk and warmth, the baby monkeys greatly preferred the cloth mother. They clung to the cloth mother even between feedings and went to it for comfort when they felt afraid.

Responsive Mothering

Psychologist **Mary Ainsworth** and her colleagues found that attachment happens through a complex set of interactions between mothers and infants. The infants of sensitive, responsive mothers have stronger attachments than the infants of insensitive mothers or mothers who respond inconsistently to their infants' needs. However, an infant's temperament also plays a role in attachment. Difficult infants who fuss, refuse to eat, and sleep irregularly tax their mothers, which makes it hard for the mothers to be properly responsive.

Attachment Styles

Ainsworth devised an experiment called the **Strange Situation** in order to study attachment behavior. She asked each mother in the sample to bring her infant to an unfamiliar room that contained various toys. After the mother and infant had spent some time in the room, a stranger entered the room and tried to play with the infant. A short while later, the mother left the room, leaving the infant with the stranger. Then the mother returned to the room, and the stranger left. A little later, the mother left the room again, briefly leaving the infant alone. Finally, the mother returned to the room.

Based on her observations of infants' behavior in the Strange Situation, Ainsworth described three types of attachment patterns:

1. **Secure attachment:** Most infants in the sample had a secure attachment to their mothers. These infants expressed

unhappiness when their mothers left but still played with the stranger. When their mothers returned, the infants looked happy. The infants displayed greater attachment to their mothers than to the stranger.

2. **Anxious-ambivalent attachment:** Some infants showed a type of insecure attachment called an anxious-ambivalent attachment. These infants became upset when their mothers left but resisted contact with their mothers when they returned.

3. **Avoidant attachment:** Other infants showed a type of insecure attachment called an avoidant attachment. These infants didn't seem upset when their mothers left and avoided their mothers when they returned. Researchers did not see a significant difference in the way these infants treated their mothers and the stranger.

Culture and Attachment Style

Culture can influence attachment style because different cultures have different child-rearing practices. Ainsworth's research in the United States showed that most of her white, middle-class sample of infants had a secure attachment to their mothers. However, in Germany, where parents encourage independence from an early age, a much higher proportion of infants display an avoidant attachment, according to Ainsworth's classification. In Japan, where infants rarely separate from their mothers, the avoidant style is nonexistent, although a higher proportion of anxious-ambivalent attachments occurred than in the United States.

SEPARATION ANXIETY

Whether they are securely attached or not, most babies do experience separation anxiety. **Separation anxiety** is the emotional distress infants show when they separate from people to whom they are attached. Separation anxiety typically begins at about six to eight months of age and reaches peak intensity when an infant is about fourteen to eighteen months old.

GENDER DEVELOPMENT

Sex isn't the same as gender. **Sex** refers to a biological distinction between males and females. An example of sex difference is the

Day Care Controversy surrounds the question of whether or not to place children in day care. Some research has suggested that babies have a greater chance of developing insecure attachments if a nonparental figure cares for them for more than twenty hours per week. However, most of the evidence suggests that day care doesn't create poor attachment. Studies have even shown that day care can have positive effects on social development.

timing of puberty. Because of biological processes, girls' sexual organs mature before those of boys. **Gender** refers to a learned distinction between masculinity and femininity. An example of gender difference is girls' and boys' attitudes toward dolls. Very early on, American society teaches boys that playing with dolls is considered a girlish thing to do. **Gender stereotypes** are societal beliefs about the characteristics of males and females.

Gender Differences

Some gender differences exist, although certainly not as many as stereotypes suggest. For example, starting in preschool, gender differences arise in play behavior. Boys prefer playing with boys and girls with girls. Boys prefer to play with boyish toys like trucks and girls with girlish toys like dolls. Different people give different answers for why this is so:

- Researchers who emphasize biological differences between the sexes say that these preferences arise from biological factors such as genetics and evolution, prenatal hormones, or brain structure.

- Researchers who focus on cognitive development believe that these preferences exist because boys and girls develop different gender schemas or mental models about gender.

- Researchers who study learning think that environment produces these preferences. They point out that almost from the moment of birth, girls and boys receive different treatment. Gender preferences, these researchers say, simply reflect what society teaches children about gender.

CHAPTER 4
DEVELOPMENT

Adolescence

Adolescence used to be automatically associated with trouble. Recently, however, researchers have found that adolescence is not always so difficult, even with all the changes that occur during this period.

PHYSICAL CHANGES

Pubescence refers to the two years before puberty. The adolescent growth spurt actually begins during pubescence, at about age eleven in girls and about age thirteen in boys. At this time, children get taller and heavier and develop secondary sex characteristics. **Secondary sex characteristics** are sex-specific physical characteristics that are not essential for reproduction. Girls develop breasts, widened pelvic bones, and wider hips. Boys develop facial hair, broader shoulders, and deeper voices.

After pubescence and at the beginning of adolescence, **puberty** occurs. Puberty is the point at which sexual organs mature. Sexual organs include the ovaries in girls and the penis and testes in boys.

Menarche, or the first menstrual period, marks the onset of puberty in girls. The average age of menarche for American girls is about twelve and a half. The beginning of **nocturnal emissions**, so-called wet dreams, marks the onset of puberty in boys. American boys typically begin to produce sperm by fourteen years of age. Girls reach full sexual maturation around age sixteen, and boys reach sexual maturity at around eighteen.

> **Earlier Onset of Puberty** Girls and boys in the United States reach puberty earlier now than they did a few generations ago, possibly because nutrition and medical care have changed over the years. In Western Europe and the United States, girls have their first menstrual periods at around age twelve or thirteen. In poorer regions of Africa, which lack proper nutrition and health care, girls may not begin to menstruate until they are between the ages of fourteen and seventeen.

Varying Maturation Rates

Puberty occurs at different rates for different people. In girls, puberty usually happens between ages ten and fifteen and in boys between ages eleven and sixteen. Early or late maturation can have the following consequences:

- Early-maturing girls and late-maturing boys tend to have more psychological and social problems than their peers.

- In girls, a correlation exists between early maturation and poorer school performance, earlier sexual activity, more unwanted pregnancies, and a higher likelihood of eating disorders.

- Both boys and girls who mature early use more alcohol and drugs and have more problems with the law than their peers.

IDENTITY

As Erik Erikson pointed out, the search for identity marks an important step in adolescence. Adolescents may go through an identity crisis, during which they struggle to understand themselves and decide their future. The psychologist **James Marcia** described four identity states, based on where people stand on the path to identity:

- **Identity foreclosure** happens when a person prematurely commits to values or roles that others prescribe.

- **Identity moratorium** happens when a person delays commitment to an identity. He or she may experiment with various values and roles.

- **Identity diffusion** occurs when a person lacks a clear sense of identity but still hasn't explored issues related to identity development.

- **Identity achievement** occurs when a person considers alternative possibilities and commits to a certain identity and path in life.

Adulthood

Certain experiences tend to occur in adulthood, including:

- Marriage
- Parenthood

- The empty nest
- The midlife crisis
- Menopause (for women)
- Aging

Not all adults go through all these experiences, and the timing of particular experiences can vary greatly from person to person. However, average ages for major life events do exist. **Social clocks** indicate the typical life events, behaviors, and issues for a particular age. Each culture and historical period has a specific social clock. A middle-class white woman living in contemporary U.S. culture may be "off time" for motherhood if she had her first child at age fifteen. In another cultural context or another historical period, however, motherhood at age fifteen may have been "on time."

A **midlife crisis** is a time of doubt and anxiety in middle adulthood. Research suggests, however, that midlife crises don't automatically happen when people reach middle age. The **empty nest** refers to the time in parents' lives when their children have grown up and left home. Parents who have other roles in addition to parenting usually find this period less difficult.

Menopause is the gradual, permanent cessation of menstruation and usually begins between ages forty-five and fifty-five. Though many women suffer uncomfortable physical symptoms during menopause, such as hot flashes, emotional reactions to menopause are far from universal: many women have strong emotional reactions, while just as many others may not. Though men don't experience menopause, they do experience a gradual decline in testosterone production and sperm count as they age.

AGING

Researchers now know quite a bit about the process of growing old. Some abilities and functions decline:

- As people age, they usually lose neurons in the brain, but this loss rarely causes problems such as **dementia**, which is a condition characterized by several significant psychological deficits.

- Vision and hearing tend to decline as people grow older.

- Some aspects of memory decrease in old age. This results from a decline in the speed of mental processing. Decrease in memory capacity is normal and is not necessarily related to dementia.

Other abilities and functions stay the same or even improve as people age:

- **Crystallized intelligence**, which is intelligence based on a life span of knowledge and skills, remains constant or increases.

- Physical exercise and mental stimulation can form new connections between neurons in the brains of older adults.

- Most people's overall sense of well-being increases as they get older.

CHAPTER 4
DEVELOPMENT

Summary

Theories of Development

- Many psychologists have proposed stage theories of development, which argue that people pass through **stages** in specific orders, with challenges related to age and different capacities emerging in each stage.

- **Sigmund Freud** first described personality development in terms of stages and believed personality developed by age five.

- **Erik Erikson** proposed a theory of psychosocial development that occurs in eight stages over a person's lifetime. He proposed that people face new challenges at each stage: **trust vs. mistrust, autonomy vs. shame and doubt, initiative vs. guilt, industry vs. inferiority, identity vs. role confusion, intimacy vs. isolation, generativity vs. self-absorption**, and **integrity vs. despair.**

- **Jean Piaget's** theory of cognitive development states that children develop **schema** or mental models to represent the world. He proposed four stages of cognitive development: the **sensorimotor period**, the **preoperational period**, the **concrete operational period**, and the **formal operational period.**

- **Lawrence Kohlberg** proposed a theory of moral development that includes three levels or stages: the **preconventional level**, the **conventional level**, and the **postconventional level.**

Prenatal Development

- **Prenatal development** occurs between conception and birth.

- Prenatal development is divided into three stages: the **germinal stage**, the **embryonic stage**, and the **fetal stage.**

Infancy and Childhood

- **Motor development** or increasing coordination of muscles improves rapidly in infancy and childhood.

- **Maturation** is genetically programmed growth and development. Maturation and experience influence motor development.

- **Temperament** refers to the personality features a person is born with. **Alexander Thomas** and **Stella Chess** proposed three basic types of temperament: easy, slow to warm up, and difficult.

- **Attachment** is the close bond between babies and their caregivers. **Margaret and Harry Harlow** concluded that attachment requires **contact comfort**, which is the comfort deriving from physical closeness.

- After conducting an experiment called the Strange Situation, **Mary Ainsworth** proposed three types of **attachment styles: secure attachment, anxious-ambivalent attachment**, and **avoidant attachment**.

- **Separation anxiety** is the emotional distress infants show when separated from people to whom they are attached.

- **Gender** is the learned distinction between masculinity and femininity. **Gender stereotypes** are societal beliefs about the characteristics of males and females.

- Depending on their perspective, researchers ascribe different causes for gender differences.

Adolescence

- **Pubescence** refers to the two years before puberty and entails growth spurts and the development of secondary sex characteristics. **Secondary sex characteristics** are sex-specific physical traits that are not essential to reproduction, such as breasts, widened hips, facial hair, and deepened voices.

- **Puberty**, the point at which sexual organs mature, occurs at the beginning of adolescence. **Menarche** refers to the first menstrual period.

- On average, puberty occurs between ages ten and fifteen for girls and eleven and sixteen for boys. Maturing before or after these ages can have adverse consequences.

- The search for identity is an important step in adolescence. James Marcia described four identity stages: **identity foreclosure, identity moratorium, identity diffusion**, and **identity achievement**.

Adulthood

- Adulthood usually includes experiences such as marriage, parenthood, the empty nest, the midlife crisis, **menopause**, and aging.

- **Social clocks** indicate the typical life events, behaviors, and concerns for a particular age.

- As people age, they tend to experience loss of neurons in the brain, a decline in vision and hearing, and decreased memory. People may also experience increased **crystallized intelligence**, which is intelligence based on accumulated knowledge and skills. Physical exercise and mental stimulation can create new neural brain connections, and older adults generally have a better sense of well-being.

CHAPTER 4
DEVELOPMENT

Sample Test Questions

1. What are schema?

2. Why would a three-year-old think a string is shorter when it is folded than when it is stretched out?

3. What are two criticisms of Kohlberg's theory of moral reasoning?

4. What important contribution did the Harlows' monkey studies make to research on attachment?

5. What is the difference between sex and gender?

6. Which of these theorists believed that people develop through a series of stages related to age?
   - A. Jean Piaget
   - B. Erik Erikson
   - C. Lawrence Kohlberg
   - D. All of the above

7. Mark stole a bar of chocolate from a convenience store when he was very hungry. He doesn't think he did anything wrong since no one noticed him stealing. Mark is probably in which of Kohlberg's stages of moral development?
   - A. Preconventional level
   - B. Conventional level
   - C. Postconventional level
   - D. None of the above

8. What is maturation?
   - A. The difference between girls and boys in the timing of puberty
   - B. Genetically programmed growth and development
   - C. The ability to focus simultaneously on several aspects of a problem
   - D. The reaction infants display when separated from people to whom they are attached

9. What is likely the main conflict faced by an adolescent, according to Erikson?
   - A. Autonomy vs. shame and doubt
   - B. Generativity vs. self-absorption
   - C. Identity vs. role confusion
   - D. Integrity vs. despair

10. *What did Piaget believe children are incapable of during the preoperational stage of development?*
    - A.   Conservation
    - B.   Hierarchical classification
    - C.   Abstract thought
    - D.   All of the above

11. *During which stage are teratogens most dangerous?*
    - A.   Germinal stage
    - B.   Embryonic stage
    - C.   Fetal stage
    - D.   Perinatal stage

12. *A baby becomes upset when her mother leaves her temporarily but resists contact with the mother when she returns. According to Ainsworth's classification, what kind of attachment pattern is this?*
    - A.   A secure attachment
    - B.   Anxious-ambivalent attachment
    - C.   Avoidant attachment
    - D.   Avoidant-ambivalent attachment

13. *What do social clocks indicate?*
    - A.   The life events, behaviors, and issues that are typical for a particular age
    - B.   The ages at which children develop specific social skills
    - C.   The age at which Erikson's sixth stage of psychosocial development would be likely to occur
    - D.   When individuals are likely to reach Kohlberg's final stage of moral development

14. *What is the primary root of temperament?*
    - A.   Biological factors
    - B.   Environmental factors
    - C.   Gender
    - D.   Culture

15. *Which of the following is true of many people as they age?*
    - A.   They experience a loss of neurons in the brain
    - B.   They experience a decline in crystallized intelligence
    - C.   They gain a better sense of well-being
    - D.   A and C

ANSWERS

1. According to Piaget, schema are mental models that represent the world.

2. According to Piaget, a three year old isn't capable of conservation. Conservation is the ability to recognize that measurable physical features of objects can remain the same even when objects look different.

3. Critics of Kohlberg's theory of moral reasoning maintain two arguments: (1) people often show reasoning that's characteristic of more than one level simultaneously, and (2) Kohlberg's theory is biased toward cultures that value individualism over community.

4. Through their study with monkeys, the Harlows showed that caregivers must provide contact comfort as well as food and warmth to encourage attachment in infants.

5. Sex refers to a biological distinction between males and females, whereas gender refers to a learned distinction between masculinity and femininity.

6. **D**	11. **B**
7. **A**	12. **B**
8. **B**	13. **A**
9. **C**	14. **A**
10. **D**	15. **D**

Sensation and Perception

- The Senses
- Vision
- Hearing
- Taste and Smell
- Position, Movement, and Balance
- Touch

5

Thanks to the nose, ears, eyes, tongue, and skin, we can imagine a day at the beach: glimmering blue sky, salty water, warm sand, and crying seagulls. Our knowledge of the world depends on the senses: vision, hearing, taste, smell, position, movement, balance, and touch. If someone bounces a basketball, our eyes and ears pick up stimuli such as light and sound waves and send neural signals to the brain. This process called sensation occurs when physical energy from objects in the world or in the body stimulates the sense organs.

However, only when the signals come together meaningfully do we actually perceive a bouncing basketball. Perception happens when the brain organizes and interprets sensory information. Sensation and perception occur together, and normally we don't distinguish between the two separate processes. We use all five of our senses and organize the information we get from them every day of our lives.

The Senses

Sensation is the process by which physical energy from objects in the world or in the body stimulates the sense organs. The brain interprets and organizes this sensory information in a process called **perception**. **Psychophysics** is the study of how the physical properties of stimuli relate to people's experience of stimuli. Research in psychophysics has revealed much information about the acuity of the senses.

MEASURING THE SENSES

Psychologists assess the acuity of the senses in three ways:

1. Measuring the absolute threshold
2. Measuring the difference threshold
3. Applying signal detection theory

The **absolute threshold** is the minimum amount of stimulation required for a person to detect the stimulus 50 percent of the time. The **difference threshold** is the smallest difference in stimulation that can be detected 50 percent of the time. The difference threshold is sometimes called the **just noticeable difference (jnd)**, and it depends on the strength of the stimulus.

> **EXAMPLE:** If someone were comparing two weak stimuli, such as two very slightly sweet liquids, he'd be able to detect quite a small difference in the amount of sweetness. However, if he were comparing two intense stimuli, such as two extremely sweet liquids, he could detect only a much bigger difference in the amount of sweetness.

Weber's Law Nineteenth-century psychologist Ernst Weber proposed a principle demonstrating the fact that we can't detect the difference between two stimuli unless they differ by a certain proportion and that this proportion is constant. In other words, the just noticeable difference for a stimulus is in a fixed proportion to the magnitude of a stimulus. Weber's Law holds true except in the most extreme kinds of stimulation.

Researchers use **signal detection theory** to predict when a weak signal will be detected. This theory considers the fact that the ability to detect a signal depends not only on the strength of the signal but also on the perceiver's experience, motivation, expectation, and degree of alertness. Different people respond differently to the same signal, and the same person may detect a particular signal at one time but not another. Furthermore, people can often detect one type of signal in a sensory modality such as hearing or vision but be oblivious to other types of signals in the same sensory modality.

SENSORY ADAPTATION

When people walk into a restaurant, they probably notice food smells right away. However, as they sit in the restaurant, the smells gradually become less noticeable. This phenomenon occurs because of sensory adaptation. **Sensory adaptation** is the decrease in sensitivity to an unchanging stimulus. The smells don't disappear—the people just become less sensitive to them.

DEVELOPMENT OF THE SENSES

Babies have all the basic sensory abilities and many perceptual skills, but these abilities develop and grow more sensitive over time. Babies can recognize the difference between a human voice and other sounds, and they can locate a sound's origin. They can recognize the difference between smells and, very early on, can recognize their mother's particular smell. As for taste, they can differentiate between sweet and salty. Babies also have fairly adept visual abilities. Soon after birth, they can distinguish objects of different colors and sizes. When they are just a few weeks old, they begin to differentiate among contrasts, shadows, and patterns, and they can perceive depth after just a few months.

SENSITIVE PERIODS

Even innate perceptual skills need the right environment to develop properly. A lack of certain experiences during sensitive periods of development will impair a person's ability to perceive the world.

> *EXAMPLE: People who were born blind but regain their vision in adulthood usually find the visual world confusing. Since these adults were blind in infancy, they missed the sensory experiences necessary for their visual system to develop fully.*

Vision

Researchers have studied **vision** more thoroughly than the other senses. Because people need sight to perform most daily activities, the sense of sight has evolved to be highly sophisticated. Vision, however, would not exist without the presence of light. **Light** is electromagnetic radiation that travels in the form of waves. Light is emitted from the sun, stars, fire, and lightbulbs. Most other objects just reflect light.

People experience light as having three features: **color**, **brightness**, and **saturation**. These three types of experiences come from three corresponding characteristics of light waves:

- The color or hue of light depends on its **wavelength**, the distance between the peaks of its waves.

- The brightness of light is related to intensity or the amount of light an object emits or reflects. Brightness depends on light **wave amplitude**, the height of light waves. Brightness is also somewhat influenced by wavelength. Yellow light tends to look brighter than reds or blues.

- Saturation or colorfulness depends on light **complexity**, the range of wavelengths in light. The color of a single wavelength is pure spectral color. Such lights are called fully saturated. Outside a laboratory, light is rarely pure or of a single wavelength. Light is usually a mixture of several different wavelengths. The greater number of spectral colors in a light, the lower the saturation. Light of mixed wavelengths looks duller or paler than pure light.

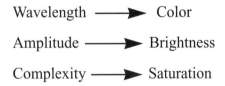

Wavelength ⟶ Color

Amplitude ⟶ Brightness

Complexity ⟶ Saturation

Rainbows and Lights

White light: *Completely unsaturated. It is a mixture of all wavelengths of light.*
The visible spectrum: *Includes the colors of the rainbow, which are red, orange, yellow, green, blue, indigo, and violet.*
Ultraviolet light: *The kind of light that causes sunburns. It has a wavelength somewhat shorter than the violet light at the end of the visible spectrum.*
Infrared radiation: *Has a wavelength somewhat longer than the red light at the other end of the visible spectrum.*

Wavelength in Centimeters

Radio	Infrared	Visible	Ultraviolet	X-ray	Gamma ray

10^4 10^2 10^{-2} 10^{-5} 10^{-6} 10^{-8} 10^{-10} 10^{-12}

STRUCTURE OF THE EYE

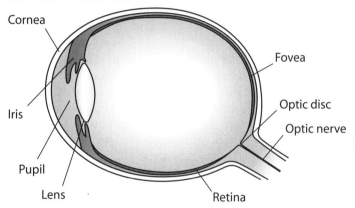

Cornea

Fovea

Optic disc

Optic nerve

Iris

Pupil

Lens

Retina

CHAPTER 5
SENSATION

The process of vision cannot be understood without some knowledge about the structure of the eye:

- The **cornea** is the transparent, protective outer membrane of the eye.

- The **iris**, the colored part of the eye, is a ring of muscle.

- The iris surrounds an opening called the **pupil**, which can get bigger or smaller to allow different amounts of light through the lens to the back of the eye. In bright light, the pupil contracts to restrict light intake; in dim light, the pupil expands to increase light intake.

- The **lens**, which lies behind the pupil and iris, can adjust its shape to focus light from objects that are near or far away. This process is called **accommodation**.

- Light passing through the cornea, pupil, and lens falls onto the retina at the back of the eye. The **retina** is a thin layer of neural tissue. The image that falls on the retina is always upside down.

- The center of the retina, the **fovea**, is where vision is sharpest. This explains why people look directly at an object they want to inspect. This causes the image to fall onto the fovea, where vision is clearest.

Eye Trouble Nearsightedness is the inability to clearly see distant objects. Farsightedness is the inability to clearly see close objects. A cataract is a lens that has become opaque, resulting in impaired vision.

Rods and Cones

The retina has millions of photoreceptors called rods and cones. **Photoreceptors** are specialized cells that respond to light stimuli. There are many more rods than cones. The long, narrow cells, called **rods**, are highly sensitive to light and allow vision even in dim conditions. There are no rods in the fovea, which is why vision becomes hazy in dim light. However, the area just outside the fovea contains many rods, and these allow peripheral vision.

Because rods are so sensitive to light, in dim lighting conditions peripheral vision is sharper than direct vision.

> EXAMPLE: *People can often see a star in the night sky if they look a little to the side of the star instead of directly at it. Looking to the side utilizes peripheral vision and makes the image of the star fall onto the periphery of the retina, which contains most of the rods.*

Cones are cone-shaped cells that can distinguish between different wavelengths of light, allowing people to see in color. Cones don't work well in dim light, however, which is why people have trouble distinguishing colors at night. The fovea has only cones, but as the distance from the fovea increases, the number of cones decreases.

Feature	Rods	Cones
Shape	Long and narrow	Cone-shaped
Sensitivity to light	High: help people to see in dim light	Low: help people to see in bright light
Help color vision	No	Yes
Present in fovea	No	Yes
Abundant in periphery of retina	Yes	No
Allow peripheral vision	Yes	No

Adaptation to Light

Dark adaptation is the process by which receptor cells sensitize to light, allowing clearer vision in dim light. **Light adaptation** is the process by which receptor cells desensitize to light, allowing clearer vision in bright light.

Connection to the Optic Nerve

Rods and cones connect via synapses to bipolar neurons, which then connect to other neurons called ganglion cells. The axons of all the ganglion cells in the retina come together to make up the **optic nerve**. The optic nerve connects to the eye at a spot in the retina called the **optic disk**. The optic disk is also called the blind spot because it has no rods or cones. Any image that falls on the blind spot disappears from view.

TRANSMISSION OF VISUAL INFORMATION

Visual information travels from the eye to the brain as follows:

- Light reflected from an object hits the retina's rods and cones.
- Rods and cones send neural signals to the bipolar cells.
- Bipolar cells send signals to the ganglion cells.

- Ganglion cells send signals through the optic nerve to the brain.

Bipolar and ganglion cells gather and compress information from a large number of rods and cones. The rods and cones that send information to a particular bipolar or ganglion cell make up that cell's receptive field.

Ganglion cell axons from the inner half of each eye cross over to the opposite half of the brain. This means that each half of the brain receives signals from both eyes. Signals from the eyes' left sides go to the left side of the brain, and signals from the eyes' right sides go to the right side of the brain. The diagram below illustrates this process.

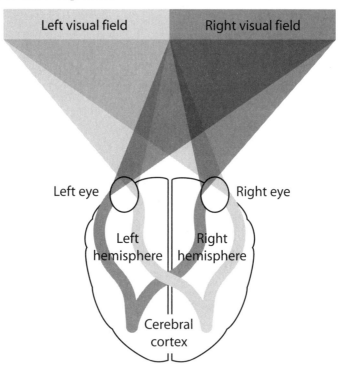

VISUAL PROCESSING IN THE BRAIN

After being processed in the thalamus and different areas of the brain, visual signals eventually reach the primary visual cortex in the occipital lobe of the brain's cerebrum. In the 1960s, David Hubel and Torsten Wiesel demonstrated that highly specialized cells called **feature detectors** respond to these visual signals in the primary visual cortex. Feature detectors are neurons that respond to specific features of the environment, such as lines and edges.

From the visual cortex, visual signals often travel on to other parts of the brain, where more processing occurs. Cells deeper down the visual processing pathway are even more specialized than those in the visual cortex. Psychologists theorize that perception occurs when a large number of neurons in different parts of the brain activate. These neurons may respond to various features of the perceived object such as edges, angles, shapes, movement, brightness, and texture.

COLOR VISION

Objects in the world seem to be brightly colored, but they actually have no color at all. Red cars, green leaves, and blue sweaters certainly exist—but their color is a psychological experience. Objects only produce or reflect light of different wavelengths and amplitudes. Our eyes and brains then convert this light information to experiences of color. Color vision happens because of two different processes, which occur in sequence:

- The first process occurs in the retina and is explained by the trichromatic theory.

- The second process occurs in retinal ganglion cells and in cells in the thalamus and visual cortex. The opponent process theory explains this process.

These two theories are explained below.

The Trichromatic Theory

Thomas Young and **Hermann von Helmholtz** proposed the **trichromatic theory**, or **Young-Helmholtz theory**. This theory states that the retina contains three types of cones, which respond to light of three different wavelengths, corresponding to red, green, or blue. Activation of these cones in different combinations and to different degrees results in the perception of other colors.

> **Color Mixing** *Mixing lights of different colors is called additive color mixing. This process adds wavelengths together and results in more light. Mixing paints, on the other hand, is called subtractive color mixing, a process that removes wavelengths so that there is less light. If red, orange, yellow, green, blue, indigo, and violet light were mixed, the result would be white light. If the same color paints were mixed together, the result would be a dark, muddy color.*

The trichromatic theory also accounts for **color blindness**, a hereditary condition that affects a person's ability to distinguish between colors. Most color-blind people are **dichromats**, which means they are sensitive to only two of the three wavelengths of light. Dichromats are usually insensitive either to red or green, but sometimes they cannot see blue.

The Opponent Process Theory

Ewald Hering proposed the **opponent process theory**. According to this theory, the visual system has receptors that react in opposite ways to three pairs of colors. The three pairs of colors are red versus green, blue versus yellow, and black versus white. Some receptors are activated by wavelengths corresponding to red light and are turned off by wavelengths corresponding to green light. Other receptors are activated by yellow light and turned off by blue light. Still others respond oppositely to black and white.

Opponent process theory explains why most people perceive four primary colors: red, green, blue, and yellow. If trichromatic theory alone fully explained color vision, people would perceive only three primary colors, and all other colors would be combinations of these three colors. However, most people think of yellow as primary rather than as a mixture of colors.

Opponent process theory also accounts for complementary or negative afterimages. **Afterimages** are colors perceived after other, complementary colors are removed.

> EXAMPLE: *If Jack stares at a picture of a red square, wave-lengths corresponding to red will activate the matching receptors in his visual system. For the sake of simplicity, these matching receptors can be referred to as red receptors. Anything that makes red receptors increase firing will be seen as red, so Jack will see the square as red. Anything that decreases the firing of red receptors will be seen as green. If Jack stares at the square for a while, the red receptors will get tired out and start to fire less. Then if he looks at a blank white sheet of paper, he will see a green square. The decreased firing of the red receptors produces an experience of a green afterimage.*

FORM PERCEPTION

The ability to see separate objects or forms is essential to daily func-tioning. Suppose a girl sees a couple in the distance with their arms around each other. If she perceived them as a four-legged, two-armed, two-headed person, she'd probably be quite disturbed. People can make sense of the world because the visual system makes sensi-ble interpretations of the information the eyes pick up.

Gestalt psychology, a school of thought that arose in Germany in the early twentieth century, explored how people organize visual information into patterns and forms. Gestalt psychologists noted that the perceived whole is sometimes more than the sum of its parts. An example of this is the **phi phenomenon**, or strobo-scopic movement, which is an illusion of movement that happens when a series of images is presented very quickly, one after another.

> EXAMPLE: *The phi phenomenon is what gives figures and objects in movies the illusion of movement. In reality, a movie is a series of still images presented in rapid succession.*

Gestalt Principles

Gestalt psychologists described several principles people use to make sense of what they see. These principles include figure and ground, proximity, closure, similarity, continuity, and simplicity:

- **Figure and ground:** One of the main ways people organize visual information is to divide what they see into figure and ground. **Figure** is what stands out, and **ground** is the background in which the figure stands. People may see an object as figure if it appears larger or brighter relative to the background. They may also see an object as figure if it differs noticeably from the background or if it moves against a static environment.

- **Proximity:** When objects lie close together, people tend to perceive the objects as a group. For example, in the graphic below, people would probably see these six figures as two groups of three.

- **Closure:** People tend to interpret familiar, incomplete forms as complete by filling in gaps. People can easily recognize the following figure as the letter *k* in spite of the gaps.

- **Similarity:** People tend to group similar objects together. In the next figure, people could probably distinguish the letter *T* because similar dots are seen as a group.

- **Continuity:** When people see interrupted lines and patterns, they tend to perceive them as being continuous by filling in gaps. The next figure is seen as a circle superimposed on a continuous line rather than two lines connected to a circle.

- **Simplicity:** People tend to perceive forms as simple, symmetrical figures rather than as irregular ones. This figure is generally seen as one triangle superimposed on another rather than a triangle with an angular piece attached to it.

DEPTH PERCEPTION

To figure out the location of an object, people must be able to estimate their distance from that object. Two types of cues help them to do this: binocular cues and monocular cues.

Binocular Cues

Binocular cues are cues that require both eyes. These types of cues help people to estimate the distance of nearby objects. There are two kinds of binocular cues: retinal disparity and convergence.

- **Retinal disparity** marks the difference between two images. Because the eyes lie a couple of inches apart, their retinas pick up slightly different images of objects. Retinal disparity increases as the eyes get closer to an object. The brain uses retinal disparity to estimate the distance between the viewer and the object being viewed.

- **Convergence** is when the eyes turn inward to look at an object close up. The closer the object, the more the eye muscles tense to turn the eyes inward. Information sent from the eye muscles to the brain helps to determine the distance to the object.

Monocular Cues

Monocular cues are cues that require only one eye. Several different types of monocular cues help us to estimate the distance of objects: interposition, motion parallax, relative size and clarity, texture gradient, linear perspective, and light and shadow.

- **Interposition:** When one object is blocking part of another object, the viewer sees the blocked object as being farther away.

- **Motion parallax** or **relative motion:** When the viewer is moving, stationary objects appear to move in different directions and at different speeds depending on their location. Relatively close objects appear to move backward. The closer the object, the faster it appears to move. Distant objects appear to move forward. The further away the object, the slower it appears to move.

- **Relative size:** People see objects that make a smaller image on the retina as farther away.

- **Relative clarity:** Objects that appear sharp, clear, and detailed are seen as closer than more hazy objects.

- **Texture gradient:** Smaller objects that are more thickly clustered appear farther away than objects that are spread out in space.

- **Linear perspective:** Parallel lines that converge appear far away. The more the lines converge, the greater the perceived distance.

- **Light and shadow:** Patterns of light and shadow make objects appear three-dimensional, even though images of objects on the retina are two-dimensional.

Creating Perspective Artists use monocular cues to give a three-dimensional appearance to two-dimensional pictures. For instance, if an artist wanted to paint a landscape scene with a straight highway on it, she would show the edges of the highway as two parallel lines gradually coming together to indicate that the highway continues into the distance. If she wanted to paint cars on the highway, she would paint bigger cars if she wanted them to seem closer and smaller cars if she wanted them to seem farther away.

PERCEPTUAL CONSTANCY

Another important ability that helps people make sense of the world is perceptual constancy. **Perceptual constancy** is the ability to recognize that an object remains the same even when it produces different images on the retina.

> EXAMPLE: *When a man watches his wife walk away from him, her image on his retina gets smaller and smaller, but he doesn't assume she's shrinking. When a woman holds a book in front of her face, its image is a rectangle. However, when she puts it down on the table, its image is a trapezoid. Yet she knows it's the same book.*

Although perceptual constancy relates to other senses as well, visual constancy is the most studied phenomenon. Different kinds of visual constancies relate to shape, color, size, brightness, and location.

- **Shape constancy:** Objects appear to have the same shape even though they make differently shaped retinal images, depending on the viewing angle.

- **Size constancy:** Objects appear to be the same size even though their images get larger or smaller as their distance decreases or increases. Size constancy depends to some extent on familiarity with the object. For example, it is common knowledge that people don't shrink. Size constancy also depends on perceived distance. Perceived size and perceived distance are strongly related, and each influences the other.

- **Brightness constancy:** People see objects as having the same brightness even when they reflect different amounts of light as lighting conditions change.

- **Color constancy:** Different wavelengths of light are reflected from objects under different lighting conditions. Outdoors, objects reflect more light in the blue range of wavelengths, and indoors, objects reflect more light in the yellow range of wavelengths. Despite this, people see objects as having the same color whether they are outdoors or indoors because of two factors. One factor is that the eyes adapt quickly to different lighting conditions. The other is that the brain interprets the color of an object relative to the colors of nearby objects. In effect, the brain cancels out the extra blueness outdoors and the extra yellowness indoors.

- **Location constancy:** Stationary objects don't appear to move even though their images on the retina shift as the viewer moves around.

VISUAL ILLUSIONS

The brain uses Gestalt principles, depth perception cues, and perceptual constancies to make hypotheses about the world. However, the brain sometimes misinterprets information from the senses and makes incorrect hypotheses. The result is an optical illusion. An **illusion** is a misinterpretation of a sensory stimulus. Illusions can occur in other senses, but most research has been done on visual illusions.

In the famous **Muller-Lyer illusion** shown here, the vertical line on the right looks longer than the line on the left, even though the two lines are actually the same length.

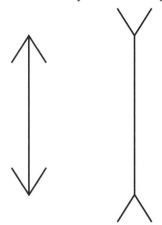

This illusion is probably due to misinterpretation of depth perception cues. Because of the attached diagonal lines, the vertical line on the left looks like the near edge of a building, and the vertical line on the right looks like the far edge of a room. The brain uses distance cues to estimate size. The retinal images of both lines are the same size, but since one appears nearer, the brain assumes that it must be smaller.

PERCEPTUAL SET

The Muller-Lyer illusion doesn't fool everyone equally. Researchers have found that people who live in cities experience a stronger illusion than people who live in forests. In other words, city-dwelling people see the lines as more different in size. This could be because buildings and rooms surround city dwellers, which prepares them to see the lines as inside and outside edges of buildings. The difference in the strength of the illusion could also be due to variations in the amount of experience people have with making three-dimensional interpretations of two-dimensional drawings.

Cultural differences in the tendency to see illusions illustrate the importance of perceptual set. **Perceptual set** is the readiness to see objects in a particular way based on expectations, experiences, emotions, and assumptions. Perceptual set influences our

CHAPTER 5
SENSATION

everyday perceptions and how we perceive **reversible figures**, which are ambiguous drawings that can be interpreted in more than one way. For example, people might see a vase or two faces in this famous figure, depending on what they're led to expect.

SELECTIVE ATTENTION

Reversible figures also illustrate the concept of **selective attention**, the ability to focus on some bits of sensory information and ignore others. When people focus on the white part of the figure, they see a vase, and when they focus on the black part of it, they see two faces. To use the language of Gestalt psychology, people can choose to make the vase figure and the face ground or vice versa.

Selective attention allows people to carry on day-to-day activities without being overwhelmed by sensory information. Reading a book would be impossible if the reader paid attention to not only the words on the page but also all the things in his peripheral vision, all the sounds around him, all the smells in the air, all the information his brain gets about his body position, air pressure, temperature, and so on. He wouldn't get very far with the book.

CONTEXT EFFECTS

Another factor that influences perception is the context of the perceiver. People's immediate surroundings create expectations that make them see in particular ways.

> **EXAMPLE:** *The figure below can be seen either as a sequence of letters, A B C, or a sequence of numbers, 12 13 14, depending on whether it is scanned across or down.*

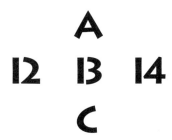

Hearing

Hearing, or audition, depends on the presence of sound waves, which travel much more slowly than light waves. **Sound waves** are changes in pressure generated by vibrating molecules. The physical characteristics of sound waves influence the three psychological features of sound: loudness, pitch, and timbre.

- Loudness depends on the **amplitude**, or height, of sound waves. The greater the amplitude, the louder the sound perceived. Amplitude is measured in decibels. The absolute threshold of human hearing is defined as 0 decibels. Loudness doubles with every 10-decibel increase in amplitude.

- Pitch, though influenced by amplitude, depends most on the frequency of sound waves. **Frequency** is the number of times per second a sound wave cycles from the highest to the

SENSATION CHAPTER 5

> **A Whisper to a Scream** *The loudness of normal human conversation is about sixty decibels. A whisper is about twenty decibels. A shout right into someone's ear is about 115 decibels. Being exposed to sounds that are over 120 decibels, even for brief periods, can damage the auditory system.*

lowest point. The higher the frequency, the higher the pitch. Frequency is measured in hertz, or cycles per second. Frequency also affects loudness, with higher-pitched sounds being perceived as louder. Amplitude and frequency of sound waves interact to produce the experiences of loudness and pitch.

> **What's Audible?** *Humans can hear sounds that are between 20 and 20,000 hertz.*

- **Timbre**, or the particular quality of a sound, depends on the **complexity** of a sound wave. A pure tone has sound waves of only one frequency. Most sound waves are a mixture of different frequencies.

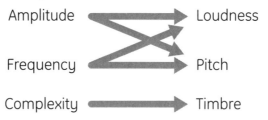

Amplitude	Loudness
Frequency	Pitch
Complexity	Timbre

THE STRUCTURE OF THE EAR

Knowing the basic structure of the ear is essential to understanding how hearing works. The ear has three basic parts: the outer ear, the middle ear, and the inner ear.

The visible part of the ear is the **pinna**, which collects sound waves and passes them along the auditory canal to a membrane called the eardrum. When sound waves hit the eardrum, it vibrates. The eardrum transmits the vibration to three bones, or **ossicles**, in the middle ear, which are called the hammer, the anvil, and the stirrup. The diagram of the ear shows how they got these names: they actually look like a hammer, an anvil, and a stirrup. In response to the vibration, these ossicles move one after another. Their function is to amplify the sound vibrations.

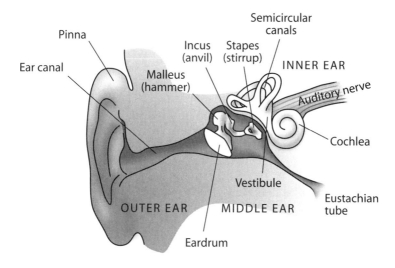

From the ossicles, vibrations move through a membrane called the oval window to the cochlea of the inner ear. The **cochlea** is a coiled, fluid-filled tunnel.

Inside the cochlea are receptors called **cilia** or hair cells that are embedded in the **basilar membrane**. The basilar membrane runs along the whole length of the coiled cochlea. Vibrations that reach the inner ear cause the fluid in the cochlea to move in waves. These waves in turn make the hair cells move.

The movement triggers impulses in neurons that connect with the hair cells. The axons of these neurons come together to form the **auditory nerve**, which sends impulses from the ear to the brain. In the brain, the thalamus and the auditory cortex, which is in the temporal lobe of the cerebrum, receive auditory information.

PITCH PERCEPTION

Two theories explain how people distinguish the pitch of different sounds: place theory and frequency theory.

Place theory explains how people discriminate high-pitched sounds that have a frequency greater than 5000 Hz. Place theory states that sound waves of different frequencies trigger receptors at different places on the basilar membrane. The brain figures out the pitch of the sound by detecting the position of the hair cells that sent the neural signal.

Frequency theory explains how people discriminate low-pitched sounds that have a frequency below 1000 Hz. According to frequency theory, sound waves of different frequencies make the whole basilar membrane vibrate at different rates and therefore cause neural impulses to be sent at different rates. Pitch is determined by how fast neural signals move along to the brain.

The detection of moderately pitched sounds, with a frequency between 1000 and 5000 Hz, is explained by both place theory and frequency theory. To discriminate among these sounds, the brain uses a code based both on where the neural impulses originated and how quickly neural impulses move.

LOCATING SOUNDS

In the same way that people use two eyes to perceive depth, people use two ears to locate the origin of sounds. The left ear receives sound waves coming from the left slightly faster than the right ear does. The signal received by the left ear may also be a little more intense than that received in the right ear, because the signal has to go around the head to enter the right ear.

Locating a sound is difficult if both ears receive a signal of exactly the same intensity at exactly the same time, as when a sound originates from directly in front, directly behind, or directly above. Turning the head or cocking it to one side can help circumvent this difficulty.

Taste and Smell

Taste and smell are chemical senses. As light waves stimulate vision and sound waves stimulate sound, chemicals stimulate taste and smell.

TASTE

Taste, or gustation, happens when chemicals stimulate receptors in the tongue and throat, on the inside of the cheeks, and on the roof of the mouth. These receptors are inside taste buds, which in turn are inside little bumps on the skin called **papillae**. Taste receptors have a short life span and are replaced about every ten days.

For a long time, researchers believed in the existence of four tastes: salty, sweet, sour, and bitter. Recently, researchers have suggested the presence of a fifth taste called umami. The spice monosodium glutamate (MSG) has an umami taste, as do many protein-rich foods. Taste is also strongly influenced by smell.

SMELL

Smell, or olfaction, happens when chemicals in the air enter the nose during the breathing process. Smell receptors lie in the top of the nasal passage. They send impulses along the olfactory nerve to the olfactory bulb at the base of the brain. Researchers theorize that there are a great many types of olfactory receptors. People perceive particular smells when different combinations of receptors are stimulated.

> **Remembrance of Smells Past** *The sense of smell is closely connected with memory. Most people have had the experience of smelling something, maybe a certain perfume or spice, and suddenly experiencing a strong emotional memory. Researchers don't know exactly why this happens, but they theorize that smell and memory trigger each other because they are processed in neighboring regions of the brain.*

CHAPTER 5
SENSATION

Position, Movement, and Balance

Kinesthesis is the sense of the position and movement of body parts. Through kinesthesis, people know where all the parts of their bodies are and how they are moving. Receptors for kinesthesis are located in the muscles, joints, and tendons.

The sense of balance or equilibrium provides information about where the body exists in space. The sense of balance tells people whether they are standing up, falling in an elevator, or riding a roller coaster. The sensory system involved in balance is called the **vestibular system.** The main structures in the vestibular system are three fluid-filled tubes called **semicircular canals**, which are located in the inner ear. As the head moves, the fluid in the semicircular canals moves too, stimulating receptors called hair cells, which then send impulses to the brain.

Touch

The sense of touch is really a collection of several senses, encompassing pressure, pain, cold, and warmth. The senses of itch and tickle are related to pressure, and burn injuries are related to pain. Touch receptors are stimulated by mechanical, chemical, and thermal energy.

Pressure seems to be the only kind of touch sense that has specific receptors.

THE GATE-CONTROL THEORY OF PAIN

Researchers don't completely understand the mechanics of pain, although they do know that processes in the injured part of the body and processes in the brain both play a role.

In the 1960s, **Ronald Melzack** and **Patrick Wall** proposed an important theory about pain called the gate-control theory of pain. **Gate-control theory** states that pain signals traveling from the body to the brain must go through a gate in the spinal cord. If the gate is closed, pain signals can't reach the brain. The gate isn't a physical structure like a fence gate, but rather a pattern of neural activity that either stops pain signals or allows them to pass. Signals from the brain can open or shut the gate. For example, focusing on pain tends to increase it, whereas ignoring the pain tends to decrease it. Other signals from the skin senses can also close the gate. This process explains why massage, ice, and heat relieve pain.

Summary

The Senses

- **Psychophysics** studies the relationship between the physical properties of stimuli and people's experience of stimuli.

- Psychologists assess the acuity of our senses by measuring the **absolute threshold** and the **difference threshold** and by applying **signal detection theory**.

- **Sensory adaptation** is the decrease in sensitivity to an unchanging stimulus.

- Babies are born with all the basic sensory abilities and some perceptual skills, which develop and become more sensitive over time.

Vision

- The sense of vision depends on **light**, which is a kind of electromagnetic radiation emitted by the sun, stars, fire, and lightbulbs.

- We experience light as color, brightness, and saturation, which depend respectively on **wavelength**, **amplitude**, and **complexity** of light waves.

- The eye is composed of the **cornea**, the **iris**, the **pupil**, the **lens**, the **retina**, and the **fovea**. The lens adjusts its shape to focus light from objects that are near or far away in a process called **accommodation**.

- **Dark and light adaptation** are processes by which receptor cells sensitize and desensitize to light, respectively.

- The retina has millions of photoreceptor cells called **rods** and **cones**. Rods and cones connect via synapses to bipolar neurons, which connect to ganglion cells. The axons of the ganglion cells make up the **optic nerve**, which connects to the eye at the **optic disk**, also called the blind spot.

- After being processed in the brain, visual signals reach the primary visual cortex, where **feature detectors** respond to the signals.

- Color is a psychological experience created when the eyes and the brain interpret light.

- **Trichromatic theory**, or the **Young-Helmholtz theory**, states that there are three types of cones in the retina, which are sensitive to light of different wavelengths corresponding to red, green, or blue. This theory accounts for **color blindness**.

- The **opponent process theory** states that receptors act in opposite ways to wavelengths associated with three pairs of colors: red vs. green, blue vs. yellow, and black vs. white. The theory accounts for the perception of four primary colors. It also accounts for **afterimages**, or colors perceived after other complementary colors are removed.

• **Gestalt psychology** proposes that the perceived whole sometimes has properties that didn't exist in the parts that make it up. An example is the **phi phenomenon**, in which an illusion of movement occurs when images are presented in a series, one after another.

• Gestalt psychologists describe principles people use to organize vision into units that make sense, including: **figure** and **ground, proximity, closure, similarity, continuity,** and **simplicity.**

• **Binocular and monocular cues** enable people to determine distance from an object.

• **Perceptual constancy** is the ability to recognize that an object is the same when it produces different images on the retina. Visual constancies relate to **shape, size, brightness, color,** and **location.**

• Visual **illusions** are misinterpretations of visual stimuli.

• **Selective attention** is the ability to focus on some pieces of sensory information and ignore others.

Hearing

• Hearing depends on **sound waves.** Sound has three features: loudness, pitch, and **timbre,** which depend respectively on wave **amplitude, frequency,** and **complexity.**

• The ear comprises the outer ear, the middle ear, and the inner ear. These parts contain the **pinna,** the eardrum, **ossicles,** oval window, **cochlea,** and **cilia.**

• Neurons in the ear form the **auditory nerve,** which sends impulses from the ear to the brain. The thalamus and auditory cortex receive auditory information.

• **Place theory** and **frequency theory** explain how people distinguish the pitch of different sounds.

Taste and Smell

• The stimuli for taste and smell are chemicals.

• Taste occurs when chemicals stimulate receptors in the tongue and throat.

• The five tastes are **salty, sweet, sour, bitter,** and **umami.**

• Smell occurs when chemicals in the air are inhaled into the nose. Smell receptors send impulses along the olfactory nerve to the brain.

Position, Movement, and Balance

- **Kinesthesis** is the sense of the position and movement of body parts.

- The sense of balance gives information about where the body exists in space and involves the vestibular system.

- The main structures of the **vestibular system** are the **semicircular canals**.

Touch

- The sense of touch encompasses **pressure, pain, cold**, and **warmth**.

- Pressure has specific receptors.

- The **gate-control theory** of pain proposes that pain signals traveling from the body to the brain pass through a gate in the spinal cord. This gate is a pattern of neural activity that prevents pain signals or admits them.

CHAPTER 5
SENSATION

Sample Test Questions

1. What are the primary tastes?

2. What is the path taken by sound waves into the ear?

3. What is accommodation?

4. How can the appearance of "afterimages" be explained?

5. Why does an animated neon sign appear to move?

6. If Alice lives near a cattle plant, she probably doesn't notice the neighborhood smell that visitors to her house complain about. What idea explains this phenomenon?
   - A. Opponent process theory
   - B. Afterimages
   - C. Sensory adaptation
   - D. Perceptual constancy

7. What is a monocular cue that helps to determine the distance of a distant object?
   - A. Motion parallax
   - B. Stroboscopic movement
   - C. Continuity
   - D. Similarity

8. What is a cue requiring the use of both eyes that helps to estimate the distance of a nearby object?
   - A. Retinal disparity
   - B. Texture gradient
   - C. Linear perspective
   - D. All of the above

9. What does perceptual constancy enable people to recognize?
   - A. Reversible figures
   - B. Afterimages
   - C. Phi phenomena
   - D. That a bus approaching on the street isn't getting bigger

10. What does perceptual set do?
    - A. Makes it likely that people will see things they assume to be true
    - B. Affects people's everyday experiences
    - C. Influences the way people see a reversible figure
    - D. All of the above

11. *What does the pitch of a sound depend on?*
    A.   The complexity and frequency of a sound wave
    B.   The amplitude and frequency of a sound wave
    C.   The amplitude and complexity of a sound wave
    D.   None of the above

12. *What theory explains how people discriminate high-pitched sounds with a frequency greater than 5000 Hz?*
    A.   Opponent-process theory
    B.   The absolute threshold
    C.   Place theory
    D.   Frequency theory

13. *Touch receptors are stimulated by which of the following?*
    A.   Mechanical energy
    B.   Chemical energy
    C.   Thermal energy
    D.   All of the above

14. *The semicircular canals are involved in which sense?*
    A.   Balance
    B.   Touch
    C.   Hearing
    D.   Smell

15. *What are feature detectors?*
    A.   Photoreceptors that enable people to see in color
    B.   Principles that people use to organize what they see into units that make sense
    C.   Neurons that respond to specific features of the environment
    D.   Instruments used by psychophysicists to measure senses

CHAPTER 5
SENSATION

ANSWERS

1. The primary tastes are salty, sour, sweet, bitter, and umami.

2. The pinna collects sound waves and passes them along the auditory canal to the eardrum. Vibrations of the eardrum move along to the ossicles and from there move through the oval window to the cochlea. The fluid in the cochlea then moves in waves, and the hair cells pick up this wave motion.

3. Accommodation is the process by which the lens of the eye adjusts in shape to focus light from objects that are near or far away.

4. According to opponent process theory, the visual system responds to three pairs of "opposed" colors. When the receptors that respond to one color, such as red, become overstimulated, the visual system perceives the opposing color, in this case green, as an afterimage.

5. The phi phenomenon, or stroboscopic movement, makes neon signs appear to move. The brain perceives a series of still images presented in rapid succession as movement.

6.	**C**	11.	**B**
7.	**A**	12.	**C**
8.	**A**	13.	**D**
9.	**D**	14.	**A**
10.	**D**	15.	**C**

States of Consciousness

- Consciousness
- Sleep
- Dreams
- Altered States

6

When we sunbathe on a warm day, we notice sensations outside our body, such as the sun shining down, as well as sensations within our body, such as relaxed muscles. Beyond this basic awareness, we are also conscious of ourselves having these experiences. Psychologists define consciousness as the awareness we have of ourselves and our environment.

Consciousness is not static: experiences constantly move in and out of our awareness as our states of mind and environments change. If we fall asleep while sunbathing, we may dream and experience thoughts, feelings, and unconscious desires that aren't always present in our waking state. Drugs and alcohol can also alter consciousness. Alcohol makes us less conscious of our physical sensations and less inhibited, and drugs such as LSD can alter consciousness even more dramatically. Our level of consciousness is, in many ways, both within and out of our control.

Consciousness

Consciousness is the awareness we have of ourselves and our environment. Different states of consciousness are associated with different patterns of brain waves. **Brain waves** are tracings of electrical activity that is going on in the brain. Scientists record brain waves using an **electroencephalograph (EEG)**, which monitors electrical activity through electrodes placed on the scalp. There are four main types of brain waves: **alpha**, **beta**, **theta**, and **delta**.

Type of Brain Wave	Corresponding Mental State
Alpha	Very relaxed or meditating
Beta	Awake and alert
Theta	Lightly asleep
Delta	Deeply asleep

Four Types of Brainwaves

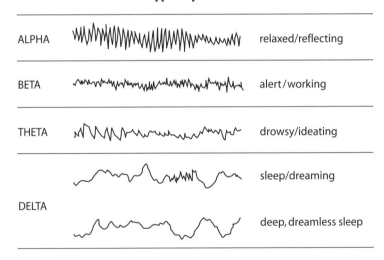

Sleep

Sleep is just one of many types of consciousness we experience, and sleep itself comprises several states of consciousness. Even when we're sleeping, our brains and bodies continue to work.

BIOLOGICAL RHYTHMS

Sleep is affected by biological rhythms or periodic physiological changes. Biological rhythms are regular, periodic changes in a body's functioning. There are three types of biological rhythms:

- **Circadian rhythms:** biological cycles that occur about every twenty-four hours. Sleep follows a circadian rhythm. Hormone secretion, blood pressure, body temperature, and urine production also have circadian rhythms.

- **Infradian rhythms:** biological cycles that take longer than twenty-four hours. For example, women's menstrual cycles occur about every twenty-eight days.

- **Ultradian rhythms:** biological cycles that occur more than once a day. Sleep follows an ultradian rhythm of about ninety minutes as well as a circadian rhythm. Alertness and hormone levels also follow ultradian rhythms.

Biological rhythms usually synchronize with environmental events such as changes in daylight. However, experiments have shown that many biological rhythms continue to have the same cycle even without cues from the environment. Such biological rhythms are **endogenous**, which means that they originate from inside the body rather than depend on outside cues.

BIOLOGICAL CLOCKS

Endogenous rhythms exist because the body has biological clocks that keep time. Biological clocks can be adjusted by environmental cues, such as changes in temperature.

In humans, the **suprachiasmatic nucleus (SCN)** is the main biological clock that regulates circadian rhythms of sleep. The SCN lies in the brain's hypothalamus. When light stimulates receptors in the retina of the eye, the receptors send signals to the SCN. The SCN then sends signals to the nearby **pineal gland**, which secretes **melatonin**, a hormone that regulates the sleep cycle.

Jet Lag

Jet lag is the fatigue and disorientation air travelers feel after a long flight. Although traveling itself drains energy, the time change also contributes to fatigue. People experience jet lag when the events in their environment are out of sync with their biological clocks.

> EXAMPLE: *A traveler leaves New York City at eight in the morning and arrives in London about seven hours later. For her, it's three in the afternoon, but because of the time change, in London it's eight in the evening. Her body, thinking it's mid-afternoon, will be confused by the lack of sunlight, and she'll experience jet lag.*

THE FUNCTION OF SLEEP

Although everyone sleeps, no one really knows *why* people sleep. Researchers have proposed several theories to explain how sleep evolved to be a necessary behavior:

- People conserve energy by sleeping periodically.

- Sleep has a protective function, as it keeps people tucked away at night, safe from predators.

- Sleep restores body tissues that are depleted during daily activities.

SLEEP RESEARCH

Sleep research has provided a lot of information about what happens to the brain and body during sleep. Researchers study sleep by monitoring subjects who spend the night in labs, and they use various instruments for different purposes:

- **Electroencephalographs (EEGs):** record brain waves

- **Electromyographs (EMGs):** record muscle activity

- **Electrooculographs (EOGs):** record eye movements

- **Electrocardiographs (EKGs):** record the activity of the heart

Other instruments monitor breathing, body temperature, and pulse.

SLEEP STAGES

During one night's sleep, people pass through several cycles of sleep, each lasting about ninety to one hundred minutes. There are five distinct stages of sleep in each cycle: 1, 2, 3, 4, and REM.

Stages 1–4

When people are relaxed and ready to fall asleep, their EEG will show mostly alpha waves. When people fall asleep, they enter into stage 1 sleep, which lasts just a few minutes. In stage 1, the EEG shows mostly theta waves. Heart rate, breathing rate, and body temperature drop, and muscles relax. Fantasies or bizarre images may float around in the mind.

After a few minutes of stage 1 sleep, people move into stage 2 sleep. Stage 2 lasts about twenty minutes and is characterized by short bursts of brain waves called **sleep spindles**. People then pass into slow-wave sleep, which occurs during stages 3 and 4. In stages 3 and 4, which together last about thirty minutes, the EEG displays mostly delta waves. People in stage 3 and 4 sleep show slow breathing and pulse rates, have limp muscles, and are difficult to rouse.

> **Sleepwalking** *Most people in stage 4 sleep are still, quiet, and difficult to rouse. Sleepwalkers, however, sometimes become physically active during stage 4. They may get up and walk around their room or even carry on a conversation, take a bath, cook, or go outside and get in their car. Because they are in a deep sleep, most sleepwalkers remember nothing of their actions when they wake up.*

REM Sleep

At the end of stage 4, people go back through the stages in reverse, from stage 4 to 3 to 2 to 1. When they reach stage 1, instead of waking up, people go into REM, or rapid eye movement, sleep. A single cycle might look like this:

1   2   3   4   3   2   REM

CHAPTER 6
CONSCIOUSNESS

REM sleep is a stage of deep sleep in which, paradoxically, brain wave activity resembles that of an alert person. REM sleep is also called paradoxical sleep.

During REM sleep, pulse rate and breathing become irregular, eyes move rapidly under closed lids, and muscles remain very relaxed. Genital arousal also happens during REM. In women, the clitoris becomes swollen with blood, and vaginal lubrication increases. In men, the penis becomes erect. EEGs show mostly beta waves during REM sleep. Although dreaming happens in other sleep stages as well, dreams are most vivid and frequent during REM sleep.

People typically go through about four sleep cycles during one night of sleep. The REM stage of sleep gets longer and longer as the night passes, while stage 3 and 4 sleep gets shorter and shorter. During the night's first sleep cycle, the REM stage lasts about ten minutes. During the night's last sleep cycle, people may spend about forty to sixty minutes in REM sleep. Non-REM sleep becomes more shallow as the night goes on, and eventually the sleeper awakens.

SLEEP DEPRIVATION

Different people need different amounts of sleep. Some people can function with fewer than six hours of sleep a night, while others can't manage without at least nine hours. Research shows that getting insufficient sleep can have negative effects on health, productivity, and performance.

Researchers have also studied the effects of insufficient REM sleep. Experiment subjects who are intentionally deprived of REM sleep tend to enter the REM stage of sleep more and more frequently during the night. After an REM-deprivation experiment has ended, subjects usually experience a **REM rebound** effect, spending more time in the REM stage on subsequent nights to make up for lost REM time.

AGING AND SLEEP

Sleep patterns change as people get older. Newborn babies spend about two-thirds of their time in sleep. As people age, they tend to sleep less. The amount of time spent in REM sleep also changes over time. In very young babies, about half of all sleep is REM sleep. As babies get older, the proportion of REM sleep decreases.

SLEEP DISORDERS

Everyone has occasional difficulty sleeping, but some people have **insomnia**, a chronic problem with falling or staying asleep. Another kind of sleep disorder is **narcolepsy**, which is a tendency to fall asleep periodically during the day. Narcolepsy can be dangerous, as people who experience it may fall asleep while driving or operating machinery.

Sleep apnea is another condition that can have negative effects on health and safety. People who have **sleep apnea** stop breathing many times during a night's sleep, and each time they stop breathing, they wake up briefly and gasp for air. This prevents them from getting enough deep sleep, which leads to irritability and sleepiness during the day. Chronic sleep apnea can also result in high blood pressure.

Dreams

The function of dreams is as much a mystery as the function of sleep.

FREUD'S DREAM THEORY

Psychoanalyst **Sigmund Freud** believed that dreams allow people to express unconscious wishes they find unacceptable in real life. He drew a distinction between the manifest content and the latent content of dreams. The **manifest content** is the plot of the dream: who's in the dream, what happens, and so on. The **latent content** is the dream's hidden meaning. According to Freud, the manifest content is a symbolic representation of the latent content. In other words, the plot acts as a disguise that masks the real meaning of the dream.

CHAPTER 6
CONSCIOUSNESS

Cigars and Tunnels   Freud theorized that many psychological problems stem from repressed sexual urges. In his dream theory, certain objects symbolize sex or genitals. The most famous Freudian symbol is the cigar, which, owing to its shape and association with men, usually represents a penis. Freudian psychiatrists would interpret tunnels and caves as vaginas.

ACTIVATION-SYNTHESIS THEORY

Another theory, called the **activation-synthesis theory**, proposes that neurons in the brain randomly activate during REM sleep. Dreams arise when the cortex of the brain tries to make meaning out of these random neural impulses. According to activation-synthesis theory, dreams are basically brain sparks.

PROBLEM-SOLVING DREAMS

Some researchers think that dreams express people's most pressing concerns and might help to solve problems in day-to-day life. If someone has an important job interview coming up, for example, he may rehearse scenarios for the interview in his dreams. If someone has relationship difficulties with a significant other, his dreams may give him clues to help solve the problem.

NEURAL HOUSEKEEPING

Some theories argue that dreams arise during the brain's routine housekeeping functions, such as eliminating or strengthening neural connections. Dreams, then, are a way of cleaning up brain files.

During **lucid dreams**, people are aware that they are dreaming and may be able to control their actions to some extent within the dream.

Altered States

Some states of consciousness don't occur naturally and must be induced in some way. These include hypnotic states, meditative states, and drug-induced states.

HYPNOSIS

Hypnosis is a procedure that opens people to the power of suggestion. A hypnotist puts a subject in an altered state by encouraging relaxation and sleepiness and often describing the sorts of physical sensations a subject should be feeling. Once a subject is in the altered state, he or she may act, perceive, think, or feel according to the hypnotist's suggestions. Not everyone can be hypnotized, and some people are more hypnotizable than others. The following chart shows what hypnosis can and can't do.

Hypnosis can:	Hypnosis can't:
Cause people to be relaxed, have a narrowed focus of attention, and be highly engaged in fantasies	Work equally effectively for everyone
Produce anesthesia and treat a range of psychological and medical problems	Force people to do things against their will
Cause hallucinations and distortions in sensory perception	Make people act in ways that would normally be beyond their physical or mental abilities
Reduce inhibitions	Reliably increase the accuracy of memories
Cause changes in behavior after the hypnosis has ended	Allow people to actually reexperience past events or lives

If hypnotized people are instructed to forget what happened during hypnosis, they later claim to have no memory of it. This phenomenon is called **posthypnotic amnesia**.

A hypnotic state isn't sleep—brain waves, for example, do not reliably change during hypnosis as they do during sleep. Researchers don't even agree that hypnosis is an altered state of consciousness. Researchers propose two main theories about hypnosis:

- **Ernest Hilgard** proposed that hypnosis causes people to dissociate or divide their consciousness into two parts. One part responds to the outside world, and the other part observes but doesn't participate. According to this theory, hypnosis can make people not react to pain because hypnosis separates the part of consciousness that registers pain from the part of consciousness that communicates with the outside world.

CHAPTER 6 CONSCIOUSNESS

- Many other researchers, such as Theodore Barber and Nicholas Spanos, think hypnosis happens when a suggestible person plays the role of a hypnotized person. According to this theory, hypnotized people simply behave as they think they are expected to.

MEDITATION

Meditation is the practice of focusing attention. People meditate to enhance awareness and gain more control of physical and mental processes. Techniques used in meditation vary and include activities such as repetitive chanting and breathing exercises.

Meditative states are associated with an increase in alpha and theta brain waves, and physical indicators of relaxation such as slowed pulse and breathing. Some researchers have found that meditation has long-term effects such as improving physical and mental health and reducing stress. However, researchers disagree about whether meditative states are unique states of consciousness. Some researchers believe relaxation techniques can produce the same kind of state produced by meditation.

PSYCHOACTIVE DRUGS

Psychoactive drugs, as opposed to medicinal drugs, have psychological effects, meaning that they change sensory experience, perception, mood, thinking, and behavior. Psychoactive drugs are sometimes called recreational drugs, though some have legitimate medical uses.

Types of Recreational Drugs

Researchers usually classify recreational drugs into four types: stimulants, sedatives, narcotics, and hallucinogens.

- **Stimulants:** drugs that stimulate the central nervous system
- **Sedatives:** drugs that slow down the central nervous system
- **Narcotics:** also called opiates; drugs that can relieve pain
- **Hallucinogens:** drugs that cause sensory and perceptual distortions

Drugs derived from the cannabis plant, such as marijuana and hashish, have features of more than one of these drug types, so researchers sometimes consider cannabis to be a separate, fifth drug type.

Drug type	Examples	Effects	Negative effects
Stimulants	Nicotine, caffeine, cocaine, amphetamines, crystal meth	Increased alertness and energy, excitation, euphoria, confidence	Anxiety, restlessness, irritability, sleeplessness, paranoia, increased aggressiveness, feelings of panic
Sedatives	Alcohol, Valium, Xanax, barbiturates, such as Seconal	Euphoria, relaxation, less anxiety	Impaired coordination, depression, lethargy, drowsiness, mood swings
Narcotics	Morphine, heroin, opium, codeine, hydrocodone, such as Vicodin	Euphoria, relaxation, less anxiety, less sensitivity to pain	Lethargy, drowsiness, nausea, impaired coordinated, constipation
Hallucinogens	LSD, mescaline, psilocybin	Euphoria, changed perception, hallucinations, insightful moments	Nausea, paranoia, anxiety, feelings of panic, mood swings, impaired judgment, jumbled thoughts
Cannabis	Marijuana, hashish	Euphoria, relaxation, increased awareness, changed perception	Sluggishness, anxiety, impaired memory

How Psychoactive Drugs Work

Psychoactive drugs work by affecting neurotransmitter function. A single drug can affect the function of more than one neurotransmitter. Drugs can:

- Cause more or less of a neurotransmitter to be released at synapses

- Block reuptake of a neurotransmitter by presynaptic cells

- Stimulate or block neurotransmitter receptors on postsynaptic cells

Hallucinations Hallucinations are sensory or perceptual experiences that happen without any external stimulus. Hallucinogenic drugs fool the brain into perceiving sights, sounds, and tastes that aren't actually present, and they may confuse a person's sense of space and time. For example, a man who takes a hallucinogenic drug may hear voices in his head.

Influences on Psychoactive Drug Effects

A given drug doesn't always have the same effect. If ten people drink beer one evening, they all may have different experiences. The effect of a drug depends on many different factors:

- The amount of the drug

- The potency of the drug

- How the drug is administered

- How much previous experience a user has with the drug

- The user's age and body weight

- The user's mood, personality, and motivation

- The environment in which the drug is used

- The user's expectations about the drug's effects

Chronic Use of Psychoactive Drugs

When people regularly use a drug, they may develop a tolerance to it. As time goes on, people with a **tolerance** need more and more of the drug to get the same effect.

When people stop using a drug after a long period of regular use, they often experience **withdrawal symptoms**. Different drugs produce different kinds of withdrawal symptoms. Not all drugs are addictive.

With chronic use, people can get physically or psychologically dependent on a drug. **Physical dependence** happens when a person must take the drug to avoid withdrawal symptoms. **Psychological dependence** is when a person keeps taking the drug because of cravings. A drug can be both physically and psychologically addictive.

Drug use can be dangerous for several reasons. Heavy or frequent use of drugs can damage body tissues and organs. Overdoses of some drugs, including sedatives, stimulants, and narcotics, can be lethal. Drugs can have dangerous indirect effects by causing people to behave in risky, accident-prone, or unhealthy ways.

Summary

Consciousness

- **Consciousness** is the awareness people have of themselves and the environment around them.

- The level and state of consciousness vary. Different states of consciousness are associated with different brain wave patterns. **Brain waves** are tracings that show the kind of electrical activity going on in the brain. Scientists use an **electroencephalograph,** or EEG, to record these waves.

- The main types of brain waves are **alpha, beta, theta,** and **delta.**

Sleep

- Types of **biological rhythms** include **circadian, infradian,** and **ultradian rhythms.**

- **Endogenous biological rhythms** originate from inside the body rather than from the outside environment.

- Biological clocks in the body regulate the sense of time.

- The **suprachiasmatic nucleus** regulates circadian rhythms of sleep.

- Different theories suggest that people sleep to conserve energy, stay safe from predators, or restore body tissues depleted during the day.

- Researchers use **EEGs, EMGs, EOGs,** and **EKGs** to record sleep patterns.

- There are five stages of sleep. At each stage, different types of brain waves function, and heart rate, breathing, and temperature vary.

- During **REM sleep,** heart rate and breathing become irregular, eyes move rapidly, and muscles relax. Dreams are most vivid during REM sleep.

- Sleep patterns change as people age, with most people needing less sleep as they get older.

- Sleep disorders include **insomnia, narcolepsy,** and **sleep apnea.**

Dreams

- **Sigmund Freud** believed that dreams allow people to express unconscious wishes. He said the **manifest content** of dreams, or the dream's plot, symbolizes the **latent content,** or hidden meaning.

- The **activation-synthesis theory** proposes that neurons in the brain randomly activate during REM sleep. Dreams arise when the cortex tries to make sense of these impulses.

- Some researchers think dreams express people's most pressing concerns, while others think dreams arise during the brain's routine housekeeping chores such as eliminating or strengthening neural connections.

Altered States

- **Altered states** are induced states of consciousness and include hypnotic states, meditative states, and drug-induced states.

- In **hypnosis**, a hypnotist makes suggestions to a person. One theory states that people in hypnosis divide their consciousness into two parts. Other theories say that people merely play a role when hypnotized.

- **Meditation** is the practice of focusing attention.

- **Psychoactive drugs** are usually used for recreational rather than medical purposes, though some have legitimate medical uses. These drugs change sensory experience, perception, mood, thinking, and behavior.

- Recreational drugs include **stimulants**, **sedatives**, **narcotics**, and **hallucinogens**.

- Drugs work by affecting neurotransmitter function in various ways.

- The effect of any drug depends on many factors such as the amount of the drug, how the drug is administered, and the user's mood, personality, and motivation.

- Chronic use of drugs can result in **tolerance**, **withdrawal symptoms**, **physical dependence**, or **psychological dependence**.

- Drug use can be dangerous.

CHAPTER 6 CONSCIOUSNESS

Sample Test Questions

1. Why is REM sleep also called paradoxical sleep?

2. What is the activation-synthesis theory of dreams?

3. What are the different classes of recreational drugs?

4. What are the two main theories about the nature of hypnosis?

5. What functions might sleep have?

6. What is an ultradian rhythm?
   - A. A biological rhythm that occurs less than once a day
   - B. A biological rhythm that occurs more than once a day
   - C. A biological rhythm that occurs once a day
   - D. A biological rhythm that occurs every other day

7. What type of brain waves predominate in stage 4 sleep?
   - A. Delta waves
   - B. Alpha waves
   - C. Theta waves
   - D. Beta waves

8. What does the suprachiasmatic nucleus do?
   - A. Secretes melatonin, which regulates the sleep cycle
   - B. Is used to measure eye activity during sleep
   - C. Is the organ that causes dreaming
   - D. Regulates circadian rhythms of sleep

9. When does the REM rebound effect occur?
   - A. When sleep spindles are occurring
   - B. As people age
   - C. After a period of REM deprivation
   - D. Mostly in newborn babies

10. What does the activation-synthesis theory propose?
    - A. Dreams arise when the cortex of the brain tries to make meaning out of random neural impulses
    - B. Dreams allow people to express unconscious wishes that are unacceptable in real life
    - C. Dreams express people's most pressing concerns
    - D. Dreams arise during the brain's routine housekeeping functions

11. *Which of the following can hypnosis not do?*
    A.   Produce anesthesia
    B.   Reduce inhibitions
    C.   Cause people to act against their will
    D.   Cause changes in behavior after hypnosis has ended

12. *Which of the following is true of meditative states?*
    A.   They are associated with an increase in delta brain waves
    B.   They are similar to states of deep sleep
    C.   They are associated with physical indicators of relaxation, such as slowed pulse
    D.   All of the above

13. *A person who has recently ingested a recreational drug cannot sleep and appears aggressive, paranoid, and restless. What might this drug have been?*
    A.   Valium
    B.   Morphine
    C.   Heroin
    D.   Crystal meth

14. *What term describes the need, as time goes on, for more and more of a drug to get the same effect?*
    A.   Physical dependence
    B.   Psychological dependence
    C.   Tolerance
    D.   Withdrawal

15. *Which of the following accurately describes people who have sleep apnea?*
    A.   They tend to be alert during the day
    B.   They stop breathing periodically during the night
    C.   They tend to sleep very heavily at night
    D.   All of the above

CHAPTER 6
CONSCIOUSNESS

ANSWERS

1.   Although REM is a stage of deep sleep in which muscles are very relaxed, paradoxically, people in REM sleep and people who are awake have similar brain wave activity.

2.   The activation-synthesis theory of dreams states that neurons in the brain randomly activate during REM sleep and that dreams arise when the cortex tries to make meaning out of these random neural impulses.

3.   The classes of recreational drugs are stimulants, sedatives, hallucinogens, narcotics, and cannabis-derived drugs.

4.   One theory proposes that hypnosis causes people to dissociate or divide their consciousness into two parts: an observing part and a participating part. Another theory proposes that hypnosis makes people play elaborate roles.

5.   The functions of sleep include conservation of energy, protection from predators, and restoration of body tissues.

6. **B**	11. **C**
7. **A**	12. **C**
8. **D**	13. **D**
9. **C**	14. **C**
10. **A**	15. **B**

Learning and Conditioning

- Classical Conditioning
- Operant Conditioning
- Biological Influences
- Cognitive Influences
- Observational Learning

A vast amount of time and effort is spent on the business of learning, and any teacher or student will agree that learning is not always a simple matter. If a teacher tells a child to stay away from kids on the swings, the child may not always remember and obey—until a few collisions teach him his lesson. A kindergartener may need to watch her father tie his shoes dozens of times before she understands how to do it herself. Psychologists define learning as a change in behavior or knowledge that results from experience.

Three kinds of learning are of particular importance to psychologists. Classical conditioning is learning that depends on associations between events, such as learning to walk far from the swings to avoid collisions. Operant conditioning is learning that depends on the consequences of behavior, such as learning that getting a good night's sleep before an exam will help to earn a good grade. Observational learning involves learning by watching others, such as learning to tie shoelaces by watching someone else do it first.

Classical Conditioning

Russian physiologist **Ivan Pavlov** was the first to describe classical conditioning. In **classical conditioning**, also called "respondent conditioning" or "Pavlovian conditioning," a subject comes to respond to a neutral stimulus as he would to another, nonneutral stimulus by learning to associate the two stimuli.

Pavlov's contribution to learning began with his study of dogs. Not surprisingly, his dogs drooled every time he gave them food. Then he noticed that if he sounded a tone every time he fed them, the dogs soon started to drool at the sound of the tone, even if no food followed it. The dogs had come to associate the tone, a neutral stimulus, with food, a nonneutral stimulus.

CONDITIONED AND UNCONDITIONED STIMULI AND RESPONSES

Psychologists use several terms to talk about classical conditioning. In Pavlov's experiment, salivation was the **unconditioned response**, which is a response that occurs naturally. Food was the **unconditioned stimulus**, the stimulus that naturally evoked salivation. The tone was the **conditioned stimulus**, the stimulus that the dogs learned to associate with food. The **conditioned response** to the tone was salivation. The conditioned response is usually the same as, or similar to, the unconditioned response.

> EXAMPLE: *Suppose Adam has a psychology class with Professor Smith, who is determined to teach him about classical conditioning. In the first class, Professor Smith whips out a revolver and shoots it into the air. The revolver is loaded with blanks, but when Adam hears the loud bang, he cringes out of surprise. Professor Smith repeats this action several times during the class. By the end of the hour, Adam cringes as soon as she whips out the revolver, expecting a bang. He cringes even if she doesn't shoot. In this scenario, the unconditioned stimulus is the bang, the unconditioned response is cringing, the conditioned stimulus is the revolver, and the conditioned response is cringing.*

ACQUISITION OF CONDITIONED RESPONSES

Subjects acquire a conditioned response when a conditioned stimulus is paired with an unconditioned stimulus. Conditioning works best if the conditioned stimulus appears just before the unconditioned stimulus and both stimuli end at about the same time. In the above example, Professor Smith's conditioning will work best if she displays the revolver right before firing and puts it away after shooting.

EXTINCTION

After Adam has been conditioned to cringe at the sight of the revolver, Professor Smith comes into the next class and pulls out the revolver again. He cringes, but she doesn't shoot. If she pulls it out again and again on several occasions without shooting, Adam will soon stop cringing when she pulls it out. This process called **extinction** is the gradual weakening and disappearance of a conditioned response. Extinction happens when the conditioned stimulus appears repeatedly without the unconditioned stimulus.

SPONTANEOUS RECOVERY

Suppose that by the end of the second class, Adam has completely stopped cringing when Professor Smith pulls out the revolver. His conditioned response has been extinguished. However, if Professor Smith comes into class later in the semester and pulls out the revolver again, Adam may still cringe, though maybe a little less than before. This is called spontaneous recovery. **Spontaneous recovery** is the reappearance of an extinguished conditioned response when the conditioned stimulus returns after a period of absence.

STIMULUS GENERALIZATION

Now suppose Professor Smith conditions Adam again to respond to the revolver as she did in the first class. Soon he cringes every time she pulls out the revolver. While Adam is in this conditioned state, the professor pulls out a cell phone. Adam is likely to cringe at that too because of **stimulus generalization**—the tendency to respond to a new stimulus as if it were the original conditioned stimulus. Stimulus generalization happens most often when the new stimulus resembles the original conditioned stimulus.

> EXAMPLE: *In the 1920s, the behaviorist **John Watson** and his colleague Rosalie Rayner did a famous study that demonstrated stimulus generalization. They gave a white rat to an eleven-month-old boy named Little Albert, who liked the rat and enjoyed playing with it. In the next stage of the experiment, the researchers repeatedly made a loud noise behind Albert while offering him the rat. Each time, Albert fell to the floor, frightened. When the researchers then offered the rat to him without making the noise, Albert showed fear of the rat and crawled away from it. The researchers were subsequently able to generalize Albert's fear to other furry, white stimuli, including a rabbit, a dog, a fur coat, a Santa Claus mask, and Watson's hair. This experiment is considered highly unethical by today's standards.*

STIMULUS DISCRIMINATION

Suppose Professor Smith used a gray revolver to condition Adam. Once Adam is conditioned, if she pulls out a brown revolver, he'll initially cringe at that, too. But suppose Professor Smith never shoots when she pulls out the brown revolver and always shoots when she pulls out the gray one. Soon, Adam will cringe *only* at the gray revolver. He is showing **stimulus discrimination**—the tendency to lack a conditioned response to a new stimulus that resembles the original conditioned stimulus.

HIGHER-ORDER CONDITIONING

Now suppose that after Adam has been conditioned to cringe at the sight of the revolver, Professor Smith comes to class one day and pulls out the revolver while yelling, "Fire!" She does this many times. Each time, Adam cringes because he is conditioned to respond to the revolver. If she then yells, "Fire!" without pulling out the revolver, Adam will still cringe due to **higher-order conditioning**—the process by which a neutral stimulus comes to act as a conditioned stimulus by being paired with another stimulus that already evokes a conditioned response.

Phobias and Conditioning A phobia is an intense, irrational fear that impairs a person's ability to function normally or participate in normal activities. Phobias, such as Little Albert's fear of rats and white, furry objects, may result from classical conditioning. For example, if someone has a near-drowning experience, he may become afraid of water in general.

Operant Conditioning

In the late nineteenth century, psychologist **Edward Thorndike** proposed the law of effect. The **law of effect** states that any behavior that has good consequences will tend to be repeated, and any behavior that has bad consequences will tend to be avoided. In the 1930s, another psychologist, **B. F. Skinner**, extended this idea and began to study operant conditioning. **Operant conditioning** is a type of learning in which responses come to be controlled by their consequences. Operant responses are often new responses.

Just as Pavlov's fame stems from his experiments with salivating dogs, Skinner's fame stems from his experiments with animal boxes. Skinner used a device called the Skinner box to study operant conditioning. A **Skinner box** is a cage set up so that an animal can automatically get a food reward if it makes a particular kind of response. The box also contains an instrument that records the number of responses an animal makes.

Psychologists use several key terms to discuss operant conditioning principles, including *reinforcement* and *punishment*.

REINFORCEMENT

Reinforcement is delivery of a consequence that increases the likelihood that a response will occur. **Positive reinforcement** is the presentation of a stimulus after a response so that the response will occur more often. **Negative reinforcement** is the removal of a stimulus after a response so that the response will occur more often. In this terminology, positive and negative don't mean good and bad. Instead, *positive* means adding a stimulus, and *negative* means removing a stimulus.

CHAPTER 7
LEARNING

PUNISHMENT

Punishment is the delivery of a consequence that decreases the likelihood that a response will occur. Positive and negative punishments are analogous to positive and negative reinforcement. **Positive punishment** is the presentation of a stimulus after a response so that the response will occur less often. **Negative punishment** is the removal of a stimulus after a response so that the response will occur less often.

Reinforcement helps to increase a behavior, while punishment helps to decrease a behavior.

PRIMARY AND SECONDARY REINFORCERS AND PUNISHERS

Reinforcers and punishers are different types of consequences:

- **Primary reinforcers**, such as food, water, and caresses, are naturally satisfying.

- **Primary punishers**, such as pain and freezing temperatures, are naturally unpleasant.

- **Secondary reinforcers**, such as money, fast cars, and good grades, are satisfying because they've become associated with primary reinforcers.

- **Secondary punishers**, such as failing grades and social disapproval, are unpleasant because they've become associated with primary punishers.

- Secondary reinforcers and punishers are also called **conditioned reinforcers and punishers** because they arise through classical conditioning.

Is It Primary or Secondary? To distinguish between primary and secondary reinforcers, people can ask themselves this question: "Would a newborn baby find this stimulus satisfying?" If the answer is yes, the reinforcer is primary. If the answer is no, it's secondary. The same idea can be applied to punishers by asking whether a baby would find the stimulus unpleasant.

SHAPING

Shaping is a procedure in which reinforcement is used to guide a response closer and closer to a desired response.

> EXAMPLE: *Lisa wants to teach her dog, Rover, to bring her the TV remote control. She places the remote in Rover's mouth and then sits down in her favorite TV-watching chair. Rover doesn't know what to do with the remote, and he just drops it on the floor. So Lisa teaches him by first praising him every time he accidentally walks toward her before dropping the remote. He likes the praise, so he starts to walk toward her with the remote more often. Then she praises him only when he brings the remote close to the chair. When he starts doing this often, she praises him only when he manages to bring the remote right up to her. Pretty soon, he brings her the remote regularly, and she has succeeded in shaping a response.*

REINFORCEMENT SCHEDULES

A **reinforcement schedule** is the pattern in which reinforcement is given over time. Reinforcement schedules can be continuous or intermittent. In **continuous reinforcement**, someone provides reinforcement every time a particular response occurs. Suppose Rover, Lisa's dog, pushes the remote under her chair. If she finds this amusing and pats him every time he does it, she is providing continuous reinforcement for his behavior. In **intermittent** or **partial reinforcement**, someone provides reinforcement on only some of the occasions on which the response occurs.

Types of Intermittent Reinforcement Schedules

There are four main types of intermittent schedules, which fall into two categories: ratio or interval. In a **ratio schedule**, reinforcement happens after a certain number of responses. In an **interval schedule**, reinforcement happens after a particular time interval.

- In a **fixed-ratio schedule**, reinforcement happens after a set number of responses, such as when a car salesman earns a bonus after every three cars he sells.

- In a **variable-ratio schedule**, reinforcement happens after a particular average number of responses. For example, a person trying to win a game by getting heads on a coin toss gets heads every two times, on average, that she tosses a penny. Sometimes she may toss a penny just once and get heads, but other times she may have to toss the penny two, three, four, or more times before getting heads.

- In a **fixed-interval schedule**, reinforcement happens after a set amount of time, such as when an attorney at a law firm gets a bonus once a year.

- In a **variable-interval schedule**, reinforcement happens after a particular average amount of time. For example, a boss who wants to keep her employees working productively might walk by their workstations and check on them periodically, usually about once a day, but sometimes twice a day, or some-times every other day. If an employee is slacking off, she reprimands him. Since the employees know there is a variable interval between their boss's appearances, they must stay on task to avoid a reprimand.

Response Patterns

These different types of reinforcement schedules result in different patterns of responses:

- Partial or intermittent schedules of reinforcement result in responses that resist extinction better than responses resulting from continuous reinforcement. Psychologists call this resistance to extinction the **partial reinforcement effect.**

- Response rate is faster in ratio schedules than in interval schedules. Ratio schedules depend on number of responses, so the faster the subject responds, the more quickly reinforcement happens.

- A fixed-interval schedule tends to result in a **scalloped response pattern**, which means that responses are slow in the beginning of the interval and faster just before reinforcement happens. If people know when reinforcement will occur, they will respond more at that time and less at other times.

- Variable schedules result in steadier response rates than fixed schedules because reinforcement is less predictable. Responses to variable schedules also cannot be extinguished easily.

EXTINCTION

As in classical conditioning, **extinction** in operant conditioning is the gradual disappearance of a response when it stops being reinforced. In the earlier example, Lisa's dog, Rover, started to put the remote under her chair regularly because she continuously reinforced the behavior with pats on his head. If she decides that the game has gone too far and stops patting him when he does it, he'll eventually stop the behavior. The response will be extinguished.

STIMULUS DISCRIMINATION

If Lisa enjoys Rover's antics with the TV remote only in the day-time and not at night when she feels tired, Rover will put the remote under her chair only during the day, because daylight has become a signal that tells Rover his behavior will be reinforced. Daylight has become a discriminative stimulus. A **discriminative stimulus** is a cue that indicates the kind of con-sequence that's likely to occur after a response. In operant condi-tioning, **stimulus discrimination** is the tendency for a response to happen only when a particular stimulus is present.

STIMULUS GENERALIZATION

Suppose Lisa's dog, Rover, began to put the remote under her chair not only during the day but also whenever a bright light was on at night, thinking she would probably pat him. This is called stimulus generalization. In operant conditioning, **stimulus generalization** is the tendency to respond to a new stimulus as if it is the original discriminative stimulus.

Biological Influences

Conditioning accounts for a lot of learning, both in humans and nonhuman species. However, biological factors can limit the capacity for conditioning. Two good examples of biological influences on conditioning are taste aversion and instinctive drift.

TASTE AVERSION

Psychologist John Garcia and his colleagues found that aversion to a particular taste is conditioned only by pairing the taste (a conditioned stimulus) with nausea (an unconditioned stimulus). If taste is paired with other unconditioned stimuli, conditioning doesn't occur.

Similarly, nausea paired with most other conditioned stimuli doesn't produce aversion to those stimuli. Pairing taste and nausea, on the other hand, produces conditioning very quickly, even with a delay of several hours between the conditioned stimulus of the taste and the unconditioned stimulus of nausea. This phenomenon is unusual, since normally classical conditioning occurs only when the unconditioned stimulus immediately follows the conditioned stimulus.

> EXAMPLE: *Joe eats pepperoni pizza while watching a movie with his roommate, and three hours later, he becomes nauseated. He may develop an aversion to pepperoni pizza, but he won't develop an aversion to the movie he was watching or to his roommate, even though they were also present at the same time as the pizza. Joe's roommate and the movie won't become conditioned stimuli, but the pizza will. If, right after eating the pizza, Joe gets a sharp pain in his elbow instead of nausea, it's unlikely that he will develop an aversion to pizza as a result. Unlike nausea, the pain won't act as an unconditioned stimulus.*

An Evolutionary Adaptation The combination of taste and nausea seems to be a special case. Researchers think that learning to quickly associate taste and nausea is an evolutionary adaptation, since this association helps people to know what foods to avoid in order to survive.

INSTINCTIVE DRIFT

Instinctive drift is the tendency for conditioning to be hindered by natural instincts. Two psychologists, Keller and Marian Breland, were the first to describe instinctive drift. The Brelands found that through operant conditioning, they could teach raccoons to put a coin in a box by using food as a reinforcer. However, they couldn't teach raccoons to put *two* coins in a box. If given two coins, raccoons just held on to the coins and rubbed them together. Giving the raccoons two coins brought out their instinctive food-washing behavior: raccoons instinctively rub edible things together to clean them before eating them. Once the coins became associated with food, it became impossible to train them to drop the coins into the box.

Cognitive Influences

Researchers once thought of conditioning as automatic and not involving much in the way of higher mental processes. However, now researchers believe that conditioning does involve some information processing.

The psychologist **Robert Rescorla** showed that in classical conditioning, pairing two stimuli doesn't always produce the same level of conditioning. Conditioning works better if the conditioned stimulus acts as a reliable signal that predicts the appearance of the unconditioned stimulus.

> EXAMPLE: *Consider the earlier example in which Adam's professor, Professor Smith, pulled out a revolver in class and shot it into the air, causing Adam to cringe. If Adam heard a gunshot only when Professor Smith pulled out her revolver, he would be conditioned to cringe at the sight of the revolver. Now suppose Professor Smith sometimes took out the revolver as before and fired it. Other times, she played an audio recording of a gunshot without taking out the revolver. The revolver wouldn't predict the gunshot sound as well now, since gunshots happen both with and without the revolver. In this case, Adam wouldn't respond as strongly to the sight of the revolver.*

The fact that classical conditioning depends on the predictive power of the conditioned stimulus, rather than just association of two stimuli, means that some information processing happens during classical conditioning. Cognitive processes are also involved in operant conditioning. A response doesn't increase just because satisfying consequences follow the response. People usually think about whether the response caused the consequence. If the response did cause the consequence, then it makes sense to keep responding the same way. Otherwise, it doesn't.

Observational Learning

People and animals don't learn only by conditioning; they also learn by observing others. **Observational learning** is the process of learning to respond in a particular way by watching others, who are called models. Observational learning is also called "vicarious conditioning" because it involves learning by watching others acquire responses through classical or operant conditioning.

> EXAMPLE: *Brian might learn not to stand too close to a soccer goal because he saw another spectator move away after getting whacked on the head by a wayward soccer ball. The other spectator stopped standing close to the soccer goal because of operant conditioning—getting clobbered by the ball acted as positive punishment for standing too close. Brian was indirectly, or vicariously, conditioned to move away.*

Bandura and the Bobo Dolls *The person best known for research on observational learning is psychologist Albert Bandura, who did some landmark experiments showing that children who watched adults behaving aggressively were more likely to behave aggressively themselves. His most famous experiment was the Bobo doll study. Bandura let a group of kindergarteners watch a film of an adult violently attacking an inflatable plastic toy shaped like Bobo the Clown by hitting it, sitting on it, hammering it, and so forth. He then let the children into a room with Bobo dolls. The children precisely imitated the adult's behavior, gleefully attacking Bobo. Their behavior was a type of observational learning.*

Summary

Classical Conditioning

- **Ivan Pavlov** was the first to describe **classical conditioning**, the type of learning in which a subject comes to respond to a neutral stimulus as he would to another stimulus by learning to associate the two stimuli.

- An **unconditioned response** is the naturally occurring response; an **unconditioned stimulus** is the stimulus that evokes an innate response. A **conditioned response** is the learned response; a **conditioned stimulus** is the learned or associated stimulus.

- A conditioned response is acquired when a conditioned stimulus is paired with an unconditioned stimulus.

- **Extinction** is the gradual weakening and disappearance of a conditioned response. **Spontaneous recovery** is the reappearance of an extinguished conditioned response when the conditioned stimulus returns after a period of absence.

- **Stimulus generalization** is the tendency to respond to a new stimulus as if it is the original conditioned stimulus. **Stimulus discrimination** is the tendency to lack a conditioned response to a new stimulus that's similar to the original conditioned stimulus.

- **Higher-order conditioning** occurs when a neutral stimulus comes to act as a conditioned stimulus by being paired with another stimulus that already evokes a conditioned response.

Operant Conditioning

- **Operant conditioning** is a type of learning in which responses come to be controlled by their consequences.

- **B. F. Skinner** used a device called a **Skinner box** to study operant conditioning in rats. He set up the boxes so that the rats could automatically get rewards or punishments for particular types of responses.

- **Reinforcement** is delivery of a consequence that increases the likelihood that a response will occur. **Positive reinforcement** is the presentation of a stimulus after a response. **Negative reinforcement** is the removal of a stimulus after a response.

- **Punishment** is the delivery of a consequence that decreases the likelihood that a response will occur. **Positive punishment** is the presentation of a stimulus after a response. **Negative punishment** is the removal of a stimulus after a response.

- **Primary reinforcers** and **punishers** are naturally satisfying and unpleasant, respectively. **Secondary reinforcers** and **punishers** are satisfying or unpleasant, respectively, because they've become associated with primary reinforcers or punishers.

- **Shaping** is a procedure in which reinforcement is used to guide a response closer and closer to a desired response.

- A **reinforcement schedule** is the pattern in which reinforcement is given over time. Reinforcement can be **continuous** or **intermittent**.

- Intermittent reinforcement schedules include **fixed-ratio**, **variable-ratio**, **fixed-interval**, and **variable-interval** schedules.

- In operant conditioning, **extinction** is the gradual disappearance of a response when it stops being reinforced.

- A **discriminative stimulus** is a cue that indicates the kind of consequence that is likely to occur after a response. **Stimulus discrimination** is the tendency for a response to occur only when a particular stimulus is present.

- In operant conditioning, **stimulus generalization** is the tendency to respond to a new stimulus as if it's the original discriminative stimulus.

Biological Influences

- Biological factors can limit conditioning.

- Aversion to a particular taste can be conditioned only by pairing the taste with nausea.

- **Instinctive drift** is the tendency for conditioning to be hindered by natural instincts.

Cognitive Influences

- Conditioning involves higher mental processes, as it depends on the predictive power of the conditioned stimulus rather than mere association of stimuli.

Observational Learning

- **Observational learning** is the process of learning to respond in a particular way by watching others, or models.

- **Albert Bandura** conducted experiments showing that children who watched adults behaving aggressively were more likely to behave aggressively themselves.

Sample Test Questions

1. In operant conditioning, what is the difference between reinforcement and punishment?

2. Which types of intermittent reinforcement schedules produce responses that are most resistant to extinction?

3. Give an example of classical conditioning, then identify the unconditioned and conditioned stimuli and responses.

4. Why is observational learning also called vicarious learning?

5. In classical conditioning, the gradual weakening and disappearance of a conditioned response is called _____, and it happens when the _____ stimulus is repeatedly presented without the _____.

6. What kind of reinforcement should you use if you want to a response to last without reinforcement long after it's been learned through operant conditioning?
    A.   Continuous
    B.   Intermittent
    C.   Either A and B
    D.   Neither A nor B

7. What is the tendency to respond to a new stimulus as if it's the original conditioned stimulus?
    A.   Stimulus discrimination
    B.   Stimulus generalization
    C.   Higher-order conditioning
    D.   Spontaneous recovery

8. A student sometimes got A's on his midterm exams last year when he used his green pen to write the exams. Now he always takes his lucky green pens to exams. How did the student's superstitious behavior arise?
    A.   Observational learning
    B.   Classical conditioning
    C.   Operant conditioning
    D.   None of the above

9. A scalloped response pattern, in which responses are slow at the beginning of a time period and then faster just before reinforcement happens, is typical of which type of reinforcement schedule?
    A.   Fixed ratio
    B.   Variable ratio
    C.   Fixed interval
    D.   Variable interval

10. *What is the procedure called in which reinforcement is used to guide a response closer and closer to a desired response?*

    A.   Stimulus discrimination

    B.   Stimulus generalization

    C.   Spontaneous recovery

    D.   Shaping

11. *Classical conditioning usually works best if which of the following occurs?*

    A.   The conditioned stimulus (CS) is presented just after the unconditioned stimulus (UCS)

    B.   The CS is presented just before the UCS

    C.   The CS is presented many hours after the UCS

    D.   All of the above are equally effective

12. *Which of the following terms means the tendency for conditioning to be limited by natural instincts?*

    A.   Instinctive drift

    B.   Innate conditioning

    C.   Natural learning

    D.   Classical conditioning

13. *With respect to taste aversion, which of the following is true?*

    A.   If taste is paired with other unconditioned stimuli, conditioning doesn't occur

    B.   Nausea paired with most other conditioned stimuli doesn't produce aversion to those stimuli

    C.   The pairing of taste and nausea produces conditioning even when there is a delay of several hours between the conditioned stimulus of the taste and the unconditioned stimulus of nausea

    D.   All of the above

14. *In operant conditioning, what is the tendency for a response to happen only when a particular stimulus is present?*

    A.   Stimulus generalization

    B.   Shaping

    C.   Response acquisition

    D.   Stimulus discrimination

15. *Students get a grade for a quiz that's given once a week. What is this an example of?*

    A.   Fixed-ratio reinforcement schedule

    B.   Variable-ratio reinforcement schedule

    C.   Fixed-interval reinforcement schedule

    D.   Variable-interval reinforcement schedule

ANSWERS

1.   Reinforcement is delivery of a consequence that increases the likelihood that a certain response will occur. Punishment is delivery of a consequence that decreases the likelihood that a certain consequence will occur.

2.   Variable schedules of reinforcement produce responses that resist extinction.

3.   Sara has always felt calm and relaxed when listening to classical music. Lately, she's been lighting a candle just before she listens to classical music. Now she doesn't even need the classical music to feel relaxed. She can just light a candle. Unconditioned stimulus = classical music; unconditioned response = relaxation; conditioned stimulus = lit candle; conditioned response = relaxation.

4.   Observational learning is also called vicarious learning because it involves learning by seeing others acquire responses through classical or operant conditioning.

5.   Extinction; conditioned; unconditioned stimulus.

6.	**B**	11.	**B**
7.	**B**	12.	**A**
8.	**C**	13.	**D**
9.	**C**	14.	**D**
10.	**D**	15.	**C**

CHAPTER 7
LEARNING

Memory

- Memory Processes
- Types of Memory
- Forgetting
- Enhancing Memory
- The Biology of Memory
- Distortions of Memory

8

Memory is just one of many phenomena that demonstrate the brain's complexity. On a basic level, memory is the capacity for storing and retrieving information, but memories are not simply recorded and neatly stored. Our memories are selected, constructed, and edited not just by us but by the world around us. We have an astounding, boundless capacity for memory, but our memories are also faulty, full of holes and distortions, and hampered by unreliable data retrieval systems.

Memory researchers explore the many mysteries of remembering. They examine why the name of a favorite elementary school teacher might leap easily to mind, while the time and place of a committee meeting prove maddeningly elusive. They try to explain why we have trouble remembering a person's name—only to recall it later, after the person is gone. We still have much to learn about how memories are made and what determines whether they last or fade away.

Memory Processes

Memory is essentially the capacity for storing and retrieving information. Three processes are involved in memory: encoding, storage, and retrieval. All three of these processes determine whether something is remembered or forgotten.

ENCODING

Processing information into memory is called **encoding**. People automatically encode some types of information without being aware of it. For example, most people probably can recall where they ate lunch yesterday, even though they didn't try to remember this information. However, other types of information become encoded only if people pay attention to it. College students will probably not remember all the material in their textbooks unless they pay close attention while they're reading.

There are several different ways of encoding verbal information:

- **Structural encoding** focuses on what words look like. For instance, one might note whether words are long or short, in uppercase or lowercase, or handwritten or typed.

- **Phonemic encoding** focuses on how words sound.

- **Semantic encoding** focuses on the meaning of words. Semantic encoding requires a deeper level of processing than structural or phonemic encoding and usually results in better memory.

STORAGE

After information enters the brain, it has to be stored or maintained. To describe the process of storage, many psychologists use the three-stage model proposed by **Richard Atkinson** and **Richard Shiffrin**. According to this model, information is stored sequentially in three memory systems: sensory memory, short-term memory, and long-term memory.

Sensory Memory

Sensory memory stores incoming sensory information in detail but only for an instant. The capacity of sensory memory is very large, but the information in it is unprocessed. If a flashlight moves quickly in a circle inside a dark room, people will see a circle of light rather than the individual points through which the flashlight moved. This happens because sensory memory holds the successive images of the moving flashlight long enough for the brain to see a circle. Visual sensory memory is called **iconic memory**; auditory sensory memory is called **echoic memory**.

Short-Term Memory

Some of the information in sensory memory transfers to **short-term memory**, which can hold information for approximately twenty seconds. Rehearsing can help keep information in short-term memory longer. When people repeat a new phone number over and over to themselves, they are rehearsing it and keeping it in short-term memory.

Short-term memory has a limited capacity: it can store about seven pieces of information, plus or minus two pieces. These pieces of information can be small, such as individual numbers or letters, or larger, such as familiar strings of numbers, words, or sentences. A method called chunking can help to increase the capacity of short-term memory. **Chunking** combines small bits of information into bigger, familiar pieces.

> EXAMPLE: *A person confronted with this sequence of twelve letters would probably have difficulty remembering it ten seconds later, because short-term memory cannot handle twelve pieces of information:*
>
> *HO TB UT TE RE DP OP CO RN IN AB OW L*
>
> *However, these letters can be easily remembered if they're grouped into six familiar words, because short-term memory can hold six pieces of information:*
>
> *HOT BUTTERED POPCORN IN A BOWL*

Working Memory

Psychologists today consider short-term memory to be a **working memory**. Rather than being just a temporary information storage system, working memory is an active system. Information can be kept in working memory while people process or examine it. Working memory allows people to temporarily store and manipulate visual images, store information while trying to make decisions, and remember a phone number long enough to write it down.

Long-Term Memory

Information can be transferred from short-term memory to long-term memory and from long-term memory back to short-term memory. **Long-term memory** has an almost infinite capacity, and information in long-term memory usually stays there for the duration of a person's life. However, this doesn't mean that people will always be able to remember what's in their long-term memory—they may not be able to *retrieve* information that's there.

Organization of Memories

Imagine what would happen if a psychology textbook weren't organized by section, by chapter, or in any other way. Imagine if the textbook didn't have a table of contents or an index. If the textbook just contained lots of information in a random order, students would have difficulty finding a particular concept, such as "encoding of memory." They'd know the information was in there somewhere, but they'd have trouble retrieving it.

Long-term memory stores much more information than a textbook, and people would never be able to retrieve the information from it if it weren't organized in some way.

Psychologists believe one way the brain organizes information in long-term memory is by category. For example, *papaya* may be organized within the semantic category *fruit*. Categories can also be based on how words sound or look. If someone is struggling to remember the word *papaya*, she may remember first that it's a three-syllable word, that it begins with the letter *p*, or that it ends with the letter *a*.

Long-term memory organizes information not only by categories but also by the information's familiarity, relevance, or connection to other information.

Where Were You When . . . Flashbulb memories are vivid, detailed memories of important events. Older people may have very clear memories of where they were and what they were doing when they heard President John F. Kennedy had been assassinated. Many people today may have a similar kind of memory of where they were when they heard the Pentagon and the World Trade Center had been attacked by terrorists.

RETRIEVAL

Retrieval is the process of getting information out of memory. **Retrieval cues** are stimuli that help the process of retrieval. Retrieval cues include associations, context, and mood.

Lost Memories The fact that people can often recall lost memories when hypnotized suggests that information in long-term memory is usually not lost—it may just be difficult to retrieve.

Associations

Because the brain stores information as networks of associated concepts, recalling a particular word becomes easier if another, related word is recalled first. This process is called **priming**.

> *EXAMPLE: If Tim shows his roommate a picture of sunbathers on a nude beach and then asks him to spell the word bear, the roommate may be more likely to spell* bare *because the picture primed him to recall that form of the word.*

Context

People can often remember an event by placing themselves in the same context they were in when the event happened.

> *EXAMPLE: If a woman loses her car keys, she may be able to recall where she put them if she re-creates in her mind exactly what she did when she last came in from parking her car.*

Mood

If people are in the same mood they were in during an event, they may have an easier time recalling the event.

Types of Memory

Psychologists often make distinctions among different types of memory. There are three main distinctions:

1. Implicit vs. explicit memory
2. Declarative vs. procedural memory
3. Semantic vs. episodic memory

IMPLICIT VS. EXPLICIT MEMORY

Sometimes information that unconsciously enters the memory affects thoughts and behavior, even though the event and the memory of the event remain unknown. Such unconscious retention of information is called **implicit memory**.

> *EXAMPLE: Tina once visited Hotel California with her parents when she was ten years old. She may not remember ever having been there, but when she makes a trip there later, she knows exactly how to get to the swimming pool.*

Explicit memory is conscious, intentional remembering of information. Remembering a social security number involves explicit memory.

DECLARATIVE VS. PROCEDURAL MEMORY

Declarative memory is recall of factual information such as dates, words, faces, events, and concepts. Remembering the capital of France, the rules for playing football, and what happened in the last game of the World Series involves declarative memory. Declarative memory is usually considered to be explicit because it involves conscious, intentional remembering.

Procedural memory is recall of how to do things such as swimming or driving a car. Procedural memory is usually considered implicit because people don't have to consciously remember how to perform actions or skills.

SEMANTIC VS. EPISODIC MEMORY

Declarative memory is of two types: semantic and episodic. **Semantic memory** is recall of general facts, while **episodic memory** is recall of personal facts. Remembering the capital of France and the rules for playing football uses semantic memory. Remembering what happened in the last game of the World Series uses episodic memory.

Forgetting

Memory researchers certainly haven't forgotten **Hermann Ebbinghaus**, the first person to do scientific studies of forgetting, using himself as a subject. He spent a lot of time memorizing endless lists of nonsense syllables and then testing himself to see whether he remembered them. He found that he forgot most of what he learned during the first few hours after learning it.

Later researchers have found that forgetting doesn't always occur that quickly. Meaningful information fades more slowly than nonsense syllables. The rate at which people forget or retain information also depends on what method is used to measure forgetting and retention. **Retention** is the proportion of learned information that is retained or remembered—the flip side of forgetting.

> **Forgetting Curve** *A forgetting curve is a graph that shows how quickly learned information is forgotten over time. Ebbinghaus made use of forgetting curves to chart his research on memory.*

MEASURES OF FORGETTING AND RETENTION

Researchers measure forgetting and retention in three different ways: recall, recognition, and relearning.

Recall

Recall is remembering without any external cues. For example, essay questions test recall of knowledge because nothing on a blank sheet of paper will jog the memory.

Recognition

Recognition is identifying learned information using external cues. For example, true or false questions and multiple-choice questions test recognition because the previously learned information is there on the page, along with other options. In general, recognition is easier than recall.

Relearning

When using the **relearning** method to measure retention, a researcher might ask a subject to memorize a long grocery list. She might measure how long he has to practice before he remembers every item. Suppose it takes him ten minutes. On another day, she gives him the same list again and measures how much time he takes to relearn the list. Suppose he now learns it in five minutes. He has saved five minutes of learning time, or 50 percent of the original time it took him to learn it. His savings score of 50 percent indicates that he retained 50 percent of the information he learned the first time.

CAUSES OF FORGETTING

Everyone forgets things. There are six main reasons for forgetting: ineffective encoding, decay, interference, retrieval failure, motivated forgetting, and physical injury or trauma.

Ineffective Encoding

The way information is **encoded** affects the ability to remember it. Processing information at a deeper level makes it harder to forget. If a student thinks about the meaning of the concepts in her textbook rather than just reading them, she'll remember them better when the final exam comes around. If the information is not encoded properly—such as if the student simply skims over the textbook while paying more attention to the TV—it is more likely to be forgotten.

Decay

According to **decay theory**, memory fades with time. Decay explains the loss of memories from sensory and short-term memory. However, loss of long-term memories does not seem to depend on how much time has gone by since the information was learned. People might easily remember their first day in junior high school but completely forget what they learned in class last Tuesday.

Interference

Interference theory has a better account of why people lose long-term memories. According to this theory, people forget information because of interference from other learned information. There are two types of interference: retroactive and proactive.

- **Retroactive interference** happens when newly learned information makes people forget old information.

- **Proactive interference** happens when old information makes people forget newly learned information.

Retrieval Failure

Forgetting may also result from failure to **retrieve** information in memory, such as if the wrong sort of **retrieval cue** is used. For example, Dan may not be able to remember the name of his fifth-grade teacher. However, the teacher's name might suddenly pop into Dan's head if he visits his old grade school and sees his fifth-grade classroom. The classroom would then be acting as a context cue for retrieving the memory of his teacher's name.

Motivated Forgetting

Psychologist **Sigmund Freud** proposed that people forget because they push unpleasant or intolerable thoughts and feelings deep into their unconscious. He called this phenomenon **repression**. The idea that people forget things they don't want to remember is also called **motivated forgetting** or psychogenic amnesia.

Physical Injury or Trauma

Anterograde amnesia is the inability to remember events that occur after an injury or traumatic event. **Retrograde amnesia** is the inability to remember events that occurred before an injury or traumatic event.

**CHAPTER 8
MEMORY**

Enhancing Memory

In spite of all these reasons for forgetting, people can still remember a vast amount of information. In addition, memory can be enhanced in a variety of ways, including rehearsal, overlearning, distributed practice, minimizing interference, deep processing, organizing information, mnemonic devices, and visual imagery.

REHEARSAL

Practicing material helps people remember it. The more people **rehearse** information, the more likely they are to remember that information.

OVERLEARNING

Overlearning, or continuing to practice material even after it is learned, also increases retention.

DISTRIBUTED PRACTICE

Learning material in short sessions over a long period is called **distributed practice** or the "spacing effect." This process is the opposite of cramming, which is also called **massed practice**. Distributed practice is more effective than cramming for retaining information.

MINIMIZING INTERFERENCE

People remember material better if they don't learn other, similar material right before or soon after their effort. One way to minimize interference is to sleep after studying material, since people can't learn new material while sleeping.

DEEP PROCESSING

People also remember material better if they pay attention while learning it and think about its meaning rather than memorize the information by rote. One way to process information deeply is to use a method called elaboration. **Elaboration** involves associating the material being learned with other material. For example, people could associate the new material with previously learned material, with an anecdote from their own lives, with a striking example, or with a movie they recently saw.

ORGANIZING MATERIAL

Organizing material in a coherent way helps people to remember it:

- Organizing material hierarchically or in categories and subcategories can be particularly helpful. The way an outline is organized, for example, usually helps people to remember the material in it.

- Chunking material into segments is also helpful. People often remember long strings of numbers, such as social security numbers, by chunking them into two-, three-, or four-digit segments.

MNEMONICS

Mnemonics are strategies for improving memory. Different kinds of mnemonics include acronyms, acrostics, the narrative method, and rhymes.

Acronyms

Acronyms are words made out of the first letters of several words. For example, to remember the colors of the spectrum, people often use the name ROY G. BIV, which gives the first letters of the colors red, orange, yellow, green, blue, indigo, and violet in the right order.

Acrostics

Acrostics are sentences or phrases in which each word begins with a letter that acts as a memory cue. For example, the rather strange phrase *Roses on yachts grow better in vinegar* also helps to remember the colors of the spectrum.

Narrative methods

Narrative methods involve making up a story to remember a list of words. For example, people could remember the colors of the rainbow in the right order by making up a short story such as this: *Red* Smith stood next to an *orange* construction cone and flagged down a *yellow* cab. He told the cabbie he was feeling very *green* and asked to be taken to a hospital. The cabbie took him to a hospital, where a nurse in a *blue* coat guided him to a room with *indigo* walls. He smelled a *violet* in a vase and passed out.

Rhymes

Rhymes are also good mnemonics. For example, the familiar rhyme that begins, "Thirty days has September . . ." is a mnemonic for remembering the number of days in each month.

VISUAL IMAGERY

Some well-known memory improvement methods involve using visual imagery to memorize or recall lists.

Method of Loci

When using the **method of loci**, people might picture themselves walking through a familiar place. They imagine each item on their list in a particular place as they walk along. Later, when they need to remember their list, they mentally do the walk again, noting the items they imagined along the path.

The Link Method

To use the **link method**, people associate items on a list with each other. For example, if a man wants to remember to buy bread, juice, and carrots at the store, he might try visualizing the peculiar image of himself eating a juice-and-bread mush using carrots as chopsticks.

Peg Word Method

When using the **peg word method**, people first remember a rhyme that associates numbers with words: one is a bun, two is a shoe, three is a tree, four is a door, five is a hive, six is sticks, seven is heaven, eight is a gate, nine is swine, ten is a hen. They then visualize each item on their list being associated with a bun, a shoe, a tree, and so on. When they need to remember the list, they first think of a bun, then see what image it's associated with. Then they think of a shoe, and so forth.

The Biology of Memory

Memory is a complicated phenomenon. Researchers still don't know exactly how it works at the physiological level. Long-term memory involves the hippocampus of the brain. Some researchers think the hippocampus binds together different elements of a memory, which are stored in separate areas of the brain. In other words, the hippocampus helps with memory organization. Other researchers think that the hippocampus helps with memory **consolidation**, or the transfer of information into long-term memory.

The brain area involved in processing a memory may determine where memories are stored. For example, memories of visual information probably end up in the visual cortex. Research suggests that there may be specific neural circuits for particular memories. Psychologists also think that memory relates to changes in neurotransmitter release from neurons, fluctuations in hormone levels, and protein synthesis in the brain.

CHAPTER 8
MEMORY

Memories on Your Nerves Long-term potentiation is a lasting change at synapses that occurs when long-term memories form. Synapses become more responsive as a result. Researchers believe long-term potentiation is the basic process behind memory and learning.

Distortions of Memory

Memories aren't exact records of events. Instead, memories are reconstructed in many different ways after events happen, which means they can be distorted by several factors. These factors include schemas, source amnesia, the misinformation effect, the hindsight bias, the overconfidence effect, and confabulation.

SCHEMAS

A **schema** is a mental model of an object or event that includes knowledge as well as beliefs and expectations. Schemas can distort memory.

> EXAMPLE: *Suppose a high school junior visits her sister's college dorm room for the first time. She's never been to a dorm before, but she's seen dorms in movies, read about them, and heard her friends talking about them. When she describes the room to another friend after the visit, she comments on how many clothes her sister had and how many huge books were on her sister's desk. In reality, the books were hidden under the bed, not out in the open. The clothes were something she actually saw, while the books were part of her dorm-room schema.*

SOURCE AMNESIA

Another reason for distorted memories is that people often don't accurately remember the origin of information.

> EXAMPLE: *After witnessing a car crash on the freeway, Sam later tells friends many details about what he saw. It turns out, however, that there is no way he could have actually seen some of the details he described and that he is, in fact, just reporting details he heard on TV about the accident. He isn't deliberately lying. He just may not be able to remember where all the different pieces of information came from.*

This inaccurate recall of the origin of information is called **source amnesia**, source misattribution, or source monitoring error.

THE MISINFORMATION EFFECT

The **misinformation effect** occurs when people's recollections of events are distorted by information given to them after the event occurred. The psychologist **Elizabeth Loftus** did influential research on the misinformation effect that showed that memory reconstructions can affect eyewitness testimony.

> EXAMPLE: *A bank robber enters a crowded bank in the middle of the day, brandishing a gun. He shoots out the security cameras and terrifies everyone. He is taking money from a teller when one of two security guards approaches the robber, draws his own weapon, and shoots. Suddenly, another shot is fired from a different direction and the security guard falls to the ground, shot. Some of the customers see that the other security guard, who was approaching the robber from the other side, mistakenly shot his partner. Later, police ask the witnesses when the robber shot the guard, and they report that he shot after the guard fired on him. Even though they saw one guard shoot the other, they are swayed by the misinformation given by the police.*

Stop or Yield In one of Loftus's early experiments, she showed research subjects a film of a simulated automobile accident at an intersection with a stop sign. Afterward, she told half the subjects that there was a yield sign at the intersection. When asked later to describe the accident, those who had received the misleading suggestion tended to claim with certainty that there was a yield sign at the intersection, while those subjects who received no misleading suggestions had a more accurate recollection.

THE HINDSIGHT BIAS

The **hindsight bias** is the tendency to interpret the past in a way that fits the present. For example, if Laura's boyfriend cheats on her, she may recall the boyfriend as always having seemed promiscuous, even if this is not true.

THE OVERCONFIDENCE EFFECT

The **overconfidence effect** is the tendency people have to over-estimate their ability to recall events correctly.

> *EXAMPLE:* Tina asks her father to tell her all about the day she was born: when her mother first went into labor, how long it took to get to the hospital, what time of day or night it was. Tina's father tells her a wonderful story about how he and her mother made a late night rush to the hospital the night of Thursday, the twelfth, and how Tracy's mother barely made it into the delivery room before Tracy emerged, and how the doctor kindly put 11:59 p.m. as the time of birth to avoid a Friday the thirteenth birthday. Years later, when glancing at an old calendar, Tracy discovers she was actually born on a Tuesday, not a Thursday.

CONFABULATION

Sometimes people claim to remember something that didn't happen or think that something happened to them when it actually happened to someone else. This phenomenon is **confabulation**.

> *EXAMPLE:* Steve is in his early twenties, and he and a room-mate have just moved to New York City. Steve has all sorts of interesting experiences. One night, he goes out to a local pub and meets Robert De Niro, who is just sitting there eating a hamburger. The two of them chat about baseball for a while and even shoot a game of pool. Later, Steve tells his room-mate about the evening. Many years later, Steve and his old roommate get together to talk about old times, and the room-mate relates the "De Niro story" as if it happened to him.

Summary

Memory Processes

- The three processes involved in memory are **encoding**, **storage**, and **retrieval**.

- **Encoding** is putting information into memory and includes **structural**, **phonemic**, and **semantic encoding**.

- In **storage**, information is maintained in a three-stage process involving **sensory memory**, **short-term memory**, and **long-term memory**.

- **Working memory** is an active system that allows people to remember, manipulate, and store information.

- Long-term memory is organized into **categories**, as well as by **familiarity**, **relevance**, and **relationship to other memories**.

- **Retrieval** is the process of getting information out of memory. **Retrieval cues** are stimuli that help get information out of memory.

- Retrieval cues include **associations**, **context**, and **mood**.

Types of Memory

- **Implicit memory** is unconscious retaining of information, whereas **explicit memory** is conscious, intentional remembering.

- **Declarative memory** is recall of factual information, whereas **procedural memory** is recall of how to do things.

- **Semantic memory** is recall of general facts, while **episodic memory** is recall of personal facts.

Forgetting

- **Hermann Ebbinghaus** was the first researcher to conduct scientific studies of forgetting. Using himself as a subject, he discovered that much information is forgotten within a few hours after learning it.

- **Retention** is the proportion of learned information that is remembered.

- Researchers use three methods to measure forgetting and retention: **recall**, **recognition**, and **relearning**.

- Causes of forgetting include ineffective **encoding**, **decay**, **interference**, **retrieval failure**, and **motivated forgetting**.

Enhancing Memory

- Memory is enhanced by **rehearsal, overlearning, distributed practice,** minimizing interference, deep processing, organizing information, **mnemonic devices,** and visual imagery.

The Biology of Memory

- The hippocampus is involved in long-term memory.
- Memories may be stored in different areas of the brain.
- There may specific neural circuits for particular memories.

Distortions of Memory

- Memories are reconstructed in many ways after events happen, which makes them prone to distortion.
- Memories can be distorted by **schema, source amnesia,** the **misinformation effect,** the **hindsight bias,** the **overconfidence effect,** and **confabulation.**

Sample Test Questions

1. What are the three processes involved in memory?

2. Why does chunking allow people to keep more information in short-term memory?

3. What kinds of retrieval cues are used to get information out of memory?

4. What are three ways of measuring forgetting and retention?

5. Define "retroactive interference" and give an example.

6. Which of the following results in memory distortion?
   - A.   The overconfidence effect
   - B.   The hindsight bias
   - C.   Confabulation
   - D.   All of the above

7. What does the misinformation effect refer to?
   - A.   Distortion of memory by information provided after an event
   - B.   Overestimation of the ability to recall events correctly
   - C.   Inaccurate recall of the origin of information
   - D.   None of the above

8. What is memory thought to be related to?
   - A.   Changes in neurotransmitter release from neurons
   - B.   Fluctuations in hormone levels
   - C.   Protein synthesis in the brain
   - D.   All of the above

9. Which of the following can enhance memory?
   - A.   Massed practice
   - B.   Staying awake for as long as possible after studying
   - C.   Rote memorization
   - D.   Rehearsing

10. What is the name for forgetting events that occurred before an injury?
   - A.   Anterograde amnesia
   - B.   Retrograde amnesia
   - C.   Source amnesia
   - D.   Interference

11. *What are three reasons people forget?*
    A.   Decay, ineffective coding, interference
    B.   Interference, retrieval failure, overlearning
    C.   Overlearning, repression, deep processing
    D.   Retrieval failure, deep processing, decay

12. *What is the idea that people forget things they don't want to remember?*
    A.   Repression
    B.   Motivated forgetting
    C.   Psychogenic amnesia
    D.   All of the above

13. *Which of the following is not true of forgetting?*
    A.   Nonsensical information is forgotten faster than meaningful information
    B.   Processing information at a deeper level makes it less likely that it will be forgotten
    C.   Decay theory provides a good explanation for loss of long-term memories
    D.   Information is sometimes forgotten because of interference from other information we learn

14. *Most people find they have no problem riding a bicycle to classes in college even though they haven't ridden one since they were young. What type of memory can account for this?*
    A.   Semantic memory
    B.   Episodic memory
    C.   Procedural memory
    D.   Explicit memory

15. *What does phonemic encoding relate to?*
    A.   How words look
    B.   How words sound
    C.   The meaning of words
    D.   The color of words on a page

ANSWERS

1.   The three processes involved in memory are encoding, storage, and retrieval.

2.   Short-term memory has a limited capacity of about seven plus or minus two pieces of information. Chunking allows people to combine many small pieces of information into fewer, bigger pieces of information. As long as people have fewer than about nine chunks of information, they will probably be able to hold that information in short-term memory.

3.   Retrieval cues that can be used to get information out of memory are associations, context, and mood.

4.   Forgetting and retention can be measured by recall, recognition, and relearning.

5.   Retroactive interference is the forgetting of old information when new information is learned. An example: Frank learned Spanish in high school. Since he took French 101 in college, however, he can't remember very much of his Spanish.

6.	**D**	11.	**A**
7.	**A**	12.	**D**
8.	**D**	13.	**C**
9.	**D**	14.	**C**
10.	**B**	15.	**B**

CHAPTER 8
MEMORY

Language and Cognition

- The Structure of Language
- Theories of Language Acquisition
- Language and Nonhuman Primates
- The Structure of Cognition
- Theories of Cognitive Development
- Problem-Solving
- Decision-Making
- Creativity

9

Cognitive psychology concerns both language and thought and has been popular only since the 1950s. Before that, many psychologists believed that the scientific method could not be applied toward study of a process as private as thinking. From ancient Greek times, only philosophers and metaphysicians studied the nature of language and thought. The metaphysician René Descartes, for example, famously argued, "I think, therefore I am."

Today, thanks to increasingly sophisticated tools for studying brain activity, cognitive psychology is a thriving science. Cognitive psychologists explore such questions as how language affects thought, whether it is possible to create a "thinking" machine, and why humans are motivated to create art.

The Structure of Language

Language is a system of symbols and rules that is used for meaningful communication. A system of communication has to meet certain criteria in order to be considered a language:

- A language uses **symbols**, which are sounds, gestures, or written characters that represent objects, actions, events, and ideas. Symbols enable people to refer to objects that are in another place or events that occurred at a different time.

- A language is meaningful and therefore can be understood by other users of that language.

- A language is **generative**, which means that the symbols of a language can be combined to produce an infinite number of messages.

- A language has rules that govern how symbols can be arranged. These rules allow people to understand messages in that language even if they have never encountered those messages before.

THE BUILDING BLOCKS OF LANGUAGE

Language is organized hierarchically, from phonemes to morphemes to phrases and sentences that communicate meaning.

Phonemes

Phonemes are the smallest distinguishable units in a language. In the English language, many consonants, such as *t*, *p*, and *m*, correspond to single phonemes, while other consonants, such as *c* and *g*, can correspond to more than one phoneme. Vowels typically correspond to more than one phoneme. For example, *o* corresponds to different phonemes depending on whether it is pronounced as in *bone* or *woman*. Some phonemes correspond to combinations of consonants, such as *ch*, *sh*, and *th*.

Morphemes

Morphemes are the smallest meaningful units in a language. In the English language, only a few single letters, such as *I* and *a*, are morphemes. Morphemes are usually whole words or meaningful parts of words, such as prefixes, suffixes, and word stems.

EXAMPLE: *The word "disliked" has three morphemes: "dis,"* *"lik," and "ed."*

Syntax

Syntax is a system of rules that governs how words can be meaningfully arranged to form phrases and sentences.

EXAMPLE: *One rule of syntax is that an article such as "the"* *must come before a noun, not after: "Read the book," not* *"Read book the."*

LANGUAGE DEVELOPMENT IN CHILDREN

Children develop language in a set sequence of stages, although sometimes particular skills develop at slightly different ages:

- Three-month-old infants can distinguish between the phonemes from any language.

- At around six months, infants begin **babbling**, or producing sounds that resemble many different languages. As time goes on, these sounds begin to resemble more closely the words of the languages the infant hears.

- At about thirteen months, children begin to produce simple single words.

- By about twenty-four months, children begin to combine two or three words to make short sentences. At this stage, their speech is usually telegraphic. **Telegraphic speech**, like telegrams, contains no articles or prepositions.

- By about age three years, children can usually use tenses and plurals.

- Children's language abilities continue to grow throughout the school-age years. They become able to recognize ambiguity and sarcasm in language and to use metaphors and puns. These abilities arise from **metalinguistic awareness**, or the capacity to think about how language is used.

> **Ambiguous Language** *Language may sometimes be used correctly but still have an unclear meaning or multiple meanings. In these cases, language is ambiguous—it can be understood in several ways.* Avoid biting dogs *is an example of an ambiguous sentence. A person might interpret it as* Keep out of the way of biting dogs *or* Don't bite dogs.

Theories of Language Acquisition

The nature vs. nurture debate extends to the topic of language acquisition. Today, most researchers acknowledge that both nature and nurture play a role in language acquisition. However, some researchers emphasize the influences of learning on language acquisition, while others emphasize the biological influences.

> **Receptive Language before Expressive Language** *Children's ability to understand language develops faster than their ability to speak it. Receptive language is the ability to understand language, and expressive language is the ability to use language to communicate. If a mother tells her fifteen-month-old child to put the toy back in the toy chest, he may follow her instructions even though he can't repeat them himself.*

ENVIRONMENTAL INFLUENCES ON LANGUAGE ACQUISITION

A major proponent of the idea that language depends largely on environment was the behaviorist **B. F. Skinner** (see pages 145 and 276 for more information on Skinner). He believed that language is acquired through principles of conditioning, including association, imitation, and reinforcement.

According to this view, children learn words by associating sounds with objects, actions, and events. They also learn words and syntax by imitating others. Adults enable children to learn words and syntax by reinforcing correct speech.

Critics of this idea argue that a behaviorist explanation is inadequate. They maintain several arguments:

- Learning cannot account for the rapid rate at which children acquire language.

- There can be an infinite number of sentences in a language. All these sentences cannot be learned by imitation.

- Children make errors, such as overregularizing verbs. For example, a child may say *Billy hitted me*, incorrectly adding the usual past tense suffix *-ed* to *hit*. Errors like these can't result from imitation, since adults generally use correct verb forms.

- Children acquire language skills even though adults do not consistently correct their syntax.

> *Neural Networks* *Some cognitive neuroscientists have created neural networks, or computer models, that can acquire some aspects of language. These neural networks are not preprogrammed with any rules. Instead, they are exposed to many examples of a language. Using these examples, the neural networks have been able to learn the language's statistical structure and accurately make the past tense forms of verbs. The developers of these networks speculate that children may acquire language in a similar way, through exposure to multiple examples.*

BIOLOGICAL INFLUENCES ON LANGUAGE ACQUISITION

The main proponent of the view that biological influences bring about language development is the well-known linguist **Noam Chomsky**. Chomsky argues that human brains have a language acquisition device (LAD), an innate mechanism or process that allows children to develop language skills. According to this view, all children are born with a universal grammar, which makes them receptive to the common features of all languages. Because of this hard-wired background in grammar, children easily pick up a language when they are exposed to its particular grammar.

Evidence for an innate human capacity to acquire language skills comes from the following observations:

- The stages of language development occur at about the same ages in most children, even though different children experience very different environments.

- Children's language development follows a similar pattern across cultures.

- Children generally acquire language skills quickly and effortlessly.

- Deaf children who have not been exposed to a language may make up their own language. These new languages resemble each other in sentence structure, even when they are created in different cultures.

Biology and Environment *Some researchers have proposed theories that emphasize the importance of both nature and nurture in language acquisition. These theorists believe that humans do have an innate capacity for acquiring the rules of language. However, they believe that children develop language skills through interaction with others rather than acquire the knowledge automatically.*

LANGUAGE, CULTURE, AND THOUGHT

Researchers have differing views about the extent to which language and culture influence the way people think. In the 1950s, **Benjamin Lee Whorf** proposed the **linguistic relativity hypothesis**. He said language *determines* the way people think. For example, Whorf said that Eskimo people and English-speaking people think about snow differently because the Eskimo language has many more words for snow than the English language does.

Most subsequent research has not supported Whorf's hypothesis. Researchers do acknowledge, however, that language can *influence* thought in subtle ways. For example, the use of sexist terminology may influence how people think about women. Two ways that people commonly use language to influence thinking are **semantic slanting** and **name calling**.

Semantic Slanting

Semantic slanting is a way of making statements so that they will evoke specific emotional responses.

> EXAMPLE: *Military personnel use the term "preemptive counterattack" rather than "invasion," since "invasion" is likely to produce more negative feelings in people.*

Name Calling

Name calling is a strategy of labeling people in order to influence their thinking. In anticipatory name calling, it is implied that if someone thinks in a particular way, he or she will receive an unfavorable label.

> EXAMPLE: *On the day a student buys a new desk, he might say, "Only a slob would pile junk on a desk like this." This might help ensure that his roommate keeps it free of junk.*

Bilingualism Although people sometimes assume that bilingualism impairs children's language development, there is no evidence to support this assumption. Bilingual children develop language at the same rate as children who speak only one language. In general, people who begin learning a new language in childhood master it more quickly and thoroughly than do people who learn a language in adulthood.

Language and Nonhuman Primates

Some researchers have tried to teach apes to use language. Because of the structure of their vocal organs, apes can't say words, but they can communicate using signs or computers. Using these means, apes can make requests, respond to questions, and follow instructions.

THE CASE OF WASHOE THE CHIMPANZEE

Researchers at Central Washington University taught a chimpanzee named Washoe to use American Sign Language (ASL) to communicate. She could sign not only single words but also meaningful combinations of words. She could follow instructions and respond to questions given in ASL. Later, Washoe's foster child, Loulis, learned signs just by watching Washoe and other chimps that had been trained to use language. Some research even suggested that language-trained chimps may use signs spontaneously to communicate with each other or to talk to themselves, although this behavior is not thoroughly documented.

CHAPTER 9
LANGUAGE & COGNITION

SKEPTICISM ABOUT APE LANGUAGE

Critics of the idea that apes can learn and use language have maintained several arguments:

- Apes, unlike people, can be trained to learn only a limited number of words and only with difficulty.

- Apes use signs or computers to get a reward, in the same way that other animals can be taught tricks. But learning tricks is not equivalent to learning language.

- Apes don't use syntax. For example, they don't recognize the difference between *Me eat apple* and *Apple eat me.*

- Trainers may be reading meanings into signs apes make and unintentionally providing cues that help them to respond correctly to questions.

Clearly, communication in nonhuman animals differs drastically from language in humans. The spontaneity, uniqueness, and reflective content of human language remains unmatched.

Nonprimates Can Communicate *Researchers have taught nonprimate animals, such as parrots, to communicate meaningfully. Parrots that participated in language acquisition studies learned to identify dozens of objects, distinguish colors, and make simple requests in English. One famous example is Alex the African gray parrot, owned by Irene Pepperberg from the University of Arizona. Alex can "speak" hundreds of words, but what makes him more unique is that he appears to do more than just vocalize. Though Pepperberg does not claim that Alex uses "language," she does believe that when Alex talks, he is expressing his thoughts, not just mimicking.*

The Structure of Cognition

Cognition, or thinking, involves mental activities such as understanding, problem solving, and decision making. Cognition also makes creativity possible.

THE BUILDING BLOCKS OF COGNITION

When humans think, they manipulate mental representations of objects, actions, events, and ideas. Humans commonly use mental representations such as concepts, prototypes, and cognitive schemas.

Concepts

A **concept** is a mental category that groups similar objects, events, qualities, or actions. Concepts summarize information, enabling humans to think quickly.

> *EXAMPLE: The concept "fish" includes specific creatures, such as an eel, a goldfish, a shark, and a flying fish.*

Prototypes

A **prototype** is a typical example of a concept. Humans use prototypes to decide whether a particular instance of something belongs to a concept.

> *EXAMPLE: Goldfish and eels are both fish, but most people will agree that a goldfish is a fish more quickly than they will agree that an eel is a fish. A goldfish fits the "fish" prototype better than an eel does.*

Cognitive Schemas

Cognitive schemas are mental models of different aspects of the world. They contain knowledge, beliefs, assumptions, associations, and expectations.

> *EXAMPLE: People may have a schema about New York that includes information they've learned about New York in school, their memories of New York, things people have told them about New York, information from movies and books about New York, what they assume to be true about New York, and so on.*

Theories of Cognitive Development

Cognitive development refers to the change in children's patterns of thinking as they grow older.

JEAN PIAGET'S STAGE THEORY

The scientist best known for research on cognitive development is **Jean Piaget** (see pages 72–75), who proposed that children's thinking goes through a set series of four major stages. Piaget believed that children's cognitive skills unfold naturally as they mature and explore their environment.

LEV VYGOTSKY'S THEORY OF SOCIOCULTURAL INFLUENCES

Psychologist **Lev Vygotsky** believed that children's sociocultural environment plays an important role in how they develop cognitively. In Vygotsky's view, the acquisition of language is a crucial part of cognitive development. After children acquire language, they don't just go through a set series of stages. Rather, their cognitive development depends on interactions with adults, cultural norms, and their environmental circumstances.

> *Private Speech* Vygotsky pointed out that children use language to control their own behavior. After children acquire language skills and learn the rules of their culture, they start to engage in private speech. They first talk to themselves out loud, and then, as they grow older, silently, giving themselves instructions about how to behave.

CURRENT RESEARCH ON COGNITIVE DEVELOPMENT

Current research indicates that children have complex cognitive abilities at much younger ages than Piaget suggested. As early as four months of age, infants appear to understand basic laws of physics. For example, a four-month-old infant can recognize that solid objects cannot pass through other solid objects and that objects roll down slopes instead of rolling up. At five months of age, infants can recognize the correct answers to addition and subtraction problems involving small numbers. These observations have led some researchers to speculate that humans are born with some basic cognitive abilities.

Critics argue that researchers who find these results are overinterpreting the behavior of the infants they study.

Problem-Solving

Problem-solving is the active effort people make to achieve a goal that cannot be easily attained.

TYPES OF PROBLEMS

Three common categories of problems include **inducing structure**, **arranging**, and **transformation**.

Inducing Structure

Some problems involve finding relationships between elements.

> *EXAMPLE:* *"Pineapple is to fruit as cabbage is to ___." In this analogy problem, the answer, "vegetable," requires people to figure out the relationship between "pineapple" and "fruit" and apply a similar relationship to "cabbage."*

Arranging

Other problems involve arranging elements in a way that fulfills certain criteria.

> *EXAMPLE:* *The answer to the problem "Arrange the letters in LEPAP to make the name of a fruit" is "APPLE."*

Transformation

Other problems involve making a series of changes to achieve a specific goal, a process called **transformation**.

> EXAMPLE: *A familiar riddle describes a situation in which a man has to take his fox, his chicken, and his tub of grain across a river in a boat. The boat will hold only him and two of his possessions at any one time. He can't leave the fox and the chicken on the riverbank by themselves because the fox will eat the chicken, and he can't leave the chicken with the grain because the chicken will eat the grain. He also can't take the fox and the chicken in the boat together because the fox will eat the chicken when he's occupied with rowing the boat. The same goes for the chicken and the grain. How will he get all three across? First he takes the fox and the grain across. He leaves the fox on the opposite bank and takes the grain back with him. He then leaves the grain on the bank and takes the chicken across. He leaves the chicken on the opposite bank and takes the fox back with him to retrieve the grain.*

APPROACHES TO PROBLEM SOLVING

There are many strategies for solving problems, included trial and error, algorithms, deductive reasoning, inductive reasoning, heuristics, dialectical reasoning, forming subgoals, using similar problems, and changing the way the problem is represented.

Trial and Error

Trial and error involves trying out different solutions until one works. This type of strategy is practical only when the number of possible solutions is relatively small.

> EXAMPLE: *It's dark, and a man is trying to figure out which button on the dashboard of his newly rented car switches on the headlights. He might press all the available buttons until he finds the right one.*

Algorithms

Algorithms are step-by-step procedures that are guaranteed to achieve a particular goal.

> *EXAMPLE: A chocolate chip cookie recipe is an algorithm for baking chocolate chip cookies.*

Deductive Reasoning

Deductive reasoning is the process by which a particular conclusion is drawn from a set of general premises or statements. The conclusion *has* to be true if the premises are true.

> *EXAMPLE: If the premises "All birds have wings" and "A penguin is a bird" are true, then the conclusion "A penguin has wings" must also be true.*

Inductive Reasoning

Inductive reasoning is the process by which a general conclusion is drawn from examples. In this case, the conclusion is likely, but not guaranteed, to be true.

> *EXAMPLE: Given the premise "All the butterflies Fred has ever seen have wingspans of less than two inches," Fred might conclude, "All butterflies have wingspans of less than two inches."*

Heuristics

A **heuristic** is a general rule of thumb that may lead to a correct solution but doesn't guarantee one.

> *EXAMPLE: A useful heuristic for finishing a timed exam might be "Do the easy questions first."*

Dialectical Reasoning

Dialectical reasoning is the process of going back and forth between opposing points of view in order to come up with a satisfactory solution.

> *EXAMPLE: A student might use dialectical reasoning when she considers the pros and cons of choosing psychology as her college major.*

Forming Subgoals

Forming subgoals involves coming up with intermediate steps to solve a problem. This is a way of simplifying a problem.

> *EXAMPLE: Susan is asked to solve the analogy problem "Prison is to inmate as hospital is to ____." Susan's subgoal could be to figure out the relationship between "prison" and "inmate." Once she achieves this subgoal, she can easily find the answer, "patient."*

Using Similar Problems

A problem is often easier to solve if it can be compared to a similar problem.

> *EXAMPLE: Mike has to give his two-year-old daughter a bath, but she resists because she is afraid of the water. Mike remembers that he convinced her to get in the kiddie pool last week by letting her take her large plastic dinosaur toy with her for "protection." He gives her the toy again, and she agrees to get in the tub.*

Changing the Way a Problem Is Represented

A problem may be easier to solve if it is represented in a different form.

> *EXAMPLE: If hundreds of guests at a banquet are trying to figure out where they are supposed to sit, written instructions might not be easy to follow. A seating chart, however, makes the seating arrangement easy to understand.*

OBSTACLES TO EFFECTIVE PROBLEM-SOLVING

Researchers have described many obstacles that prevent people from solving problems effectively. These obstacles include irrelevant information, functional fixedness, mental set, and making assumptions.

Irrelevant Information

Focusing on irrelevant information hinders problem-solving.

> *EXAMPLE: A familiar children's riddle goes like this: As I was going to St. Ives, I met a man with seven wives. Every wife had seven sacks, every sack had seven cats, every cat had seven kits. How many were going to St. Ives? People may think of this as a complicated math problem, but in reality, only one person, the "I," is headed to St. Ives. The seven wives and their respective entourages are headed the other way.*

Functional Fixedness

Functional fixedness is the tendency to think only of an object's most common use in solving a problem.

> *EXAMPLE: Rachel's car breaks down while she is driving through the desert. She is terribly thirsty. She finds several soda bottles in the trunk but no bottle opener. She doesn't think of using the car key to open the bottles because of functional fixedness.*

Mental Set

A **mental set** is a tendency to use only those solutions that have worked in the past.

> *EXAMPLE: When Matt's flashlight hasn't worked in the past, he's just shaken it to get it to work again. One day when it doesn't come on, he shakes it, but it still doesn't work. He would be subject to mental set if he keeps shaking it without checking whether it needs new batteries.*

LANGUAGE & COGNITION

CHAPTER 9

Making Assumptions

Making assumptions about constraints that don't exist prevent people from solving problems effectively.

> **EXAMPLE:** *Another familiar riddle goes as follows: A father and his son are driving on a highway and get into a terrible accident. The father dies, and the boy is rushed to the hospital with major injuries. When he gets to the hospital, a surgeon rushes in to help the boy but stops and exclaims, "I can't operate on this boy—he's my son!" How can this be? If people have a hard time answering, they may be making a false assumption. The surgeon is the boy's mother.*

Decision-Making

Decision-making involves weighing alternatives and choosing between them.

People don't always make rational decisions. In the 1950s, economist Herbert Simon proposed that people's capacity to process and evaluate multiple alternatives limits their ability to make rational decisions. Because it is difficult to simultaneously evaluate all possible options, people tend to focus on only a few aspects of the available options. This can result in less than optimal decisions. Two types of decisions are decisions about preferences and risky decisions. People generally use a variety of different approaches when making these types of decisions.

DECISIONS ABOUT PREFERENCES

Some decisions require people to make choices about what they would prefer.

> **EXAMPLE:** *Josh needs to choose which of two armchairs to buy. He must decide which one he likes better.*

People may use additive or elimination strategies when making decisions about preferences.

Additive Strategies

When using an **additive strategy**, a person lists the attributes of each element of the decision, weights them according to importance, adds them up, and determines which one is more appealing based on the result.

> *EXAMPLE: To decide which armchair to buy, Josh may list the features he considers important in an armchair. For example, he might list attractiveness, comfort, and price. Then, for each armchair, he rates each feature on a scale from +5 to –5. He also weights each feature according to its importance. For instance, if he considers comfort to be twice as important as price, he multiplies the ranking for comfort by 2. Josh then adds up the ratings for each armchair. The chair with the highest ranking wins.*

Elimination Strategies

Another strategy for making decisions about preferences is called **elimination by aspects**, which involves eliminating alternatives based on whether they do or do not possess aspects or attributes the decision maker has deemed necessary or desirable. People often use this type of strategy when a large number of options and features have to be evaluated.

> *EXAMPLE: When using this strategy to choose his armchair, Josh sets a minimum criterion for each feature he thinks is important. For example, minimum criteria for attractiveness, comfort, and price of an armchair might be blue color, soft fabric, and under $300, respectively. He then compares the two armchairs according to these minimum criteria, starting with the most important criterion. An armchair that doesn't meet a criterion gets eliminated, and the remaining one wins.*

RISKY DECISIONS

When making choices about preferences, people select between known features of alternatives. In other types of decisions, however, they have to decide between unknown outcomes. This type of decision-making involves taking risks.

> EXAMPLE: *If Eric is trying to decide whether to buy a $5 raffle ticket, a risk is involved, since he has only a 1 in 1000 chance of winning a $500 prize.*

People make risky decisions by judging the probability of outcomes. Strategies people use to make risky decisions include calculating expected value, estimating subjective utility, and using heuristics.

Expected Value

One strategy for making a risky decision is to calculate the **expected value** of the decision. People calculate the expected value by adding the value of a win times the probability of a win to the value of a loss times the probability of a loss.

> EXAMPLE: *For Eric, the value of a win is +$495 ($500 prize – $5 cost), and the value of a loss is –$5. The probability of winning is 1/1000 and the probability of losing is 999/1000. Therefore the expected value is –3.5. That means Eric can expect to lose $3.50 for every raffle ticket he buys.*

Subjective Utility

Even when decisions have negative expected values, people still make such decisions. Some researchers believe that this occurs because people make some decisions by estimating **subjective utility**, or the personal value of a decision's outcome.

> EXAMPLE: *Eric may still buy the raffle ticket because having the ticket lets him dream about buying a stereo he's always wanted.*

Availability Heuristic

People often use heuristics to estimate probabilities. One heuristic people frequently use is the **availability heuristic**. When people use this rule-of-thumb strategy, they estimate probability based on how readily they can remember relevant instances of an event. If people can quickly remember instances of some event, then they will estimate that event as being quite likely.

> *EXAMPLE: If Eric can think of several friends who have won raffles, he will judge that he is likely to win the raffle.*

Representativeness Heuristic

People also use the **representativeness heuristic** to estimate probability. The representativeness heuristic is a rule-of-thumb strategy that estimates the probability of an event based on how typical that event is. For example, if Eric the raffle ticket buyer lives in the United States, has several tattoos, and often wears dark sunglasses and a leather jacket, is it more likely that he owns a motorcycle or a car? If people use the representativeness heuristic, they may judge that Eric is more likely to own a motorcycle. This happens because the description of Eric is more representative of motorcycle owners.

BIAS IN DECISION-MAKING

People often make flawed decisions. There are many biases that account for bad decision-making.

The Tendency to Ignore Base Rates

When using the representativeness heuristic, people frequently ignore the base rate, or the total number of events.

> *EXAMPLE: If people judged that Eric is more likely to be a motorcycle owner than a car owner because he has tattoos, they were subject to the tendency to ignore base rates. The total number of car owners in the United States far exceeds the number of motorcycle owners, so it is really more likely that Eric owns a car.*

The Gambler's Fallacy

The representativeness heuristic can also make people susceptible to the gambler's fallacy. The **gambler's fallacy** is the false belief that a chance event is more likely if it hasn't happened recently.

This belief is false because the laws of probability don't apply to individual independent events.

> *EXAMPLE: Mindy tosses a coin and get heads. Because of this, she believes that on her second toss, she'll get tails, since 50 percent of her tosses should yield tails. This belief is incorrect. Over a series of tosses, she can estimate that the probability of tails will be about 50 percent, but this logic can't be correctly applied to a single toss.*

Overestimating the Improbable and Underestimating the Probable

Using the availability heuristic can cause people to overestimate improbable events. This happens because rare but memorable events come to mind easily.

> *EXAMPLE: Recalling a few dramatic TV reports of plane crashes could make people overestimate the likelihood of a plane crash.*

Using the availability heuristic can also cause people to underestimate likely events. This can happen when events are hard to visualize and don't easily come to mind.

> *EXAMPLE: Beth may have unprotected sex because she doesn't think anyone she knows has a sexually transmitted disease (STD), and she doesn't know what the symptoms of an STD might be. In reality, the majority of the adult American population has contracted one or more STDs, and Beth has a very high chance of contracting one herself through unprotected sex.*

Minimizing Risk

People sometimes make irrational decisions in an effort to minimize risk. An event is more likely to be chosen if it's framed in terms of winning rather than losing.

> *EXAMPLE: People are more likely to buy a raffle ticket if they hear they have a 1 in 1000 chance of winning than if they hear they have a 999 in 1000 chance of losing.*

Confirmation Bias and Belief Perseverance

Confirmation bias is the tendency for people to look for and accept evidence that supports what they want to believe and to ignore or reject evidence that refutes their beliefs. When people reject evidence that refutes their beliefs, it can also be called **belief perseverance**, because rejecting contradicting evidence makes it easy for people to hold on to their beliefs.

> EXAMPLE: *If Carl is a believer in herbal nutritional supplements, he may willingly accept research that supports their benefits while ignoring or rejecting research that disproves their benefits.*

The Overconfidence Effect

The **overconfidence effect** is the tendency for people to be too certain that their beliefs, decisions, and estimates are correct. People can minimize the effects of overconfidence by collecting a lot of information and evaluating it carefully before making a decision.

> EXAMPLE: *At the outset of the Civil War, young Southern men eagerly enlisted in the Confederate Army, believing their superior gallantry would help them make speedy work of the Union soldiers.*

Creativity

Creativity is the ability to generate novel, valuable ideas. People need a minimum level of intelligence to be creative, but not all people who get high scores on intelligence tests are creative.

DIVERGENT VS. CONVERGENT THINKING

Creativity is characterized by **divergent thinking**. In divergent thinking, people's thoughts go off in different directions as they try to generate many different solutions to a problem.

In **convergent thinking**, on the other hand, people narrow down a list of possibilities to arrive at a single right answer.

> *EXAMPLE: Cindy would have to use divergent thinking if her professor asked her to think of a hundred different uses for a fork. She uses convergent thinking when she considers the list of possibilities on a multiple-choice question and picks the one correct answer.*

CHARACTERISTICS OF CREATIVE PEOPLE

Researchers have identified several characteristics that creative people share:

- **Expertise:** Creative people usually have considerable training, knowledge, and expertise in their field.

- **Nonconformity:** Creative people tend to think independently and have relatively little concern for what others think of them.

- **Curiosity:** Creative people tend to be open to new experiences and willing to explore unusual events.

- **Persistence:** Creative people are usually willing to work hard to overcome obstacles and take risks.

- **Intrinsic motivation:** Creative people tend to be motivated more by intrinsic rewards, such as a sense of accomplishment or satisfaction of curiosity, rather than by extrinsic rewards, such as money or social approval.

ENVIRONMENTAL INFLUENCES ON CREATIVITY

People can best realize their creative potential if they are in circumstances that promote creativity. Families, organizations, and institutions promote creativity when they allow people to have control over problem solving and task completion, minimize judgment and evaluation of work, and encourage new ways of doing things.

Summary

The Structure of Language

- **Language** is a system of symbols and rules used for meaningful communication.

- A language uses **symbols** and **syntax** and is meaningful and **generative**.

- Language is organized hierarchically from **phonemes** to **morphemes** to phrases and sentences.

- Children develop language in a set sequence of stages.

Theories of Language Acquisistion

- Behaviorist **B. F. Skinner** strongly supported the idea that language depends largely on environment.

- Skinner believed that people acquire language through principles of conditioning.

- Critics argue the inadequacy of behaviorist explanations.

- Some cognitive neuroscientists have created **neural networks** that can acquire some aspects of language by encountering many examples of language. They think children may acquire language in the same way.

- **Noam Chomsky** is the main proponent of the importance of biological influences on language development.

- Chomsky proposed that human brains have a **language acquisition device** that allows children to acquire language easily.

- Some researchers believe that language is both biologically and environmentally determined.

- The **linguistic relativity hypothesis** states that language determines the way people think.

- Today, researchers believe language influences, rather than determines, thought.

- Two ways that people use language to influence thinking are **semantic slanting** and **name calling**.

- People master a new language better if they begin learning it in childhood.

- Nonhuman animals can learn some aspects of language.

Language and Nonhuman Primates

- Some researchers have tried to teach apes to use language.

- Apes can communicate, but researchers are divided on whether this communication can really be considered "learning language."

The Structure of Cognition

- **Cognition** involves activities such as understanding, **problem solving,** **decision making,** and being creative.

- People use mental representations such as **concepts, prototypes,** and **cognitive schemas** when they think.

Theories of Cognitive Development

- **Jean Piaget** believed that children's cognitive skills unfold naturally as they mature and explore their environment.

- **Lev Vygotsky** believed that children's sociocultural environment plays an important role in cognitive development.

- Some researchers have shown that humans are born with some basic cognitive abilities.

Problem-Solvinvg

- **Problem-solving** is the active effort people make to achieve a goal that is not easily attained.

- Three common types of problems involve **inducing structure, arranging,** and **transformation.**

- Some approaches to problem-solving are **trial and error, deductive** and **inductive reasoning,** use of **algorithms** and **heuristics, dialectical reasoning, creation of subgoals, use of similar problems,** and **changes in the way the problems are represented.**

- Researchers have identified many obstacles to effective problem-solving, such as **focus on irrelevant information, functional fixedness, mental set,** and **assumptions about unnecessary constraints.**

Decision-Making

- Decision-making involves weighing alternatives and choosing among them.
- **Additive strategies** and **elimination strategies** are ways of making decisions about preferences.
- Using **expected value, subjective utility,** the **availability heuristic,** and the **representativeness heuristic** are all ways of making risky decisions.
- Using the representativeness heuristic can make people susceptible to **biases,** such as the **tendency to ignore base rates** and the **gambler's fallacy.**
- Using the availability heuristic can make people susceptible to **overestimating the improbable** or **underestimating the probable.**
- In an effort to minimize risk, people also make decision-making errors, such as the **overconfidence effect,** the **confirmation bias,** and **belief perseverance.**

Creativity

- **Creativity** is the ability to generate novel, useful ideas.
- Creativity is characterized by **divergent,** rather than **convergent,** thinking.
- Some characteristics of creative people are **expertise, nonconformity, curiosity, persistence,** and **intrinsic motivation.**
- People can best realize their creative potential if they are in environmental circumstances that promote creativity.

Sample Test Questions

1. Maria is applying for a job at an ad agency. At the interview, she's asked to list some creative things she can do with a diamond necklace. One of the things she lists is Put it in the trash basket. Can this be considered a creative solution? Why or why not?

2. What criteria can be used to determine whether a particular system of communication is a language?

3. What revolutionary idea did Noam Chomsky propose regarding language?

4. A mansion and a tent are both houses, but people would probably agree that a mansion is a house more quickly than they would agree that a tent is a house. Why is this the case?

5. What are two strategies for making decisions about preferences?

6. Jen decides to buy a lottery ticket. She knows her chances of winning are very small, only 1 in 10 million. But if she wins, she'll get $10,000 in cash, and knowing that means that she can dream about going on a luxury cruise. What was her decision probably based on?
   - A. Expected value
   - B. Subjective utility
   - C. An additive strategy
   - D. An elimination strategy

7. When coming back from the dry cleaners, Joe finds he's locked himself out of his car. He uses a coat hanger to pry the lock of his car open. He thought of using the coat hanger in this way because he was not subject to which of the following?
   - A. Dialectical reasoning
   - B. Functional fixedness
   - C. The gambler's fallacy
   - D. The tendency to ignore base rates

8. A company labels its frozen entrees 75% fat free rather than contains 25% fat so that people will view them more positively. What is this is an example of?
   - A. A prototype
   - B. A phoneme
   - C. Subjective utility
   - D. Semantic slanting

9. When children first start to speak in sentences, what is usually true of their speech?

    A.   It is similar to babbling

    B.   It is exceptionally soft

    C.   It is telegraphic

    D.   It is in many languages

10. Which is an observation that supports Noam Chomsky's ideas about language acquisition?

    A.   Children's language development follows a similar pattern across cultures

    B.   Children acquire language quickly and effortlessly

    C.   The stages of language development occur at about the same ages in most children

    D.   All of the above

11. What is the system of rules that governs how words can be meaningfully arranged to form phrases and sentences?

    A.   Language

    B.   Syntax

    C.   Morpheme

    D.   Phoneme

12. When Frank follows the step-by-step instructions for assembling a desk he just bought, which problem-solving strategy is he using?

    A.   Heuristic

    B.   Inductive reasoning

    C.   Deductive reasoning

    D.   Algorithm

13. Janet has used drug A to treat headaches for a long time. She has found it to be effective and has felt no negative side effects. When research reports suggest that the drug is ineffective and dangerous, she ignores it. What is this an example of?

    A.   The tendency to ignore base rates

    B.   Functional fixedness

    C.   The confirmation bias

    D.   Subjective utility

14. *Paul decides to buy earthquake insurance for his house in Wyoming because he remembers the devastation caused to houses by an earthquake in California in the 1990s. This is an example of a decision-making bias that results from using which of the following?*

    A.   The availability heuristic
    B.   The representativeness heuristic
    C.   An elimination strategy
    D.   An additive strategy

15. *A twelve-year-old child enjoys using puns. This enjoyment indicates that she has which of the following?*

    A.   Semantic slanting
    B.   Cognitive schemas
    C.   Deductive reasoning
    D.   Metalinguistic awareness

CHAPTER 9
LANGUAGE & COGNITION

ANSWERS

1. Maria's solution cannot be considered creative, because a creative solution must be both novel and useful. Putting a diamond necklace in the trash may be novel, but most people wouldn't consider it useful.

2. A language must use symbols and syntax and be meaningful and generative.

3. Noam Chomsky proposed that humans are born with an innate language acquisition device that allows them to acquire language easily.

4. Mansions fit most people's prototypes of the concept *house* better than tents do.

5. Two strategies for making preference decisions are additive strategies and elimination strategies.

6.	**B**	11.	**B**
7.	**B**	12.	**D**
8.	**D**	13.	**C**
9.	**C**	14.	**A**
10.	**D**	15.	**D**

Intelligence

- Theories of Intelligence
- Intelligence Testing
- The Influence of Heredity and Environment

Few people agree on exactly what "intelligence" is or how to measure it. The nature and origin of intelligence are elusive, and the value and accuracy of intelligence tests are often uncertain. Researchers who study intelligence often argue about what IQ tests really measure and whether or not Einstein's theories and Yo Yo Ma's cello playing show different types of intelligence.

Intelligence is a particularly thorny subject, since research in the field has the potential to affect many social and political decisions, such as how much funding the U.S. government should devote to educational programs. People who believe that intelligence is mainly inherited don't see the usefulness in special educational opportunities for the underprivileged, while people who believe that environment plays a large role in intelligence tend to support such programs. The importance and effects of intelligence are clear, but intelligence does not lend itself to easy definition or explanation.

Theories of Intelligence

A typical dictionary definition of **intelligence** is "the capacity to acquire and apply knowledge." Intelligence includes the ability to benefit from past experience, act purposefully, solve problems, and adapt to new situations. Intelligence can also be defined as "the ability that intelligence tests measure." There is a long history of disagreement about what actually constitutes intelligence.

Savant Syndrome Savant syndrome, observed in some individuals diagnosed with autism or mental retardation, is characterized by exceptional talent in one area of functioning, such as music or math, and poor mental functioning in all other areas.

THE G FACTOR

Charles Spearman proposed a **general intelligence factor**, g, which underlies all intelligent behavior. Many scientists still believe in a general intelligence factor that underlies the specific abilities that intelligence tests measure. Other scientists are skeptical, because people can score high on one specific ability but show weakness in others.

EIGHT TYPES OF INTELLIGENCE

In the 1980s and 1990s, psychologist **Howard Gardner** proposed the idea of not one kind of intelligence but eight, which are relatively independent of one another. These eight types of intelligence are:

1. **Linguistic:** spoken and written language skills

2. **Logical–mathematical:** number skills

3. **Musical:** performance or composition skills

4. **Spatial:** ability to evaluate and analyze the visual world

5. **Bodily-kinesthetic:** dance or althletic abilities

6. **Interpersonal:** skill in understanding and relating to others

7. **Intrapersonal:** skill in understanding the self

8. **Nature:** skill in understanding the natural world

Gardner believes that each of these domains of intelligence has inherent value but that culture and context may cause some domains to be emphasized over others. Critics of the idea of multiple intelligences maintain that these abilities are talents rather than kinds of intelligence.

TRIARCHIC THEORY OF INTELLIGENCE

Also in the 1980s and 1990s, **Robert Sternberg** proposed a **triarchic theory of intelligence** that distinguishes among three aspects of intelligence:

- **Componential intelligence**: the ability assessed by intelligence tests
- **Experiential intelligence**: the ability to adapt to new situations and produce new ideas
- **Contextual intelligence**: the ability to function effectively in daily situations

EMOTIONAL INTELLIGENCE

Some researchers distinguish **emotional intelligence** as an ability that helps people to perceive, express, understand, and regulate emotions. Other researchers maintain that this ability is a collection of personality traits such as empathy and extroversion, rather than a kind of intelligence.

Intelligence Testing

The **psychometric approach** to intelligence emphasizes people's performance on standardized aptitude tests. **Aptitude tests** predict people's future ability to acquire skills or knowledge. **Achievement tests**, on the other hand, measure skills and knowledge that people have already learned.

TYPES OF TESTS

Intelligence tests can be given individually or to groups of people. The best-known individual intelligence tests are the Binet-Simon scale, the Stanford-Binet Intelligence Scale, and the Wechsler Adult Intelligence Scale.

The Binet-Simon Scale

Alfred Binet and his colleague Theodore Simon devised this general test of mental ability in 1905, and it was revised in 1908 and 1911. The test yielded scores in terms of mental age. **Mental age** is the chronological age that typically corresponds to a particular level of performance.

> EXAMPLE: *A ten-year-old child whose score indicates a mental age of twelve performed like a typical twelve-year-old.*

The Stanford-Binet Intelligence Scale

In 1916, **Lewis Terman** and his colleagues at Stanford University created the Stanford-Binet Intelligence Scale by expanding and revising the Binet-Simon scale. The Stanford-Binet yielded scores in terms of intelligence quotients. The **intelligence quotient (IQ)** is the mental age divided by the chronological age and multiplied by 100. IQ scores allowed children of different ages to be compared.

> EXAMPLE: *A ten-year-old whose performance resembles that of a typical twelve-year-old has an IQ of 120 (12 divided by 10 times 100).*

There are two problems with the intelligence quotient approach:

1. The score necessary to be in the top range of a particular age group varies, depending on age.
2. The scoring system had no meaning for adults. For example, a fifty-year-old man who scores like a thirty-year-old can't accurately be said to have low intelligence.

The Stanford-Binet was revised in 1937, 1960, 1973, and 1986.

Wechsler Adult Intelligence Scale

David Wechsler published the first test for assessing intelligence in adults in 1939. The Wechsler Adult Intelligence Scale contains many items that assess nonverbal reasoning ability and therefore depends less on verbal ability that does the Stanford-Binet. It also provides separate scores of verbal intelligence and nonverbal or performance intelligence, as well as a score that indicates overall intelligence.

The term *intelligence quotient,* or *IQ,* is also used to describe the score on the Wechsler test. However, the Wechsler test presented scores based on a normal distribution of data rather than the intelligence quotient. The **normal distribution** is a symmetrical bell-shaped curve that represents how characteristics like IQ are distributed in a large population. In this scoring system, the mean IQ score is set at 100, and the standard deviation is set at 15. The test is constructed so that about two-thirds of people tested (68 percent) will score within one standard deviation of the mean, or between 85 and 115.

On the Wechsler test, the IQ score reflects where a person falls in the normal distribution of IQ scores. Therefore, this score, like the original Stanford-Binet IQ score, is a relative score, indicating how the test taker's score compares to the scores of other people. Most current intelligence tests, including the revised versions of the Stanford-Binet, now have scoring systems based on the normal distribution. About 95 percent of the population will score between 70 and 130 (within two standard deviations from the mean), and about 99.7 percent of the population will score between 55 and 145 (within three standard deviations from the mean).

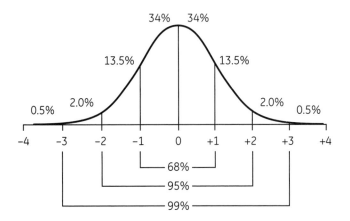

Group Intelligence Tests

Individual intelligence tests can be given only by specially trained psychologists. Such tests are expensive and time-consuming to administer, and so educational institutions often use tests that can be given to a group of people at the same time. Commonly used group intelligence tests include the Otis-Lennon School Ability Test and the Lorge-Thorndike Intelligence Test.

Biological Tests of Intelligence

Some researchers have suggested that biological indices such as reaction time and perceptual speed relate to intelligence as measured by IQ tests:

- **Reaction time:** the amount of time a subject takes to respond to a stimulus, such as by pushing a button when a light is presented.

- **Perceptual speed:** the amount of time a person takes to accurately perceive and discriminate between stimuli. For example, a test of perceptual speed might require a person to determine which of two lines is shorter when pairs of lines flash very briefly on a screen.

THE INFLUENCE OF CULTURE

Many psychologists believe that cultural bias can affect intelligence tests, for the following reasons:

- Tests that are constructed primarily by white, middle-class researchers may not be equally relevant to people of all ethnic groups and economic classes.

- Cultural values and experiences can affect factors such as attitude toward exams, degree of comfort in the test setting, motivation, competitiveness, rapport with the test administrator, and comfort with problem solving independently rather than as part of a team effort.

- Cultural stereotypes can affect the motivation to perform well on tests.

CHARACTERISTICS OF IQ TESTS

Some characteristics of IQ tests are standardization, norms, percentile scores, standardization samples, reliability, and validity.

Standardization

Intelligence tests are **standardized**, which means that uniform procedures are used when administering and scoring the tests. Standardization helps to ensure that people taking a particular test all do so under the same conditions. Standardization also allows test takers to be compared, since it increases the likelihood that any difference in scores between test-takers is due to ability rather than the testing environment. The SAT and ACT are two examples of standardized tests.

Norms and Percentile Scores

Researchers use norms when scoring the tests. **Norms** provide information about how a person's test score compares with the scores of other test takers. Norms allow raw test scores to be converted into percentile scores. A **percentile score** indicates the percentage of people who achieved the same as or less than a particular score. For example, if someone answered twenty items correctly on a thirty-item vocabulary test, he receives a raw score of 20. He consults the test norms and finds that a raw score of 20 corresponds with a percentile score of 90. This means that he scored the same as or higher than 90 percent of people who took the same test.

Standardization Samples

Psychologists come up with norms by giving a test to a standardization sample. A **standardization sample** is a large group of people that is representative of the entire population of potential test takers.

Reliability

Most intelligence tests have good reliability. **Reliability** is a test's ability to yield the same results when the test is administered at different times to the same group of people. For more on reliability, see page 14.

Validity

Validity is a test's ability to measure what it is supposed to measure. For more on validity, see page 14. Although intelligence tests cannot be considered good measures of general intelligence or general mental ability, they are reasonably valid indicators of the type of intelligence that enables good academic performance.

Critical Views on Intelligence Testing Critics of widespread intelligence testing point out that politicians and the public in general misuse and misunderstand intelligence tests. They argue that these tests provide no information about how people go about solving problems. Also, say the critics, these tests do not explain why people with low intelligence scores can function intelligently in real-life situations. Advocates of intelligence testing point out that such tests can identify children who need special help, as well as gifted children who can benefit from opportunities for success.

The Influence of Heredity and Environment

Today, researchers generally agree that heredity and environment have an interactive influence on intelligence. Many researchers believe that there is a **reaction range** to IQ, which refers to the limits placed on IQ by heredity. Heredity places an upper and lower limit on the IQ that can be attained by a given person. The environment determines where within these limits the person's IQ will lie.

Despite the prevailing view that both heredity and environment influence intelligence, researchers still have different opinions about how much each contributes and how they interact.

HEREDITARY INFLUENCES

Evidence for hereditary influences on intelligence comes from the following observations:

- Family studies show that intelligence tends to run in families.

- Twin studies show a higher correlation between identical twins in IQ than between fraternal twins. This holds true even when identical twins reared apart are compared to fraternal twins reared together.

- Adoption studies show that adopted children somewhat resemble their biological parents in intelligence.

Family studies, twin studies, and adoption studies, however, are not without problems. See pages 36–38 for more information about the drawbacks of such studies.

Heritability of Intelligence

Heritability is a mathematical estimate that indicates how much of a trait's variation in a population can be attributed to genes. Estimates of the heritability of intelligence vary, depending on the methods used. Most researchers believe that heritability of intelligence is between 60 percent and 80 percent.

Heritability estimates apply only to groups on which the estimates are based. So far, heritability estimates have been based mostly on studies using white, middle-class subjects. Even if heritability of IQ is high, heredity does not necessarily account for differences *between* groups. Three important factors limit heritability estimates:

1. Heritability estimates don't reveal anything about the extent to which genes influence a single person's traits.

2. Heritability depends on how similar the environment is for a group of people.

3. Even with high heritability, a trait can still be influenced by environment.

ENVIRONMENTAL INFLUENCES

Evidence for environmental influences on intelligence comes from the following observations:

- Adoption studies demonstrate that adopted children show some similarity in IQ to their adoptive parents.

- Adoption studies also show that siblings reared together are more similar in IQ than siblings reared apart. This is true even when identical twins reared together are compared to identical twins reared apart.

- Biologically unrelated children raised together in the same home have some similarity in IQ.

- IQ declines over time in children raised in deprived environments, such as understaffed orphanages or circumstances of poverty and isolation. Conversely, IQ improves in children who leave deprived environments and enter enriched environments.

- People's performance on IQ tests has improved over time in industrialized countries. This strange phenomenon, which is known as the **Flynn effect**, is attributed to environmental influences. It cannot be due to heredity, because the world's gene pool could not have changed in the seventy years or so since IQ testing began.

Possible Causes of the Flynn Effect *The precise cause for the Flynn effect is unclear. Researchers speculate that it may be due to environmental factors such as decreased prevalence of severe malnutrition among children, enhancing of skills through television and video games, improved schools, smaller family sizes, higher level of parental education, or improvements in parenting.*

CULTURAL AND ETHNIC DIFFERENCES

Studies have shown a discrepancy in average IQ scores between whites and minority groups in the United States. Black, Native American, and Hispanic people score lower, on average, than white people on standardized IQ tests. Controversy exists about whether this difference is due to heredity or environment.

Hereditary Explanations

A few well-known proponents support hereditary explanations for cultural and ethnic differences in IQ:

* In the late 1960s, researcher Arthur Jensen created a storm of controversy by proposing that ethnic differences in intelligence are due to heredity. He based his argument on his own estimate of about 80 percent heritability for intelligence.

* In the 1990s, researchers Richard Herrnstein and Charles Murray created a similar controversy with their book, *The Bell Curve.* They also suggested that intelligence is largely inherited and that heredity at least partly contributes to ethnic and cultural differences.

Environmental Explanations

Many researchers believe that environmental factors primarily cause cultural and ethnic differences. They argue that because of a history of discrimination, minority groups comprise a disproportionately large part of the lower social classes, and therefore cultural and ethnic differences in intelligence are really differences among social classes. People in lower social classes have a relatively deprived environment. Children may have:

- Fewer learning resources
- Less privacy for study
- Less parental assistance
- Poorer role models
- Lower-quality schools
- Less motivation to excel intellectually

Some researchers argue that IQ tests are biased against minority groups and thus cause the apparent cultural and ethnic differences.

However, not all minority groups score lower than whites on IQ tests. Asian Americans achieve a slightly higher IQ score, on average, than whites, and they also show better school performance. Researchers suggest that this difference is due to Asian American cultural values that encourage educational achievement.

Summary

Theories of Intelligence

- **Intelligence** is the capacity to acquire and apply knowledge.

- Intelligence includes the ability to benefit from experience, act purposefully, solve problems, and adapt to new situations.

- **Charles Spearman** proposed a **general intelligence factor**, g, that underlies all intelligent behavior.

- **Howard Gardner** proposed that there are eight domains of intelligence.

- **Robert Sternberg** distinguished among three aspects of intelligence.

- **Emotional intelligence** helps people to perceive, express, understand, and regulate emotions.

Intelligence Testing

- The most commonly used individual tests of intelligence are the **Binet-Simon scale**, the **Stanford-Binet Scale**, and the **Wechsler Adult Intelligence Scale**.

- The Binet-Simon scale yielded scores in terms of **mental age**.

- The original Stanford-Binet test yielded scores in terms of **intelligence quotient**, or **IQ**.

- The Wechsler test yields scores based on a **normal distribution**.

- Although the term *IQ* is still used, current intelligence tests present scores based on a normal distribution.

- Group intelligence tests are often used in educational settings.

- Some researchers have suggested that there are biological indices of intelligence, such as **reaction time** and **perceptual speed**.

- Many psychologists believe that **cultural bias** affects intelligence tests.

- Intelligence tests are **standardized**.

- **Norms** provide information about how a score compares with other people's scores.

- Intelligence tests are very reliable.

- Intelligence tests are reasonably valid measures of academic ability.

- Intelligence tests have both critics and advocates.

The Influence of Heredity and Environment

- There is dispute about how and how much heredity and environment affect intelligence.

- Evidence for hereditary influences come from **family studies**, **twin studies**, and **adoption studies**.

- **Heritability** estimates for intelligence vary depending on the method used for estimation.

- Evidence for environmental influences comes from **adoption studies**, **studies of environmental deprivation**, and the **Flynn effect**.

- There is probably a reaction range for IQ. **Reaction range** refers to limits set on IQ by heredity. Environment determines where IQ will lie within these limits.

- There is a discrepancy in IQ scores between whites and some minority groups.

- There are both hereditary and environmental explanations for this discrepancy.

- The higher IQ test scores and better school performance of Asian Americans may be due to cultural factors.

Sample Test Questions

1. What is the difference between aptitude tests and achievement tests?

2. How might IQ tests be culturally biased?

3. What is the benefit of standardizing IQ tests?

4. Why was the intelligence quotient inadequate as a way to represent scores on intelligence tests?

5. What kinds of evidence suggest that there are hereditary influences on intelligence?

6. Bob achieved a score of 100 on the current version of the Wechsler Adult Intelligence Scale. What does his score mean?
   A. He answered 100 questions correctly
   B. He completed 100 questions, whether correctly or incorrectly
   C. He has 100 units of intelligence
   D. He achieved an average IQ score compared to other people

7. A nine-year-old child with a mental age of twelve would have what IQ?
   A. 133
   B. 75
   C. 108
   D. 120

8. Which of the following statements is true of heritability?
   A. Heritability estimates indicate how genes influence an individual's traits
   B. Heritability depends on how similar the environment is for a group of people
   C. A highly heritable trait cannot be influenced by environment
   D. If heritability of a trait is high, then heredity must account for differences in that trait between groups

9. The Flynn effect suggests that which of the following is true?
   A. Environment influences IQ
   B. Heredity influences IQ
   C. There are discrepancies in average IQ between cultural groups
   D. There are no discrepancies in average IQ between cultural groups

10. *What does the term* reaction range *refer to?*
    A.   The limits placed on IQ by heredity
    B.   The limits placed on IQ by environment
    C.   A commonly used biological index of intelligence
    D.   None of the above

11. *What percentage of all people who take the Wechsler Adult Intelligence Scale will achieve a score between 70 and 130?*
    A.   It is impossible to say
    B.   68 percent
    C.   95 percent
    D.   99 percent

12. *Howard Gardner is notable for which of the following?*
    A.   Creating the Wechsler Adult Intelligence Scale
    B.   Revising the Stanford-Binet
    C.   Research on multiple intelligences
    D.   Writing *The Bell Curve*

13. *What is one biological index of intelligence?*
    A.   g
    B.   Heritability
    C.   Performance IQ
    D.   Reaction time

14. *Which of the following provides the best evidence of environmental influence on intelligence?*
    A.   There is a higher positive correlation in IQ between identical twins reared apart than between fraternal twins raised together
    B.   There is a positive correlation between the IQ of adopted children and their biological parents
    C.   There is a positive correlation between the IQ of biologically unrelated children raised in the same home
    D.   There is a higher positive correlation in IQ between identical twins than between fraternal twins

15. *The reliability of a test is its ability to do which of the following?*
    A.   Measure what it's supposed to measure
    B.   Yield the same results when given a second time
    C.   Give an unbiased score
    D.   All of the above

ANSWERS

1. Aptitude tests predict people's future ability to acquire skills or knowledge. Achievement tests measure skills and knowledge that people have already learned.

2. IQ tests might be culturally biased in three ways: 1. Tests that are constructed primarily by white, middle-class researchers may not be equally relevant to people of all ethnic groups and economic classes. 2. Cultural values and experiences can affect factors such as attitude toward exams, degree of comfort in the test setting, motivation, competitiveness, rapport with the test administrator, and comfort with problem solving independently rather than as part of a team effort. 3. Cultural stereotypes can affect the motivation to perform well on tests.

3. Standardization is a procedure that's used to help ensure that all people taking the same test do so under similar conditions. The benefit is that it allows for comparisons among test takers, since differences in scores among test takers are then likely caused by ability rather than environment.

4. The intelligence quotient was inadequate as a way to represent scores on intelligence tests for two reasons: 1. The score necessary to be in the top range of a particular age group varied, depending on age. 2. The scoring system was not meaningful for adults.

5. Three kinds of evidence suggest that there are hereditary influences on intelligence: 1. Family studies show that intelligence tends to run in families. 2. Twin studies show that there is a higher correlation between identical twins in IQ than between fraternal twins. This is true even when identical twins reared apart are compared to fraternal twins reared together. 3. Adoption studies show that adopted children and their biological parents are somewhat similar in intelligence.

6.	D	11.	C
7.	A	12.	C
8.	B	13.	D
9.	A	14.	C
10.	A	15.	B

Emotion

11

The source of our emotions remains elusive. No one knows exactly where emotions come from, what makes us feel the way we do, or whether we can fully control the way we feel. Emotion is intimately related to cognition and culture, and it affects us physically: our bodies react to different emotional states, and we often show emotion physically. Researchers have proposed many theories about the source, purpose, and expression of emotion.

In many ways, our emotions define our existence—without them, most of us would not feel truly alive. We've all felt fear of a lurking stranger, pride at scoring well on a test, love, sadness, and loneliness. And between emotional extremes are the ups and downs of everyday life: frustration in a traffic jam, contentment over a satisfying lunch, amusement at a cartoon. We have much to learn about emotion—but we have also learned simply by being human and feeling things every day.

Theories of Emotion

Emotion is a complex, subjective experience accompanied by biological and behavioral changes. Emotion involves feeling, thinking, activation of the nervous system, physiological changes, and behavioral changes such as facial expressions.

Different theories exist regarding how and why people experience emotion. These include evolutionary theories, the **James-Lange theory**, the **Cannon-Bard theory**, Schacter and Singer's **two-factor theory**, and **cognitive appraisal**.

EVOLUTIONARY THEORIES

More than a century ago, in the 1870s, **Charles Darwin** proposed that emotions evolved because they had adaptive value. For example, fear evolved because it helped people to act in ways that enhanced their chances of survival. Darwin believed that facial expressions of emotion are innate (hard-wired). He pointed out that facial expressions allow people to quickly judge someone's hostility or friendliness and to communicate intentions to others.

Recent evolutionary theories of emotion also consider emotions to be innate responses to stimuli. Evolutionary theorists tend to downplay the influence of thought and learning on emotion, although they acknowledge that both can have an effect. Evolutionary theorists believe that all human cultures share several primary emotions, including happiness, contempt, surprise, disgust, anger, fear, and sadness. They believe that all other emotions result from blends and different intensities of these primary emotions. For example, terror is a more intense form of the primary emotion of fear.

THE JAMES-LANGE THEORY

In the 1880s, two theorists, psychologist **William James** and physiologist **Carl Lange**, independently proposed an idea that challenged commonsense beliefs about emotion. This idea, which came to be known as the **James-Lange theory**, is that people experience emotion because they perceive their bodies' physiological responses to external events. According to this theory, people don't cry because they feel sad. Rather, people feel sad because they cry, and, likewise, they feel happy because they smile. This theory suggests that different physiological states correspond to different experiences of emotion.

THE CANNON-BARD THEORY

The physiologist **Walter Cannon** disagreed with the James-Lange theory, posing three main arguments against it:

1. People can experience physiological arousal without experiencing emotion, such as when they have been running. (The racing heart in this case is not an indication of fear.)

2. Physiological reactions happen too slowly to cause experiences of emotion, which occur very rapidly. For example, when someone is in a dark alley alone, a sudden sound usually provokes an immediate experience of fear, while the physical "symptoms" of fear generally follow that feeling.

3. People can experience very different emotions even when they have the same pattern of physiological arousal. For example, a person may have a racing heart and rapid breathing both when he is angry and when he is afraid.

Cannon proposed his own theory of emotion in the 1920s, which was extended by another physiologist, **Philip Bard**, in the 1930s. The resulting **Cannon-Bard theory** states that the experience of emotion happens at the same time that physiological arousal happens. Neither one causes the other. The brain gets a message that causes the experience of emotion at the same time that the autonomic nervous system gets a message that causes physiological arousal.

SCHACHTER AND SINGER'S TWO-FACTOR THEORY

In the 1960s, **Stanley Schachter** and **Jerome Singer** proposed a different theory to explain emotion. They said that people's experience of emotion depends on two factors: physiological arousal and the cognitive interpretation of that arousal. When people perceive physiological symptoms of arousal, they look for an environmental explanation of this arousal. The label people give an emotion depends on what they find in their environment.

> EXAMPLE: *If a person finds herself near an angry mob of people when she is physiologically aroused, she might label that arousal "anger." On the other hand, if she experiences the same pattern of physiological arousal at a music concert, she might label the arousal "excitement."*

Schachter and Singer agree with the James-Lange theory that people infer emotions when they experience physiological arousal. But they also agree with the Cannon-Bard theory that the same pattern of physiological arousal can give rise to different emotions.

COGNITIVE APPRAISAL

The psychologist **Richard Lazarus**'s research has shown that people's experience of emotion depends on the way they appraise or evaluate the events around them.

> EXAMPLE: *If Tracy is driving on a winding road by the edge of a high cliff, she may be concerned about the danger of the road. Her passenger, on the other hand, thinks about the beauty of the view. Tracy will probably feel frightened, while her passenger may feel exhilarated.*

The Biological Bases of Emotion

The experience of emotion is accompanied by activation of two major areas of the nervous system: the brain and the autonomic nervous system.

ACTIVATION OF BRAIN REGIONS

The area of the brain known as the **limbic system** is highly involved in emotion. One structure in the limbic system, called the **amygdala**, plays a particularly important role in regulating emotion.

Researchers believe that sensory information about emotion-evoking events moves along two pathways in the brain. The information goes first to the thalamus and from there moves simultaneously to the amygdala and the cortex of the brain. The amygdala processes the information quickly and sends signals to the hypothalamus, which in turn activates the autonomic nervous system. The cortex, on the other hand, processes the information more slowly, allowing people to appraise or evaluate the event.

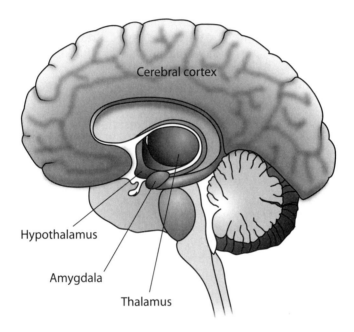

Cerebral cortex

Hypothalamus

Amygdala

Thalamus

EXAMPLE: *When information travels from the sense organs to the thalamus to the amygdala, people respond instantaneously, without thinking, to events in their environment. A parent may snatch her child away from a curb without thinking if she hears the sound of squealing tires coming toward them.*

The Amygdala Damage to the amygdala results in an inability to appropriately process fear. Animals with damaged amygdalas cannot develop conditioned fear responses. People with damaged amygdalas can't recognize fear in other people, though they may be able to experience fear themselves.

ACTIVATION OF THE AUTONOMIC NERVOUS SYSTEM

The **autonomic nervous system** controls all the automatic functions in the body. See pages 51–52 for more information about the autonomic nervous system.

When an emotion-evoking event happens, the **sympathetic** branch of the autonomic nervous system, which prepares the body for action, begins to work. It sends signals to the adrenal gland, which secretes the hormones epinephrine and norepinephrine. These hormones in turn prepare a person to face the challenges of the event. The following physical responses are indicative signs in a man or woman:

- Blood pressure, heart rate, respiration rate, and blood sugar levels increase and prepare a person for action.

- Pupils dilate to let in more light for vision.

- The digestive processes slow down so that energy can be directed to the crisis at hand.

Autonomic Nervous System *The autonomic nervous system is made up of two parts: the sympathetic and parasympathetic nervous systems. Unlike the* **sympathetic nervous system***, which prepares the body for action, the* **parasympathetic nervous system** *keeps the body still. The sympathetic nervous system involves expending energy, while the parasympathetic nervous system works to keep energy in the body.*

Measuring Emotion

Researchers often use autonomic responses to measure emotion. One frequently used autonomic response is called the galvanic skin response. The **galvanic skin response** is an increase in the skin's rate of electrical conductivity, which occurs when subjects sweat during emotional states. Researchers also use indicators such as blood pressure, muscle tension, heart rate, and respiration rate to measure emotion.

Polygraph Tests

The **polygraph**, or **lie detector**, is a device used to detect deception. In reality, the polygraph cannot detect deception. Instead, it measures autonomic indices of emotion. A subject is hooked up to the device and asked a series of neutral questions such as *What is your name? Where do you live?* and so on. The polygraph records the autonomic responses as the subject answers these questions, establishing the baseline, or normal pattern of autonomic activation. Then the subject answers other questions that can determine guilt or innocence, such as *Where were you on the night of the murder?*

In theory, when lying, the subject feels emotions such as nervousness or anxiety, and the polygraph records accompanying changes in autonomic activation. In practice, the polygraph is not very effective. Polygraph tests have a high error rate for two main reasons:

- Many people who are not engaging in deception feel nervous or anxious when asked questions concerning their guilt or innocence.

- People who are engaging in deception can often "trick" the polygraph by acting tense during neutral questions so that their baseline responses resemble their responses during the critical period of questioning.

DIFFERENCES AMONG EMOTIONS

The release of the hormones epinephrine and norepinephrine accompanies many emotional states, but emotions differ at the biological level:

- Different emotions have different patterns of brain activation.

- Different neurotransmitters are involved in different emotions.

- Different emotions have different patterns of autonomic nervous system activity.

Expression of Emotion

People express emotions not only through speech but also through nonverbal behavior, or body language. Nonverbal behavior includes facial expressions, postures, and gestures.

THE BASIC EMOTIONS

The psychologist **Paul Ekman** and his colleagues have identified six basic emotions: happiness, sadness, anger, fear, surprise, and disgust. Worldwide, most people can identify the facial expressions that correspond to these emotions.

> **The Catharsis Hypothesis** *The catharsis hypothesis suggests that anger can be decreased by releasing it through aggressive actions or fantasies. However, although catharsis helps in some cases, researchers have generally found that catharsis does not decrease anger in the long term. In fact, aggressive actions or fantasies can sometimes increase anger.*

THE FACIAL-FEEDBACK HYPOTHESIS

Some researchers have proposed that the brain uses feedback from facial muscles to recognize emotions that are being experienced. This idea is known as the **facial-feedback hypothesis**. It follows from this hypothesis that making the facial expression corresponding to a particular emotion can make a person feel that emotion. Studies have shown that this phenomenon does indeed occur.

For example, if people smile and try to look happy, they will feel happiness to some degree.

GENDER DIFFERENCES

Some research suggests that the genders differ in how much emotion they express. In North America, women appear to display more emotion than men. Anger is an exception—men tend to express anger more than women, particularly toward strangers.

This gender difference in expressiveness is not absolute. It depends on gender roles, cultural norms, and context:

- For both men and women, having a nontraditional gender role leads to increased emotional expressiveness.

- In some cultures, women and men are equally expressive.

- In some contexts, men and women do not differ in expressiveness. For example, neither men nor women are likely to express anger toward someone more powerful than themselves.

Emotion and Culture

Some aspects of emotion are universal to all cultures, while other aspects differ across cultures.

SIMILARITIES AMONG CULTURES

Ekman and his colleagues have found that people in different cultures can identify the six basic emotions: happiness, sadness, anger, fear, surprise, and disgust. The physiological indicators of emotion are similar in people from different cultures.

Facial Expressions Are Innate Both people who can see and people who have been blind since birth have similar facial expressions of emotions. This observation suggests that facial expressions are innate, since blind people could not have learned these expressions by observing others.

DIFFERENCES AMONG CULTURES

Although many emotions and expressions of emotions are universal, some differences exist among cultures:

- **Categories of emotions:** People in different cultures categorize emotions differently. Some languages have labels for emotions that are not labeled in other languages.

    EXAMPLE: Tahitians do not have a word for sadness. *Germans have a word,* schadenfreude, *indicating joy at someone else's misfortune, that has no equivalent in English.*

- **Prioritization of emotions:** Different cultures consider different emotions to be primary.

    EXAMPLE: Shame is considered a key emotion in some non-Western cultures, but it is less likely to be considered a primary emotion in many Western cultures.

- **Different emotions evoked:** The same situation may evoke different emotions in different cultures.

    EXAMPLE: A pork chop served for dinner might evoke disgust in the majority of people in Saudi Arabia, while it's likely to provoke happiness in many people in the United States.

- **Differences in nonverbal expressions:** Nonverbal expressions of emotion differ across cultures, due partly to the fact that different cultures have different display rules. **Display rules** are norms that tell people whether, which, how, and when emotions should be displayed.

    EXAMPLE: In the United States, male friends usually do not embrace and kiss each other as a form of greeting. Such behavior would make most American men uncomfortable or even angry. In many European countries, however, acquaintances normally embrace and kiss each other on both cheeks, and avoiding this greeting would seem unfriendly.

- **Power of cultural norms:** Cultural norms determine how and when to show emotions that are not actually felt. Acting out an emotion that is not felt is called **emotion work**.

    EXAMPLE: In some cultures, it is appropriate for people who attend a funeral to show extreme grief. In others, it is appropriate to appear stoic.

Happiness

Happiness is a basic human emotion, but people often make assumptions about happiness that empirical research does not support. For example, people often assume that most people feel unhappy and dissatisfied with their lives, but research shows this is not true. Most people describe themselves as fairly happy even if they are in less than ideal circumstances. Surprisingly, researchers have not found a consistent positive correlation between happiness and factors such as wealth, age, intelligence, physical attractiveness, or parenthood—factors that many people commonly associate with happiness.

Although circumstances do not reliably predict happiness, some circumstances do correlate with increased happiness. These include having a good social network, being married, having a satisfying job, and having strong religious convictions. These circumstances, however, are only correlated with happiness. As explained on page 10, correlation does not necessarily mean causation. Research also shows that happiness tends to depend on people's expectations of life and on how people compare themselves to their peers.

Subjective Well-being *Rather than focusing only on negative reactions to unfavorable circumstances, researchers today have begun to study subjective well-being.* **Subjective well-being** *is the perception people have about their happiness and satisfaction with life. Subjective well-being depends more on attitudes to external circumstances than on the circumstances themselves. That is, factors such as wealth or employment don't matter as much as how we feel about our wealth or employment.*

Summary

Theories of Emotion

- **Emotion** is a complex, subjective experience that is accompanied by biological and behavioral changes.
- **Charles Darwin** proposed that emotional expressions are hard-wired and that emotions evolved because they had **adaptive value.**
- Current evolutionary theorists believe that emotions are **innate.**
- The **James-Lange theory** states that people experience emotion because they perceive their bodies' physiological responses to external events.
- The **Cannon-Bard theory** states that the experience of emotion and the accompanying physiological arousal happen at the same time.
- **Schachter and Singer's two-factor theory** states that people's experience of emotion depends on physiological arousal and the cognitive interpretation of that arousal.
- People's experience of emotion depends on how they evaluate their environment.

The Biological Bases of Emotion

- Emotion involves activation of the brain and the **autonomic nervous system.**
- Information about emotion-evoking events moves along two pathways in the brain.
- The pathway that goes to the **amygdala** allows people to respond rapidly to events.
- The pathway that goes to the **cortex** allows people to appraise events more slowly.
- Researchers use **autonomic responses** to measure emotion.
- The **polygraph**, or lie detector, is a device that detects changes in autonomic arousal. It is often inaccurate in determining whether or not a person is lying.
- Different emotions differ in **pattern of brain activation, neurotransmitters released**, and **autonomic nervous system activity.**

Expression of Emotion

- People worldwide can identify six primary emotions: **happiness, sadness, anger, fear, surprise,** and **disgust.**

- The **facial-feedback hypothesis** states that the brain uses feedback from facial muscles to recognize emotions that are being experienced.

- The two genders express different amounts of emotion. This difference depends on gender roles, culture, and context.

Emotion and Culture

- People in different cultures can identify six basic emotions.

- There are **universal physiological indicators** of emotion.

- People in different cultures categorize emotions differently.

- Different cultures consider different emotions to be **primary.**

- The same situation may evoke different emotions in different cultures.

- Nonverbal expressions of emotion differ across cultures.

- **Cultural norms** determine how and when to display emotions that are not actually felt.

Happiness

- **Subjective well-being** depends more on attitudes toward circumstances than on the circumstances themselves.

- Circumstances such as **social support, marriage, job satisfaction,** and **religiosity** are positively correlated with happiness.

- Happiness tends to depend on **people's expectations of life** and on **the way they compare themselves to others.**

Sample Test Questions

1. What are some arguments against the James-Lange theory?

2. What are the neural pathways for information about emotion-evoking events?

3. What is the facial-feedback hypothesis, and why is it relevant to someone having a bad day?

4. Why are lie detectors often ineffective at determining whether someone is lying?

5. What aspects of emotion are similar across cultures?

6. Which one of the following is not one of the six universally recognizable, basic emotions described by Ekman and his colleagues?
   A. Surprise
   B. Fear
   C. Disgust
   D. Anxiety

7. Polygraphs detect which of the following?
   A. Hormone changes
   B. Cognitive appraisal
   C. Emotional experience
   D. Autonomic arousal

8. During emotional states, epinephrine and norepinephrine are released because of activation of which of the following?
   A. Sympathetic nervous system
   B. Cortex
   C. Thalamus
   D. Amygdala

9. What are display rules?
   A. Norms that inform people about appropriate emotional expression
   B. Rules that describe how polygraphs display data
   C. Norms for displaying autonomic responses during polygraph tests
   D. Displays of emotion that are not really felt

10. What is the part of the limbic system involved in regulating emotion?
    A. The cortex
    B. The hypothalamus
    C. The amygdala
    D. The adrenal

11. *Keri feels relaxed after an hour spent caught in traffic because she sees it as an opportunity to listen to some good music. In the same situation, Jill feels frustrated and anxious because she sees it as a waste of valuable time. The difference in the way they feel can be attributed to which of the following?*
    A.   Different expressions of emotion
    B.   Different biological responses to situations
    C.   Different cognitive appraisals
    D.   Different emotion work

12. *According to the Cannon-Bard theory, what is the relationship between physiological arousal and the experience of emotion?*
    A.   People experience emotion because they experience physiological arousal
    B.   The experience of emotion and physiological arousal occur simultaneously
    C.   People have physiological arousal because they experience emotion
    D.   None of the above

13. *The statement* We are afraid because we tremble *is explained by which theory of emotion?*
    A.   Darwin's theory
    B.   The two-factor theory
    C.   The James-Lange theory
    D.   The Cannon-Bard theory

14. *What is the galvanic skin response?*
    A.   An increase in the skin's electrical conductivity
    B.   A response that occurs when subjects secrete sweat
    C.   A way of measuring emotion
    D.   All of the above

15. *Differences among emotions at the biological level are characterized by which of the following?*
    A.   Activation of different brain areas, different cognitive appraisals, different patterns of autonomic activity
    B.   Different patterns of autonomic activity, different nonverbal behaviors, different neurotransmitters
    C.   Different neurotransmitters, different patterns of autonomic activity, activation of different brain areas
    D.   Activation of different brain areas, different nonverbal behaviors, different neurotransmitters

ANSWERS

1.   There are three main arguments against the James-Lange theory: 1. People can experience physiological arousal without experiencing emotion. 2. Physiological reactions happen too slowly to be the cause of experiences of emotion, which occur very rapidly. 3. People can experience very different emotions even when they have the same pattern of physiological arousal.

2.   The information goes first to the thalamus, and from there it moves simultaneously to the amygdala and the cortex of the brain. The amygdala processes the information quickly and sends signals to the hypothalamus, which in turn activates the autonomic nervous system. The cortex, on the other hand, processes the information more slowly, allowing us to appraise or evaluate the event.

3.   The facial-feedback hypothesis is the idea that the brain uses feedback from facial muscles to recognize emotions that are being experienced. Making the facial expression corresponding to a particular emotion can make a person feel that emotion. So a person having a bad day might feel better if he or she put on a happy expression.

4.   Lie detectors are often ineffective for two main reasons: 1. Many people who are not lying feel nervous or anxious when asked questions concerning their guilt or innocence. 2. People who are lying can often trick the polygraph by acting tense when neutral questions are asked so that their baseline responses resemble their responses during the critical period of questioning.

5.   People in many different cultures can identify the six basic emotions: happiness, sadness, anger, fear, surprise, and disgust. Also, the physiological indicators of emotion are similar in people from different cultures.

6.	**D**	11.	**C**
7.	**D**	12.	**B**
8.	**A**	13.	**C**
9.	**A**	14.	**D**
10.	**C**	15.	**C**

Motivation

- What Is Motivation?
- Hunger
- Sexual Drive
- Achievement

A dog's motivation seems straightforward: offer the dog a treat, and it will perform all sorts of tricks. Human motivations, however, are far more complicated. Food and sex motivate us, just like they do most animals, but we often do amazing, brave, horrifying, or death-defying things because of the importance we ascribe to intangible principles.

Millions of people around the world fast for religious or personal reasons, ignoring hunger. Some people enter eating contests, which challenge them to ignore their full stomachs and eat huge amounts of food. King Edward VIII of England gave up his throne to marry an American divorcée, and Roman Catholic priests give up sex for their calling. Why would people do these things? Food, sex, and achievement are motivations for all of us, but motivation can also be as unique as each individual.

What Is Motivation?

A **motive** is an impulse that causes a person to act. **Motivation** is an internal process that makes a person move toward a goal. Motivation, like intelligence, can't be directly observed. Instead, motivation can only be inferred by noting a person's behavior.

Researchers have proposed theories that try to explain human motivation. These theories include **drive reduction theories** and Maslow's **hierarchy of needs theory**.

DRIVE REDUCTION THEORIES

Drive reduction theories of motivation suggest that people act in order to reduce needs and maintain a constant physiological state. For example, people eat in order to reduce their need for food. The idea of homeostasis is central to drive reduction theories. **Homeostasis** is the maintenance of a state of physiological equilibrium.

Drive reduction theories fail to explain several aspects of motivation:

- People sometimes aren't motivated by internal needs.

    EXAMPLE: Some people fast for long periods for political causes, despite feeling extreme hunger.

- Sometimes, people continue being motivated even when they have satisfied internal needs.

    EXAMPLE: People sometimes eat even when they don't feel hungry.

- People are often motivated by external incentives as well as internal needs.

    EXAMPLE: If a person is hungry, he or she may choose to eat a salad rather than a cheeseburger because he or she wants to be slimmer.

Intrinsic and Extrinsic Motivation

A motivation may be intrinsic, extrinsic, or both. **Intrinsic motivation** is the motivation to act for the sake of the activity alone. For example, people have intrinsic motivation to write poetry if they do it simply because they enjoy it. **Extrinsic motivation**, on the other hand, is the motivation to act for external rewards. For example, people have extrinsic motivation to write if they do so in the hopes of getting published, being famous, or making money.

> **Incentives** An **incentive** is an environmental stimulus that pulls people to act in a particular way. Getting an A on an exam may be an incentive that pulls a student toward studying.

MASLOW'S HIERARCHY OF NEEDS

In the 1970s, the psychologist **Abraham Maslow** suggested that people are motivated by a **hierarchy of needs:**

- First, most basic level: physiological needs, such as the need for food, water, safety, and security.

- Second level: needs for social interaction, such as the need to belong.

- Third level: needs for esteem, which include the need for respect from oneself and others.

- Fourth level: needs for self-actualization, or realizing one's full potential.

Maslow believed people pay attention to higher needs only when lower needs are satisfied.

Critics argue that Maslow's theory doesn't explain why higher needs often motivate people even when lower needs are unsatisfied.

> *EXAMPLE: Ray lives in a very dangerous neighborhood and constantly worries about safety. He makes little money at his job in civil-rights law, but he enjoys it because he believes that his true calling is to fight injustice.*

Critics also point out that people are sometimes simultaneously motivated by needs at different levels.

> EXAMPLE: *Angie might be motivated to join a theater club both because she wants to be part of a close community and because she wants to be respected for her acting skills.*

Types of Needs

People have innate needs and learned needs, both of which are influenced by society and culture. People have a limited number of innate needs, which include needs for food, water, oxygen, and elimination of wastes. There are, however, a relatively large number of learned needs, including needs for achievement, autonomy, and power. These needs are determined by **values**, or people's perceptions of what is important in life.

Hunger

Hunger is a complicated motivation; people don't eat only because they need food. Many factors, both biological and environmental, influence hunger. These factors interact with one another in many ways.

BIOLOGICAL FACTORS

Researchers believe certain genetic differences among individuals play a role in hunger. The brain, the digestive system, and hormones are all involved in influencing hunger at the biological level.

Genetic Differences Among Individuals

Researchers theorize that people have a genetically influenced **set point** for body weight. If a person's weight rises too far above his set point, his appetite decreases, or he uses up more energy. His weight then returns to its set point. If, on the other hand, his weight falls too far below his set point, his appetite increases, or he uses less energy. Once again, he returns to his set point.

The set point is maintained not only by food intake and energy expenditure but also by the body's basal metabolic rate, another genetically influenced variable. **Basal metabolic rate** is the rate at which a person at complete rest uses energy.

Some researchers disagree about set points and believe that people can reset their normal weight if they add or lose pounds slowly. They also point out that people usually gain weight when they have easy access to rich foods.

The Brain

Researchers believe three areas in the hypothalamus play a key role in regulating hunger:

1. The lateral hypothalamus is involved in recognizing hunger. In rats, damage to the lateral hypothalamus results in loss of interest in eating.

2. The ventromedial nucleus of the hypothalamus is involved in recognizing satiety or fullness. In rats, damage to the ventromedial nucleus results in excessive eating and weight gain.

3. The paraventricular nucleus of the hypothalamus is also involved in hunger regulation. When the paraventricular nucleus of a rat is damaged, the rat will eat a very large quantity of food at each meal.

The Digestive System

The digestive system influences hunger in several ways. For instance, after a meal, the stomach and intestines send nerve impulses to the brain to help people recognize that they are full.

The body converts food to **glucose**, a simple sugar that acts as an energy source for cells. The level of glucose in the blood affects hunger. Low blood glucose increases hunger; high blood glucose decreases hunger.

Hormones

The hormone **insulin** also plays an important role in regulating hunger. Insulin allows cells to access glucose in the blood. When the pancreas secretes insulin, hunger increases.

Diabetes is a condition caused by a deficiency of insulin. People who have diabetes take injections of insulin. Without these injections, their cells would be unable to use the glucose in their blood.

Another hormone involved in hunger regulation is **leptin**. Fat cells in the body secrete leptin and release it into the blood. When the leptin level in the blood is high, hunger decreases.

ENVIRONMENTAL FACTORS

Many environmental factors influence hunger, including the availability of rich foods, taste preferences, habits, memory, stress, and cultural attitudes.

- **Availability of rich foods:** People tend to gain weight when rich foods are plentiful.

- **Preferences:** Some taste preferences appear to be innate, such as the preference for fatty foods. However, people acquire most taste preferences through conditioning or observational learning. People tend to prefer familiar foods. These preferences have an influence on hunger and food intake.

- **Habits:** People learn habits, such as when and how much they eat. These habits also influence hunger and food intake.

- **Memory:** The memory of what people last ate and when they ate it influences hunger.

- **Stress:** The increased physiological arousal associated with stressful situations can stimulate hunger in some people. In other people, stress decreases hunger.

- **Cultural attitudes:** Cultural attitudes about ideal body size and shape have a strong influence on what and how much people eat.

Eating Disorders *The prevalence of the eating disorders anorexia nervosa and bulimia nervosa in weight-conscious cultures shows that cultural factors can have a negative influence on hunger and body weight. Anorexia nervosa is characterized by extremely low body weight and a distorted body image. Bulimia nervosa is characterized by bouts of binging, followed by compensatory behaviors such as purging, fasting, or heavy exercise to rid the body of food. Both disorders can be life-threatening.*

Sexual Drive

Unlike hunger, sexual drive does not motivate people to fulfill a basic biological need. A lack of food leads to death; a lack of sex, on the other hand, does not. Both biological and psychological factors strongly influence sexual drive.

KINSEY'S STUDIES

One of the first researchers to give a modern account of human sexuality was **Alfred Kinsey**. In the 1940s, he and his colleagues interviewed more than 18,000 U.S. men and women about their sexual behavior and attitudes. In his comprehensive reports about human sexuality, Kinsey denounced the repressive social attitudes of his time, which he said bore little relation to actual sexual practices. Kinsey provided statistics showing that sexual practices varied widely and that even in the 1940s there was a high prevalence of masturbation and premarital sex. These statistics shocked many people of his day.

Critics of Kinsey's research maintained three arguments:

- Kinsey's sample was not random. Instead, it consisted largely of well-educated, white city dwellers.

- Kinsey and his colleagues used questionable methods to gather their data, especially asking leading questions when interviewing subjects.

- Kinsey may have let his own beliefs influence his results.

MASTERS AND JOHNSON'S STUDIES

Other pioneers of sexual research were **William Masters** and **Virginia Johnson**. In the 1960s, they studied several hundred male and female volunteers who agreed to either masturbate or have intercourse in a laboratory. Masters and Johnson hooked up the volunteers to instruments that measured various physiological indicators during sexual activity. Using the results of these studies, they described the sexual response cycle.

The Sexual Response Cycle

Masters and Johnson divided the human sexual response cycle into four phases:

1. **Excitement phase:** Physiological arousal increases quickly. Muscle tension, heart rate, blood pressure, and breathing rate increase. In men, the penis gets erect and the testes swell. In women, the clitoris hardens and swells, the vaginal lips open, and the vagina lubricates.

2. **Plateau phase:** Physiological arousal continues. In women, the clitoris retracts under the clitoral hood. Men may secrete a small amount of fluid from the penis.

3. **Orgasm phase:** Physiological arousal peaks. Men ejaculate seminal fluid. Both men and women experience muscular contractions in the pelvic area, along with a sensation of pleasure.

4. **Resolution phase:** Physiological responses return to normal levels. Men then go through a refractory period that can vary in length, during which they are not responsive to stimulation. The refractory period tends to get longer as men age.

Critics of Masters and Johnson's research maintained two arguments:

- Masters and Johnson studied a biased sample of people. The sample included only people who were both willing and able to perform sexual acts in a laboratory setting.

- Masters and Johnson didn't pay attention to individual differences. In reality, people's sexual responses vary according to factors such as age, amount of sexual experience, and cultural background.

The Role of Testosterone Sexual drive is related to testosterone level in both men and women, but the relationship is a complex one. Sexual activity increases testosterone levels, and testosterone levels increase sex drive.

PSYCHOLOGICAL FACTORS IN SEXUAL MOTIVATION

Hormones alone cannot cause sexual arousal. Psychological factors are also highly influential.

- **Erotic stimuli:** Both men and women can become sexually aroused by external and internal erotic stimuli. External erotic stimuli include sexually exciting material that is read, heard, or seen. Internal erotic stimuli include thoughts, fantasies, and memories of past sexual experiences. What is considered erotic varies according to the individual, historical period, and cultural context.

- **Desires:** People have an infinite number of desires that influence the motivation for sex, including to procreate, to express love, to have physical enjoyment, to cope with difficult situations and emotions, to validate one's desirability, and to do what peers do.

- **Cultural context:** Having a strong influence on sexual behavior, cultures inform people about **sexual scripts**, or implicit rules that allow a person to judge the appropriate sexual behavior for a given situation. For example, people follow sexual scripts when deciding whether they should initiate sexual activity or wait to receive a partner's advances.

A culture's social and economic structure determines the gender roles that men and women adopt. These gender roles in turn determine people's attitude toward sexual activity. In some cultures, for instance, women need marriage to get access to status and wealth. In such cultures, a woman is less likely to be interested in sex for its own sake, since casual sex can damage her reputation and reduce her chances of marriage.

Sex and the Brain Psychological influences are clearly powerful motivators for sex, and the brain is highly involved in sexual arousal. People who have lost all sensation in their genitals because of spinal injuries, for example, are still capable of sexual desire.

**CHAPTER 12
MOTIVATION**

GENDER DIFFERENCES IN SEXUAL BEHAVIOR AND PARTNER CHOICE

Many researchers have found that some differences exist between men and women in sexual behavior and partner choice, though all men and all women do not behave the same way or feel the same things.

Men	Women
More interested in sex; initiate and think about sex more often	Less interested in sex
Want sex with more partners	Not as interested in sex with many partners
Desire sex without emotional commitment	Desire sex with emotional commitment
Focus on youth and physical attractiveness when choosing a sex partner	Focus on social and economic status when choosing a sex partner
Feel more jealous when partner is physically unfaithful	Feel more jealous when partner is emotionally unfaithful

Evolutionary Explanations

Some theorists use evolutionary theory to explain these gender differences. Their explanations are generally based on Robert Trivers's idea that men and women make different parental investments in order to produce offspring. From a biological standpoint, men invest no more than the energy required for intercourse. Women, on the other hand, invest time and energy in pregnancy and breast feeding. Because of these biological differences, females can produce only a limited number of offspring, whereas males can potentially produce virtually unlimited offspring.

Males can increase their reproductive success by producing as many offspring as possible. Evolutionary theory predicts that men tend to choose attractive, youthful partners because these qualities imply good health and an ability to reproduce successfully. Females increase their reproductive success by being highly discriminating when choosing mates. They try to select males who have the most access to material resources, because such males can contribute the most to caring for offspring.

Furthermore, men must contend with paternity uncertainty—they can never be certain that they are the fathers of their partners' offspring. Evolutionary theorists predict that men would therefore tend to have concerns about their partners' sexual infidelity. Women, on the other hand, *can* be certain that their offspring are their own, though they cannot be certain that their partners will provide for their offspring. Therefore, they are more likely to be concerned about the emotional fidelity of their partners.

Problems with Evolutionary Explanations

Many people criticize the use of evolutionary explanations of gender differences in sexual behavior. Some critics argue that alternative explanations can account equally well for the observed gender differences. For example, women's history of social and economic subservience may have taught them to place a high value on their partners' access to material resources. Men's preferences and behaviors may likewise be a product of socialization. See page 43 for more information on problems with evolutionary explanations.

SEXUAL ORIENTATION

Sexual orientation is such a controversial subject that people cannot even agree about how the term *sexual orientation* should be defined. Some people argue over whether it refers to sexual behavior, sexual attraction, emotional attraction, or all three.

Researchers define sexual orientation in a variety of ways, which means there is no clear idea about what proportion of the population is homosexual. Researchers also have many different opinions regarding how much biological and environmental factors contribute to sexual orientation.

Possible Biological Factors

Researchers have many ideas about the possible biological factors of homosexuality:

- **Hormones:** Some researchers have suggested that homosexuals and heterosexuals have different levels of various hormones in the blood. However, research in this area has failed consistently to find hormonal variations that could account for differences in sexual orientation.

- **Genes:** Others have proposed that there is a genetic basis for predisposition to homosexuality. To investigate the possibility of a genetic basis, researchers have studied the sexual orientations of the identical, fraternal, and adoptive siblings of homosexual people. This research has shown that the identical twins of homosexuals are much more likely to be homosexual than the fraternal twins of homosexuals. In turn, the fraternal twins of homosexuals are more likely to be homosexual than the adoptive siblings of homosexuals.

- **Prenatal factors:** Some researchers have focused on prenatal environment. These researchers believe that the level of hormones present during a critical period in prenatal development can affect the organization of the brain, which in turn can influence sexual orientation. Research shows that women who were exposed to high prenatal levels of androgens are more likely to be homosexual. Critics point out that not all women who were exposed to prenatal androgens became homosexual and that many homosexual women were not exposed to androgens prenatally.

- **Brain differences:** One researcher, Simon LeVay, examined anatomical differences in the brains of homosexual and heterosexual men. He found that a specific area of the hypothalamus tended to be smaller in homosexual men and in heterosexual women than in heterosexual men.

Environmental Factors

Many researchers believe biological factors alone can't explain the origin of homosexuality. For example, there is only about a 50 percent chance that the identical twins of homosexual men will also be homosexual. Therefore, some other factor must make the other 50 percent heterosexual. Although this other factor remains unknown, researchers have proposed a number of environmental situations that might influence sexual orientation:

- An ineffectual, distant father and an overly close, domineering mother

- Seduction in childhood by a homosexual adult
- Same-sex sexual play as children

Many of these proposals lack empirical support.

At this time, no one knows exactly what determines sexual orientation. Possibly, men and women develop homosexual orientations through various pathways. It is also possible that the cause of homosexual orientation differs from individual to individual.

> **Sexual Orientation in the Animal World** Humans are not the only species to engage in homosexual or bisexual activity. Biologists have documented that animals belonging to hundreds of different species engage in homosexual or bisexual behavior. Many, both male and female, form exclusive, long-term homosexual pairs.

**CHAPTER 12
MOTIVATION**

Achievement

An **achievement motive** is an impulse to master challenges and reach a high standard of excellence. Both personality and situational factors influence achievement motivation.

Researchers often use the **Thematic Apperception Test (TAT)** to measure people's need for achievement. The TAT consists of a set of ambiguous pictures, such as one of a woman standing in the doorway of a room. Researchers ask subjects to make up stories about these pictures. Some subjects' stories consistently contain themes that relate to achievement. Researchers consider these subjects to have a high need for achievement.

PERSONALITY FACTORS

High-achievement motivation tends to lead to particular personality features. These include persistence, ability to delay gratification, and competitiveness:

- **Persistence:** High achievers tend to be very persistent and work hard to attain goals they set for themselves.

- **Ability to delay gratification:** High achievers tend to have a greater ability to delay gratifying their impulses in the short term in order to reach long-term goals.

- **Competitiveness:** High achievers tend to select careers that give them opportunities to compete with other people.

Self-Fulfilling Prophecies Expectations can result in self-fulfilling prophecies. If a student expects to get an A on a term paper, she'll work hard, and her work will be more likely to earn her an A.

SITUATIONAL FACTORS

Some situational factors also affect achievement motivation. They include the expectation of success, incentives, control, and opportunity:

- **Expectation of success:** People are more likely to have a high expectation of success if they have a feeling of **self-efficacy**, or confidence in their own ability to meet challenges effectively. People can acquire self-efficacy by dealing with difficulties and learning from mistakes. Having good role models and getting constructive feedback and encouragement also help to build self-efficacy.

- **Incentives:** Incentives reward people for their competence and motivate them to achieve. However, incentives can also decrease people's intrinsic motivation if people focus on getting incentives rather than doing tasks for their own sake.

- **Control:** People tend to have more motivation to achieve if they feel they have control over some aspects of their work.

- **Opportunity:** People are motivated to achieve only when they have the opportunity to achieve.

High Achievers Prefer Moderately Difficult Tasks People with a high need for achievement tend to prefer moderately difficult tasks. Such tasks allow people to succeed and to see themselves as competent for having succeeded. Very difficult tasks tend to prevent success, and very easy tasks don't allow people to feel competent when they succeed.

THE POWER OF GOALS

Goals are most likely to increase motivation to achieve if they are specific, challenging but achievable, and positive:

- **Goals should be specific.** The more specific the goals, the more effective they are as motivators.

    EXAMPLE: *If Steve is trying to get all his reading done for a final exam, a specific goal, such as* I will finish one chapter each week, *is more effective than a more diffuse goal, such as* I will make sure I'm ready for my final.

- **Goals should be challenging but achievable.** Goals have to be difficult enough to be challenging but easy enough to be reachable.

    EXAMPLE: *If Kelly has been struggling to maintain a C average in a class all semester, a goal such as* I will make a B on the final exam *will be more motivational than a goal such as* I will get an A in this class.

- **Goals should be positive.** It is better for people to frame goals in terms of what they *will* do rather than in terms of what they *will not* do.

    EXAMPLE: *A goal such as* I will study for an hour every weekday evening *is likely to be more effective than a goal such as* I will not go out on weekday evenings.

Summary

What Is Motivation?

- **Motivation** is an internal process that makes a person move toward a goal.

- Motivation may be **extrinsic**, **intrinsic**, or both.

- **Drive reduction theories of motivation** suggest that people act in order to reduce needs and maintain a constant physiological state.

- **Abraham Maslow** proposed that there is a **hierarchy of needs** and that people pay attention to higher needs only when lower ones are satisfied.

- Needs may be **innate** or **learned**. Learned needs are determined by **values**. Both innate and learned needs are influenced by society and culture.

Hunger

- A genetically influenced **set point** may allow people to keep their weight constant.

- The **lateral hypothalamus** and the **ventromedial** and **paraventricular nuclei** of the hypothalamus play key roles in regulating hunger.

- The digestive system and hormones such as **insulin** and **leptin** also regulate hunger.

- Environmental influences on hunger include **availability of foods**, **preferences**, **habits**, **memory**, **stress**, and **cultural attitudes**.

Sexual Drive

- **Alfred Kinsey** was one of the first people to give a modern account of human sexuality.

- **William Masters** and **Virginia Johnson** described the human sexual response.

- The sexual response cycle has four phases: **excitement**, **plateau**, **orgasm**, and **resolution**.

- Testosterone increases sex drive, and sexual activity increases testosterone.

- Psychological influences on sex drive include **internal and external erotic stimuli**, **desires**, and **cultural context**.

- Researchers have found that there are some gender differences in sexual behavior and partner choice. Both evolutionary and sociocultural explanations can account for these differences.

- Estimates of the prevalence of homosexuality vary, and the causes of homosexuality remain unclear.

- Researchers have suggested that biological factors including **hormone levels, genes, prenatal environment**, and **brain anatomy** could influence sexual orientation.

- Psychologists have proposed several theories about how environment might influence homosexuality, but research has failed to support these theories.

Achievement

- Researchers often use the **thematic apperception test (TAT)** to measure the need for achievement.

- People who have a high **achievement motivation** tend to be persistent and hardworking. They are able to delay gratification to meet long-term goals, and they tend to choose careers that allow them to compete with others.

- People achieve the most when they have **high expectations of success, incentives that reward competence, control over tasks, opportunities to achieve**, and **effective goals**.

- Goals are most effective when they are **specific, moderately difficult**, and **framed in terms of what must be done** rather than what must be avoided.

Sample Test Questions

1. Why might drive reduction theories be inadequate for explaining motivation?

2. What findings suggest that there may be a genetic basis for the predisposition to homosexuality?

3. What is Maslow's theory of motivation?

4. What are some criticisms of Kinsey's research on human sexuality?

5. Some research suggests that women tend to pick marriage partners based on wealth and status, whereas men tend to pick partners based on youthfulness and attractiveness. How do evolutionary theorists explain this difference?

6. If someone has intrinsic motivation to go for a jog every evening, she is most likely to jog for which reason?
   - A. She likes the way she feels when she jogs
   - B. She wants to please her mother by losing some weight
   - C. She wants other people to admire her for jogging
   - D. All of the above

7. What influences set points for body weight?
   - A. Basal metabolic rate
   - B. Food intake
   - C. Energy output
   - D. All of the above

8. Which of the following is likely to be true?
   - A. When the level of glucose in the blood falls, people always feel hungry
   - B. When the level of glucose in the blood is low, whether or not people feel hungry may depend on environmental factors
   - C. Blood glucose level is not related to hunger
   - D. When people eat, their blood glucose level falls

9. According to Masters and Johnson, men go through a refractory period in which phase?
   - A. Plateau
   - B. Resolution
   - C. Excitement
   - D. Orgasm

10. *Which statement best describes the relationship between testosterone level and sex?*
    A.   Sexual activity decreases testosterone
    B.   Testosterone increases sex drive
    C.   Testosterone increases sex drive and sexual activity increases testosterone
    D.   Testosterone increases sex drive and sexual activity decreases testosterone

11. *There are many gender differences in sexual behavior. Critics of evolutionary explanations are likely to attribute these differences to which of the following?*
    A.   Differences in parental investment
    B.   Differences in genetic makeup
    C.   Differences in socialization
    D.   None of the above

12. *A person with an injury in the ventromedial nucleus of the hypothalamus might exhibit what kind of behavior?*
    A.   Eating very small meals
    B.   Eating only salty foods
    C.   Loss of interest in eating
    D.   Excessive eating and weight gain

13. *In order for a goal to be effective at increasing motivation, what should it be?*
    A.   Very difficult to reach
    B.   Specific
    C.   Framed in terms of what should be avoided
    D.   Easily attained

14. *A disadvantage of incentives is that they may do which of the following?*
    A.   Increase motivation in general
    B.   Decrease intrinsic motivation
    C.   Decrease extrinsic motivation
    D.   Decrease opportunities for achievement

15. *What are sexual scripts?*
    A.   Stories on sexual themes that people are asked to write when tested with the TAT
    B.   Implicit rules about appropriate sexual behavior
    C.   Theories that evolutionary theorists use to explain sexual behavior
    D.   Theories that psychologists use to explain the origins of sexual orientation

CHAPTER 12
MOTIVATION

ANSWERS

1.   Drive reduction theories are inadequate for explaining motivation for three reasons: A. They don't explain why people sometimes aren't motivated by internal needs. B. They don't explain why people don't stop being motivated when internal needs are satisfied. C. They don't explain why people are often motivated by external incentives as well as internal needs.

2.   Research has shown that the identical twins of homosexuals are much more likely to be homosexual than the fraternal twins of homosexuals. In turn, the fraternal twins of homosexuals are more likely to be homosexual than the adoptive siblings of homosexuals.

3.   Maslow proposed that people are motivated by a hierarchy of needs and that people pay attention to higher-level needs only when lower-level needs are satisfied. The most basic needs are physiological needs and needs for safety and security. The next needs are for social interaction, followed by needs for esteem. The last needs are for self-actualization.

4.   Critics of Kinsey's research maintain that his sample was biased; that he used questionable methods, such as asking leading questions when interviewing subjects; and that he may have let his own beliefs influence his results.

5.   Evolutionary theorists base their explanation on the difference in parental investment between males and females. Males invest less to produce offspring than do females. Males can increase their reproductive success by producing as many offspring as possible. Evolutionary theory predicts that men tend to choose partners who are attractive and youthful because these qualities imply good health and an ability to reproduce successfully. Females increase their reproductive success by being highly discriminating when choosing mates. They try to select males who have the most access to material resources, because such males can contribute the most to caring for offspring.

6. **A**	11. **C**
7. **D**	12. **D**
8. **B**	13. **B**
9. **B**	14. **B**
10. **C**	15. **B**

Personality

13

Personality—it's who we are. Our personalities determine how we act and react, as well as how we interact with and respond to the world. Despite much research, the origins of personality are still a mystery, though there are many theories that attempt to explain them. Some researchers propose that children learn personality from their parents; others believe personality is fixed from birth. Some theories address how environment, genetics, and culture influence the development of personality.

What does it mean to have "personality"? Someone with personality could be funny, passionate, daring, extroverted, aggressive, egotistical, hot-tempered, or insecure. He or she might be altruistic, humble, mellow, shy, or wary. He or she might even be all or any of these things at different times and in different places, depending on the situation. Researchers have developed many ways of assessing personality, but even if we do gain an understanding of *how* we are, the question of *why* we're that way remains.

Personality Traits

Personality is the collection of characteristic thoughts, feelings, and behaviors that are associated with a person. Personality **traits** are characteristic behaviors and feelings that are consistent and long lasting.

> *Traits vs. States* Unlike traits, which are stable characteristics, **states** are temporary behaviors or feelings that depend on a person's situation and motives at a particular time. The difference between traits and states is analogous to the difference between climate and weather. Los Angeles has a warm climate, but on some days it may have cool weather. In the same way, a person who has the trait of calmness may experience a state of anxiety on a day when he or she faces a difficult challenge.

ANCIENT GREEK IDEAS

The ancient Greeks believed that people's personalities depended on the kind of **humor**, or fluid, most prevalent in their bodies. The ancient Greeks identified four humors—blood, phlegm, black bile, and yellow bile—and categorized people's personalities to correspond as follows:

- **Sanguine:** Blood. Cheerful and passionate.
- **Phlegmatic:** Phlegm. Dull and unemotional.
- **Melancholic:** Black bile. Unhappy and depressed.
- **Choleric:** Yellow bile. Angry and hot-tempered.

The Greek theory of personality remained influential well into the eighteenth century.

CATTELL'S SIXTEEN TRAITS

Like the ancient Greeks, modern researchers believe in the existence of a few basic personality traits. Combinations of these basic traits, they believe, form other traits. Psychologist Raymond Cattell used a statistical procedure called **factor analysis** to identify basic personality traits from a very long list of English words that identified traits. Factor analysis allowed Cattell to cluster these traits into groups according to their similarities. He found that personality is made up of sixteen basic dimensions.

THE BIG FIVE TRAITS

Other researchers have since clustered personality traits into even fewer categories. Today, many psychologists believe that all personality traits derive from five basic personality traits, which are commonly referred to as the **Big Five**:

1. Neuroticism

2. Extraversion

3. Openness to experience

4. Agreeableness

5. Conscientiousness

The Big Five traits remain quite stable over the life span, particularly after the age of thirty. Although researchers identified the Big Five traits by using a list of English words, these traits seem to be applicable in many countries.

Criticisms of the Big Five Model

Critics of the Big Five have various arguments against the model:

- Some critics think that more than five traits are needed to account for the wide personality differences among people.

- Other critics argue that five traits are too many. For example, they point out that openness correlates positively with extraversion. These critics argue that just three traits— neuroticism, extraversion, and agreeableness—should be enough to fully describe personality.

- Still other critics argue that the Big Five are somewhat arbitrary because they depend on the words used in the statistical analysis that produced them. A different list of words may have yielded different basic traits.

- Some psychologists have questioned the research supporting the stability of the Big Five traits across cultures. They argue that the research could be biased because the use of Western tests is more likely to uncover cultural similarities than differences.

Psychodynamic Theories

Many psychologists have proposed theories that try to explain the origins of personality. One highly influential set of theories stems from the work of Austrian neurologist **Sigmund Freud**, who first proposed the theory of psychoanalysis. Collectively, these theories are known as **psychodynamic theories**. Although many different psychodynamic theories exist, they all emphasize unconscious motives and desires, as well as the importance of childhood experiences in shaping personality.

SIGMUND FREUD'S THEORY OF PSYCHOANALYSIS

In the late 1800s and early 1900s, Freud developed a technique that he called **psychoanalysis** and used it to treat mental disorders. He formed his theory of psychoanalysis by observing his patients. According to psychoanalytic theory, personalities arise because of attempts to resolve conflicts between unconscious sexual and aggressive impulses and societal demands to restrain these impulses.

The Conscious, the Preconscious, and the Unconscious

Freud believed that most mental processes are unconscious. He proposed that people have three levels of awareness:

- The **conscious** contains all the information that a person is paying attention to at any given time.

    EXAMPLE: The words Dan is reading, the objects in his field of vision, the sounds he can hear, and any thirst, hunger, or pain he is experiencing at the moment are all in his conscious.

- The **preconscious** contains all the information outside of a person's attention but readily available if needed.

    EXAMPLE: Linda's telephone number, the make of her car, and many of her past experiences are in her preconscious.

- The **unconscious** contains thoughts, feelings, desires, and memories of which people have no awareness but that influence every aspect of their day-to-day lives.

    EXAMPLE: Stan's unconscious might contain angry feelings toward his mother or a traumatic incident he experienced at age four.

Freud believed that information in the unconscious emerges in slips of the tongue, jokes, dreams, illness symptoms, and the associations people make between ideas.

> **The Freudian Slip** Cathy calls up her mother on Mother's Day and says, "You're the beast, Mom," when she consciously intended to say, "You're the best, Mom." According to psychoanalytic theory, this slip of the tongue, known as a Freudian slip, reveals her unconscious anger toward her mother.

The Id, the Ego, and the Superego

Freud proposed that personalities have three components: the id, the ego, and the superego.

- **Id:** a reservoir of instinctual energy that contains biological urges such as impulses toward survival, sex, and aggression. The id is unconscious and operates according to the **pleasure principle**, the drive to achieve pleasure and avoid pain. The id is characterized by **primary process thinking**, which is illogical, irrational, and motivated by a desire for the immediate gratification of impulses.

- **Ego:** the component that manages the conflict between the id and the constraints of the real world. Some parts of the ego are unconscious, while others are preconscious or conscious. The ego operates according to the **reality principle**, the awareness that gratification of impulses has to be delayed in order to accommodate the demands of the real world. The ego is characterized by **secondary process thinking**, which is logical and rational. The ego's role is to prevent the id from gratifying its impulses in socially inappropriate ways.

- **Superego:** the moral component of personality. It contains all the moral standards learned from parents and society. The superego forces the ego to conform not only to reality but also to its ideals of morality. Hence, the superego causes people to feel guilty when they go against society's rules. Like the ego, the superego operates at all three levels of awareness.

Conflict

Freud believed that the id, the ego, and the superego are in constant conflict. He focused mainly on conflicts concerning sexual and aggressive urges because these urges are most likely to violate societal rules.

Anxiety

Internal conflicts can make a person feel anxious. In Freud's view, anxiety arises when the ego cannot adequately balance the demands of the id and the superego. The id demands gratification of its impulses, and the superego demands maintenance of its moral standards.

Defense Mechanisms

To manage these internal conflicts, people use defense mechanisms. **Defense mechanisms** are behaviors that protect people from anxiety. There are many different kinds of defense mechanisms, many of which are automatic and unconscious:

- **Repression:** keeping unpleasant thoughts, memories, and feelings shut up in the unconscious.

    EXAMPLE: Nate witnessed his mother being beaten by a mugger when he was seven years old. As an adult, he does not remember this incident.

- **Reaction formation:** behaving in a way that is opposite to behavior, feelings, or thoughts that are considered unacceptable.

    EXAMPLE: Lisa feels sexually attracted to her roommate's boyfriend but does not admit this to herself. Instead, she constantly makes very disparaging comments about the boyfriend and feels disgusted by the way he acts.

- **Projection:** attributing one's own unacceptable thoughts or feelings to someone else.

    EXAMPLE: Mario feels angry toward his father but is not aware of it. Instead, he complains that he cannot be around his father because his father is such an angry man.

- **Rationalization:** using incorrect but self-serving explanations to justify unacceptable behavior, thoughts, or feelings.

    EXAMPLE: Sylvia runs a red light while driving. She justifies this by telling herself she was already in the intersection when the light changed to red.

- **Displacement:** transferring feelings about a person or event onto someone or something else.

    EXAMPLE: Seth is angry at his professor for giving him a bad grade. He leaves class and shouts angrily at a passerby who accidentally bumps into him.

- **Denial:** refusing to acknowledge something that is obvious to others.

    EXAMPLE: Kate's use of alcohol starts to affect her academic performance, her job, and her relationships. However, she insists that she drinks only to relieve stress and that she does not have an alcohol problem.

- **Regression:** reverting to a more immature state of psychological development.

  EXAMPLE: When six-year-old Jameel gets less attention from his parents because of a new baby brother, he suddenly starts to wet his bed at night.

- **Sublimation:** channeling unacceptable thoughts and feelings into socially acceptable behavior.

  EXAMPLE: Priya deals with her angry feelings toward her family by writing science-fiction stories about battles between civilizations.

Psychosexual Stages of Development

Freud believed that personality solidifies during childhood, largely before age five. He proposed five stages of psychosexual development: the oral stage, the anal stage, the phallic stage, the latency stage, and the genital stage. He believed that at each stage of development, children gain sexual gratification, or sensual pleasure, from a particular part of their bodies. Each stage has special conflicts, and children's ways of managing these conflicts influence their personalities.

If a child's needs in a particular stage are gratified too much or frustrated too much, the child can become fixated at that stage of development. **Fixation** is an inability to progress normally from one stage into another. When the child becomes an adult, the fixation shows up as a tendency to focus on the needs that were over-gratified or over-frustrated.

Freud's Psychosexual Stages of Development

Stage	Age	Sources of pleasure	Result of fixation
Oral stage	Birth to roughly twelve months	Activities involving the mouth, such as sucking, biting, and chewing	Excessive smoking, overeating, or dependence on others

Freud's Psychosexual Stages of Development

Stage	Age	Sources of pleasure	Result of fixation
Anal stage	Age two, when the child is being toilet trained	Bowel movements	An overly controlling (anal-retentive) personality or an easily angered (anal-expulsive) personality
Phallic stage	Age three to five	The genitals	Guilt or anxiety about sex
Latency Stage	Age five to puberty	Sexuality is latent, or dormant, during this period	No fixations at this stage
Genital stage	Begins at puberty	The genitals; sexual urges return	No fixations at this stage

CHAPTER 13 PERSONALITY

Oedipus Complex Freud believed that the crucially important **Oedipus complex** also developed during the phallic stage. The Oedipus complex refers to a male child's sexual desire for his mother and hostility toward his father, whom he considers to be a rival for his mother's love. Freud thought that a male child who sees a naked girl for the first time believes that her penis has been cut off. The child fears that his own father will do the same to him for desiring his mother—a fear called **castration anxiety**. Because of this fear, the child represses his longing for his mother and begins to identify with his father. The child's acceptance of his father's authority results in the emergence of the superego.

During his lifetime, Freud had many followers who praised his theory, but his ideas, particularly his emphasis on children's sexuality, also drew criticism. Some of Freud's followers broke away from him because of theoretical disagreements and proposed their own theories. These theorists are called neo-Freudians. Some important neo-Freudians were Carl Jung, Alfred Adler, and object-relations theorists.

CARL JUNG'S ANALYTICAL PSYCHOLOGY

Until the 1910s, **Carl Jung** was a follower and close friend of Freud's. Like Freud, Jung believed that unconscious conflicts are

> **Penis Envy and Womb Envy** Freud believed that the successful resolution of the Oedipus complex played a crucial role in the formation of the superego and the personality. However, he did not have a plausible account of how this developmental phase applied to girls. Freud believed that because girls do not have a penis, they don't have the same motivation to develop a strong superego. Instead, they develop **penis envy**, or a sense of discontent and resentment resulting from their wish for a penis. This gender-biased idea has raised strong criticism from many psychologists, including the psychoanalyst Karen Horney. Horney proposed that it was more likely that men have **womb envy** because of their inability to bear children.

important in shaping personality. However, he believed the unconscious has two layers: the **personal unconscious**, which resembled Freud's idea, and the **collective unconscious**, which contains universal memories of the common human past.

Jung called these common memories archetypes. **Archetypes** are images or thoughts that have the same meaning for all human beings. Jung said that archetypes exist in dreams as well as in art, literature, and religion across cultures.

> EXAMPLE: *The archetype of the "powerful father" can be seen in the Christian conception of God, the Zeus of Greek mythology, and popular movies such as* The Godfather.

ALFRED ADLER'S INDIVIDUAL PSYCHOLOGY

Alfred Adler, another follower of Freud and a member of his inner circle, eventually broke away from Freud and developed his own school of thought, which he called **individual psychology**. Adler believed that the main motivations for human behavior are not sexual or aggressive urges but strivings for superiority. He pointed out that children naturally feel weak and inadequate in comparison to adults. This normal feeling of inferiority drives them to adapt, develop skills, and master challenges. Adler used the term **compensation** to refer to the attempt to shed normal feelings of inferiority.

However, some people suffer from an exaggerated sense of inferiority, or an **inferiority complex**, which can be due either to being spoiled or neglected by parents. Such people **overcompensate**, which means that rather than try to master challenges, they try to cover up their sense of inferiority by focusing on outward signs of superiority such as status, wealth, and power.

OBJECT-RELATIONS THEORIES

The object-relations school of psychoanalysis emerged in the 1950s, led by a group of psychoanalysts that included D. W. Winnicott and Melanie Klein. The term **object relations** refers to the relationships that people have with others, who are represented mentally as objects with certain attributes. Object-relations theorists believe that people are motivated most by attachments to others rather than by sexual and aggressive impulses. According to these theorists, the conflict between autonomy and the need for other people plays a key role in shaping personality.

Criticisms of Psychodynamic Theories

Freud's original ideas have little popularity today, but many psychologists do adhere to neo-Freudian ideas. However, other psychologists criticize psychodynamic theories for various reasons:

- Some critics argue that psychodynamic theories are not falsifiable (see pages 8–9) and therefore unscientific. In response to this criticism, proponents of psychodynamic theories point out that empirical evidence does support some psychodynamic concepts. For example, empirical research shows that there are unconscious mental processes, that people have mental representations of other people, and that people use unconscious defense mechanisms to protect themselves from unpleasant emotions such as anxiety.

- Other critics argue that psychodynamic theories are made by generalizing from a small number of patients to the whole human population. Relying only on case studies can lead to faulty conclusions.

- Still others argue that most psychodynamic theories are not based on studies that follow people from childhood to adulthood. Instead, psychodynamic theorists listen to descriptions of an adult patient's past and draw conclusions about the relevance of childhood experiences. However, as described on pages 172–174, memories are not always reliable.

Behaviorist Theories

The school of behaviorism emerged in the 1910s, led by **John B. Watson**. Unlike psychodynamic theorists, behaviorists study only observable behavior. Their explanations of personality focus on learning. Skinner, Bandura, and Walter Mischel all proposed important behaviorist theories.

B. F. SKINNER'S IDEAS

As described in Chapter 7, "Learning and Conditioning," **B. F. Skinner** is well known for describing the principles of operant conditioning. Skinner believed that the environment determines behavior. According to his view, people have consistent behavior patterns because they have particular kinds of **response tendencies**. This means that over time, people learn to behave in particular ways. Behaviors that have positive consequences tend to increase, while behaviors that have negative consequences tend to decrease.

Skinner didn't think that childhood played an especially important role in shaping personality. Instead, he thought that personality develops over the whole life span. People's responses change as they encounter new situations.

> *EXAMPLE: When Jeff was young, he lived in the suburbs. He developed a liking for fast driving because his friends enjoyed riding with him and he never got speeding tickets. After he left college, though, he moved to the city. Whenever he drove fast, he got a speeding ticket. Also, his new friends were much more cautious about driving in fast cars. Now Jeff doesn't like to drive fast and considers himself to be a cautious person.*

ALBERT BANDURA'S IDEAS

Albert Bandura pointed out that people learn to respond in particular ways by watching other people, who are called models. See Chapter 7, "Learning and Conditioning," for more information on Bandura's research on observational learning.

Although Bandura agrees that personality arises through learning, he believes that conditioning is not an automatic, mechanical process. He and other theorists believe that cognitive processes like thinking and reasoning are important in learning. The kind of behaviorism they advocate is called social-cognitive learning.

Whom Do We Imitate? *Research has shown that people are more likely to imitate some models than others. People tend to imitate models they like or admire and models they consider attractive and powerful. People are also more likely to imitate models who seem similar to themselves. Furthermore, if people see models being rewarded for their behavior, they will be more likely to imitate those models. Advertisers often use these research results when they design ads. For example, ads that try to persuade young adults to purchase a certain brand of soft drink often show young, attractive models who are being rewarded with good times for their soda-drinking behavior.*

WALTER MISCHEL'S IDEAS

Walter Mischel, like Bandura, is a social-cognitive theorist. Mischel's research showed that situations have a strong effect on people's behavior and that people's responses to situations depend on their thoughts about the likely consequences of their behavior. Mischel's research caused considerable debate because it cast doubt on the idea of stable personality traits. Mischel himself did not want to abandon the idea of stable personality traits. He believed that researchers should pay attention to both situational and personal characteristics that influence behavior.

Today, most psychologists acknowledge that both a person's characteristics and the specific situation at hand influence how a person behaves. Personal characteristics include innate temperaments, learned habits, and beliefs. The environment includes opportunities, rewards, punishments, and chance occurrences. Personality results from a two-way interaction between a person's characteristics and the environment. This process of interaction is called **reciprocal determinism**. People's characteristics influence the kind of environment in which they find themselves. Those environments, in turn, influence and modify people's personal characteristics.

CRITICISMS OF BEHAVIORAL APPROACHES

Critics of the behavioral approach to personality maintain three arguments:

- Behaviorist researchers often do animal studies of behavior and then generalize their results to human beings. Generalizing results in this way can be misleading, since humans have complex thought processes that affect behavior.

- Behaviorists often underestimate the importance of biological factors.

- By emphasizing the situational influences on personality, some social-cognitive theorists underestimate the importance of personality traits.

Humanistic Theories

Some psychologists at the time disliked psychodynamic and behaviorist explanations of personality. They felt that these theories ignored the qualities that make humans unique among animals, such as striving for self-determination and self-realization. In the 1950s, some of these psychologists began a school of psychology called **humanism**.

Humanistic psychologists try to see people's lives as those people would see them. They tend to have an optimistic perspective on human nature. They focus on the ability of human beings to think consciously and rationally, to control their biological urges, and to achieve their full potential. In the humanistic view, people are responsible for their lives and actions and have the freedom and will to change their attitudes and behavior.

Two psychologists, Abraham Maslow and Carl Rogers, became well known for their humanistic theories.

ABRAHAM MASLOW'S THEORY

The highest rung on **Abraham Maslow**'s ladder of human motives is the need for **self-actualization**. Maslow said that human beings strive for self-actualization, or realization of their full potential, once they have satisfied their more basic needs. Maslow's hierarchy of needs theory is described on page 247.

Maslow also provided his own account of the healthy human personality. Psychodynamic theories tend to be based on clinical case studies and therefore lack accounts of healthy personalities. To come up with his account, Maslow studied exceptional historical figures, such as Abraham Lincoln and Eleanor Roosevelt, as well as some of his own contemporaries whom he thought had exceptionally good mental health.

Maslow described several characteristics that self-actualizing people share:

- Awareness and acceptance of themselves
- Openness and spontaneity
- The ability to enjoy work and see work as a mission to fulfill
- The ability to develop close friendships without being overly dependent on other people
- A good sense of humor
- The tendency to have peak experiences that are spiritually or emotionally satisfying

CARL ROGERS'S PERSON-CENTERED THEORY

Carl Rogers, another humanistic psychologist, proposed a theory called the **person-centered theory**. Like Freud, Rogers drew on clinical case studies to come up with his theory. He also drew from the ideas of Maslow and others. In Rogers's view, the **self-concept** is the most important feature of personality, and it includes all the thoughts, feelings, and beliefs people have about themselves. Rogers believed that people are aware of their self-concepts.

CHAPTER 13
PERSONALITY

Congruence and Incongruence

Rogers said that people's self-concepts often do not exactly match reality. For example, a person may consider himself to be very honest but often lies to his boss about why he is late to work. Rogers used the term **incongruence** to refer to the discrepancy between the self-concept and reality. **Congruence**, on the other hand, is a fairly accurate match between the self-concept and reality.

According to Rogers, parents promote incongruence if they give their children conditional love. If a parent accepts a child only when the child behaves a particular way, the child is likely to block out experiences that are considered unacceptable. On the other hand, if the parent shows unconditional love, the child can develop congruence. Adults whose parents provided conditional love would continue in adulthood to distort their experiences in order to feel accepted.

Results of Incongruence

Rogers thought that people experience anxiety when their self-concepts are threatened. To protect themselves from anxiety, people distort their experiences so that they can hold on to their self-concept. People who have a high degree of incongruence are likely to feel very anxious because reality continually threatens their self-concepts.

> EXAMPLE: *Erin believes she is a very generous person, although she is often stingy with her money and usually leaves small tips or no tips at restaurants. When a dining companion comments on her tipping behavior, she insists that the tips she leaves are proportional to the service she gets. By attributing her tipping behavior to bad service, she can avoid anxiety and maintain her self-concept of being generous.*

CRITICISMS OF HUMANISTIC THEORIES

Humanistic theories have had a significant influence on psychology as well as pop culture. Many psychologists now accept the idea that when it comes to personality, people's subjective experiences have more weight than objective reality. Humanistic psychologists' focus on healthy people, rather than troubled people, has also been a particularly useful contribution.

However, critics of humanistic theories maintain several arguments:

- Humanistic theories are too naïvely optimistic and fail to provide insight into the evil side of human nature.

- Humanistic theories, like psychodynamic theories, cannot be easily tested.

- Many concepts in humanistic psychology, like that of the self-actualized person, are vague and subjective. Some critics argue that this concept may reflect Maslow's own values and ideals.

- Humanistic psychology is biased toward individualistic values.

Biological Approaches

Psychologists agree that environmental factors interact with genetic factors to form personality. Some psychologists have proposed theories that emphasize these genetic influences on personality.

HANS EYSENCK'S THEORY

Psychologist **Hans Eysenck** believes that genetics are the primary determinate of personality, although he thinks conditioning also plays a role. According to Eysenck, personality traits are hierarchical, with a few basic traits giving rise to a large array of more superficial traits. Genetically determined differences in physiological functioning make some people more vulnerable to behavioral conditioning. Eysenck suggests that introverted people have higher levels of physiological arousal, which allows them to be conditioned by environmental stimuli more easily. Because of this, such people develop more inhibitions, which make them more shy and uneasy in social situations.

Empirical evidence for genetic contributions to personality comes mainly from two kinds of studies: studies of children's temperaments and heritability studies.

STUDIES OF TEMPERAMENT

Temperament refers to innate personality features or dispositions. Babies show particular temperaments soon after birth. Temperaments that researchers have studied include reactivity, which refers to a baby's excitability or responsiveness, and soothability, which refers to the ease or difficulty of calming an upset baby.

Researchers have studied children from infancy to adolescence and found that temperaments remain fairly stable over time. However, temperaments can also be modified over time by environmental factors.

HERITABILITY STUDIES

Heritability studies also provide evidence for genetic contributions to personality. **Heritability** is a mathematical estimate that indicates how much of a trait's variation in a population can be attributed to genes. For more information about heritability, see page 35.

Twin studies help researchers to determine heritability, as described in Chapter 2, "Evolution and Genes." Researchers have shown that identical twins raised together are more similar than fraternal twins raised together in traits such as positive emotionality, negative emotionality, and constraint. Identical twins separated early in life and raised apart are more similar in these traits than are fraternal twins raised together. Both of these research findings suggest the existence of a genetic component to personality.

Behavioral geneticists have shown, after doing studies in many different countries, that the heritability of personality traits is around .5, which means that 50 percent of the variation in personality traits in a group of people can be attributed to genetic differences among those people.

The Influence of Family Environment Surprisingly, research shows that sharing a family environment doesn't lead to many similarities in personality. There is no or little correlation between the personality traits of adopted children and their adoptive parents. Researchers think this is because parents don't act the same way with all their children. Children's temperaments influence how a parent behaves toward them, and a child's gender and place in a birth order can also affect how that child is treated.

ENVIRONMENTAL INFLUENCES

The environment also has important influences on personality. These include peer relationships and the kinds of situations a child encounters. As described on page 277, under "Walter Mischel's Ideas," the interactions between innate characteristics and environmental factors are two-way. Children's temperaments are likely to influence their peer relationships and the situations they encounter. Similarly, peers and situations can modify children's personality characteristics.

EVOLUTIONARY APPROACHES

Evolutionary theorists explain personality in terms of its adaptive value. Theorists such as David Buss have argued that the Big Five personality traits are universally important because these traits have given humans a reproductive advantage.

Culture and Personality

Cultural psychologists have noted that some aspects of personality differ across cultural groups. For example, Americans and Asians have slightly different conceptions of self. American culture promotes a view of the self as independent. American children tend to describe themselves in terms of personal attributes, values, and achievements, and they learn to be self-reliant, to compete with others, and to value their uniqueness.

Many Asian cultures, such as those of Japan and China, promote a view of the self as interdependent. Children from these cultures tend to describe themselves in terms of which groups they belong to. They learn to rely on others, to be modest about achievements, and to fit into groups.

Researchers believe that culture influences aggressiveness in males. In places where there are plentiful resources and no serious threats to survival, such as Tahiti or Sudest Island near New Guinea, males are not socialized to be aggressive. Culture also influences altruism. Research shows that children tend to offer support or unselfish suggestions more frequently in cultures where they are expected to help with chores such as food preparation and caring for younger siblings.

Challenges for Cultural Psychology Cultural psychologists face the difficult challenge of studying and describing differences among cultures without stereotyping any particular culture. Ideally, cultural psychologists acknowledge that all members of a culture don't behave similarly. Variation exists within every culture, in terms of both individuals and subcultures. Cultural psychologists also try not to exaggerate differences among cultures.

Assessing Personality

Doctors, researchers, and employers use personality assessments for a variety of reasons:

- Clinical psychologists often use assessments as aids for diagnosing psychological disorders.

  EXAMPLE: A psychologist might administer personality tests to a patient with a varied set of symptoms to narrow down possible diagnoses. In such a case, a psychologist would typically use a battery of tests in addition to interviewing the patient.

- Some mental health providers use tests to decide how best to counsel people about normal problems of daily living.

  EXAMPLE: A counselor might administer a personality test in order to help a person choose a career.

- Some organizations use assessments to select personnel to hire, although this practice is decreasing in popularity.

    EXAMPLE: A consulting firm might assess job candidates in order to decide which candidates would be likely to perform well under pressure.

- Researchers frequently use tests in the course of studying personality traits.

    EXAMPLE: A researcher studying the correlation between risk taking and criminality might administer a personality test to a sample of prison inmates.

Three important ways of assessing personality include objective tests, projective tests, and assessment centers.

OBJECTIVE PERSONALITY TESTS

Objective personality tests are usually self-report inventories. **Self-report inventories** are paper-and-pen tests that require people to answer questions about their typical behavior. Commonly used objective tests include the MMPI-2, the 16PF, and the NEO Personality Inventory.

The MMPI-2

The **Minnesota Multiphasic Personality Inventory (MMPI)** was developed in the 1940s and revised in the 1980s. The revised version is called the MMPI-2. The MMPI-2 contains a list of 567 questions. People taking the test must answer these questions with *true, false,* or *cannot say.*

The MMPI was originally developed to help clinical psychologists diagnose psychological disorders. To interpret the MMPI-2, psychologists divide the answers to questions into fourteen subscales. Ten of these subscales are clinical subscales, which give information about different aspects of the test taker's personality. The other four subscales are validity subscales, which indicate whether the test taker was careless or deceptive when answering questions. A score on any single subscale doesn't provide a clear indication of a specific psychological disorder. Rather, the score profile, or pattern of responses across subscales, indicates specific psychological disorders.

The 16PF

The **Sixteen Personality Factor Questionnaire (16PF)** is a test that assesses sixteen basic dimensions of personality. It consists of a list of 187 questions.

The NEO Personality Inventory

The **NEO Personality Inventory** measures the Big Five traits: extraversion, openness to experience, agreeableness, conscientiousness, and neuroticism.

Advantages and Disadvantages of Self-Report Inventories

Self-report inventories are useful because they allow psychologists to get precise answers to standardized questions. In other words, all subjects who take a test answer the same questions, and all subjects have to select answers from the same range of options. Inventories are also objective, which means that different people scoring the same test would score them in the same way. However, these scores might be interpreted differently by different people.

There are several disadvantages to self-report inventories as well:

- Self-report inventories often contain transparent questions, which means subjects can figure out what a psychologist wants to measure. Therefore, subjects can lie intentionally and fake personality traits they don't really have. Researchers who develop tests address this problem by including **lie scales** in tests, which provide information about the likelihood that a subject is lying.

- The social desirability bias can affect responses on self-report inventories. In other words, when filling out an inventory, people might state what they wish were true, rather than what *is* true. Test developers can minimize this bias by dropping questions that are likely to evoke it.

- People sometimes don't understand the questions on the test. Test developers try to address this issue by wording questions very clearly so that they have only one possible interpretation.

- People sometimes don't remember aspects of the experience they are asked about.

PROJECTIVE PERSONALITY TESTS

Projective personality tests require subjects to respond to ambiguous stimuli, such as pictures and phrases, that can be interpreted in many different ways. Projective tests are based on the **projective hypothesis**, which is the idea that people interpret ambiguous stimuli in ways that reveal their concerns, needs, conflicts, desires, and feelings.

Clinical psychologists and researchers often use two projective tests: the Rorschach test and the Thematic Apperception Test.

The Rorschach Test

The **Rorschach test** consists of a series of ten inkblots. Psychologists ask subjects to look at the inkblots and describe what they see, and the psychologists then use complex scoring systems to interpret the subjects' responses. Scores are based on various characteristics of responses, such as the originality of the response and the area of the blot described in the response. The Rorschach gives psychologists information about the subject's personality traits and the situational stresses the subject may be experiencing.

The Thematic Apperception Test

The **Thematic Apperception Test (TAT)** consists of a series of pictures containing a variety of characters and scenes. Psychologists ask subjects to make up stories about each picture and look for themes that run through the subjects' responses. For example, a person with a high need for achievement may consistently come up with stories that have achievement-related themes.

Advantages and Disadvantages of Projective Tests

Projective tests are useful because they allow psychologists to assess unconscious aspects of personality. Projective tests are also not transparent: subjects cannot figure out how their responses will be interpreted. Therefore, subjects cannot easily fake personality traits on a projective test.

A serious disadvantage of projective tests is that they have questionable reliability and validity. Despite this flaw, many researchers and clinicians find that such tests give them useful information.

ASSESSMENT CENTERS

Assessment centers allow psychologists to assess personality in specific situations. In assessment centers, subjects are made to face situations in which they must use particular types of traits and skills, and their performance is then assessed. Assessment centers work on the well-accepted idea that the best predictor of future behavior is past behavior in similar situations. For example, a corporation may select a person for a managerial position by placing candidates in a simulated managerial situation for half a day and assessing their performance.

Assessment centers are useful for selecting personnel for positions of responsibility because they predict how people will act in challenging situations. However, assessment centers are expensive and time consuming.

Summary

Personality Traits

- **Personality** is the collection of characteristic thoughts, feelings, and behaviors that make up a person.

- Personality **traits** are consistent and long lasting, while **states** are temporary.

- The Greeks thought that four types of humors corresponded to personality types.

- Raymond Cattell used **factor analysis** to cluster traits into sixteen groups.

- Many psychologists believe that there are five basic traits.

- These **Big Five** traits include neuroticism, extraversion, openness to experience, agreeableness, and conscientiousness.

Psychodynamic Theories

- **Psychodynamic theories** are based on **Sigmund Freud**'s theory of **psychoanalysis** and emphasize unconscious motives and the importance of childhood experiences in shaping personality.

- Freud believed that the mind has three levels of awareness: the **conscious**, the **preconscious**, and the **unconscious**.

- Information in the unconscious emerges in slips of the tongue, jokes, dreams, illness symptoms, and associations between ideas.

- The personality is made up of three components that are in constant conflict: the **id**, the **ego**, and the **superego**.

- The **id** contains biological impulses, is governed by the **pleasure principle**, and is characterized by **primary process thinking**.

- The **ego** manages the conflict between the id and reality. It is governed by the **reality principle** and is characterized by **secondary process thinking**.

- The **superego** is the moral component of the personality.

- Anxiety arises when the ego is unable to balance adequately the demands of the id and superego.

- People use **defense mechanisms** to protect themselves from anxiety.

- Freud proposed that children go through five stages of development, each characterized by sexual gratification from a particular part of the body.

- **Fixation** is an inability to progress normally from one developmental stage to another.

- The **Oedipus complex** is a critical phase of development that occurs in the phallic stage. It refers to a male child's sexual desire for his mother and his hostility toward his father.

- According to **Carl Jung**'s analytical psychology, people have a **personal unconscious** and a **collective unconscious**. The latter contains universal memories of people's common human past.

- According to **Alfred Adler's individual psychology**, the main motivations for behavior are strivings for superiority.

- **Object relations** theorists believe that people are motivated most by attachments to people.

- Critics of psychodynamic theories argue that these theories are not falsifiable, that they generalize from a few patients to all people, and that they rely on retrospective accounts.

Behaviorist Theories

- Behaviorist explanations of personality focus on learning.

- **B. F. Skinner** believed that people's personalities arise from **response tendencies** and that consequences shape the responses.

- **Albert Bandura** said that people learn responses by watching others. He believes that thinking and reasoning are important in learning.

- **Walter Mischel**'s research showed that people behave differently in different situations.

- Psychologists agree that personality is formed through a two-way interaction between personal characteristics and the environment. This interaction is called **reciprocal determinism**.

- Critics argue that behaviorists often generalize inappropriately from animal studies to humans and that they often underestimate biological factors.

Humanistic Theories

- **Humanistic** theories emphasize subjective viewpoints when studying personality. They have an optimistic view that focuses on humans' rationality, consciousness, and freedom.

- **Abraham Maslow** studied the healthy personality and described the characteristics of the **self-actualizing** personality.

- **Carl Rogers**'s person-centered theory suggests that the **self-concept** is the most important feature of personality. Children's self-concepts match reality if their parents give them unconditional love. Rogers said that people experience anxiety when reality threatens their self-concepts.

- Critics argue that humanistic theories and concepts are too naïvely optimistic, vague, difficult to test, and biased toward individualistic values.

Biological Approaches

- **Hans Eysenck** believes that genetics largely determine personality.
- Studies of **temperament** and **heritability** provide the most empirical evidence for genetic contributions to personality.
- Environment influences peer relationships and situations.
- Sharing a family environment does not lead to many similarities in personality.
- Evolutionary theorists explain personality in terms of its adaptive value.

Culture and Personality

- American culture promotes a view of the self as independent, while Asian cultures generally promote a view of the self as interdependent.
- Culture influences both aggressiveness in males and altruism.
- Cultural psychologists face the challenge of avoiding stereotypes and acknowledging universal features while studying differences among cultures.

Assessing Personality

- **Personality assessments** are used to help diagnose psychological disorders, counsel people about normal day-to-day problems, select personnel for organizations, and conduct research.
- **Objective personality tests** are usually **self-report inventories**. They include the **MMPI-2**, the **16PF**, and the **NEO Personality Inventory**.
- **Projective personality tests** require subjects to respond to ambiguous stimuli. They include the **Rorschach test** and the **Thematic Apperception Test**.
- **Assessment centers** allow psychologists to assess personality in specific situations.
- Each way of assessing personality has its advantages and disadvantages.

Sample Test Questions

1. What are the Big Five traits?

2. What are psychodynamic theories?

3. In Freud's view, what causes anxiety?

4. Describe Maslow's self-actualizing personality.

5. Is sharing a family environment likely to lead to similarities in personality? Why or why not?

6. What is the MMPI-2?
   - A. An objective personality test
   - B. A self-report inventory
   - C. A test designed for people who have psychological disorders
   - D. All of the above

7. According to Freud, during what stage does the superego emerge?
   - A. Genital
   - B. Oral
   - C. Phallic
   - D. Anal

8. Attributing one's own unacceptable thoughts or feelings to someone else is called what?
   - A. Reaction formation
   - B. Projection
   - C. Displacement
   - D. Sublimation

9. What is the part of the personality that compels people to act in perfect accordance with moral ideals?
   - A. The id
   - B. The superego
   - C. The pleasure principle
   - D. The reality principle

10. Which theorist focused on the importance of the self-concept in personality?
    - A. Carl Rogers
    - B. Alfred Adler
    - C. Walter Mischel
    - D. Hans Eysenck

11. *Which one of the following statements about humanistic theories is false?*
- A. They do not provide insight into the evil side of human nature
- B. They are biased because they are based on individualistic values
- C. They are based on studies of people with psychological disorders
- D. They are difficult to test empirically

12. *Studies of temperament provide evidence for which of the following?*
- A. The concept of congruence
- B. Maslow's concept of the self-actualizing person
- C. Sublimation
- D. Genetic contributions to personality

13. *When he was young, Greg's father was consistently promoted at work for his diligence. Greg saw this and learned to be a conscientious worker himself. This fact could most easily provide evidence for whose theory of personality?*
- A. Sigmund Freud
- B. Albert Bandura
- C. Abraham Maslow
- D. Hans Eysenck

14. *What is an advantage of projective personality tests?*
- A. Different people would score them the same way
- B. They are very reliable
- C. They are not transparent to the subject
- D. They have lie scales that indicate whether subjects are being deceptive

15. *Which of Jung's beliefs differed from Freud's theories?*
- A. Everyone has a collective unconscious
- B. The unconscious is important in shaping personality
- C. The main motivation for behavior is a striving for superiority
- D. Behavior depends on the consequences that follow it

ANSWERS

1. The Big Five traits are neuroticism, extraversion, openness to experience, agreeableness, and conscientiousness.

2. Psychodynamic theories are based on the work of Sigmund Freud. They all emphasize unconscious motives and desires and the importance of childhood experiences in shaping personality.

3. In Freud's view, anxiety is caused by the inability of the ego to balance adequately the demands of the id and the superego.

4. Self-actualizing people tend to be both aware and accepting of themselves. They are open and spontaneous. They tend to enjoy their work and typically feel they have a mission to fulfill. They have close friendships without being overly dependent on other people. They also tend to have a good sense of humor. They are more likely than other people to have peak experiences that are spiritually or emotionally satisfying.

5. Sharing a family environment is not likely to lead to similarities in personality. This is probably because parents don't act the same way with all their children. Children's temperaments influence how a parent behaves toward them. A child's gender and place in a birth order can also affect how that child is treated.

6. **D**	11. **C**
7. **C**	12. **D**
8. **B**	13. **B**
9. **B**	14. **C**
10. **A**	15. **A**

Stress, Coping, and Health

- **Stress and Stressors**
- **Coping**
- **Stress and Disease**

14

We all experience stress, but we don't all find the same situations stressful. Some people find flying in planes highly stressful, while others take up skydiving as a hobby. Some people thrive in fast-paced, deadline-heavy careers, while others prefer less stimulating work. Stress means different things for different people, and everyone has their own way of coping with it. In some cases, people can worry themselves sick—literally—and some research links stress directly to illness.

Today, most researchers use a biopsychosocial model to explain disease. According to the biopsychosocial model, physical illness results from a complicated interaction among biological, psychological, and sociocultural factors. In recent decades, the recognition that psychological factors can affect health has given rise to a new branch of psychology called health psychology. Health psychologists study ways of promoting and maintaining health. Their research focuses on the relationship between psychosocial factors and the emergence, progression, and treatment of illness.

Stress and Stressors

Stress is difficult to define because researchers approach it in different ways. Some use the term *stress* to refer to circumstances that threaten well-being or to refer to the response people have to threatening circumstances. Others think of stress as the process of evaluating and coping with threatening circumstances. Yet others use the term to refer to the experience of being threatened by taxing circumstances. This chapter will use the term *stress* in the last sense: the experience of being threatened by taxing circumstances.

APPRAISAL

Researchers agree that stress is subjective. People don't have the same response to the same circumstances. Instead, stress depends on how people appraise or evaluate environmental events. If people believe that a challenge will severely tax or exceed their resources, they experience stress.

TYPES OF STRESSORS

Stressors are psychologically or physically demanding events or circumstances. Research links stressors to increased susceptibility to physical illnesses such as heart disease as well as to psychological problems such as anxiety and depression.

Stressors don't always increase the risk of illness. They tend to affect health more when they are chronic, highly disruptive, or perceived as uncontrollable. Researchers who study stress usually distinguish among three types of stressors:

- **Catastrophic events:** Large earthquakes, hurricanes, wars

- **Major life changes, positive or negative:** Marriage, divorce, death of a parent, beginning a new job, starting college

- **Minor hassles:** Standing in line, traffic jams, noisy environments

Health, Wealth, and Power People who live in conditions of poverty and powerlessness have an increased risk of poor health. Many factors make such people more susceptible to illness. For instance, poor people tend to have low access to preventive care. When ill, they often do not have access to good medical care. Their nutrition tends to be poor, since high-fat, high-salt foods are cheaper and more easily available than many healthy foods. They also encounter many chronic environmental stressors, including high crime rates, discrimination, and poor housing conditions.

INTERNAL SOURCES OF STRESS

Exposure to difficult circumstances doesn't produce stress by itself. Rather, stress occurs when people experience frustration, conflict, or pressure:

- **Frustration** is the experience of being thwarted when trying to achieve a goal.

  EXAMPLE: A student worked very hard on a term paper with the hope of getting an A but ends up with a B.

- **Conflict** occurs when people have two or more incompatible desires or motives. Conflict can occur in three forms:

1. The **approach-approach conflict**, the least stressful, occurs when people try to choose between two desirable alternatives.

   EXAMPLE: A student tries to decide between two interesting classes.

2. The **approach-avoidance conflict**, typically more stressful and quite common, occurs when people must decide whether to do something that has both positive and negative aspects.

   EXAMPLE: A boy invites a girl to a party. She finds him attractive, but going to the party means she won't have time to study for one of her final exams.

CHAPTER 14
STRESS

3. The **avoidance-avoidance conflict**, also typically stressful, occurs when people have to choose between two undesirable options.

> EXAMPLE: *Because of his financial situation, a man might have to choose whether to keep his nice-looking car, which breaks down frequently, or buy a badly dented, but reliable, used one.*

- **Pressure** occurs when people feel compelled to behave in a particular way because of expectations set by themselves or others.

> EXAMPLE: *A high school student wants to be accepted by the popular crowd at school, so she tries hard to distance herself from her old friends because the popular crowd considers them geeky or undesirable.*

THE PHYSIOLOGY OF STRESS

The experience of stress is accompanied by many physiological changes.

Selye's General Adaptation Syndrome

Hans Selye, a pioneer in the field of stress research, proposed that stressors of many different kinds result in a nonspecific bodily response. He said the body's stress response consists of a **general adaptation syndrome**, which has three stages: alarm, resistance, and exhaustion.

STAGE 1. In the **alarm stage**, an organism recognizes a threatening situation. The sympathetic nervous system activates, giving rise to the fight-or-flight response. Digestive processes slow down, blood pressure and heart rate increase, adrenal hormones are released, and blood is drawn away from the skin to the skeletal muscles.

STAGE 2. The **resistance stage** occurs when stress continues. Physiological arousal stabilizes at a point that is higher than normal.

STAGE 3. If stress is prolonged, organisms reach the **exhaustion stage**. The body's resources run out, and physiological arousal decreases. In this stage, organisms become more susceptible to disease.

> **Modification of Selye's Theory:** Research has supported Selye's idea that prolonged stress can cause physical deterioration. Research has also shown, however, that the bodily response to stress isn't as nonspecific as Selye believed. Different kinds of stressors produce subtly different bodily responses. Also, different people respond to the same stressor differently, depending on their gender, medical condition, and genetic predisposition to problems such as high blood pressure and obesity.

Pathways from the Brain

In stressful situations, the brain sends signals to the rest of the body along two pathways.

In the first pathway, the hypothalamus of the brain activates the sympathetic division of the autonomic nervous system, which in turn stimulates the inner part of the adrenal glands, which is called the **adrenal medulla**. The adrenal medulla releases hormones called **catecholamines**, which include epinephrine and norepinephrine. The action of the catecholamines results in the fight-or-flight response.

In the second pathway, the hypothalamus sends signals to the pituitary gland. The pituitary releases **adrenocorticotropic hormone (ACTH)**, which in turn stimulates the outer part of the adrenal glands, which is called the **adrenal cortex**. The adrenal cortex then releases hormones called **corticosteroids**, which include cortisol. Corticosteroids increase blood sugar levels, providing energy. Corticosteroids also help to limit tissue inflammation in case injuries occur.

Coping

Coping refers to efforts to manage stress. Coping can be adaptive or maladaptive. Adaptive coping strategies generally involve confronting problems directly, making reasonably realistic appraisals of problems, recognizing and changing unhealthy emotional reactions, and trying to prevent adverse effects on the body. Maladaptive coping includes using alcohol or drugs to escape problems.

Some researchers believe that people have characteristic ways of coping, even in different sorts of situations. Other researchers believe that people use different coping styles in different situations and that people's ways of coping change over time.

COPING STRATEGIES

There are many different coping strategies. Some common ones include:

- Relaxation
- Humor
- Releasing pent-up emotions by talking or writing about them
- Exercise
- Getting social support
- Reappraising an event or changing perspective on the problem
- Spirituality and faith
- Problem solving
- Comparing oneself to others who are worse off
- Altruism or helping others
- Using defense mechanisms
- Aggressive behavior
- Self-indulgent behavior, such as overeating, smoking, and excessive use of alcohol or drugs

The Frustration-Aggression Hypothesis *Several years ago, some researchers proposed the frustration-aggression hypothesis, which states that aggression is always caused by frustration. Today, researchers believe that frustration doesn't always lead to aggression and that it can lead to other responses, such as apathy. However, frustration does sometimes lead to aggressive behavior.*

FACTORS THAT IMPROVE COPING

Some people cope more effectively than others. Some important factors that influence coping are social support, optimism, and perceived control:

- **Social support:** Many studies show that having good social support correlates with better physical and mental health. Researchers believe that supportive social networks buffer the effects of stressful circumstances. In stressful situations, a social network can provide a person with care and comfort, access to helpful resources, and advice about how to evaluate and manage problems.

- **Optimism:** A tendency to expect positive outcomes, optimism is associated with better physical health. Optimistic people are more likely to find social support, appraise events in less threatening ways, take good care of themselves when sick, and use active coping strategies that focus on problem solving.

- **Perceived control:** The term **locus of control** refers to people's perception of whether or not they have control over circumstances in their lives. People with an **internal locus of control** tend to believe they have control over their circumstances. People with an **external locus of control** tend to believe that fate, luck, or other people control circumstances. Having an internal locus of control is associated with better physical and emotional health.

Primary and Secondary Control Some researchers have pointed out that people in different cultures have different kinds of perceived control. The Western approach emphasizes the importance of primary control. When faced with a problematic situation, people in Western cultures tend to focus on changing the situation so that the problem no longer exists. A different approach, seen in many Asian cultures, emphasizes secondary control. When faced with a problematic situation, people in these cultures focus on accommodating the situation by changing their perspective on it. Both kinds of control can be beneficial.

CHAPTER 14
STRESS

Stress and Disease

Chronic stress is linked to the development of many psychological problems, such as depression, anxiety, and schizophrenia. A large body of research also indicates that stress is linked to a variety of physical problems, including cancer, heart disease, rheumatoid arthritis, genital herpes, periodontal disease, yeast infections, and the common cold, to name just a few.

STRESS AND IMMUNE FUNCTION

Stress affects the functioning of the immune system, as do age, nutrition, and genetic factors. The **immune system** is the body's defense against harmful agents such as bacteria, viruses, and other foreign substances. It communicates constantly with the brain and the endocrine system. The immune system has many different kinds of disease-fighting cells, including B lymphocytes, T lymphocytes, and macrophages:

- **B lymphocytes** are formed in the bone marrow and release antibodies. Antibodies are protein molecules that travel through the blood and lymph and defend the body against bacteria and cancer cells.

- **T lymphocytes** are formed in the thymus gland and defend the body against cancer cells, viruses, and other foreign substances.

- **Macrophages** destroy foreign substances by absorbing them.

Stress affects the immune system in many ways. For instance, hormones that are released in response to stress can inhibit the activity of lymphocytes.

THE LINK BETWEEN EMOTIONS AND ILLNESS

Researchers have linked negative emotional states to disease.

Depression

Recent research suggests that depression makes people more vulnerable to heart disease.

Type A Behavior and Hostility

Researchers have identified a type of personality, called the **type A personality**, that is associated with a higher risk of coronary heart disease. People with type A personalities tend to be competitive, impatient, easily angered, and hostile. People with **type B personalities**, on the other hand, are relaxed, patient, easygoing, and amiable.

Type A personalities may be more prone to heart disease for several reasons:

- Type A people tend to be more physiologically reactive than type B people. In challenging situations, type A people have higher pulse rates, blood pressure, and hormone levels. This physiological reactivity can impair health in the long term. For instance, frequent release of stress hormones increases the likelihood of **atherosclerosis**, or hardening of the arteries because of cholesterol deposits.

- Type A people may encounter more stressors. For example, because of their behavior, they may be more likely to have marital stress and work-related problems.

- Type A people may have less social support because of their characteristic ways of relating to people.

- Type A people may pay less attention to health-promoting behaviors such as getting exercise and resting when tired. They also smoke more and consume more caffeine.

Hostility, a key type A personality feature, relates most to increased risk of heart disease. A tendency to get angry easily is associated not only with heart disease but also impaired immune function and high blood pressure.

Emotional Inhibition

People who have a tendency to suppress emotions such as fear, anxiety, and anger have a higher risk of becoming ill than people who can acknowledge and express their feelings.

CHAPTER 14 STRESS

LIFESTYLES THAT ENDANGER HEALTH

People's lifestyles can endanger their health. Three features of problematic lifestyles include smoking, not exercising, and eating poorly.

Smoking

Smoking increases the risk of many cardiovascular and lung diseases, including heart disease, hypertension, stroke, bronchitis, and emphysema. Smoking also increases the risk of cancers of the lung, mouth, bladder, kidney, larynx, esophagus, and pancreas. Although formal smoking cessation programs don't help most people quit, many people eventually do stop smoking. Research shows that many people quit only after several unsuccessful attempts.

Lack of Exercise

Lack of exercise can also have strong negative effects. Regular exercise leads to longer life expectancy, promotes cardiovascular health, decreases obesity-related problems such as diabetes and respiratory problems, and decreases the risk of colon, breast, and reproductive system cancers.

Poor Nutrition

Research shows that bad eating habits contribute to health problems:

- Chronic overeating increases the risk of heart disease, hypertension, stroke, respiratory problems, arthritis, and back problems.

- Low-fiber diets and diets that increase serum cholesterol levels are linked to heart disease.

- Eating too much salt may contribute to high blood pressure.

- High-fat, low-fiber diets are linked to cancers of the colon, prostate, and breast.

- A low-calcium diet may contribute to osteoporosis.

GETTING MEDICAL TREATMENT

Once people develop symptoms of illness, their behavior influences whether their health will improve or worsen. People's behavior can have an impact at three different stages.

Seeking Medical Help

People who are highly anxious, who score high on the personality trait of neuroticism, who are very health-conscious, and who are very aware of bodily sensations tend to report more physical symptoms than other people.

Delaying seeking medical help can have serious consequences, as early diagnosis can improve the treatment of many health problems. Despite this, people often delay seeking medical help for several reasons:

- Fear of appearing ridiculous if their symptoms turn out to be benign

- Reluctance to bother their physicians

- The tendency to minimize symptoms

- Unwillingness to have a medical appointment interfere with other plans.

Communicating Effectively

People often have trouble communicating effectively with health care providers. Communication difficulties frequently happen for the following reasons:

- Medical providers often use jargon and unclear explanations when talking to patients.

- Patients sometimes forget to ask questions they should have asked.

- People sometimes forget to mention symptoms they have or avoid mentioning the extent of their problems for fear of a serious diagnosis.

- People are sometimes passive in their interactions with health care providers because they feel intimidated by health care providers' authority.

Adhering to Treatment Regimens

People's chances of recovery decrease if they don't adhere to the treatment regimens that their health care providers prescribe. People don't adhere to medical advice for three main reasons:

- Not understanding the instructions they are given

- Not following treatment regimens that are unpleasant or interfere significantly with daily routines

- Not following advice if they are displeased about their interactions with their health care provider

Summary

Stress and Stressors

- **Stress** is defined differently by different researchers.
- One definition of stress is the experience of being threatened by taxing circumstances.
- Stress depends on how environmental events are appraised.
- Stressors can be associated with poor health if they are chronic, highly disruptive, or perceived as uncontrollable.
- Three types of stressors are **catastrophic events, major life changes**, and **minor hassles.**
- Stress is produced when people experience **frustration, conflict,** or **pressure.**
- **Hans Selye** proposed that the stress response consists of a **general adaptation syndrome,** which has three stages: alarm, resistance, and exhaustion.
- In stressful situations, the brain sends signals to the rest of the body along two pathways.

Coping

- **Coping** refers to efforts to manage stress.
- Coping can be **adaptive** or **maladaptive.**
- **Adaptive coping** involves direct confrontation of problems, realistic appraisals, recognizing and modifying unhealthy emotional reactions, and protecting bodily health.
- **Maladaptive coping** includes behaviors such as using alcohol and drugs to escape problems.
- There are many different coping strategies.
- Factors that improve coping include **social support, optimism,** and **perceived control.**

Stress and Disease

- Chronic stress is linked to the development of many psychological and physical problems.
- Stress can affect the **immune system.**
- Depression, type A behavior and hostility, and emotional inhibition are associated with health problems.

- Lifestyle features that endanger health include smoking, poor nutrition, and lack of exercise.

- After developing illness symptoms, people's behavior influences the likelihood that they will get better.

- People often delay seeking medical treatment for a variety of reasons.

- Health care providers and patients often have communication problems.

- People sometimes don't adhere to treatment regimens.

Sample Test Questions

1. Describe the general adaptation syndrome proposed by Hans Selye.

2. Describe the two pathways by which the brain sends stress signals to the rest of the body.

3. Why might the type A personality be more susceptible to heart disease?

4. What are some reasons why people might not follow medical advice for a given condition?

5. What are some possible reasons for the link between optimism and better physical health?

6. Stressors are more likely to affect health if they are which of the following?
   - A. Long lasting
   - B. Highly disruptive
   - C. Difficult to control
   - D. All of the above

7. Which of the following statements is true?
   - A. The stress response is nonspecific
   - B. Different kinds of stressors produce exactly the same response
   - C. Different people respond to the same stressor differently
   - D. All of the above

8. Which factors improve coping?
   - A. Social support
   - B. Optimism
   - C. Perceived control
   - D. All of the above

9. Ali is trying to decide whether to give up his current part-time job. He dislikes the job, but if he gives it up, he will have no spending money. This is an example of what kind of conflict?
   - A. An approach-approach conflict
   - B. An approach-avoidance conflict
   - C. An avoidance-avoidance conflict
   - D. None of the above

10. Jackie has been denied a promotion at work. She is not an effective worker, but she believes she did not get the promotion because her supervisor has a grudge against her. This suggests that Jackie has which of the following?
    A.   A pessimistic personality
    B.   An external locus of control
    C.   A type A personality
    D.   A type B personality

11. Research shows which of the following is true about smoking?
    A.   Many people are able to stop smoking
    B.   Smoking cessation programs are highly effective
    C.   People who quit smoking usually do so on the first try
    D.   All of the above

12. Which behavior has been linked to poor health?
    A.   Suppressing negative emotions
    B.   Hostility
    C.   Overeating
    D.   All of the above

13. What does secondary control involve?
    A.   Changing locus of control
    B.   Trying to change one's perspective on a situation
    C.   Trying to change a problematic situation
    D.   None of the above

14. What does the frustration-aggression hypothesis state?
    A.   Aggression always precedes frustration
    B.   Aggression and frustration occur simultaneously
    C.   Aggression is always caused by frustration
    D.   Aggression always follows frustration

15. When is a person more likely to have difficulty coping with a stressful situation?
    A.   When he is over the age of fifty
    B.   When he expects a positive outcome
    C.   When he thinks he does not have control over the situation
    D.   When he has a good social support network

ANSWERS

1. The general adaptation syndrome occurs when an organism is exposed to a stressor. It has three stages. In the alarm stage, an organism recognizes a threatening situation. The sympathetic nervous system is activated, giving rise to the fight-or-flight response. Digestive processes slow down, blood pressure and heart rate increase, adrenal hormones are released, and blood is drawn away from the skin to the skeletal muscles. In the resistance stage, which occurs when stress continues, physiological arousal stabilizes at a point that is higher than normal. If stress is prolonged, the organism reaches the exhaustion stage. The body's resources get used up, and physiological arousal decreases. In this stage, organisms are more susceptible to disease.

2. In the first pathway, the hypothalamus of the brain activates the sympathetic division of the autonomic nervous system, which in turn stimulates the adrenal medulla. The adrenal medulla releases catecholamines, which results in the fight-or-flight response. In the second pathway, the hypothalamus sends signals to the pituitary gland. The pituitary releases ACTH, which in turn stimulates the adrenal cortex. The adrenal cortex then releases corticosteroids, which give a boost of energy and reduce tissue inflammation in case injuries occur.

3. Type A people have higher pulse rates, blood pressure, and hormone levels when faced with stress. The release of stress hormones can cause hardening of the arteries over time. Furthermore, type A people may encounter more stressors. For example, because of their behavior toward other people, they may be more likely to have marital stress and work-related problems. As a result, type A people may be less likely to have friends they can turn to when they are in trouble or under stress. Finally, type A people also smoke more and consume more caffeine instead of exercising and focusing on healthy living.

4. First, people sometimes don't understand the instructions they are given. People also may not follow treatment regimens if they are unpleasant or interfere significantly with daily routines. Finally, people may not follow advice if they are displeased about their interactions with their health care provider.

5. People who are optimistic are more likely to find social support, appraise events in less threatening ways, take good care of themselves when sick, and use active coping strategies that focus on problem solving.

6.	D	11.	A
7.	C	12.	D
8.	D	13.	B
9.	B	14.	C
10.	B	15.	C

CHAPTER 14
STRESS

Psychological Disorders

When people think of mental illness, they often think of imaginary voices or terrifying killers like Charles Manson. However, psychological disorders are not always that dramatic—or that clear-cut. Suppose a person drinks heavily on weekends and doesn't spend any time with his family. Another person keeps to a strict diet in order to stay thin and still isn't satisfied with her body weight. Do these people have mental disorders?

The question of what classifies as a mental disorder is often difficult to answer. Psychologists use many criteria to evaluate and diagnose these disorders, and they use a detailed system to classify them into categories. The origins of psychological disorders are varied and often unclear, and understanding these disorders involves an understanding of biology, culture, and personality. Many factors help make us who we are, and those same factors may, in certain people, prove precarious.

What Is a Psychological Disorder?

Several criteria exist for defining a psychological disorder. Some-times a person needs to meet only one criterion to be diagnosed as having a psychological disorder. In other cases, more than one of the following criteria may be met:

- Violation of cultural standards behavior

  EXAMPLE: Ted's delusion that he is a prophet causes him to stand at street corners lecturing people about the morality of their behavior.

- Exhibition of behavior harmful to self or others

  EXAMPLE: Bethanne's excessive use of alcohol makes her unable to hold down a job.

- Experiencing distress

  EXAMPLE: David suffers from chronic and painful anxiety.

MODEL OF PSYCHOLOGICAL DISORDERS

Psychologists use different conceptual models for understanding, describing, and treating psychological disorders.

The Medical Model

The **medical model** is a way of describing and explaining psycho-logical disorders as if they are diseases. Many terms used to discuss psychological disorders come from the medical model. **Diagnosis** refers to the process of distinguishing among disorders. **Etiology** refers to the cause or origin of a disorder. **Prognosis** refers to a pre-diction about the probable course and outcome of a disorder.

Critics argue that this model is not suitable for describing psychological problems. They say that psychological problems are not illnesses but rather behaviors and experiences that are morally or socially deviant.

The Vulnerability-Stress Model

The **vulnerability-stress model** states that psychological disorders result from an interaction between biological and environmental factors. According to this model, individuals who have a biological vulnerability to a particular disorder will have the disorder only if certain environmental stressors are present.

The Learning Model

The **learning model** theorizes that psychological disorders result from the reinforcement of abnormal behavior.

The Psychodynamic Model

The **psychodynamic model** states that psychological disorders result from maladaptive defenses against unconscious conflicts.

DISORDER ASSESSMENT

Psychologists use two methods to assess a psychological disorder: objective testing and projective testing. **Objective tests** are usually pencil-and-paper standardized tests such as the **Minnesota Multiphasic Personality Inventory (MMPI)**. **Projective tests** require psychologists to make judgments based on a subject's responses to ambiguous stimuli. Word association tests or the **Rorschach test**, in which subjects interpret a series of inkblots, are examples of projective tests. (See pages 285–287 for more information on these tests.)

Classification

Psychologists and psychiatrists have classified psychological disorders into categories. Classification allows clinicians and researchers to describe disorders, predict outcomes, consider treatments, and encourage research into their etiology.

Insanity *Insanity is not a diagnostic label that psychologists use. Rather, it is a legal term that refers to the inability to take responsibility for one's actions. The law does not consider most people with psychological disorders to be insane. People can use an insanity defense only if they were unable to distinguish right from wrong at the time they committed a crime.*

THE DSM

Psychologists and psychiatrists use a reference book called the *Diagnostic and Statistical Manual of Mental Disorders* (DSM) to diagnose psychological disorders. The American Psychiatric Association published the first version of the *DSM* in 1952. It has been revised several times, and the newest version is commonly referred to as the *DSM-IV*.

The *DSM-IV* uses a multi-axial system of classification, which means that diagnoses are made on several different axes or dimensions. The *DSM* has five axes:

1. Axis I records the patient's primary diagnosis.

2. Axis II records long-standing personality problems or mental retardation.

3. Axis III records any medical conditions that might affect the patient psychologically.

4. Axis IV records any significant psychosocial or environmental problems experienced by the patient.

5. Axis V records an assessment of the patient's level of functioning.

Psychologists and Psychiatrists *People sometimes use the words psychologist and psychiatrist interchangeably, but they are not the same. Psychologist is a broad term that refers to anyone with advanced training in psychology who conducts psychological testing, research, or therapy. A psychiatrist has a medical degree and treats patients with mental and emotional disorders. A psychiatrist can also prescribe medication.*

CRITICISMS OF THE DSM

Although the *DSM* is used worldwide and considered a very valuable tool for diagnosing psychological disorders, it has been criticized for several reasons:

- Some critics believe it can lead to normal problems of living being turned into "diseases." For example, a child who displays the inattentive and hyperactive behavior normally seen in young children could be diagnosed with attention-deficit/hyperactivity disorder by an overzealous clinician. In earlier versions of the *DSM*, homosexuality was listed as a disorder.

- Some critics argue that including relatively minor problems such as caffeine-induced sleep disorder in the *DSM* will cause people to liken these problems to serious disorders such as schizophrenia or bipolar disorder.

- Other critics argue that giving a person a diagnostic label can be harmful because a label can become a self-fulfilling prophecy. A child diagnosed with attention-deficit/ hyperactivity disorder may have difficulty overcoming his problems if he or other people accept the diagnosis as the sole aspect of his personality.

- Some critics point out that the *DSM* makes the process of diagnosing psychological disorders seem scientific when, in fact, diagnosis is highly subjective.

In general, psychologists view the *DSM* as a valuable tool that, like all tools, has the potential for misuse. The *DSM* contains many categories of disorders, and the following sections will cover a few of these categories.

CHAPTER 15 DISORDERS

Culture and Psychological Disorders Most of the major disorders listed in the DSM are found worldwide, although cultural factors often influence the symptoms and course of disorders. Culture-bound disorders, on the other hand, are limited to specific cultural contexts. They may or may not be linked to DSM diagnostic categories. One example of a culture-bound syndrome described in the DSM is dhat, a condition that occurs in India and is characterized by anxiety, hypochondria, discharge of semen, whitish urine color, weakness, and exhaustion. Similar conditions exist in Sri Lanka and China.

Anxiety Disorders

Anxiety is a common and normal occurrence. However, a chronic, high level of anxiety indicates an anxiety disorder.

COMMON ANXIETY DISORDERS

Some of the more common anxiety disorders include:

- **Generalized Anxiety Disorder:** A person with **generalized anxiety disorder** experiences persistent and excessive anxiety or worry that lasts at least six months.

- **Specific Phobia:** A person who has **specific phobia** experiences intense anxiety when exposed to a particular object or situation. The person often avoids the feared object or situation because of a desire to escape the anxiety associated with it.

- **Social Phobia:** A person who has **social phobia** experiences intense anxiety when exposed to certain kinds of social or performance situations. As a result, the person often avoids these types of situations.

- **Panic Disorder and Agoraphobia:** A person with **panic disorder** experiences recurrent, unexpected panic attacks, which cause worry or anxiety. During a **panic attack,** a person has symptoms such as heart palpitations, sweating, trembling, dizziness, chest pain, and fear of losing control, going crazy, or dying. Panic disorder can occur with or without agoraphobia. **Agoraphobia** involves anxiety about losing control in public places, being in situations from which escape would be difficult or embarrassing, or being in places where there might be no one to help if a panic attack occurred.

- **Obsessive-compulsive Disorder:** A person with **obsessive-compulsive disorder** experiences obsessions, compulsions, or both. **Obsessions** are ideas, thoughts, impulses, or images that are persistent and cause anxiety or distress. A person usually feels that the obsessions are inappropriate but uncontrollable. **Compulsions** are repetitive behaviors that help to prevent or relieve anxiety.

- **Post–traumatic Stress Disorder (PTSD):** A person with this disorder persistently re-experiences a highly traumatic event and avoids stimuli associated with the trauma. Symptoms include increased arousal such as insomnia, irritability, difficulty concentrating, hypervigilance, or exaggerated startle response.

ROOTS OF ANXIETY DISORDERS

Many different interactive factors influence the development of anxiety disorders.

Biological Factors

Many biological factors can contribute to the onset of anxiety disorders:

- **Genetic predisposition:** Twin studies suggest that there may be genetic predispositions to anxiety disorders. Researchers typically use concordance rates to describe the likelihood that a disorder might be inherited. A **concordance rate** indicates the percentage of twin pairs who share a particular disorder. Research has shown that identical twins have a higher concordance rate for anxiety disorders than fraternal twins.

- **Differing sensitivity:** Some research suggests that people differ in sensitivity to anxiety. People who are highly sensitive to the physiological symptoms of anxiety react with even more anxiety to these symptoms, which sets off a worsening spiral of anxiety that can result in an anxiety disorder.

- **Neurotransmitters:** Researchers believe there is a link between anxiety disorders and disturbances in neural circuits that use the neurotransmitters GABA and serotonin. GABA limits nerve cell activity in the part of the brain associated with anxiety. People who do not produce enough GABA or whose brains do not process it normally may feel increased anxiety. Inefficient processing of serotonin may also contribute to anxiety.

- **Brain damage:** Some researchers have suggested that damage to the hippocampus can contribute to PTSD symptoms.

SSRIs and Anxiety Disorders *Selective serotonin reuptake inhibitors (SSRIs) are a class of drug commonly used to treat anxiety disorders. They raise the level of serotonin in the brain by preventing it from being reabsorbed back into cells that released it. Serotonin is a neurotransmitter that affects sleep, alertness, appetite, and other functions. Abnormal levels of serotonin can lead to mood disorders.*

Conditioning and Learning

Research shows that conditioning and learning also play a role in anxiety disorders:

- **Classical conditioning:** People can acquire anxiety responses, especially phobias, through classical conditioning and then maintain them through operant conditioning. A neutral stimulus becomes associated with anxiety by being paired with an anxiety-producing stimulus. After this classical conditioning process has occurred, a person may begin to avoid the conditioned anxiety-producing stimulus. This leads to a decrease in anxiety, which reinforces the avoidance through an operant conditioning process. For example, a near drowning experience might produce a phobia of water. Avoiding oceans, pools, and ponds decreases anxiety about water and reinforces the behavior of avoidance.

- **Evolutionary predisposition:** Researchers such as **Martin Seligman** have proposed that people may be more likely to develop conditioned fears to certain objects and situations. According to this view, evolutionary history biologically prepares people to develop phobias about ancient dangers, such as snakes and heights.

- **Observational learning:** People also may develop phobias through observational learning. For example, children may learn to be afraid of certain objects or situations by observing their parents' behavior in the face of those objects or situations.

Cognitive Factors

Some researchers have suggested that people with certain styles of thinking are more susceptible to anxiety disorders than others. Such people have increased susceptibility for several reasons:

- They tend to see threats in harmless situations.

- They focus too much attention on situations that they perceive to be threatening.

- They tend to recall threatening information better than nonthreatening information.

Personality Traits

The personality trait of neuroticism is associated with a higher likelihood of having an anxiety disorder.

Mood Disorders

Mood disorders are characterized by marked disturbances in emotional state, which affect thinking, physical symptoms, social relationships, and behavior. If mood is viewed as a continuum, mood disorders occur when a person experiences moods that lie at either extreme of the continuum. Mood disorders are of two basic types: unipolar or bipolar. People with unipolar disorders experience moods that are at the depressive end of the continuum. People with bipolar disorders experience moods that are at both ends of the continuum.

Mood disorders are generally episodic, which means they tend to come and go. The duration of the disturbed emotional state and the pattern of its occurrence determine how a mood disorder is diagnosed.

DYSTHYMIC DISORDER

A person with **dysthymic disorder** experiences a depressed mood for a majority of days over at least two years.

MAJOR DEPRESSIVE DISORDER

Major depressive disorder is characterized by at least one major depressive episode. A **major depressive episode** is a period of at least two weeks in which a person experiences some or all of the following symptoms:

- Constant sadness or irritability

- Loss of interest in almost all activities

- Changed sleeping or eating patterns

- Low energy

- Feelings of worthlessness or guilt

- Difficulty concentrating

- Recurrent thoughts about suicide

Major depressive disorder is much more common in women than in men.

> **Suicide** People who are extremely depressed typically do not commit suicide. In the depths of a depressive episode, people usually feel too unmotivated and apathetic to form a suicide plan and carry it out. Suicide is more likely when a depressed person begins the process of recovery and becomes more energetic. Research shows that women are more likely to attempt suicide than men, but men are more likely to be successful at carrying out a suicide.

BIPOLAR DISORDERS

Bipolar disorders involve at least one distinct period when a person exhibits manic symptoms. Manic symptoms include any or all of the following:

- Irritability

- Feelings of being high

- Decreased need for sleep

- Inflated self-esteem or grandiosity

- Fast and pressured speech

- Agitation
- Increased interest in pleasurable activities that have the potential for harmful consequences.

People with bipolar disorders usually also experience major depressive episodes. Men and women are equally likely to suffer from bipolar disorders.

ETIOLOGY OF MOOD DISORDERS

Researchers believe that many different influences interact to produce mood disorders.

Biological Factors

Biological influences include the following:

- **Genetic predisposition:** Twin studies suggest that people can be genetically predisposed to major depressive disorder and bipolar disorders. Concordance rates for both major depressive disorder and bipolar disorders are higher for identical twins than fraternal twins. Genetic factors seem to be implicated more in depression among women than among men.
- **Neurotransmitters:** Research shows that the neurotransmitters norepinephrine and serotonin are involved in mood disorders.
- **Brain structure:** Some research indicates that people with chronic depression tend to have a smaller hippocampus and amygdala in the brain, perhaps because of an excess of the stress hormone cortisol.

Cognitive Factors

Many researchers have studied the various cognitive factors involved in depression:

- **Learned helplessness:** The psychologist **Martin Seligman** proposed that depression results from **learned helplessness,** or a tendency to give up passively in the face of unavoidable stressors. Seligman pointed out that people who have a pessimistic explanatory style are likely to experience depression.

- **Self-blame:** Depressed people tend to attribute negative events to internal, stable, and global factors. When a problem occurs, they blame themselves rather than situational factors. They believe the problem is likely to be permanent, and they overgeneralize from the problem to their whole lives.

- **Low self-esteem:** Some researchers have suggested that a pessimistic worldview is only one of several factors that contribute to depression. They say that other factors such as low self-esteem and stress also play an important role. All these lead to hopelessness, which then leads to depression.

- **Rumination:** Rumination, or brooding about problems, is associated with longer periods of depression. Some researchers believe that women have higher rates of depression because they tend to ruminate more than men.

Although many researchers believe negative thinking makes people susceptible to depression, most also acknowledge a two-way relationship between depression and negative thinking. Negative thinking makes people susceptible to depression, and depression makes people more likely to think negatively.

Interpersonal Factors

Various interpersonal influences are also linked to depression:

- **Lack of social network:** Depressed people tend to have less social support than other people, and the relationship between social support and depression is likely to be two-way. People with poor social skills may be more likely to develop depression. Once people are depressed, they tend to be unpleasant companions, which further reduces their social support.

- **Loss of an important relationship:** Some researchers have suggested that depression can result when people lose important relationships.

Environmental Stressors

The onset and course of mood disorders may be influenced by stress. Stress also affects people's responses to treatment and whether they are likely to have a relapse. Some researchers have suggested that women are more vulnerable to depression because they tend to experience more stress in the form of discrimination, poverty, and sexual abuse and because they may have less satisfying work and family lives than men.

Even if people are usually happy and have friends and family to rely on, they can still become depressed. Major catastrophes and personal traumas can also contribute to depression. For instance, living in a war zone, having a home destroyed by fire, suffering from a chronically painful or debilitating illness, going through a divorce, or losing a loved one can all bring on depression.

Eating Disorders

Eating disorders are characterized by the following:

- Problematic eating patterns

- Extreme concerns about body weight

- Inappropriate behaviors aimed at controlling body weight.

The two main types of eating disorders are anorexia nervosa and bulimia nervosa.

The large majority of eating disorders occur in females and are much more common in industrialized countries where people idealize thinness and have easy access to food. Eating disorders are also much more common in younger women.

ANOREXIA NERVOSA

The main features of **anorexia nervosa** are a refusal to maintain a body weight in the normal range, intense fear about gaining weight, and highly distorted body image. In postpubescent women, another symptom of anorexia nervosa is absence of menstrual periods. Anorexia nervosa can result in serious medical problems, including anemia, kidney and cardiovascular malfunctions, dental problems, and osteoporosis.

BULIMIA NERVOSA

The main features of **bulimia nervosa** are habitual binge eating and unhealthy efforts to control body weight, including vomiting, fasting, excessive exercise, or use of laxatives, diuretics, and other medications. People with bulimia nervosa tend to evaluate themselves largely according to their body weight and shape. Unlike people with anorexia nervosa, people with bulimia nervosa typically have body weight in the normal range.

Bulimia nervosa can have serious medical consequences, including fluid and electrolyte imbalances and dental and gastrointestinal problems.

ETIOLOGY OF EATING DISORDERS

Many different factors influence the development of eating disorders.

Biological Factors

Some evidence suggests a genetic vulnerability to eating disorders:

- Identical twins are more likely to both suffer from an eating disorder than are fraternal twins.

- Biological relatives of people with bulimia nervosa and anorexia nervosa appear to have an increased risk of developing the disorders.

Personality Factors

Some researchers have noted that people with eating disorders are more likely to have certain personality traits:

- People with anorexia nervosa tend to be obsessive, rigid, neurotic, and emotionally inhibited.

- People with bulimia nervosa tend to be impulsive and oversensitive and have poor self-esteem.

Cultural Factors

Cultural factors strongly influence the onset of eating disorders. One example is the high value placed on thinness in industrial countries.

Family Influences

Family environment may also influence the onset of eating disorders:

- Some theorists have suggested that eating disorders are related to insufficient autonomy within the family.
- Others have proposed that eating disorders might be affected by mothers who place too much emphasis on body weight.

Cognitive Factors

People with eating disorders show distortions of thinking, such as the tendency to think in rigid all-or-none terms. It is unclear whether this type of thinking causes the eating disorders or results from the eating disorders.

Stress

The onset of anorexia nervosa is often associated with stressful events such as leaving home for college.

Somatoform Disorders

Somatoform disorders are characterized by real physical symptoms that cannot be fully explained by a medical condition, the effects of a drug, or another mental disorder. People with somatoform disorders do not fake symptoms or produce symptoms intentionally.

Three common somatoform disorders are somatization disorder, conversion disorder, and hypochondriasis.

SOMATIZATION DISORDER

Somatization disorder was formerly called *hysteria* or *Briquet's syndrome*. People with somatization disorder experience a wide variety of physical symptoms, such as pain and gastrointestinal, sexual, and pseudoneurological problems. The disorder usually affects women, begins before age thirty, and continues for many years.

CONVERSION DISORDER

Conversion disorder is characterized by symptoms that affect voluntary motor functioning or sensory functioning. These symptoms cannot be explained medically. A conflict or other stressor precedes the onset or exacerbation of these symptoms, which implies a relationship between the symptoms and psychological factors.

> EXAMPLE: *After being sexually assaulted, a young girl loses the ability to speak. Her inability to speak has no medical explanation.*

HYPOCHONDRIASIS

People with **hypochondriasis** are preoccupied with fears that they have a serious disease. They base these fears on misinterpretations of physical symptoms. People with this disorder continue to worry about having a serious medical problem even after they receive reassurances to the contrary. People with hypochondriasis, however, are not delusional—they can acknowledge that their worries might be excessive.

ETIOLOGY OF SOMATOFORM DISORDERS

Personality, cognitive factors, and learning appear to be involved in the etiology of somatoform disorders.

Personality Factors

Some researchers have suggested that people with histrionic personality traits are more likely to develop somatoform disorders. **Histrionic** people enjoy being the center of attention. They tend to be self-focused, excitable, highly open to suggestion, very emotional, and dramatic.

Cognitive Factors

Researchers have proposed that several cognitive factors contribute to somatoform disorders:

* People with these disorders may pay too much attention to bodily sensations.

* They may make catastrophic conclusions when they experience minor symptoms.

* They may have distorted ideas about good health and expect healthy people to be free of any symptoms or discomfort.

Learning

People with somatoform disorders may learn to adopt a sick role because they are reinforced for being sick. Rewards that help to maintain sickness include attention and sympathy from others and avoidance of work and family challenges.

Substance-Related Disorders

The *DSM* describes many substance-related disorders, which occur when a person is intoxicated by, withdrawing from, using, abusing, or dependent on one or more drugs. Two common types of substance-related disorders are substance abuse and substance dependence.

CHAPTER 15 DISORDERS

SUBSTANCE ABUSE

The *DSM* defines **substance abuse** as a maladaptive pattern of drug use that results in repeated negative consequences such as legal, social, work-related, or school-related problems. A drug abuser may even use drugs in situations in which it is physically dangerous to do so.

SUBSTANCE DEPENDENCE

Substance dependence, or drug addiction, involves continuing to use a drug despite persistent physical or psychological costs. A person who is addicted to drugs may make several unsuccessful attempts to give up the drug and may even develop tolerance for the drug. **Tolerance** is the gradual need for more and more of the drug to get the same effect. The person may also experience **withdrawal symptoms** such as sweating, nausea, muscle pain, shakiness, and irritability when he or she stops taking the drug.

ETIOLOGY OF SUBSTANCE-DEPENDENCE

Many researchers believe biology and environment interact to produce substance dependence.

Biological Influences

Several lines of research have examined genetic predispositions to drug dependence. Researchers think there may be a genetic predisposition to one particular type of alcoholism: the type that begins in adolescence and that is associated with impulsive, antisocial, and criminal behavior. With other types of alcoholism, many genes may interact to play a role.

Genes may influence traits such as impulsivity, which can make a person more likely to become alcoholic. Genes may also influence the level of dopamine in the brain. Researchers have suggested that high dopamine levels may in turn influence the susceptibility to alcoholism.

Just as biological factors may make a person susceptible to dependence, heavy use of drugs can affect a person's biological makeup. For example, excessive drug use can reduce the number of dopamine receptors in the brain. Since dopamine is involved in feeling pleasure, the reduced number of receptors can then make a person dependent on the drug. The person will crave more of the drug in order to feel the same amount of pleasure.

Environmental Influences

Research findings suggest that certain environmental factors play a key role in substance dependence:

- **Cultural norms:** The pattern of drug dependence varies according to cultural norms. For example, alcohol dependence is rarer in countries where children learn to drink responsibly and in moderation and where excessive drinking by adults is considered improper. Alcohol dependence is more common in societies that condone adult drunkenness and forbid children to drink.

- **Social policy:** Governmental policies that totally prohibit alcohol consumption tend to increase rates of alcohol dependence.

- **Variation in symptoms:** The existence of withdrawal symptoms after discontinuing a drug depends on many factors, including a person's expectations and context. This suggests that dependence is not just a biological phenomenon.

- **Reasons for drug use:** A person's tendency toward drug addiction depends not only on the properties of the drug but also on the reasons a person uses the drug. For example, people who receive prescription narcotics in hospitals for postsurgical pain may not become addicted, while others who use narcotics to escape stress may become addicted.

Schizophrenia

Schizophrenia is one of several psychotic disorders described in the *DSM*. People with psychotic disorders lose contact with reality and often have delusions or hallucinations. People with schizophrenia have a wide range of symptoms, which can be classified into positive or negative symptoms.

POSITIVE SYMPTOMS

Positive symptoms involve the presence of altered behaviors. Examples of positive symptoms include delusions, hallucinations, disorganized speech, and disorganized behavior. **Delusions** are false beliefs that are strongly held despite contradictory evidence. **Hallucinations** are sensory or perceptual experiences that happen without any external stimulus. Hallucinations can occur in any sensory modality, but auditory hallucinations are most common in schizophrenia. Disorganized speech can also take many forms. For example, a person with schizophrenia may produce *word salad*, which consists of words and sentences strung together in an incoherent way. Examples of disorganized behavior include inappropriate gestures or laughter, agitated pacing, or unpredictable violence.

NEGATIVE SYMPTOMS

Negative symptoms involve an absence or reduction of normal behavior. Negative symptoms include emotional flatness, social withdrawal, spare or uninflected speech, and lack of motivation.

SUBTYPES OF SCHIZOPHRENIA

Schizophrenia is classified into four subtypes, depending on the symptoms present at the time of evaluation:

1. **Paranoid type:** Characterized by marked delusions or hallucinations and relatively normal cognitive and emotional functioning. Delusions are usually persecutory, grandiose, or both. **Persecutory delusions** involve a belief that one is being oppressed, pursued, or harassed in some way. **Grandiose delusions** involve the belief that one is very important or famous. This subtype usually happens later in life than the other subtypes. Prognosis may also be better for this subtype than for other subtypes.

CHAPTER 15
DISORDERS

2. **Disorganized type:** Characterized by disorganized behavior, disorganized speech, and emotional flatness or inappropriateness.

3. **Catatonic type:** Characterized by unnatural movement patterns such as rigid, unmoving posture or continual, purposeless movements, or by unnatural speech patterns such as absence of speech or parroting of other people's speech.

4. **Undifferentiated type:** Diagnosis given to a patient that does not meet criteria for paranoid, disorganized, or catatonic schizophrenia.

ETIOLOGY OF SCHIZOPHRENIA

As with other psychological disorders, researchers have studied the etiology of schizophrenia from different perspectives.

Biological Factors

Research suggests that genes, neurotransmitters, and brain abnormalities play a role in the onset of schizophrenia:

- **Genetic predisposition:** Substantial evidence suggests that there is a genetically inherited predisposition to schizophrenia. For example, there is a concordance rate of about 48 percent for identical twins. The concordance rate for fraternal twins is considerably less, about 17 percent. Concordance rate refers to the percentage of both people in a pair having a certain trait or disorder. A person who has two parents with schizophrenia has about a 46 percent chance of developing schizophrenia. This probability is very high compared to the roughly 1 percent chance of developing schizophrenia in the general population.

- **Neurotransmitters:** Some researchers have proposed that schizophrenia is related to an overabundance of the neurotransmitter dopamine in the brain. Other researchers have suggested that both serotonin and dopamine may be implicated. The neurotransmitter glutamate may also play a role in the disorder. Underdevelopment of glutamate neurons results in the overactivity of dopamine neurons.

- **Brain structure:** Some researchers have suggested that schizophrenia may involve an inability to filter out irrelevant information, which leads to being overwhelmed by stimuli. With this idea in mind, researchers have looked for brain abnormalities in schizophrenia patients. The brains of people with schizophrenia do differ structurally from the brains of normal people in several ways. For example, they are more likely to have enlarged ventricles, or fluid-filled spaces. They are also more likely to have abnormalities in the thalamus and reduced hippocampus volume.

- **Brain injury:** Another line of research suggests that injuries to the brain during sensitive periods of development can make people susceptible to schizophrenia later on in life. For example, researchers believe that viral infections or malnutrition during the prenatal period and complications during the birthing process can increase the later risk of schizophrenia. Some researchers have suggested that abnormal brain development during adolescence may also play a role in schizophrenia.

Stress

Many researchers believe stress plays a role in bringing on schizophrenia in people who are already biologically vulnerable to this disorder.

Dissociative Disorders

Dissociative disorders are characterized by disturbances in consciousness, memory, identity, and perception.

Three kinds of dissociative disorders are dissociative amnesia, dissociative fugue, and dissociative identity disorder.

DISSOCIATIVE AMNESIA

The main feature of **dissociative amnesia** is an inability to remember important personal information, usually about something traumatic or painful. The memory loss is too extensive to be explained by normal forgetfulness.

DISSOCIATIVE FUGUE

People with **dissociative fugue** suddenly leave their homes and disappear unexpectedly. They do not remember their past and are confused about their identity. Sometimes, they may assume entirely new identities.

DISSOCIATIVE IDENTITY DISORDER

Dissociative identity disorder was formerly called "multiple personality disorder." In this disorder, certain aspects of identity, consciousness, and memory are not integrated. People with dissociative identity disorder cannot remember important personal information and have two or more identities or personality states that control their behavior. Often, each of these identities has a separate name, personal history, set of characteristics, and self-image.

The Dissociative Identity Disorder Controversy Dissociative identity disorder is a controversial diagnosis. Some psychologists believe that the disorder is very rare and that the increase in its prevalence since the 1980s is due to overdiagnosis. These theorists point out that the presentation of dissociative identity disorder often changes according to its representation in the media, such as in the book Sybil. Others have suggested that clinicians sometimes induce this disorder in highly suggestible people. Some psychologists, however, believe that dissociative identity disorder is not rare and has only been unrecognized and underdiagnosed in the past.

ETIOLOGY OF DISSOCIATIVE DISORDERS

Many researchers believe that severe stress plays a role in the onset of dissociative disorders. However, they cannot explain why only a small minority of people who experience severe stress develop such disorders.

Personality Disorders

Personality disorders are stable patterns of experience and behavior that differ noticeably from patterns that are considered normal by a person's culture. Symptoms of a personality disorder remain the same across different situations and manifest by early adulthood. These symptoms cause distress or make it difficult for a person to function normally in society. There are many types of personality disorders, including the following:

- **Schizoid personality disorder:** entails social withdrawal and restricted expression of emotions

- **Borderline personality disorder:** characterized by impulsive behavior and unstable relationships, emotions, and self-image

- **Histrionic personality disorder:** involves attention-seeking behavior and shallow emotions

- **Narcissistic personality disorder:** characterized by an exaggerated sense of importance, a strong desire to be admired, and a lack of empathy

- **Avoidant personality disorder:** includes social withdrawal, low self-esteem, and extreme sensitivity to negative evaluation

- **Antisocial personality disorder:** characterized by a lack of respect for other people's rights, feelings, and needs, beginning by age fifteen. People with antisocial personality disorder are deceitful and manipulative and tend to break the law frequently. They often lack empathy and remorse but can be superficially charming. Their behavior is often aggressive, impulsive, reckless, and irresponsible. Antisocial personality disorder has been referred to in the past as sociopathy or psychopathy.

ETIOLOGY OF ANTISOCIAL PERSONALITY DISORDER (APD)

Researchers have proposed that the following biological factors might be related to the etiology of antisocial personality disorder:

- People with this disorder may have central nervous system abnormalities that prevent them from experiencing anxiety in stressful situations. Because they feel no anxiety, they never learn to avoid behavior with negative consequences.

- Such people may also have a genetically inherited inability to control impulses.

- Some researchers have suggested that antisocial personality disorder may be caused by brain damage. Injuries to the prefrontal cortex, which is involved in planning and impulse control, may be particularly involved.

As with other disorders, however, biological factors alone are often not enough to cause APD. Environmental factors, such as family abuse or dysfunction, also play a large role in the development of APD. Generally, it is the combination of these environmental factors with the biological vulnerability that brings on the disorder.

Summary

What Is a Psychological Disorder?

- Criteria for defining psychological disorders depend on whether cultural norms are violated, whether behavior is maladaptive or harmful, and whether there is distress.

- The **medical model** describes and explains psychological disorders as if they are diseases.

- The **vulnerability-stress model** states that disorders are caused by an interaction between biological and environmental factors.

- The **learning model** theorizes that psychological disorders result from the reinforcement of abnormal behavior.

- The **psychodynamic model** states that psychological disorders result from maladaptive defenses against unconscious conflicts.

- Psychologists use **objective** and **projective tests** to assess psychological disorders.

Classification

- **Classification** allows psychologists to describe disorders, predict outcomes, consider treatments, and study etiology.

- **Insanity** is a legal term, not a diagnostic label.

- Psychologists and psychiatrists use the *DSM* to diagnose psychological disorders.

- The *DSM* uses a **multi-axial system of classification**.

- The *DSM* is a useful tool but has been criticized for several reasons.

- Most of the major disorders in the *DSM* are found worldwide.

- **Culture-bound syndromes** are limited to specific cultural contexts.

Anxiety Disorders

- A chronic, high level of anxiety may be a sign of an **anxiety disorder**.

- **Generalized anxiety disorder** involves persistent and excessive anxiety for at least six months.

- Having a **specific phobia** means becoming anxious when exposed to a specific circumstance.

- **Social phobia** is characterized by anxiety in social or performance situations.

- A person with **panic disorder** experiences recurrent, unexpected panic attacks.

- **Agoraphobia** involves anxiety about having panic attacks in difficult or embarrassing situations.

- **Obsessive-compulsive disorder** entails **obsessions**, **compulsions**, or both.

- **Post–traumatic stress disorder** is a set of psychological and physiological responses to a highly traumatic event.

- Biological factors implicated in the onset of anxiety disorders include **genes, different sensitivity to anxiety, the neurotransmitters GABA and serotonin,** and **brain damage.**

- Conditioning and learning may contribute to the development of phobias.

- Some styles of thinking may make people more susceptible to anxiety disorders.

- **Neuroticism** is associated with anxiety disorders.

Mood Disorders

- **Mood disorders** are characterized by marked disturbances in emotional state, which cause physical symptoms and affect thinking, social relationships, and behavior.

- Mood disorders may be **unipolar** or **bipolar**.

- People with **dysthymic disorder** have depressed mood for at least two years.

- **Major depressive disorder** involves at least one period with significant depressive symptoms.

- **Bipolar disorders** involve at least one period with manic symptoms and usually depressive periods as well.

- Biological influences on mood disorders include **genes, the neurotransmitters norepinephrine and serotonin,** and **brain abnormalities.**

- There is a two-way relationship between negative thinking and depression.

- Cognitive characteristics of depressed people include **learned helplessness; a pessimistic worldview; hopelessness; a tendency to make internal, stable, global attributions;** and a **tendency to ruminate.**

- There is a two-way relationship between social support and depression.

- **Depression** may be related to experiences of loss.

- The onset and course of mood disorders may be influenced by stress.

**CHAPTER 15
DISORDERS**

Eating Disorders

- **Eating disorders** are characterized by problematic eating patterns, concerns about body weight, and inappropriate efforts to control weight.

- **Anorexia nervosa** entails very low body weight, fear of gaining weight, and distorted body image.

- **Bulimia nervosa** involves binge eating and unhealthy efforts to control body weight.

- Some people may have a genetic vulnerability to eating disorders.

- Eating disorders may be associated with particular personality traits.

- Cultural factors strongly influence the onset of eating disorders.

- Lacking autonomy in the family and having an overly weight-conscious mother may influence the onset of eating disorders.

- People with eating disorders tend to have certain distortions of thinking.

- The onset of anorexia nervosa may be associated with stressful events.

Somatoform Disorders

- **Somatoform disorders** are characterized by real physical symptoms that cannot be fully explained by a medical condition, the effects of a drug, or another mental disorder.

- A person with **somatization disorder** has many different, recurrent physical symptoms.

- **Conversion disorder** involves symptoms that affect voluntary motor functioning or sensory functioning.

- People with **hypochondriasis** constantly fear that they may have a serious disease.

- People with **histrionic personality** traits may be more likely to develop somatoform disorders.

- Several cognitive factors may contribute to somatoform disorders.

- People with somatoform disorders may learn to adopt a sick role.

Substance-Related Disorders

- Many substance-related disorders are described in the *DSM*.

- **Substance abuse** is a maladaptive pattern of drug use that results in repeated, negative legal, social, occupational, or academic consequences.

- **Substance dependence** involves continuing to use a drug despite persistent harmful physical or psychological consequences.

- The **disease model of addiction** holds that addiction is a disease that must be treated medically.

- The **learning model of addiction** holds that addiction is a way of coping with stress.

- Genes may produce a predisposition to substance dependence.

- Several lines of evidence suggest that environmental factors play a key role in substance dependence.

Schizophrenia

- **Schizophrenia** is a psychotic disorder that includes **positive** and **negative symptoms**. There are several subtypes of schizophrenia.

- The **paranoid type** is characterized by marked **delusions** or **hallucinations** and relatively normal cognitive and emotional functioning.

- The **disorganized type** involves disorganized behavior, disorganized speech, and emotional flatness or inappropriateness.

- The **catatonic type** is characterized by unnatural movement or speech patterns.

- A **diagnosis** of **undifferentiated type** applies if diagnostic criteria are not met for any of the above three subtypes.

- Research suggests that **genes, neurotransmitters,** and **brain abnormalities** are involved in the onset of schizophrenia.

- Stress may help to induce schizophrenia in people who are already biologically vulnerable to the disorder.

Dissociative Disorders

- **Dissociative disorders** are characterized by disturbances in consciousness, memory, identity, and perception.

- **Dissociative fugue** involves sudden and unexpected travel away from home, failure to remember the past, and confusion about identity.

- People with **dissociative identity disorder** fail to remember important personal information and have two or more identities or personality states that control behavior.

- Dissociative identity disorder is a controversial diagnosis. Psychologists disagree about why its prevalence has risen since the 1980s.

- Severe stress may play a role in the onset of dissociative disorders.

Personality Disorders

- **Personality disorders** are stable patterns of experience and behavior that differ noticeably from patterns that are considered normal by a person's culture.

- People with **schizoid personality disorder** are socially withdrawn and have restricted expression of emotions.

- **Borderline personality disorder** involves impulsive behavior and unstable relationships, emotions, and self-image.

- **Histrionic personality disorder** is characterized by attention-seeking behavior and shallow emotions.

- People with **narcissistic personality disorder** have an exaggerated sense of importance, a strong desire to be admired, and a lack of empathy.

- **Avoidant personality disorder** involves social withdrawal, low self-esteem, and extreme sensitivity to being evaluated negatively.

- **Antisocial personality disorder** begins at age fifteen and includes a lack of respect for other people's rights, feelings, and needs.

- **Abnormalities in physiological arousal**, a **genetically inherited inability to control impulses**, and **brain damage** may be involved in the development of antisocial personality disorder.

- Environmental influences are also likely to influence the development of antisocial personality disorder.

Sample Test Questions

1. Describe the DSM's multi-axial system of classification.

2. What criteria are commonly used to determine whether a person might have a psychological disorder?

3. What is the vulnerability-stress model?

4. What are some cognitive characteristics of depressed people?

5. Describe the disease model and the learning model of addiction.

6. A person's tendency to become addicted to a drug depends not only on the properties of the drug but also on the reason the person uses the drug. What does this observation suggest?
   A. There is a genetic predisposition to drug addiction
   B. Psychological factors influence drug addiction
   C. Drug addiction depends on the biochemistry of a drug
   D. None of the above

7. Which is likely true about people with somatoform disorders?
   A. They intentionally produce their symptoms
   B. They have symptoms that are caused by a medical condition
   C. They may pay too much attention to bodily symptoms
   D. They do not experience real symptoms

8. People with obsessive-compulsive disorder often do which of the following?
   A. Experience anxiety-producing thoughts, impulses, or images
   B. Have panic attacks
   C. Have false beliefs that they hold despite contradictory evidence
   D. Have sensory or perceptual experiences that occur without an external stimulus

9. Which disorder is characterized by an inability to remember a traumatic incident?
   A. Post–traumatic stress disorder
   B. Conversion disorder
   C. Schizophrenia
   D. Dissociative amnesia

10. Which of the following might contribute to the onset of antisocial personality disorder?
    A. Abnormal physiological arousal
    B. An inability to control impulses
    C. Brain damage
    D. All of the above

11. Which subtype of schizophrenia often involves relatively normal cognitive functioning?
    A. The paranoid type
    B. The disorganized type
    C. The catatonic type
    D. The undifferentiated type

12. Which is likely true about people with anorexia nervosa?
    A. They do not binge eat
    B. They tend to be relatively physically healthy
    C. They tend to be rigidly confident that they won't gain weight
    D. They do not have normal body weight

13. Which of the following is likely to be implicated in the etiology of schizophrenia?
    A. A histrionic personality type
    B. Learned helplessness
    C. Dopamine
    D. All of the above

14. What is a culture-bound disorder?
    A. A disorder that is bound to occur in most cultures
    B. A disorder specific to a particular cultural context
    C. A disorder not included in one of the DSM's diagnostic categories
    D. Any disorder whose onset is highly influenced by cultural factors

15. Insanity refers to which of the following?
    A. The inability to take responsibility for one's actions
    B. The existence of a psychological disorder
    C. A defense available to someone who committed a crime and who has a psychological disorder
    D. A specific diagnostic category in the DSM

ANSWERS

1. The patient's primary diagnosis is usually recorded on axis I. Long-standing personality problems or mental retardation are recorded on axis II. Any medical conditions that might affect the patient's psychologically are recorded on axis III. Any significant psychosocial or environmental problems experienced by the patient are recorded on axis IV. An assessment of the patient's level of functioning is recorded on axis V.

2. Three main criteria are commonly used to determine whether a person might have a psychological disorder: A. The person's behavior violates culturally determined standards or acceptability. B. The person's behavior is maladaptive or harmful to that person or others. C. The person suffers from distress.

3. The vulnerability-stress model states that disorders are caused by an interaction between biological and environmental factors. According to this model, individuals who have a biological vulnerability to a particular disorder will have the disorder only if certain environmental stressors are present.

4. Depressed people usually have a pessimistic explanatory style; a tendency to attribute negative events to internal, global, and stable factors; and a tendency to ruminate about problems.

5. The disease model holds that addiction is a disease that has to be treated medically. According to this model, an addict remains an addict forever and can function in society only by abstaining completely from drug use. The learning model holds that addiction is not a disease but a way of coping with stress. According to this model, addicts can learn to cope with stress in other ways. Once people learn to use other coping strategies, they can drink in moderation without reverting to addiction.

6.	**B**	11.	**A**
7.	**C**	12.	**D**
8.	**A**	13.	**C**
9.	**D**	14.	**B**
10.	**D**	15.	**A**

Psychological Treatment

16

Cartoon characterizations of psychological treatment typically involve a client lying tensely on a couch while a poker-faced therapist sits nearby, taking notes. Real treatments for psychological problems rarely fit this image. Hundreds of different treatments exist, including medication, electric shock, and surgery. Some types involve unorthodox and often strange procedures, such as making rapid eye movements.

Talk therapy is another common type of treatment. Therapists vary in their style and approach from client to client, and although some therapists still have their clients lie on couches, most therapists sit face-to-face with them. Some therapists take a relatively passive, listening role in therapy sessions, while others actively discuss problems or even argue with clients. All these treatments have different rationales and varying degrees of success. The type of treatment used and the effectiveness of that treatment sometimes depend as much on the client as on the treatment itself.

Types of Treatment

There are many different types of treatment for psychological disorders, all of which fit into three broad types: insight therapies, behavior therapies, and biomedical therapies.

- **Insight therapies** involve complex conversations between therapists and clients. The aim is to help clients understand the nature of their problems and the meaning of their behaviors, thoughts, and feelings. Insight therapists may use a variety of approaches, including psychodynamic, cognitive, or humanistic.

- **Behavior therapies** also involve conversations between therapists and clients but attempt to directly influence maladaptive behaviors. Behavior therapies are based on learning principles. (See Chapter 7 for more information on learning.)

- **Biomedical therapies** involve efforts to directly alter biological functioning through medication, electric shock, or surgery.

Psychotherapy

Psychotherapy is the treatment of psychological problems through confidential verbal communications with a mental health professional. All psychotherapies offer hope that a problem will improve, present new perspectives on the problem, and encourage an empathic relationship with a therapist. The approach a psychotherapist uses depends on his or her theoretical orientation. Types of approaches include psychodynamic, cognitive, humanistic, and behavioral.

PSYCHODYNAMIC APPROACHES

All of the many psychodynamic therapies derive from the treatment called *psychoanalysis*, which **Sigmund Freud** developed and used in the late 1800s and early 1900s. (See Chapter 13 for more information on Freud and his theory of psychoanalysis.)

Types of Mental Health Professionals

• *Clinical and counseling psychologists have a doctoral degree as well as specialized training for diagnosing and treating psychological disorders and problems of daily living.*

• *Psychiatrists are physicians. They have a medical degree and specialize in diagnosing and treating psychological disorders. Psychiatrists tend to focus on biomedical therapies, although they sometimes also provide psychotherapy.*

• *Psychiatric social workers and psychiatric nurses also provide psychotherapy, often in institutional settings, such as hospitals and social service organizations. They sometimes practice independently as well.*

• *Counselors who provide psychotherapy services usually work in schools, colleges, and social service organizations.*

Psychoanalytic treatment focuses on uncovering unconscious motives, conflicts, and defenses that relate to childhood experiences. Freud believed that people experience anxiety because of conflicts among the **id, ego**, and **superego**. To manage these conflicts, people use defense mechanisms, which can often be self-defeating and unsuccessful at fully controlling anxiety.

Psychoanalytic Techniques

In the traditional form of psychoanalysis, clients meet with a psychoanalyst several times a week for many years. The psychoanalyst sits out of view of the client, who sometimes lies on a couch.

Some techniques commonly used in psychoanalysis include free association, dream analysis, and interpretation:

- **Free association:** Psychoanalysts encourage clients to say anything that comes to mind. Clients are expected to put all thoughts into words, even if those thoughts are incoherent, inappropriate, rude, or seemingly irrelevant. Free associations reveal the client's unconscious to the psychoanalyst.

- **Dream analysis:** Dreams also reveal the subconscious. Clients describe their dreams in detail, and the psychoanalyst interprets the latent content, or the hidden meaning, of these dreams.

- **Interpretation:** A key technique in psychoanalysis, interpretation refers to the psychoanalyst's efforts to uncover the hidden meanings in the client's free associations, dreams, feelings, memories, and behavior. Psychoanalysts are trained to make interpretations carefully and only when a client is ready to accept them. Ideally, such interpretations increase the client's insight.

Psychoanalytic Concepts

Three important concepts involved in psychoanalysis are transference, resistance, and catharsis:

- **Transference** refers to the process by which clients relate to their psychoanalysts as they would to important figures in their past. Psychoanalysts usually encourage transference because it helps them to uncover the client's hidden conflicts and helps the client to work through such conflicts.

    > EXAMPLE: *A client who is resentful about her mother's authority over her might show angry, rebellious behavior toward the psychoanalyst.*

- **Resistance** refers to the client's efforts to block the progress of treatment. These efforts are usually unconscious. Resistance occurs because the client experiences anxiety when unconscious conflicts begin to be uncovered.

    > EXAMPLE: *Resistance can take many different forms, such as coming late to sessions, forgetting to pay for sessions, and expressing hostility toward the psychoanalyst.*

- **Catharsis** is the release of tension that results when repressed thoughts or memories move into the patient's conscious mind.

    > EXAMPLE: *Jane has a repressed childhood memory of being punished by her father after walking into her parents' bedroom while they were having sex. This memory comes into her conscious mind while she is undergoing psychotherapy. Subsequently, she feels a release of tension and is able to relate the incident to her current aversion toward sex.*

Current Psychodynamic Therapies

Today, the classical form of psychoanalysis is rarely practiced. Psychodynamic therapies, however, are widely used for treating the full range of psychological disorders. Psychodynamic therapies differ in their specific approaches, but they all focus on increasing insight by uncovering unconscious motives, conflicts, and defenses.

Interpretation and the concepts of transference and resistance are important features of psychodynamic therapies. Unlike traditional psychoanalysts, psychodynamic therapists usually sit face-to-face with their clients. Sessions typically occur once or twice a week, and treatment usually does not last as long as psychoanalysis.

COGNITIVE APPROACHES

Cognitive therapies aim to identify and change maladaptive thinking patterns that can result in negative emotions and dysfunctional behavior. Psychologist **Aaron Beck** first developed cognitive therapy to treat depression, although cognitive therapies are now used to treat a wide range of disorders. Beck's cognitive therapy helps clients test whether their beliefs are realistic.

Cognitive therapists such as Beck believe that depression arises from errors in thinking. According to this theory, depressed people tend to do any of the following:

- Blame themselves for negative events. They underestimate situational causes.

- Pay more attention to negative events than to positive ones.

- Are pessimistic.

- Make inappropriately global generalizations from negative events.

Cognitive Therapy Techniques

Cognitive therapists try to change their clients' ways of thinking. In therapy, clients learn to identify automatic negative thoughts and the assumptions they make about the world. **Automatic thoughts** are self-defeating judgments that people make about themselves. Clients learn to see these judgments as unrealistic and to consider other interpretations for events they encounter.

> **Rational-Emotive Therapy** *Rational-emotive therapy is a type of cognitive-behavioral therapy started by the psychologist* **Albert Ellis** *In this therapy, the therapist directly challenges the client's irrational beliefs. Ellis's therapy hinges on the idea that people's feelings are influenced not by negative events but by their catastrophic thoughts and beliefs about these events. Ellis points out that catastrophic thinking is based on irrational assumptions about what one must do or be. His therapy aims to identify catastrophic thinking and change the irrational assumptions that underlie it.*

BEHAVIORAL APPROACHES

Whereas insight therapies focus on addressing the problems that underlie symptoms, behavior therapists focus on addressing symptoms, which they believe *are* the real problem. Behavior therapies use learning principles to modify maladaptive behaviors. Many therapists combine behavior therapy and cognitive therapy into an approach known as cognitive-behavior therapy.

Behavior therapies are based on two assumptions:

- Behavior is learned.

- Behavior can be changed by applying the principles of classical conditioning, operant conditioning, and observational learning. (See Chapter 7 for more information.)

Behavior therapies are designed for specific types of problems. Three important types of behavior therapies include systematic desensitization, aversion therapy, and social skills training.

Systematic Desensitization

Systematic desensitization is a treatment designed by the psychologist **Joseph Wolpe**. It uses counterconditioning to decrease anxiety symptoms. This therapy works on the assumption that anxiety arises through classical conditioning. That is, a neutral stimulus begins to arouse anxiety when it is paired with an unconditioned stimulus that evokes anxiety.

EXAMPLE: *A person might develop a fear of high places after experiencing an avalanche on a mountain trail. The avalanche is the unconditioned stimulus, and any high place becomes the conditioned stimulus, producing anxiety similar to that evoked by the avalanche.*

Systematic desensitization aims to replace the conditioned stimulus with a response, such as relaxation, that is incompatible with anxiety. If psychotherapists can teach their clients to relax whenever they encounter an anxiety-producing stimulus, the anxiety will gradually decrease.

Exposure Therapies *Systematic desensitization is a type of exposure therapy.* **Exposure therapies** *are commonly used to treat phobias. These therapies recognize the fact that people maintain phobias by avoiding anxiety-producing situations, and they involve eliminating anxiety responses by having clients face a real or imagined version of the feared stimulus. In recent years, therapists have started using virtual reality devices to help clients experience feared stimuli.*

*   **Flooding** *is a more extreme type of exposure therapy than systematic desensitization. In flooding, exposure to anxiety-producing stimuli is sudden rather than gradual. For example, the person with the fear of heights would be taken to a mountain trail. No avalanche happens, so the person's anxiety is extinguished.*

Systematic desensitization involves a series of steps, which occur over several therapy sessions:

1. The therapist and client make up an anxiety hierarchy. The hierarchy lists stimuli that the client is likely to find frightening. The client ranks the stimuli from least frightening to most frightening.

2. The therapist teaches the client how to progressively and completely relax his body.

3. Next, the therapist asks the client to first relax and then imagine encountering the stimuli listed in the anxiety hierarchy, beginning with the least-frightening stimulus. If the client feels anxious while imagining a stimulus, he is asked to stop imagining the stimulus and focus on relaxing. After some time, the client becomes able to imagine all the stimuli on the hierarchy without anxiety.

4. Finally, the client practices encountering the real stimuli.

EMDR *Eye movement desensitization and reprocessing (EMDR) is a method that some therapists use to treat problems such as post-traumatic stress disorder and panic attacks. This treatment is a type of exposure therapy in which clients move their eyes back and forth while recalling memories that are to be desensitized. Many critics of EMDR claim that the treatment is no different from a standard exposure treatment and that the eye movements do not add to the effectiveness of the procedure.*

Aversion Therapy

In **aversion therapy**, a stimulus that evokes an unpleasant response is paired with a stimulus that evokes a maladaptive behavior.

> EXAMPLE: *A therapist might give an alcoholic a nausea-producing drug along with alcoholic drinks.*

Therapists use aversion therapy to treat problems such as deviant sexual behavior, substance abuse, and overeating. One major limitation of this type of therapy is that people know that the aversive stimulus occurs only during therapy sessions. Aversion therapy is usually used in combination with other treatments.

Criticisms of Aversion Therapy Many doctors and psychologists criticize aversion therapy as both inhumane and ineffective. Therapists have sometimes used aversion therapy for controversial ends. For example, in the past, therapists used aversion therapy to "treat" homosexuality.

Social Skills Training

Social skills training aims to enhance a client's relationships with other people. Techniques used in social skills training include modeling, behavioral rehearsal, and shaping:

- **Modeling** involves having clients learn specific skills by observing socially skilled people.

- **Behavioral rehearsal** involves having the client role-play behavior that could be used in social situations. The therapist provides feedback about the client's behavior.

- **Shaping** involves having the client approach progressively more difficult social situations in the real world.

Token Economies *A **token economy*** *is a behavior modification program based on operant conditioning principles. Token economies are sometimes successfully used in institutional settings, such as schools and psychiatric hospitals. People receive tokens for desirable behaviors, such as getting out of bed, washing, and cooperating. These tokens can be exchanged for rewards, such as candy or TV-watching time.*

HUMANISTIC APPROACHES

Humanistic therapies are derived from the school of humanistic psychology (see Chapter 13). Humanistic therapists try to help people accept themselves and free themselves from unnecessary limitations. The influence of humanistic therapies led to the use of the term *clients*, rather than *patients*, in referring to people who seek therapy. Humanistic therapists tend to focus on the present situation of clients rather than their past.

The best-known humanistic therapy is client-centered therapy.

Client-Centered Therapy

Client-centered, or person-centered, **therapy** was developed by the psychologist **Carl Rogers**. (See Chapter 13 for more information on Carl Rogers.) It aims to help clients enhance self-acceptance and personal growth by providing a supportive emotional environment. This type of therapy is nondirective, which means that the therapist does not direct the course and pace of therapy. Client-centered therapists believe that people's problems come from **incongruence**, or a disparity between their self-concept and reality. Incongruence arises because people are too dependent on others for approval and acceptance. When people have incongruence, they feel anxious. They subsequently try to maintain their self-concept by denying or distorting reality.

In client-centered therapy, people learn to adopt a more realistic self-concept by accepting who they are and thus becoming less reliant on the acceptance of others. To do this, therapists have to be genuine, empathic, and provide **unconditional positive regard**, which is nonjudgmental acceptance of the client. Client-centered therapists use **active listening** to show empathy by accurately mirroring, or reflecting, the thoughts and feelings of the client. They help the client to clarify these thoughts and feelings by echoing and restating what the client has said.

> **Integrative Approaches to Therapy** Many therapists use an **integrative approach**, which means they use the perspectives and techniques of many different schools of psychology rather than adhering rigidly to one school. For example, a therapist might use a psychodynamic approach to understand the unconscious motivations influencing a client's behavior, a client-centered approach when interacting empathically with the client, and a cognitive-behavioral approach to suggest strategies that may help the client cope with problems.

> **Existential Therapies** **Existential therapies** aim to help clients find meaning in their lives. They address concerns about death, alienation from other people, and freedom. Existential therapists, like humanistic therapists, believe that people are responsible for their own lives.

Family Therapies

In **family therapy**, a therapist sees two or more members of a family at the same time. Family therapies work on the assumption that people do not live in isolation but as interconnected members of families. A problem that affects one person in the family must necessarily affect the whole family, and any change a person makes will inevitably affect the whole family. Family therapists help people to identify the roles they play in their families and to resolve conflicts within families. Family therapists sometimes use family trees to help family members identify intergenerational patterns of behavior.

In **couples therapy**, therapists help couples identify and resolve conflicts. Therapists usually see both members of a couple at the same time. Family and couples therapists may use psychodynamic, cognitive, behavioral, or humanistic approaches.

Group Therapies

In group therapy, a therapist meets with several people at once. Psychotherapy groups usually have between four and fifteen people. Group therapies are cost-effective for clients and time saving for therapists.

Self-Help Groups **Self-help groups**, such as Alcoholics Anonymous, resemble therapy groups except that they do not have a therapist. These groups allow people to feel less alone in dealing with their problems. Self-help group participants both give and receive help and can usually attend the group free of charge. Self-help groups are used very widely.

FEATURES OF PSYCHOTHERAPY GROUPS

Groups may be homogeneous or heterogeneous. In homogeneous groups, all members share one or more key characteristics. For example, a group may be composed of people who are all suffering from depression or people who are between the ages of twenty and thirty. Many groups are heterogeneous and contain people who differ in age, type of problem, gender, and so on.

THE THERAPIST'S ROLE

The therapist usually screens people to determine whether they would be suitable for a group, excluding people who are likely to be highly disruptive. In the group, the therapist's role is to promote a supportive environment, set goals, and protect the clients from harm.

THE ROLE OF GROUP MEMBERS

Group members discuss their problems and experiences with one another and consider different ways of coping. They provide each other with acceptance, support, and honest feedback. A therapy group is a place where people can practice coping strategies and ways of relating to others. Therapy groups also help people to realize they are not alone in their suffering.

Biomedical Therapies

Biomedical therapies include drug therapy, electroconvulsive therapy, and psychosurgery.

DRUG THERAPIES

Drug therapy, or **psychopharmacotherapy**, aims to treat psychological disorders with medications. Drug therapy is usually combined with other kinds of psychotherapy. The main categories of drugs used to treat psychological disorders are antianxiety drugs, antidepressants, and antipsychotics.

Antianxiety Drugs

Antianxiety drugs include a class of drugs called **benzodiazepines**, or tranquilizers. Two commonly used benzodiazepines are known by the brand names Valium and Xanax. The generic names of these drugs are diazepam and alprazolam, respectively:

- **Effects:** Benzodiazepines reduce the activity of the central nervous system by increasing the activity of GABA, the main inhibitory neurotransmitter in the brain. Benzodiazepines take effect almost immediately after they are administered, but their effects last just a few hours. Psychiatrists prescribe these drugs for panic disorder and anxiety.

- **Side effects:** Side effects may include drowsiness, lightheadedness, dry mouth, depression, nausea and vomiting, constipation, insomnia, confusion, diarrhea, palpitations, nasal congestion, and blurred vision. Benzodiazepines can also cause drug dependence. Tolerance can occur if a person takes these drugs for a long time, and withdrawal symptoms often appear when the drug use is discontinued.

Antidepressant Drugs

Antidepressants usually take a few weeks to have an effect. There are three classes of antidepressants: monoamine oxidase inhibitors, tricyclics, and selective serotonin reuptake inhibitors.

- **Monoamine oxidase inhibitors (MAOIs):** Include phenelzine (Nardil).

- **Tricyclics:** Include amitriptyline (Elavil). Tricyclics generally have fewer side effects than the MAOIs.

- **Selective serotonin reuptake inhibitors (SSRIs):** The newest class of antidepressants, including paroxetine (Paxil), fluoxetine (Prozac), and sertraline (Zoloft).

Antidepressants are typically prescribed for depression, anxiety, phobias and obsessive-compulsive disorder.

- **Effects:** MAOIs and tricyclics increase the level of the neurotransmitters norepinephrine and serotonin in the brain. SSRIs increase the level of serotonin.

- **Side effects:** Although antidepressants are not addictive, they often have side effects such as headache, dry mouth, constipation, nausea, weight gain, and feelings of restlessness. Of the three classes of antidepressants, MAOIs generally have the most side effects. People who take MAOIs also have to restrict their diet, because MAOIs interact negatively with foods that contain the amino acid tyramine, such as beer and some cheeses and meats. SSRIs have fewer side effects than the other two classes of antidepressants. However, SSRIs can cause sexual dysfunction, and if they are discontinued abruptly, withdrawal symptoms occur.

Antipsychotic Drugs

Antipsychotic drugs are used to treat schizophrenia and other psychotic disorders. They include chlorpromazine (Thorazine), thioridazine (Mellaril), and haloperidol (Haldol). Antipsychotic drugs usually begin to take effect a few days after they are administered.

- **Effects:** Antipsychotic drugs, or neuroleptics, reduce sensitivity to irrelevant stimuli by limiting the activity of the neurotransmitter dopamine. Many antipsychotic drugs are most useful for treating positive symptoms of schizophrenia, such as hallucinations and delusions. However, a new class of antipsychotic drugs, called **atypical antipsychotic drugs**, also help treat the negative symptoms of schizophrenia. They reduce the activity of both dopamine and serotonin. Atypical antipsychotic drugs include clozapine (Clozaril), olanzapine

(Zyprexa), and quetiapine (Seroquel). Atypical antipsychotic drugs can sometimes be effective for schizophrenia patients who have not responded to the older antipsychotic drugs.

- **Side effects:** Side effects include drowsiness, constipation, dry mouth, tremors, muscle rigidity, and coordination problems. These side effects often make people stop taking the medications, which frequently results in a relapse of schizophrenia. A more serious side effect is **tardive dyskinesia**, a usually permanent neurological condition characterized by involuntary movements. To avoid tardive dyskinesia, the dosage of antipsychotics has to be carefully monitored. The atypical antipsychotics have fewer side effects than the older antipsychotic drugs and are less likely to cause tardive dyskinesia. In addition, relapse rates are lower if people continue to take the drug. However, the relapse rate is higher with these drugs if people discontinue the drug.

Lithium One drug used in the treatment of bipolar disorders is **lithium**.
Effects: Lithium prevents mood swings in people with bipolar disorders. Researchers have suggested that lithium may affect the action of norepinephrine or glutamate.
Side effects: Lithium can cause tremors or long-term kidney damage in some people. Doctors must carefully monitor the level of lithium in a patient's blood. A level that is too low is ineffective, and a level that is too high can be toxic. Discontinuing lithium treatment abruptly can increase the risk of relapse. Recently developed alternatives to lithium include the drugs carbamazepine (Tegretol) and divalproex (Depakote).

CRITICISMS OF DRUG THERAPIES

Drug therapies are effective for many people with psychological disorders, especially for those who suffer from severe disorders that cannot be treated in other ways. However, drug therapies have been criticized for several reasons:

- Their effects are superficial and last only as long as the drug is being administered.

- Side effects can often be more severe and troubling than the disorder for which the drug was given. This can cause patients to discontinue the drugs and experience relapses.

- Patients often respond well to new drugs when they are first released into the market because of the enthusiasm and high expectations surrounding the drug. But such placebo effects tend to wane over time.

- The **therapeutic window** for drugs, or the amount of the drug that is required for an effect without toxicity, varies according to factors such as gender, age, and ethnicity. This makes it difficult for physicians to determine the right dose of a drug.

- New drugs, even those approved for long-term use, are often tested on only a few hundred people for a few weeks or months. This means that the risks of taking drugs long-term are unknown.

- Some critics point out that because of pressure from managed care companies, physicians may overprescribe drugs rather than recommend psychotherapy.

- Drugs are tested only on certain populations, for certain conditions. Physicians, however, sometimes prescribe a drug for conditions and populations that were not included in the testing.

- Researchers who study the effectiveness of medications may be biased because they often have financial ties to pharmaceutical companies.

- Freely prescribing drugs for psychological disorders gives the impression that such disorders can be treated only biochemically. However, the biological abnormalities present in such disorders can often be treated by changing thoughts and behavior.

ELECTROCONVULSIVE THERAPY

Electroconvulsive therapy (ECT) is used mainly for the treatment of severe depression. Electrodes are placed on the patient's head, over the temporal lobes of the brain. Anesthetics and muscle relaxants help minimize discomfort to the patient. Then an electric current is delivered for about one second. The patient has a convulsive seizure and becomes unconscious, awakening after about an hour. The typical number of ECT sessions varies from six to twenty, and they are usually done while a patient is hospitalized.

ECT is a controversial procedure. Research suggests that there are short-term side effects of ECT, such as attention deficits and memory loss. Critics of ECT believe that it is often used inappropriately and that it can result in permanent cognitive problems. Proponents of ECT, however, believe that it does not cause long-term cognitive problems, loss of memory, or brain damage. They believe that it is highly effective and that it is underused because of negative public ideas surrounding it.

PSYCHOSURGERY

Psychosurgery is brain surgery to treat a psychological disorder. The best-known form of psychosurgery is the prefrontal lobotomy. A **lobotomy** is a surgical procedure that severs nerve tracts in the frontal lobe. Surgeons performed lobotomies in the 1940s and 1950s to treat highly emotional and violent behavior. The surgery often resulted in severe deficits, including apathy, lethargy, and social withdrawal.

Lobotomies are now rarely performed, but some neurosurgeons perform **cingulotomies**, which involve destruction of part of the frontal lobes. These surgeries are usually performed on patients who have severe depressive or anxiety disorders and who do not respond to other treatments. The effectiveness of these surgeries is unclear.

TRANSCRANIAL MAGNETIC STIMULATION

Transcranial magnetic stimulation (TMS) is a recently developed, noninvasive procedure. It involves stimulating the brain by means of a magnetic coil held to a person's skull near the left prefrontal cortex. It is used to treat severe depression.

Effectiveness of Treatment

Research has shown that many people with psychological disorders benefit from treatment. Effectiveness depends on the specific disorder being treated and the skill of the therapist.

WAYS OF ASSESSING EFFECTIVENESS

The effectiveness of a particular therapeutic approach can be assessed in three ways: client testimonials, providers' perceptions, and empirical research.

Client Testimonials

Clients who get treatment for psychological problems often testify to their effectiveness. However, such testimonials can be unreliable for several reasons:

- **Regression toward the mean:** People often go into treatment because they are in extreme distress. When their distress becomes less extreme, they may attribute this to the treatment's effectiveness. But even without treatment, extreme distress tends to decrease. The tendency for extreme states to move toward the average when assessed a second time is called **regression toward the mean**.

- **The placebo effect:** People often feel better after being in treatment because of their expectations that they will improve. (See Chapter 1 for more information on placebo effects.)

- **The justification of effort effect:** People may believe that treatment was effective because they spent time, effort, and money on it. If people work hard to reach a goal, they are likely to value the goal more. This phenomenon is called **justification of effort**.

Providers' Perceptions

Treatment providers can say whether a treatment is effective, but this can be unreliable for several reasons:

- Regression toward the mean affects providers' perceptions of success. They may believe that a client who entered treatment in crisis became less extremely distressed because of the treatment. However, such an improvement may have occurred without any intervention.

- Providers' perceptions may be biased because clients often emphasize improvements in order to justify discontinuing treatment.

- Providers may also have biased perceptions because they continue to hear from past clients only when those clients were satisfied with treatment. They don't often hear from clients who found treatment ineffective.

Empirical Research

Another way to assess effectiveness is through careful empirical research. Research has shown that some treatments are more effective for a particular problem than a placebo or no treatment. These treatments are known as **empirically validated treatments**. Researchers have to conduct two or more studies in order to conclude that a specific treatment is effective for a particular problem.

Research shows that psychotherapy works for many psychological problems. Although people who do not receive therapy also sometimes improve with time, people who do receive therapy are more likely to improve. Research also shows that all approaches to therapy are about equally effective, though certain kind of therapies do seem somewhat more effective for specific problems.

Specific Disorder	Most Effective Treatment
Panic disorders	Cognitive therapy
Specific phobias	Systematic desensitization
Obsessive-compulsive disorder	Behavior therapy or medication
Depression	Cognitive therapy
Post–traumatic stress disorder and agoraphobia	Exposure treatment

Therapist Factors Research shows that the effectiveness of therapy does not depend on the level of training or experience of the therapist or on the type of mental health professional providing therapy. However, the effectiveness of therapy does depend on the skill of the therapist. The most effective therapists tend to be empathic, genuine, and warm.

WHO BENEFITS FROM TREATMENT?

Clients who are likely to benefit from therapy share some common features:

- Motivation to get better
- Family support
- Tendency to deal actively with problems rather than avoid them

Clients who are less likely to benefit from therapy also share some features:

- Hostility and negativity
- Personality disorders
- Psychotic disorders

CAN THERAPY BE HARMFUL?

Under some conditions, therapy can be harmful to the client. Clients may be harmed if:

- Therapists engage in unethical behavior, such as by having sexual relationships with clients
- Therapists act according to personal prejudices or are ignorant of cultural differences between themselves and their clients
- Therapists coerce clients into doing things they don't want to do
- Therapists use techniques that research has not demonstrated as being effective
- Therapists lead their clients to produce false memories of past traumas through careless use of techniques such as hypnosis or free association

Seeking Treatment

Although many people experience psychological problems over their lifetime, not everyone seeks treatment. Not everyone is willing to get psychotherapy for problems they experience. More women than men get psychotherapy, and people who are more educated and who have medical insurance are also more likely to seek treatment.

BARRIERS TO GETTING TREATMENT

People may not seek treatment even if they feel they need it. Common barriers to getting treatment are:

- Concerns about the cost of treatment

- Lack of health insurance

- The stigma associated with getting psychological treatment

PSYCHOTHERAPY FOR CULTURAL AND ETHNIC MINORITIES

Modern psychotherapy is based on individualistic values, and many researchers have argued that such therapy may not be readily applied to ethnic minorities in the United States. Ethnic and cultural minorities may face several barriers to receiving psychotherapy:

- Some cultural groups may be hesitant to seek help from professionals, particularly in institutional settings such as hospitals and clinics. They may instead prefer to seek informal help from family, friends, elders, and priests.

- Cultural minorities may find it difficult to get psychotherapy services because therapists who speak their language are unavailable.

- Therapists trained to treat mainly white, middle-class clients may not be familiar with or responsive to the needs of clients from different ethnic and cultural backgrounds.

Treatment Trends

Two current trends that affect the treatment of psychological disorders are managed care and deinstitutionalization.

MANAGED CARE

Managed care is an arrangement in which an organization, such as a health maintenance organization (HMO), acts as an intermediary between a person seeking health care and a treatment provider. People buy insurance plans from HMOs and then pay only a small copayment each time they get healthcare services. Prior to managed care, health care was done through fee-for-service arrangements. In **fee-for-service** arrangements, people pay for any health care services they believe they need. They may then be reimbursed by insurance companies or government health care programs, such as Medicaid and Medicare.

The advantages of managed care are that consumers pay lower fees to providers and that money is not usually spent on medically unnecessary services.

Criticisms of Managed Care

Managed care systems have many critics who argue that HMOs compromise the quality of health care in the following ways:

- Consumers are often denied treatment they need, or the length of treatment is inappropriately limited.

- Managed care creates barriers to accessing health care services by requiring people to get referrals through their primary care providers or by authorizing only a small number of therapy sessions at a time.

- Because of cost issues, the professionals who provide treatment are often less well-trained to treat severe disorders. For example, they may be counselors with master's degrees rather than doctoral-level psychologists or psychiatrists.

- Physicians might be required to prescribe older, less effective drugs rather than new drugs in order to keep costs down.

- Clients' confidentiality may be threatened because HMOs require therapists to disclose details about the clients' problems in order to have treatment authorized.

The Community Mental Health Movement

In the past, people with psychological disorders typically received inpatient treatment at **mental hospitals**, or medical institutions that specialize in providing such treatment. In the 1950s, however, it began to be clear that mental hospitals often made psychological problems worse instead of better. Mental hospitals were very crowded and had few properly trained professionals, and they were often in less populated areas, giving patients little access to support from their friends and families.

In the 1950s, the **community mental health movement** started. This movement advocated treating people with psychological problems in their own communities, providing treatment through outpatient clinics, and preventing psychological disorders before they arose.

Because of the community mental health movement, deinstitutionalization became popular. **Deinstitutionalization** refers to providing treatment through community-based outpatient clinics rather than inpatient hospitals. Although people are still hospitalized for serious psychological problems, inpatient stays are usually relatively short and occur in psychiatric wings of general hospitals, rather than in mental hospitals far away from people's communities.

- **Advantages of deinstitutionalization:** Treatment at outpatient clinics is less costly than inpatient care and often just as effective. Also, people often prefer the freedom of community-based treatment to inpatient hospitals.

- **Disadvantages of deinstitutionalization:** It has contributed to homelessness, since some people released from inpatient facilities have nowhere to go. Also, it has led to what is referred to as a "revolving door" population of chronically mentally ill people who are periodically hospitalized, released, and rehospitalized.

Summary

Types of Treatment

- Treatment for psychological disorders can be categorized into **insight therapies, behavior therapies,** and **biomedical therapies.**
- All psychotherapies offer **hope, new perspectives on a problem,** and an **empathic relationship with a therapist.**
- Many types of professionals provide psychological treatment.

Psychotherapy

- All psychodynamic therapies are based on **Sigmund Freud's** psychoanalytic treatment.
- **Psychoanalytic treatment** focuses on uncovering unconscious motives, conflicts, and defenses.
- Three techniques used in psychoanalysis are **free association, dream analysis,** and **interpretation.**
- The concepts of **transference** and **resistance** are important features of psychoanalysis and current psychodynamic therapies.
- **Cognitive therapies** attempt to identify and change maladaptive thinking patterns.
- Cognitive therapists believe that depression arises from **errors in thinking.**
- Cognitive therapists help clients to identify and change **automatic thoughts** and **assumptions about the world.**
- **Albert Ellis's rational-emotive therapy** is based on the idea that people's feelings are influenced by their catastrophic thoughts and beliefs about events.
- Behavior therapists focus on addressing symptoms rather than the underlying causes. They use learning principles to modify behavior.
- **Systematic desensitization** is a type of **exposure therapy** that uses counterconditioning to decrease anxiety. It is effective at treating phobias.
- **Flooding** is an exposure therapy in which patients are suddenly exposed to a feared object or situation.
- **EMDR** is an exposure treatment for post-traumatic stress disorder and panic attacks. The eye movements do not appear to add to the effectiveness of the treatment.
- In **aversion therapy**, a stimulus that evokes an unpleasant response is paired with a stimulus that evokes a maladaptive behavior.
- **Social skills training** for improving relationships with people uses techniques such as modeling, behavioral rehearsal, and shaping.

- A **token economy** is a behavior modification program based on operant conditioning principles.

- **Humanistic therapists** try to help people accept themselves and free themselves from unnecessary limitations.

- In **client-centered therapy**, therapists provide a supportive emotional environment that helps clients enhance self-acceptance and personal growth.

- Humanistic therapists believe that it is important to be genuine and empathic and provide **unconditional positive regard.**

Family Therapies

- In **family therapy**, a therapist sees two or more members of a family at the same time. Family therapies are based on the idea that people live as interconnected members of families.

- In **couples therapy**, therapists help couples to identify and resolve conflicts.

Group Therapies

- In **group therapy**, a therapist meets with several people at once.

- Groups may be homogeneous or heterogeneous.

- In group therapy, the therapist **screens participants, promotes a supportive environment, sets goals,** and **protects clients from harm.**

- Group members provide each other with acceptance, support, and honest feedback.

- **Self-help groups** are similar to therapy groups, except that they do not have a therapist.

Biomedical Therapies

- In **drug therapy**, psychological disorders are treated with medications. These medications are often effective but have many side effects.

- **Antianxiety drugs** include **benzodiazepines**, which reduce central nervous system activity.

- **Antidepressants** include **MAOIs, tricyclics,** and **SSRIs.** These drugs affect the levels of the neurotransmitters serotonin and epinephrine.

- **Antipsychotic drugs** are used to treat schizophrenia and other psychotic drugs. They reduce dopamine activity.

- Unlike the older antipsychotic drugs, the newer **atypical antipsychotic drugs** help treat the negative symptoms of schizophrenia. These drugs reduce serotonin activity as well as dopamine.

- **Lithium** is used to treat bipolar disorders.

- Drug therapies have been criticized for several reasons.

- **ECT** is used to treat severe depression. It is a controversial procedure.

- **Lobotomies** are performed only rarely to treat psychological disorders, but **cingulotomies** are sometimes done.

- **TMS** is a recently developed noninvasive procedure for treating severe depression.

Effectiveness of Treatment

- **Client testimonials** and **providers' perceptions** are not reliable ways of assessing the effectiveness of treatments.

- Empirical research shows that psychotherapy is effective for many problems.

- All approaches to therapy are equally effective, but some approaches are more effective than others for specific problems.

- Effectiveness does not depend on the therapist's level of training, experience, or education but does depend on therapist skill. Effective therapists are **empathic, genuine**, and **warm**.

- Clients who benefit from therapy tend to be people who are motivated, who are active problem solvers, and who have family support.

- Under some conditions, therapy can be harmful to clients, such as if the therapist acts unethically or coerces the client in any way.

CHAPTER 16 TREATMENT

Seeking Treatment

• People who seek psychotherapy are more likely to be women, to be more educated, and to have medical insurance.

• People may not seek treatment because of cost concerns, lack of insurance, or fear of stigma.

• Cultural and ethnic minorities often face barriers to receiving psychotherapy.

Treatment Trends

• In managed care systems, consumers pay lower fees to providers and money is not spent on unnecessary medical services. However, critics argue that managed care compromises quality of care in many ways.

• There has been a trend toward deinstitutionalization over the past several decades.

• Deinstitutionalization has both advantages and disadvantages.

Sample Test Questions

1. What are some characteristics of people who are likely to benefit from therapy?

2. What are the steps involved in systematic desensitization treatment?

3. What is free association?

4. What are some errors in thinking that underlie depression, according to cognitive therapists?

5. According to humanistic therapists, what underlies psychological problems?

6. What is one difference between self-help groups and therapy groups?
   A. Participants only give help in self-help groups
   B. Participants only receive help in self-help groups
   C. Self-help groups don't have a professional leader
   D. Self-help groups can't help people feel less alone in dealing with problems

7. Which treatment produces the serious side effect known as tardive dyskinesia?
   A. Antianxiety drugs
   B. Antidepressant drugs
   C. Antipsychotic drugs
   D. Lithium

8. From an empirical point of view, how can the effectiveness of a therapy best be determined?
   A. By doing controlled studies
   B. By asking therapists whether the therapy is successful
   C. By asking clients how they felt about the therapy
   D. All of the above

9. The effectiveness of therapy depends to some extent on which of the following?
   A. The theoretical orientation of the therapist
   B. The therapist's skill
   C. The therapist's gender
   D. All of the above

10. Many critics argue that the average person receives poorer quality treatment for psychological problems because of which of the following?
   A. Deinstitutionalization
   B. Managed care
   C. Token economies
   D. The therapeutic window

11. A therapist who pays particular attention to transference during therapy is likely to have which approach?

    A.   A psychodynamic approach

    B.   A cognitive approach

    C.   A humanistic approach

    D.   A behavioral approach

12. A therapist who tries to decrease incongruence in the client is likely to have which approach?

    A.   A psychodynamic approach

    B.   A cognitive approach

    C.   A humanistic approach

    D.   A behavioral approach

13. A therapist who uses classical conditioning principles to treat a spider phobia is likely to have which approach?

    A.   A psychodynamic approach

    B.   A cognitive approach

    C.   A humanistic approach

    D.   A behavioral approach

14. A therapist whose main task is to encourage clients to test their assumptions against reality is likely to have which approach?

    A.   A psychodynamic approach

    B.   A cognitive approach

    C.   A humanistic approach

    D.   A behavioral approach

15. Social skills training typically involves which of the following?

    A.   Antipsychotic drugs or lithium

    B.   Behavioral rehearsal

    C.   Dream analysis

    D.   All of the above

ANSWERS

1. People who benefit from therapy are generally motivated to get better, have family support, and deal actively with problems rather than avoid them.

2. In systematic desensitization treatment, the therapist and client first make up an anxiety hierarchy. The hierarchy lists stimuli that the client is likely to find frightening. The client then ranks the stimuli from least frightening to most frightening. Next, the therapist teaches the client how to progressively and completely relax his body. The therapist then asks the client to relax and then imagine encountering the stimuli listed in the anxiety hierarchy, beginning with the least frightening stimulus. If the client feels anxious while imagining a stimulus, he is asked to stop imagining the stimulus and focus on relaxing. After some time, the client becomes able to imagine all the stimuli on the hierarchy without anxiety. Finally, the client practices encountering the real stimuli.

3. Free association is a technique in psychoanalysis that involves saying anything that comes to mind. Clients are expected to put all thoughts into words, even if those thoughts are incoherent, inappropriate, rude, or seemingly irrelevant. Free associations reveal the client's unconscious to the psychoanalyst.

4. According to cognitive therapists, depressed people tend to blame themselves for negative events and underestimate situational causes; tend to pay more attention to negative events than to positive ones; tend to be pessimistic; and tend to make inappropriately global generalizations from negative events.

5. Client-centered therapists believe people's problems come from incongruence, or a disparity between their self-concept and reality. Incongruence arises because people are too dependent on others for approval and acceptance. When there is incongruence, people feel anxious. They then try to maintain their self-concept by denying or distorting reality.

6.	C	11.	A
7.	C	12.	C
8.	A	13.	D
9.	B	14.	B
10.	B	15.	B

Social Psychology

- Impressions
- Stereotypes and Prejudice
- Attribution
- Attitudes
- Social Influence
- Attraction
- Obedience and Authority
- Groups
- Helping Behavior

17

When we read the newspaper, listen to the TV news, or browse an online news site, we see hundreds of examples of how people affect others. The media tells us which Hollywood actors are beautiful. The public reacts when a fifty-six-year-old woman gives birth to twins. A former janitor amasses a fortune and leaves it to the school where he worked.

Social psychologists try to explain how other people influence our thoughts, feelings, and behavior; how we form impressions of other people; and why stereotypes and prejudice flourish. They study how people manage to persuade, influence, and attract us. Obedience to authorities, group functioning, and helpfulness are part of social psychology as well. Social psychology acknowledges that we move in and out of one another's lives, directly and indirectly, and all parties are, in some way, affected.

Impressions

People form impressions, or vague ideas, about other people through the process of **person perception**.

THE INFLUENCE OF PHYSICAL APPEARANCE

Physical appearance has a strong effect on how people are perceived by others. Two aspects of physical appearance are particularly important: attractiveness and baby-faced features.

Attractiveness

Research shows that people judge attractive-looking people as having positive personality traits, such as sociability, friendliness, poise, warmth, and good adjustment. There is, however, little actual correlation between personality traits and physical attractiveness.

People also tend to think that attractive-looking people are more competent. Because of this bias, attractive people tend to get better jobs and higher salaries.

Baby-Faced Features

People's attractiveness does not have much influence on judgments about their honesty. Instead, people tend to be judged as honest if they have baby-faced features, such as large eyes and rounded chins. Baby-faced people are often judged as being passive, helpless, and naïve. However, no correlation exists between being baby-faced and actually having these personality traits.

Evolutionary theorists believe the qualities attributed to baby-faced people reflect an evolved tendency to see babies as helpless and needing nurture. Such a tendency may have given human ancestors a survival advantage, since the babies of people who provided good nurturing were more likely to live on to reproduce.

COGNITIVE SCHEMAS

When people meet, they form impressions of each other based on their **cognitive schemas**. People use cognitive schemas to organize information about the world. Cognitive schemas help to access information quickly and easily.

Social schemas are mental models that represent and categorize social events and people. For example, certain social schemas tell people what it means to be a spectator at a baseball game. There are also social schemas for categories of people, such as *yuppie* or *geek*. These social schemas affect how people perceive events and others. Once a social schema is activated, it may be difficult to adjust a perception of a person or event.

Stereotypes and Prejudice

Cognitive schemas can result in stereotypes and contribute to prejudice.

STEREOTYPES

Stereotypes are beliefs about people based on their membership in a particular group. Stereotypes can be positive, negative, or neutral. Stereotypes based on gender, ethnicity, or occupation are common in many societies.

> EXAMPLES: *People may stereotype women as nurturing or used car salespeople as dishonest.*

The Stability of Stereotypes

Stereotypes are not easily changed, for the following reasons:

- When people encounter instances that disconfirm their stereotypes of a particular group, they tend to assume that those instances are atypical subtypes of the group.

  > EXAMPLE: *Ben stereotypes gay men as being unathletic. When he meets Al, an athletic gay man, he assumes that Al is not a typical representative of gay people.*

- People's perceptions are influenced by their expectations.

  EXAMPLE: Liz has a stereotype of elderly people as mentally unstable. When she sees an elderly woman sitting on a park bench alone, talking out loud, she thinks that the woman is talking to herself because she is unstable. Liz fails to notice that the woman is actually talking on a cell phone.

- People selectively recall instances that confirm their stereotypes and forget about disconfirming instances.

  EXAMPLE: Paul has a stereotype of Latin Americans as academically unmotivated. As evidence for his belief, he cites instances when some of his Latin American classmates failed to read required class material. He fails to recall all the times his Latin American classmates did complete their assignments.

Functions

Stereotypes have several important functions:

- They allow people to quickly process new information about an event or person.
- They organize people's past experiences.
- They help people to meaningfully assess differences between individuals and groups.
- They help people to make predictions about other people's behavior.

Everyday Use of Stereotypes The word stereotype has developed strong negative connotations for very good reasons. Negative stereotypes of different groups of people can have a terrible influence on those people's lives. However, most people do rely on stereotypes nearly every day to help them function in society. For example, say a woman has to work late and finds herself walking home alone on a dark city street. Walking toward her is a group of five young men talking loudly and roughhousing. The woman crosses the street and enters a convenience store until the young men pass, then continues on her way. Most people would say she acted prudently, even though she relied on a stereotype to guide her behavior.

Dangers

Stereotypes can lead to distortions of reality for several reasons:

- They cause people to exaggerate differences among groups.

- They lead people to focus selectively on information that agrees with the stereotype and ignore information that disagrees with it.

- They tend to make people see other groups as overly homogenous, even though people can easily see that the groups they belong to are heterogeneous.

Evolutionary Perspectives

Evolutionary psychologists have speculated that humans evolved the tendency to stereotype because it gave their ancestors an adaptive advantage. Being able to decide quickly which group a person belonged to may have had survival value, since this enabled people to distinguish between friends and enemies.

Xenophobia Some evolutionary psychologists believe that xenophobia, the fear of strangers or people different from oneself, has genetic roots. They argue that humans are to some extent programmed by their genes to respond positively to genetically similar people and negatively to genetically different people.

PREJUDICE

A **prejudice** is a negative belief or feeling about a particular group of individuals. Prejudices are often passed on from one generation to the next.

Functions

Prejudice is a destructive phenomenon, and it is pervasive because it serves many psychological, social, and economic functions:

CHAPTER 17 SOCIAL PSYCHOLOGY

- Prejudice allows people to avoid doubt and fear.

  EXAMPLE: Rachel's parents came from a working-class background but are now wealthy business owners. Rachel might develop a dislike of the working class because she does not want to be identified with working-class people. She believes such an association would damage her claim to upper-class social status.

- Prejudice gives people scapegoats to blame in times of trouble.

  EXAMPLE: Glen blames his unemployment on foreign nationals whom he believes are incompetent but willing to work for low wages.

- Prejudice can boost self-esteem.

  EXAMPLE: A poor white farmer in the nineteenth-century South could feel better about his own meager existence by insisting on his superiority to African-American slaves.

- Evolutionary psychologists suggest that prejudice allows people to bond with their own group by contrasting their own groups to outsider groups.

  EXAMPLE: Most religious and ethnic groups maintain some prejudices against other groups, which help to make their own group seem more special.

- Prejudice legitimizes discrimination because it apparently justifies one group's dominance over another.

  EXAMPLE: Pseudoscientific arguments about the mental inferiority of African Americans allowed whites to feel justified in owning slaves.

Measuring Prejudice

Researchers find it difficult to measure prejudice. One reason for this is that people differ in the type and extent of prejudice they harbor. For example, a person who makes demeaning comments about a particular ethnic group may be bigoted or just ignorant. Also, people often do not admit to being prejudiced.

People may often have implicit unconscious prejudices even when they do not have explicit prejudices. Researchers assess implicit prejudice in three ways:

- Some researchers assess attitudes that suggest prejudice, such as a strong emotional objection to affirmative action.

- Some researchers observe behavior rather than assess attitudes. People's behavior in stressful situations may be particularly useful at revealing implicit prejudice.

- Some researchers assess the unconscious associations people have about particular groups.

Ingroups and Outgroups

People's social identities depend on the groups they belong to. From a person's perspective, any group he belongs to is an **ingroup**, and any group he doesn't belong to is an **outgroup**. People generally have a lower opinion of outgroup members and a higher opinion of members of their own group. People who identify strongly with a particular group are more likely to be prejudiced against people in competing outgroups.

People tend to think that their own groups are composed of different sorts of people. At the same time, they often think that everyone in an outgroup is the same. According to the **contact hypothesis**, prejudice declines when people in an ingroup become more familiar with the customs, norms, food, music, and attitudes of people in an outgroup. Contact with the outgroup helps people to see the diversity among its members.

CHAPTER 17
SOCIAL PSYCHOLOGY

Competition and Cooperation Hostility between an ingroup and an outgroup increases when groups compete. Researchers have found that hostility between groups decreases when those groups have to cooperate in order to reach a shared goal. In such a situation, people in the two groups tend to feel that they belong to one larger group rather than two separate groups.

Reducing Prejudice

Research shows that prejudice and conflict among groups can be reduced if four conditions are met:

- The groups have equality in terms of legal status, economic opportunity, and political power.
- Authorities advocate equal rights.
- The groups have opportunities to interact formally and informally with each other.
- The groups cooperate to reach a common goal.

Kurt Lewin and the AJC Kurt Lewin is widely considered the father of social psychology. He developed many concepts that both psychologists and the general public now take for granted, including his "field theory" that a person's behavior is determined both by that person's character and by his current environment. Lewin also did important work in the area of majority-minority relations. In the mid-1940s, the American Jewish Council (AJC) began talking with Lewin about ways to reduce anti-Semitism. Shortly before his death in 1947, Lewin became chief consultant for the AJC's Commission on Community Interrelations, a groundbreaking organization designed to combat prejudice through community intervention.

Attribution

Attributions are inferences that people make about the causes of events and behavior. People make attributions in order to understand their experiences. Attributions strongly influence the way people interact with others.

TYPES OF ATTRIBUTIONS

Researchers classify attributions along two dimensions: internal vs. external and stable vs. unstable. By combining these two dimensions of attributes, researchers can classify a particular attribution as being internal-stable, internal-unstable, external-stable, or external-unstable.

Internal vs. External

Attribution theory proposes that the attributions people make about events and behavior can be classed as either internal or external. In an **internal**, or dispositional, **attribution**, people infer that an event or a person's behavior is due to personal factors such as traits, abilities, or feelings. In an **external**, or situational, **attribution**, people infer that a person's behavior is due to situational factors.

> EXAMPLE: *Maria's car breaks down on the freeway. If she believes the breakdown happened because of her ignorance about cars, she is making an internal attribution. If she believes that the breakdown happened because her car is old, she is making an external attribution.*

Stable vs. Unstable

Researchers also distinguish between stable and unstable attributions. When people make a **stable attribution**, they infer that an event or behavior is due to stable, unchanging factors. When making an **unstable attribution**, they infer that an event or behavior is due to unstable, temporary factors.

> EXAMPLE: *Lee gets a D on his sociology term paper. If he attributes the grade to the fact that he always has bad luck, he is making a stable attribution. If he attributes the grade to the fact that he didn't have much time to study that week, he is making an unstable attribution.*

ATTRIBUTION BIAS

When people make an attribution, they are guessing about the causes of events or behaviors. These guesses are often wrong. People have systematic biases, which lead them to make incorrect attributions. These biases include the fundamental attribution error, the self-serving bias, and the just world hypothesis.

The Fundamental Attribution Error

The **fundamental attribution error** is the tendency to attribute other people's behavior to internal factors such as personality traits, abilities, and feelings. The fundamental attribution error is also called the correspondence bias, because it is assumed that other people's behavior corresponds to their personal attributes. When explaining their own behavior, on the other hand, people tend to attribute it to situational factors.

> *EXAMPLE: Alexis falls asleep in class. Sean attributes her behavior to laziness. When he fell asleep in class last week, however, he attributed his own behavior to the all-nighter he pulled finishing a term paper.*

The Self-Serving Bias

The **self-serving bias** is the tendency to attribute successes to internal factors and failures to situational factors. This bias tends to increase as time passes after an event. Therefore, the further in the past an event is, the more likely people are to congratulate themselves for successes and to blame the situation for failures.

> *EXAMPLE: Chad wins a poetry competition but fails to get the poem published in a magazine he sent it to. He attributes his success in the competition to his talent. He attributes his failure to get it published to bad luck.*

The Just World Hypothesis

The **just world hypothesis** refers to the need to believe that the world is fair and that people get what they deserve. The just world hypothesis gives people a sense of security and helps them to find meaning in difficult circumstances.

People are less generous about other people than about themselves. Other people's successes tend to be attributed to situational factors and their failures to internal factors.

> EXAMPLE: *Chad's friend Diana does manage to get a poem published in a magazine. However, she did not receive a prize in a poetry competition she entered. Chad attributes Diana's publication success to good luck and her failure to her underdeveloped writing abilities.*

Unfortunately, the just world hypothesis also leads to a tendency to blame the victim. When something tragic or terrible happens to someone, people often reassure themselves by deciding that the person must have done something to provoke or cause the event.

> EXAMPLE: *Anthony gets into a car wreck. His friends believe that Anthony must have been driving drunk.*

CULTURAL INFLUENCES ON ATTRIBUTION STYLE

Research suggests that cultural values and norms affect the way people make attributions. In particular, differences in attribution style exist between individualist and collectivist cultures. People in individualist cultures place a high value on uniqueness and independence, believe in the importance of individual goals, and define themselves in terms of personal attributes. People in collectivist cultures, on the other hand, place a high value on conformity and interdependence, believe in the importance of group goals, and define themselves in terms of their membership in groups. North American and Western European cultures tend to be individualistic, while Asian, Latin American, and African cultures tend to be collectivist.

People in collectivist cultures tend to be less susceptible to the fundamental attribution error than people in individualist cultures. People from collectivist cultures are more likely to believe that a person's behavior is due to situational demands rather than to personal attributes. People from collectivist cultures are also less susceptible to the self-serving bias.

The Self-Effacing Bias

Research suggests that people who are from a collectivist culture, such as the Japanese culture, tend to have a **self-effacing bias** when making attributions. That is, they tend to attribute their successes to situational factors rather than to personal attributes, and, when they fail, they blame themselves for not trying hard enough.

Attitudes

Attitudes are evaluations people make about objects, ideas, events, or other people. Attitudes can be positive or negative. **Explicit attitudes** are conscious beliefs that can guide decisions and behavior. **Implicit attitudes** are unconscious beliefs that can still influence decisions and behavior. Attitudes can include up to three components: cognitive, emotional, and behavioral.

> *EXAMPLE: Jane believes that smoking is unhealthy, feels disgusted when people smoke around her, and avoids being in situations where people smoke.*

DIMENSIONS OF ATTITUDES

Researchers study three dimensions of attitude: strength, accessibility, and ambivalence.

- **Attitude strength:** Strong attitudes are those that are firmly held and that highly influence behavior. Attitudes that are important to a person tend to be strong. Attitudes that people have a vested interest in also tend to be strong. Furthermore, people tend to have stronger attitudes about things, events, ideas, or people they have considerable knowledge and information about.

- **Attitude accessibility:** The accessibility of an attitude refers to the ease with which it comes to mind. In general, highly accessible attitudes tend to be stronger.

- **Attitude ambivalence:** Ambivalence of an attitude refers to the ratio of positive and negative evaluations that make up that attitude. The ambivalence of an attitude increases as the positive and negative evaluations get more and more equal.

THE INFLUENCE OF ATTITUDES ON BEHAVIOR

Behavior does not always reflect attitudes. However, attitudes do determine behavior in some situations:

- If there are few outside influences, attitude guides behavior.

    EXAMPLE: Wyatt has an attitude that eating junk food is unhealthy. When he is at home, he does not eat chips or candy. However, when he is at parties, he indulges in these foods.

- Behavior is guided by attitudes specific to that behavior.

    EXAMPLE: Megan might have a general attitude of respect toward seniors, but that would not prevent her from being disrespectful to an elderly woman who cuts her off at a stop sign. However, if Megan has an easygoing attitude about being cut off at stop signs, she is not likely to swear at someone who cuts her off.

- Behavior is guided by attitudes that come to mind easily.

    EXAMPLE: Ron has an attitude of mistrust and annoyance toward telemarketers, so he immediately hangs up the phone whenever he realizes he has been contacted by one.

THE INFLUENCE OF BEHAVIOR ON ATTITUDES

Behavior also affects attitudes. Evidence for this comes from the foot-in-the-door phenomenon and the effect of role playing.

The Foot-in-the-Door Phenomenon

People tend to be more likely to agree to a difficult request if they have first agreed to an easy one. This is called the **foot-in-the-door phenomenon**.

> EXAMPLE: *Jill is more likely to let an acquaintance borrow her laptop for a day if he first persuades her to let him borrow her textbook for a day.*

Social Norms and Social Roles

Social norms are a society's rules about appropriate behavior. Norms exist for practically every kind of situation. Some norms are explicit and are made into laws, such as the norm While driving, you may not run over a pedestrian. Other norms are implicit and are followed unconsciously, such as You may not wear a bikini to class.

Social roles are patterns of behavior that are considered appropriate for a person in a particular context. For example, gender roles tell people how a particular society expects men and women to behave. A person who violates the requirements of a role tends to feel uneasy or to be censured by others. Role requirements can change over time in a society.

The Effect of Role Playing and the "Prison Study"

People tend to internalize roles they play, changing their attitudes to fit the roles. In the 1970s, the psychologist Philip Zimbardo conducted a famous study called the **prison study**, which showed how roles influence people. Zimbardo assigned one group of college student volunteers to play the role of prison guards in a simulated prison environment. He provided these students with uniforms, clubs, and whistles and told them to enforce a set of rules in the prison. He assigned another group of students to play the role of prisoners. Zimbardo found that as time went on, some of the "guard" students became increasingly harsh and domineering. The "prisoner" students also internalized their role. Some broke down, while others rebelled or became passively resigned to the situation. The internalization of roles by the two groups of students was so extreme that Zimbardo had to terminate the study after only six days.

ATTITUDE CHANGE

Researchers have proposed three theories to account for attitude change: learning theory, dissonance theory, and the elaboration likelihood model.

Learning Theory

Learning theory says that attitudes can be formed and changed through the use of learning principles such as classical conditioning, operant conditioning, and observational learning:

- **Classical conditioning:** The emotional component of attitudes can be formed through classical conditioning. For example, in a billboard ad, a clothing company pairs a sweater with an attractive model who elicits a pleasant emotional response. This can make people form a positive attitude about the sweater and the clothing company.

- **Operant conditioning:** If someone gets a positive response from others when she expresses an attitude, that attitude will be reinforced and will tend to get stronger. On the other hand, if she gets a negative response from others, that attitude tends to get weaker.

- **Observational learning:** Seeing others display a particular attitude and watching people be reinforced for expressing a particular attitude can make someone adopt those attitudes.

Dissonance Theory

Leon Festinger's dissonance theory proposes that people change their attitudes when they have attitudes that are inconsistent with each other. Festinger said that people experience **cognitive dissonance** when they have related cognitions that conflict with one another. Cognitive dissonance results in a state of unpleasant tension. People try to reduce the tension by changing their attitudes.

> EXAMPLE: *Sydney is against capital punishment. She participates in a debate competition and is assigned to a team that has to argue for capital punishment. Subsequently, she is more amenable to the idea of capital punishment.*

SOCIAL PSYCHOLOGY

CHAPTER 17

The phenomenon called justification of effort also results from cognitive dissonance. **Justification of effort** refers to the idea that if people work hard to reach a goal, they are likely to value the goal more. They justify working hard by believing that the goal is valuable.

The Elaboration Likelihood Model

The elaboration likelihood model holds that attitude change is more permanent if the elaborate and thought-provoking persuasive messages are used to change the attitude. Basically, if someone can provide a thorough, thought-provoking persuasive message to change an attitude, he is more likely to succeed than if he provides a neutral or shallow persuasive message.

> EXAMPLE: *Ten teenagers who smoke are sent to an all-day seminar on the negative consequences of smoking. Many of the students subsequently give up the habit.*

Social Influence

People influence each other constantly, in a variety of different ways.

SOCIAL INFLUENCE STRATEGIES

One social influence strategy is the foot-in-the-door technique (see the "Attitudes" section for a complete explanation). Three other strategies include manipulating the reciprocity norm, the lowball technique, and feigned scarcity.

Manipulation of the Reciprocity Norm

The **reciprocity norm** is an implicit rule in many societies that tells people they should return favors or gifts given to them. A person or group can manipulate this norm to make it more likely that people will buy a product or make a donation.

> EXAMPLE: *If a wildlife preservation organization sends Harry a pad of notepaper personalized with his name, he may feel obligated to send them the donation they want.*

The Lowball Technique

The **lowball technique** involves making an attractive proposition and revealing its downsides only after a person has agreed to it.

> EXAMPLE: *A car salesperson tells Sheila that a car she is interested in buying costs $5,000. After she has committed to buying the car, the salesperson points out that adding a stereo, an air conditioner, and floor mats will cost an extra $3,000.*

Feigned Scarcity

Researchers have found that when something is hard to get, people want it more. This observation is often manipulated by groups and people who want to sell something. They imply that a product is in scarce supply, even when it is not, in order to increase demand for it.

> EXAMPLE: *A grocery store advertises a brand of yogurt for a reduced price, noting in the ad that there is a limited supply.*

ELEMENTS OF PERSUASION

People often try to change others' attitudes through persuasion. There are four elements involved in persuasion: the source, the receiver, the message, and the channel.

The Source

The person who sends a communication is called the source. Persuasion is most successful when a source is both likable and credible. Credible sources are those that are trustworthy or that have expertise.

An expert source is particularly likely to increase persuasion when a communication is ambiguous.

Sources are considered less trustworthy if they seem to have a vested interest in persuading people. On the other hand, sources seem more trustworthy if they provide counterarguments for their position.

The Message

A message is the content of a piece of communication. Some messages are more persuasive than others:

- Messages that provide both arguments and counterarguments for a position are more persuasive than one-sided messages.

- Messages that arouse fear are likely to be persuasive if people think that rejecting the message will bring about a highly undesirable consequence and that accepting the message will prevent a highly undesirable consequence.

The Receiver

The target of a persuasive message is called a receiver. Certain factors influence the persuasiveness of a message for receivers:

- If receivers are forewarned about a message, they are less likely to be persuaded by it.

- Receivers are more likely to be persuaded by messages that are compatible with their own existing attitudes.

- Receivers are less likely to be persuaded by messages that try to alter a strongly held attitude.

The Channel

The channel is the medium used to send the message. Newspapers, television, the Internet, radio, movies, direct mail, word of mouth, magazines, and billboard advertisements are just a few of the different media through which people might encounter a persuasive message. The medium can influence the persuasiveness of the message.

> *EXAMPLE: An article in a newspaper about the dangers of a popular herbal supplement may be more persuasive than a website devoted to the same topic.*

MEANS OF PERSUASION

Some effective means of persuading people include:

- Repetition of the message
- Endorsement of the message by an admired or attractive individual
- Association of the message with a pleasant feeling

Coercive Persuasion Persuasion is coercive when it limits people's freedom to make choices that are in their best interest and prevents them from reasoning clearly. Cults use coercive techniques to persuade their members to adopt ideas and practices. Coercive persuasion often involves practices such as placing people in emotionally or physically stressful situations, telling people their problems all stem from one cause, having a leader who is expected to be adored and obeyed, encouraging people to identify strongly with a new group, entrapping people so that they have to increase their participation in the group, and controlling people's access to outside information.

Attraction

Interpersonal attraction refers to positive feelings about another person. It can take many forms, including liking, love, friendship, lust, and admiration.

INFLUENCES

Many factors influence whom people are attracted to. They include physical attractiveness, proximity, similarity, and reciprocity:

- **Physical attractiveness:** Research shows that romantic attraction is primarily determined by physical attractiveness. In the early stages of dating, people are more attracted to partners whom they consider to be physically attractive. Men are more likely to value physical attractiveness than are women.

  People's perception of their own physical attractiveness also plays a role in romantic love. The **matching hypothesis** proposes that people tend to pick partners who are about equal in level of attractiveness to themselves.

- **Proximity:** People are more likely to become friends with people who are geographically close. One explanation for this is the mere exposure effect. The **mere exposure effect** refers to people's tendency to like novel stimuli more if they encounter them repeatedly.

- **Similarity:** People also tend to pick partners who are similar to themselves in characteristics such as age, race, religion, social class, personality, education, intelligence, and attitude.

  This similarity is seen not only between romantic partners but also between friends. Some researchers have suggested that similarity causes attraction. Others acknowledge that people may be more likely to have friends and partners who are similar to themselves simply because of accessibility: people are more likely to associate with people who are similar to themselves.

- **Reciprocity:** People tend to like others who reciprocate their liking.

ROMANTIC LOVE

Many researchers focus on one particular form of attraction: romantic love.

Kinds of Romantic Love

Researchers have proposed that romantic love includes two kinds of love: passionate love and compassionate love. These two kinds of love may occur together, but they do not always go hand in hand in a relationship:

- **Passionate love:** Involves absorption in another person, sexual desire, tenderness, and intense emotion.

- **Compassionate love:** Involves warmth, trust, and tolerance of another person. Compassionate love is sometimes considered to have two components: intimacy and commitment. **Intimacy** is the warm, close, sharing aspect of a relationship. **Commitment** is the intent to continue the relationship even in the face of difficulties. Researchers believe commitment is a good predictor of the stability of a relationship.

Attachment Styles

Some researchers study the influence of childhood attachment styles on adult relationships. Many researchers believe that as adults, people relate to their partners in the same way that they related to their caretakers in infancy. (See Chapter 4 for more information on attachment styles.)

Cultural Similarities and Differences

There are both similarities and differences among cultures in romantic attraction. Researchers have found that people in many different cultures place a high value on mutual attraction between partners and the kindness, intelligence, emotional stability, dependability, and good health of partners.

However, people in different cultures place a different value on romantic love within a marriage. People in individualistic cultures often believe romantic love is a prerequisite for marriage. In many collectivist cultures, people often consider it acceptable for family members or third parties to arrange marriages.

Evolutionary Perspectives

Evolutionary psychologists speculate that the tendency to be attracted to physically attractive people is adaptive. Many cultures value particular aspects of physical attractiveness, such as facial symmetry and a small waist-to-hip ratio. Evolutionary psychologists point out that facial symmetry can be an indicator of good health, since many developmental abnormalities tend to produce facial asymmetries. A small waist-to-hip ratio, which produces an "hourglass" figure, indicates high reproductive potential.

As predicted by the parental investment theory described in Chapters 2 and 12, men tend to be more interested in their partners' youthfulness and physical attractiveness. Evolutionary psychologists think that this is because these characteristics indicate that women will be able to reproduce successfully. Women, on the other hand, tend to value partners' social status, wealth, and ambition, because these are characteristics of men who can successfully provide for offspring.

Obedience and Authority

Obedience is compliance with commands given by an authority figure. In the 1960s, the social psychologist **Stanley Milgram** did a famous research study called the obedience study. It showed that people have a strong tendency to comply with authority figures.

MILGRAM'S OBEDIENCE STUDY

Milgram told his forty male volunteer research subjects that they were participating in a study about the effects of punishment on learning. He assigned each of the subjects to the role of teacher. Each subject was told that his task was to help another subject like himself learn a list of word pairs. Each time the learner made a mistake, the teacher was to give the learner an electric shock by flipping a switch. The teacher was told to increase the shock level each time the learner made a mistake, until a dangerous shock level was reached.

Throughout the course of the experiment, the experimenter firmly commanded the teachers to follow the instructions they had been given. In reality, the learner was not an experiment subject but Milgram's accomplice, and he never actually received an electric shock. However, he pretended to be in pain when shocks were administered.

Prior to the study, forty psychiatrists that Milgram consulted told him that fewer than 1 percent of subjects would administer what they thought were dangerous shocks to the learner. However, Milgram found that two-thirds of the teachers did administer even the highest level of shock, despite believing that the learner was suffering great pain and distress. Milgram believed that the teachers had acted in this way because they were pressured to do so by an authority figure.

FACTORS THAT INCREASE OBEDIENCE

Milgram found that subjects were more likely to obey in some circumstances than others. Obedience was highest when:

- Commands were given by an authority figure rather than another volunteer

- The experiments were done at a prestigious institution

- The authority figure was present in the room with the subject

- The learner was in another room

- The subject did not see other subjects disobeying commands

In everyday situations, people obey orders because they want to get rewards, because they want to avoid the negative consequences of disobeying, and because they believe an authority is legitimate. In more extreme situations, people obey even when they are required to violate their own values or commit crimes. Researchers think several factors cause people to carry obedience to extremes:

- People justify their behavior by assigning responsibility to the authority rather than themselves.

- People define the behavior that's expected of them as routine.

- People don't want to be rude or offend the authority.

- People obey easy commands first and then feel compelled to obey more and more difficult commands. This process is called entrapment, and it illustrates the foot-in-the-door phenomenon.

Groups

Social psychologists consider a **group** to be composed of two or more people who interact and depend on each other in some way. Examples of groups include a baseball team, an Internet listserv, a college psychology class, and a cult.

FEATURES OF GROUPS

Groups usually have the following features:

- Norms that determine appropriate behavior
- Roles that are assigned to people that determine what behaviors and responsibilities people should take on
- A communication structure that determines who talks to whom within the group
- A power structure that determines how much authority and influence group members have

> EXAMPLE: *A college psychology class has norms, such as when people should arrive for class. The professor's role includes teaching, inviting discussion, and administering exams. The students' role is to attend class, listen to lectures, read materials, and pose questions. The communication structure of the class demands that students listen without talking to each other while the professor lectures. The power structure gives the professor more authority than any of the students. Some students also may have more authority and influence than other students, such as those who are more familiar with the class material.*

CONFORMITY

Conformity is the process of giving in to real or imagined pressure from a group. In the 1950s, the psychologist **Solomon Asch** did a famous study that demonstrated that people often conform.

Asch's Conformity Study

Asch recruited male undergraduate subjects for the study and told them that he was doing research on visual perception. He placed each subject in a room with six accomplices. The subject thought that the six were also subjects. The seven people were then given a series of easy tasks. In each task, they looked at two cards, one with a single line on it and the other with three lines of different lengths. The people were asked to decide which line on the second card was the same length as the line on the first card. On the first two tasks, the accomplices announced the correct answer to the group, as did the subject. On the next twelve tasks, the accomplices picked a line on the second card that was clearly a wrong answer. When put in this situation, more than one-third of the subjects conformed to the choices made by their group.

Factors that Influence Conformity

Asch and other researchers have found that many factors influence conformity:

- **Group size:** Asch found that group size influenced whether subjects conformed. The bigger the group, the more people conformed, up to a certain point. After group size reached a certain limit, conformity didn't increase any further.

- **Group unanimity:** Asch also found that subjects were much more likely to conform when a group agreed unanimously. If even one other person in the group disagreed with the group, a subject was much less likely to conform. This was true even when the other dissenter disagreed with the subject as well as the group.

Researchers have found that conformity also increases when:

- A person feels incompetent or insecure
- The person admires the group

- The group can see how the person behaves

Reasons for Conforming

People have many reasons for conforming:

- They want to be accepted by the group, or they fear rejection by the group. In this case, the group is exerting **normative social influence**.

- The group provides them with information. In this case, the group is exerting **informational social influence**.

- They want a material or social reward, such as a pay raise or votes.

- They admire the group and want to be like other group members.

PRODUCTIVITY IN GROUPS

Research shows that productivity tends to decline when a group of people are working on a task together. This happens for two reasons: insufficient coordination and social loafing.

Insufficient Coordination

When many people work on a task, their efforts may not be sufficiently coordinated. Several people may end up doing the same portion of the task, and some portions of the task may be neglected.

Social Loafing

Social loafing, which contributes to declines in the productivity of a group, is the reduced effort people invest in a task when they are working with other people. **Diffusion of responsibility** contributes to social loafing. A person does not feel as responsible for working on a task if several others are also present, since responsibility is distributed among all those present.

Social loafing is particularly likely to happen in the following circumstances:

- When the group is large
- When it is difficult to evaluate individual contributions to a task
- When people expect their coworkers to pick up the slack

Social Facilitation

In some circumstances, individuals perform better when other people are present. This phenomenon is called **social facilitation**. Social facilitation is more likely to occur on easy tasks. On difficult tasks, people are likely to perform worse in the presence of others.

GROUP DECISION-MAKING

Members of a group are often required to make decisions together. Three concepts related to group decision-making are groupthink, group polarization, and minority influence.

Groupthink

Groupthink is the tendency for a close-knit group to emphasize consensus at the expense of critical thinking and rational decision-making. In a groupthink situation, group members squash dissent, exert pressure to conform, suppress information from outside the group, and focus selectively on information that agrees with the group's point of view.

Groupthink is more likely to occur when groups have certain characteristics:

- High cohesiveness. **Group cohesiveness** is the strength of the liking and commitment group members have toward each other and to the group.
- Isolation from outside influences
- A strong leader
- The intent to reach a major decision

Group Polarization

The dominant point of view in a group often tends to be strengthened to a more extreme position after a group discussion, a phenomenon called **group polarization**. When a group starts out with a dominant view that is relatively risky, the group is likely to come to a consensus that is even riskier. This phenomenon is called **risky shift**.

Minority Influence

A committed minority viewpoint can change the majority opinion in a group. Group members are more likely to be influenced by a minority opinion when the minority holds the opinion firmly.

> Deindividuation *When people are in a large group that makes them feel aroused and anonymous, they may experience **deindividuation**. When people become deindividuated, they lose their inhibitions and their sense of responsibility and are not self-conscious about their behavior. Deindividuation is a major reason for the violence that sometimes happens in mobs.*

Helping Behavior

Social psychologists study the circumstances in which people offer help to others.

THE BYSTANDER EFFECT

Research shows that people are less likely to offer help to someone in distress if other people are also present. This is called the **bystander effect**. The probability that a person will receive help decreases as the number of people present increases.

Diffusion of responsibility contributes to the bystander effect. A person does not feel as responsible for helping someone if several others are also present, since responsibility is distributed among all those present.

INFLUENCES ON HELPING

Researchers have proposed that bystanders who witness an emergency will help only if three conditions are met:

- They notice the incident.
- They interpret the incident as being an emergency situation.
- They assume responsibility for helping.

Researchers suggest that people are most likely to help others in certain circumstances:

- They have just seen others offering help.
- They are not in a hurry.
- They share some similarities with the person needing help.
- They are in a small town or a rural setting.
- They feel guilty.
- They are not preoccupied or focused on themselves.
- They are happy.
- The person needing help appears deserving of help.

REASONS FOR HELPING OTHERS

Some social psychologists use the **social exchange theory** to explain why people help others. They argue that people help each other because they want to gain as much as possible while losing as little as possible. The social responsibility norm also explains helping behavior. The **social responsibility norm** is a societal rule that tells people they should help others who need help even if doing so is costly.

Another norm that explains helping behavior is the **reciprocity norm,** which is the implicit societal rule that says people must help those who have helped them.

Social Traps When people act in their own interest, they can sometimes help others as well. However, in other circumstances, people can harm themselves and others by acting in their own self-interest. This sort of situation is called a **social trap.** Global warming is an example of a social trap: it is occurring because people act in their own self-interest when they buy fuel-inefficient cars.

Summary

Impressions

- People form impressions about others through the process of **person perception**.
- People's physical appearance strongly influences the way they are perceived by others.
- People are particularly influenced by **physical attractiveness** and **baby-faced features**.
- **Social schemas** affect how people perceive events and other people.

Stereotypes and Prejudice

- **Stereotypes** are beliefs about people based on their membership in a particular group.
- Stereotypes tend to be difficult to change.
- Stereotyping has some important functions, but it can also distort reality in dangerous ways.
- Evolutionary psychologists believe that people evolved the tendency to stereotype because it gave their ancestors an adaptive advantage.
- A **prejudice** is a negative belief or feeling about a particular group of individuals.
- Prejudice is pervasive because it serves many social and psychological functions.
- Researchers find it difficult to measure prejudice. They often measure **implicit** rather than **explicit prejudice**.
- People who identify strongly with their **ingroup** are more likely to be prejudiced against people in **outgroups**.
- Research shows that there are effective ways to reduce prejudice.

Attribution

- **Attributions** are inferences people make about the causes of events and behavior.
- Attributions can be classified along two dimensions: **internal vs. external** and **stable vs. unstable**.
- People often make incorrect attributions because of the **fundamental attribution error**, the **self-serving bias**, and the **just world hypothesis**.
- Cultural values and norms affect the way people make attributions.

Attitudes

- **Attitudes** are evaluations people make about objects, ideas, events, or other people. They can be **explicit** or **implicit** and can include beliefs, emotions, and behavior.
- Attitudes vary according to **strength, accessibility,** and **ambivalence.**
- Attitudes do not always affect behavior.
- The **foot-in-the-door phenomenon** and the **prison study** show that behavior can affect attitudes.
- Theories that account for attitude change are **learning theory, dissonance theory,** and the **elaboration likelihood model.**

Social Influence

- Some common social influence strategies are the **foot-in-the-door technique,** the **lowball technique, manipulation of the reciprocity norm,** and **feigning scarcity.**
- Persuasion involves a **source,** a **receiver,** a **message,** and a **channel.**
- Credible, likable sources are more likely to be persuasive.
- Many features of the source, receiver, and message influence persuasion.
- **Coercive persuasion** involves limiting freedom to choose and preventing clear reasoning.

Attraction

- **Interpersonal attraction** refers to positive feelings about another person.
- **Physical attractiveness, proximity, similarity,** and **reciprocity** influence attraction.
- **Romantic love** includes **passionate** and **compassionate love.**
- **Compassionate love** includes **intimacy** and **commitment.**
- Infant attachment styles tend to be reproduced in adult relationships.
- There are both similarities and differences among cultures in romantic attraction.
- Evolutionary psychologists speculate that the tendency to be attracted to physically attractive people is adaptive.

Obedience and Authority

- **Obedience** is compliance with commands given by an authority figure.
- **Stanley Milgram**'s obedience study showed that people have a strong tendency to comply with authority figures.
- The degree of obedience depends on many situational factors.
- People sometimes carry obedience to extremes.

Groups

- A **group** is a social unit composed of two or more people who interact and depend on each other in some way.
- Groups tend to have **distinct norms, roles, communication structures,** and **power structures**.
- **Conformity** is the process of giving in to real or imagined pressure from a group.
- **Solomon Asch** did a famous study that showed that people often conform and that social roles influence behavior.
- Factors that influence conformity include **group size and unanimity, level of competence, liking for the group,** and **group observation of the behavior**.
- People conform because of **normative social influence,** because of **informational social influence,** because **they want to gain rewards,** and because **they identify with the group**.
- **Insufficient coordination** and **social loafing** contribute to lowered productivity in groups.
- **Social facilitation** may occur in some group situations.
- **Groupthink, group polarization,** and **minority influence** affect decision-making in groups.
- **Deindividuation** sometimes occurs in large, anonymous, arousing groups.

Helping Behavior

- People are less likely to offer help in the presence of other people.
- Bystanders are more likely to help people in some circumstances than others.
- Explanations for helping behavior include **social exchange theory,** the **social responsibility norm,** and the **reciprocity norm**.
- A **social trap** is a situation in which acting in one's own self-interest can harm both the actor and others.

Sample Test Questions

1. Suppose Jessica severely sprains her ankle after stumbling off a curb and has trouble walking. Would a social psychologist expect her to be more likely to get help on a street in New York City or on a small side street in rural Wyoming? Why?

2. Why do researchers find prejudice hard to measure?

3. What are the differences in attribution style between individualist and collectivist cultures?

4. What is Philip Zimbardo's prison study, and what did it demonstrate?

5. In Stanley Milgram's obedience study, what circumstances resulted in the highest levels of obedience?

6. When is a person less likely to conform?
   A.   When the group is unanimous
   B.   When the person feels incompetent
   C.   When the group cannot see how the person behaves
   D.   When the person admires the group

7. People are likely to invest less effort in a task when they are working with others. What is this phenomenon called?
   A.   Social facilitation
   B.   Social loafing
   C.   Deindividuation
   D.   The bystander effect

8. What is group polarization?
   A.   The tendency for a dominant point of view in a group to be strengthened to a more extreme position after a group discussion
   B.   The strength of the liking and commitment group members have toward each other and to a group
   C.   The tendency of a close-knit group to emphasize consensus at the expense of critical thinking and rational decision making
   D.   A situation in which one harms oneself and others by acting in one's self-interest

9. Research shows that romantic attraction is determined primarily by which characteristic?
   A.   Partners' personality
   B.   Partners' commitment
   C.   Partners' intimacy
   D.   Partners' physical attractiveness

10. *Attraction is influenced by which of the following?*
    A. Whether people live or work in the same neighborhood
    B. How similar people are to each other
    C. Whether liking is reciprocated
    D. All of the above

11. *When are people more likely to be persuaded by a message?*
    A. If they are forewarned about the message
    B. If they like the person sending the message
    C. If they think the person sending the message has a vested interest in the point of view expressed in the message
    D. All of the above

12. *Suppose Suzie persuades her roommate to make her a cup of tea, then gets her roommate to cook for a week. What is this strategy called?*
    A. The lowball technique
    B. Social facilitation
    C. The foot-in-the-door technique
    D. Social loafing

13. *If people work hard to reach a goal, they are likely to justify their hard work by valuing the goal highly. What is this tendency called?*
    A. Justification of effort
    B. Cognitive dissonance
    C. Risky shift
    D. Diffusion of responsibility

14. *Justin sees his psychology professor arguing angrily with a worker at the local post office. From this, he assumes that his professor is a hostile person. What does his assumption illustrate?*
    A. The just world hypothesis
    B. The fundamental attribution error
    C. The matching hypothesis
    D. The bystander effect

15. *Which of the following statements is true?*
    A. Baby-faced people tend to be relatively passive
    B. Physically attractive people tend to have more pleasing personalities
    C. Physically attractive people tend to have better career prospects
    D. People tend to judge physically attractive people as being lazy

CHAPTER 17 SOCIAL PSYCHOLOGY

ANSWERS

1.   Social psychology research suggests that Jessica is more likely to get help in rural Wyoming because of the bystander effect. People are less likely to offer help to someone who needs it if other people are also present, and the probability that a person will receive help decreases as the number of people present increases. A person does not feel as responsible for helping someone if several others are also present, since responsibility is distributed among all those present.

2.   People differ in the type and extent of prejudice they harbor. Also, people often do not admit to being prejudiced.

3.   People in collectivist cultures tend to be less susceptible to the fundamental attribution error than people in individualist cultures. People from collectivist cultures are more likely to believe that a person's behavior is due to situational demands rather than to personal attributes. Finally, people from collectivist cultures are also less susceptible to the self-serving bias.

4.   The prison study showed how people are influenced by roles. Zimbardo assigned one group of college student volunteers to play the role of prison guards in a simulated prison environment. He provided these students with uniforms, clubs, and whistles and told them to enforce a set of rules in the prison. He assigned another group of students to play the role of prisoners. Zimbardo found that as time went on, some of the "guard" students became increasingly harsh and domineering, while the "prisoner" students also internalized their role: some broke down and others rebelled or became passively resigned to the situation.

5.   In Milgram's obedience study, the highest levels of obedience occurred in the following circumstances: A. When commands were given by an authority figure rather than another volunteer. B. When experiments were done at a prestigious institution. C. When the authority figure was present in the room with the subject. D. When the learner was in another room. E. When the subject did not see other subjects disobeying commands.

6. C	11. B
7. B	12. C
8. A	13. A
9. D	14. B
10. D	15. C

Major Figures

Note from SparkNotes: Not all of the people mentioned in the text are listed here. We've narrowed the list to include only those figures you're most likely to be tested on.

Adler, Alfred (1870–1937) An Austrian psychiatrist and one of Freud's close associates. Adler broke away from Freud because of theoretical disagreements. He believed that social motives, rather than sexual drives, motivated people the most. He formed his own school of thought, which he called individual psychology. In Adler's view, strivings for superiority drive people's behavior. He thought mental disorders were characterized by extreme feelings of inferiority and a desire for superiority over others.

Asch, Solomon (1907–1996) A psychologist who investigated social conformity by studying how people reacted when their perceptions of events were challenged by others. Asch found that most individuals changed their own opinions in order to agree with the group, even when the majority was clearly wrong.

Atkinson, Richard (1938–) and **Richard Shiffrin** (1936–) Two influential memory researchers who developed a three-stage model of memory storage.

Bandura, Albert (1925–) A researcher who focused on observational learning, or modeling. Bandura showed that children learn behavior by watching others. He did a famous study involving Bobo dolls that demonstrated that children don't need punishment or reward to learn.

Beck, Aaron (1921–) A developer of cognitive therapy, which is now used for disorders ranging from depression to panic attacks, addictions, and eating disorders. Beck initially received psychoanalytic training but became disenchanted with the approach of psychoanalysis. His cognitive approach to therapy emphasizes using rational thoughts to overcome fears rather than trying to uncover the unconscious meaning of those fears. In addition to writing several books, Beck has developed a questionnaire called the Beck Depression Inventory for assessing depression.

Binet, Alfred (1857–1911) A developer of the Binet-Simon scale, along with his colleague **Theodore Simon**. Binet intended the test to predict school performance. He did not believe that it measured innate intelligence.

Cannon, Walter (1871–1945) The psychologist who, along with colleague Philip Bard (1898–1977), developed the Cannon-Bard theory of emotion, which holds that physical and emotional stimuli happen simultaneously, with no causal relationship.

Chomsky, Noam (1928–) A linguist and Massachusetts Institute of Technology professor who revolutionized ideas about language. Chomsky performed research that led to the decline of behaviorist theories about language acquisition and encouraged researchers to study the biological bases of behavior. He proposed that humans are born with an innate language acquisition device that allows them to acquire language skills easily.

Darwin, Charles (1809–1882) A British naturalist best known for his contributions to evolutionary theory. Darwin outlined his theory of natural selection in his influential book *On the Origin of Species*. His ideas shaped the course of evolutionary studies, including evolutionary psychology.

Ebbinghaus, Hermann (1850–1909) A philosopher, psychologist, and author of *On Memory*. Ebbinghaus began conducting research on memory in 1878. His work challenged the view that higher mental processes such as memory couldn't be studied scientifically.

Ekman, Paul (1934–) An expert in emotional research and nonverbal communication. Ekman is particularly well-known for his studies of emotional expression and the physiology of the face.

Ellis, Albert (1913–) An American psychologist who developed a form of cognitive-behavioral therapy known as rational-emotive therapy. Ellis was trained as a psychoanalyst but found the psychoanalytic approach too limiting. His rational-emotive therapy is based on the idea that self-defeating thoughts cause psychological problems.

Erikson, Erik (1902–1994) A key contributor to the study of development across the life span. Erikson proposed a theory that people go through eight distinct stages of development. Erikson published his most influential book, *Childhood and Society*, in 1950, and his book *Gandhi's Truth*, published in 1969, won both the Pulitzer Prize and the National Book Award.

Eysenck, Hans (1916–1997) A psychologist whose research focused on the genetic foundations of personality. Eysenck believed that conditioning was important in personality formation but that personality grew largely out of genetic differences.

Festinger, Leon (1919–1989) An influential psychologist who developed the theory of cognitive dissonance. Festinger's research examined the efforts people made in order to view their attitudes, beliefs, and behaviors as consistent.

Freud, Sigmund (1856–1939) An Austrian neurologist and pioneer in the field of psychoanalysis. Freud's comprehensive theory of psychoanalysis sought to explain the structure of the human mind, human attitudes and behavior, mental disorders, and the origins of civilization. Freud's ideas, particularly his emphasis on sexuality, were highly controversial in the repressive Victorian era in which he lived. He published a revolutionary book called *The Interpretation of Dreams* in 1900 and a more concise version of his theories called *On Dreams* in 1903. His ideas have had an enormous influence on Western thought, but they continue to be controversial today.

Galton, Sir Francis (1822–1911) A British scholar who advocated eugenics, the study of human improvement through selective breeding. Galton was interested in the idea that intelligence is inherited. He believed that intelligence is related to sensory ability and attempted to assess intelligence by measuring sensory abilities such as sensitivity to sound, color perception, and reaction time. Although he failed to correlate intelligence with these sensory abilities, his work paved the way for subsequent research on assessing mental abilities.

Gardner, Howard (1943–) A developmental psychologist whose research focuses on creativity in adults and children. Gardner proposed a theory of multiple intelligences, which has been highly influential among educators.

Helmholtz, Hermann von (1821–1894) The inventor of the ophthalmoscope, an instrument for examining the eye. Von Helmholtz lent further support to Young's theories of color. He also developed a sophisticated theory of harmony.

Hering, Ewald (1834–1918) The developer of the opponent process theory of color vision, which accounted for some phenomena not explained by the Young-Helmholtz theory.

Hilgard, Ernest (1904–2001) A psychologist who became famous in the 1950s for his research on hypnosis. Hilgard was president of the International Society of Hypnosis in the 1970s. During that time, he studied the use of hypnosis in the treatment of children suffering from cancer.

Hodgkin, Sir Alan (1914–1998) and **Sir Andrew Fielding Huxley** (1917–) Recipients of the Nobel Prize in Physiology or Medicine in 1963 for their work on information transmission in neurons. Hodgkin and Huxley studied giant squid, whose neurons have giant axons.

Hubel, David (1926–) and **Torsten Wiesel** (1924–) Two Harvard University researchers who received the Nobel Prize in Physiology or Medicine for their discoveries about information processing in the visual system. By recording impulses from individual brain cells of cats and monkeys, Hubel and Wiesel demonstrated that specialized cells in the mammalian brain respond to complex visual features of the environment.

James, William (1842–1910) An American philosopher and psychologist. James believed that the experience of emotion arises from bodily expression. For example, according to his view, people are sad because they cry. Another researcher, **Carl Lange** (1834–1900), independently proposed the same theory of emotion. The James-Lange theory was published in 1884, and James's landmark book, *The Principles of Psychology*, was published in 1890. He also wrote two other important books, *The Varieties of Religious Experience* and *Pragmatism*.

Jung, Carl (1875–1961) A Swiss psychologist and psychiatrist who was a friend and follower of Freud. Jung broke away from Freud in the early 1910s because of a bitter theoretical disagreement and began his own school of thought, which he called analytical psychology. Jung believed that Freud placed too much emphasis on the sexual drive of humans. He thought the will to live was a stronger motivation than sexual drive. Jung also disagreed with Freud about the nature of the unconscious mind. He thought that in addition to the personal unconscious, there is a collective unconscious that contains universal human memories.

Kinsey, Alfred (1894–1956) A leading sex researcher. Kinsey, a biologist, shocked the American public by publishing *Sexual Behavior in the Human Male* (1948), a best-selling summary of his research into sexual behavior. He next published *Sexual Behavior in the Human Female* (1953).

Kohlberg, Lawrence (1927–1987) A major figure in moral psychology and moral education. Kohlberg had a passionate commitment to building a just society, and this commitment fueled his research. He drew on philosophy and sociology as well as psychology to argue that people go through sequential stages of moral judgment.

Lazarus, Richard (1922-2002) The psychologist whose theory of emotion centered on the concept of appraisal, or how a person evaluates the personal impact of an event. Lazarus conducted several studies on the link between emotion and cognition.

Lewin, Kurt (1890-1947) The founder of the field of social psychology. Lewin launched the Research Center for Group Dynamics at the Massachusetts Institute of Technology in 1946. He studied interaction among races in particular and is famous for the development of "field theory," which holds that human behavior is determined both by the person and the environment.

Loftus, Elizabeth (1944-) A memory researcher renowned for establishing how the misinformation effect might affect the criminal justice system.

Marcia, James (1937-) The psychologist who described four identity states, based on where people stand on the path to identity. The four states are identity foreclosure, identity moratorium, identity diffusion, and identity achievment.

Maslow, Abraham (1908-1970) A leader in the field of humanistic psychology. Maslow believed that human beings' needs are arranged like a ladder. He said that basic needs such as the needs for oxygen, food, and water are at the bottom of this ladder, while higher needs such as the need to achieve one's full potential are at the top of the ladder. Maslow thought people paid attention to higher needs only when their lower needs were satisfied.

Masters, William (1915-2001), and **Virginia Johnson** (1925-) Researchers whose work changed people's perceptions of human sexuality. Physician Masters and psychologist Johnson based their book *The Human Sexual Response* on an eleven-year project that investigated human sexuality. In Masters and Johnson's laboratory studies, research subjects wore instruments that monitored their physiological signs while they engaged in sexual activities.

Melzack, Ronald (1929-) and **Patrick Wall** (1925-2001) The developers of the gate-control theory of pain, which states that perception of pain is related to past experience of pain. Melzack and Wall's theory led to the discovery of endorphins and other natural painkillers produced by the body.

Milgram, Stanley (1933–1984) The conductor of a famous, controversial research study of obedience to authority. Milgram found that his experiment subjects were often so obedient to an authority figure that they were willing to cause serious harm and suffering to others. In order to do his experiment, Milgram had to deceive his subjects. Many people objected to his use of deception and questioned the ethics of his research because he made subjects believe that they were inflicting pain on other people.

Mischel, Walter (1930–) A social-cognitive theorist whose research focuses on personality formation. Mischel's work has called into question the idea of stable personality traits.

Pavlov, Ivan (1849–1936) A doctor best known for his research on the conditioned reflex. Pavlov made his most famous discovery while studying how dog saliva related to the function of the stomach. He found that when he repeatedly gave a dog food after ringing a bell, the dog began to salivate for false alarms too. The bell rang, and the dog salivated, even with no food in sight. Pavlov won a Nobel Prize for his work in 1904.

Piaget, Jean (1896–1980) A pioneer in the field of child psychology. Piaget argued that children develop their thinking capacity in stages and that the progression through these stages depends on a genetically determined timetable. His research changed the way people viewed education, showing that children actively explore the world and develop their own hypotheses about what they observe. In 1923, he published *The Language and Thought of the Child*, the first of his many psychology books.

Rescorla, Robert (1935–) An influential modern theorist of classical conditioning. Rescorla has made numerous refinements to classical conditioning theories.

Rogers, Carl (1902–1987) An American psychologist who proposed the person-centered or client-centered theory of psychology. Rogers asserted that people's self-concepts determine their behavior and relationships with others. Rogers also believed that the relationship between a therapist and client was crucial in the treatment of psychological disorders. He thought that a therapist's unconditional positive regard could help clients to undergo psychotherapeutic personality change.

Schachter, Stanley (1922–1997), and **Jerome Singer** (1924–) The developers of the two-factor theory of emotion. Schachter and Singer believed that emotions come both from physiological stimuli and the cognitive interpretation of that stimuli.

Seligman, Martin (1942–) Pioneer in the field of "positive psychology," the study of what makes people happy and good, in contrast to traditional clinical psychology, which focuses on what makes people distressed. Seligman is the former president of the American Psychological Association. As a graduate student, Seligman, along with his colleagues, discovered the phenomenon of learned helplessness in dogs.

Selye, Hans (1907–1982) A Viennese-born endocrinologist who pioneered the field of stress research. While doing laboratory research on rat subjects, Selye found that many different types of stressors, such as heat, cold, electric shock, and restraint, produced the same physiological response. He concluded that the physiological response to stress is nonspecific.

Skinner, B. F. (1904–1990) A psychologist who built on Pavlov's work to develop theories of operant behavior. Skinner wrote *The Behavior of Organisms* in 1938, in which he described his work on operant behavior. He wrote several other books as well, including a popular though controversial novel, *Walden Two*. Skinner studied operant conditioning by using the Skinner box.

Spearman, Charles (1863–1945) A psychologist who theorized the existence of a general type of intelligence, the "g" factor, that underlies all types of intelligence.

Sperry, Roger (1913–1994) A pioneer in the study of lateralization, the fact that the right and left hemispheres of the brain regulate different functions. Sperry and his colleagues examined people who had gone through split-brain surgery, an operation that separates the two brain hemispheres.

Sternberg, Robert (1949–) The developer of a triarchic theory of intelligence. Sternberg proposed that there are three aspects to intelligence: componential, experiential, and contextual.

Terman, Lewis (1877–1956) A developer of the Stanford-Binet Intelligence Scale in 1916, a revision of the Binet-Simon scale. Terman believed in the existence of innate differences in intelligence and supported the eugenics movement of his time. He advocated widespread use of intelligence tests.

Thorndike, Edward (1874-1949) The psychologist who formulated the law of effect, among other theories of learning. Thorndike primarily focused on animal behavior.

Trivers, Robert (1943-) A sociobiologist who studies sexual and social behavior with respect to evolutionary history. Trivers forwarded the theory that gender differences in sexual behavior have a genetic root.

Vygotsky, Lev (1896-1934) A Russian psychologist who studied the development of thought. Vygotsky took a sociocultural approach to explaining cognitive development. He believed that social interactions with adults play a critical role in the development of children's cognitive skills.

Watson, John (1878-1958) The founder of a school of psychology known as behaviorism. Watson studied the effects of conditioning on children. One of his most famous experiments involved conditioning a child named Little Albert to fear white, furry objects.

Wechsler, David (1896-1981) The former chief psychologist at New York's Bellevue Hospital who designed the first intelligence test specifically for adults. Wechsler called the test the Wechsler Adult Intelligence Scale. Wechsler also devised a test for children called the Wechsler Intelligence Scale for Children.

Whorf, Benjamin Lee (1897-1941) A linguist who hypothesized that language has a marked impact on thought. Whorf conducted famous studies of Native American languages.

Wolpe, Joseph (1915-1997) A psychiatrist who helped develop the procedure known as systematic densensitization, which is highly effective in treating phobias. Wolpe believed that most behavior was learned and therefore could be unlearned. Wolpe also developed the behavior therapy known as assertiveness training.

Young, Thomas (1773-1829) An early developer of color theory. Young studied the structure of the eye, the effects of light on the eye, and the nature of light itself.

Glossary

A

Absolute refractory period The period during which a neuron lies dormant after an action potential has been completed.

Absolute threshold The minimum amount of stimulation needed for a person to detect the stimulus 50 percent of the time.

Accommodation The process by which the shape of an eye's lens adjusts to focus light from objects nearby or far away. Also: the modification of a schema as new information is incorporated.

Acetylcholine A neurotransmitter involved in muscle movement, attention, arousal, memory, and emotion.

Achievement motive An impulse to master challenges and reach a high standard of excellence.

Achievement tests An assessment that measures skills and knowledge that people have already learned.

Acronym A word made out of the first letters of several words.

Acrostic A sentence or phrase in which each word begins with a letter that acts as a memory cue.

Action potential A short-lived change in electric charge inside a neuron.

Activation-synthesis theory A theory proposing that neurons in the brain activate randomly during REM sleep.

Active listening A feature of client-centered therapy that involves empathetic listening, by which the therapist echoes, restates, and clarifies what the client says.

Adaptation An inherited characteristic that increases in a population because it provides a survival or reproductive advantage.

Adaptive behaviors Behaviors that increase reproductive success.

Additive strategy The process of listing the attributes of each element of a decision, weighing them according to importance, adding them up, and determining which one is more appealing based on the result.

Adoption studies Studies in which researchers examine trait similarities between adopted children and their biological and adoptive parents to figure out whether that trait might be inherited.

Adrenal cortex The outer part of the adrenal glands, which secretes corticosteroids.

Adrenal medulla The inner part of the adrenal glands, which secretes catecholamines.

Adrenocorticotropic hormone (ACTH) A hormone released by the pituitary gland that stimulates release of corticosteroids from the adrenal cortex.

Afferent nerves Bundles of axons that carry information from muscles and sense organs to the central nervous system.

Afterimage A color we perceive after another color is removed.

Age of viability The point at which a fetus has some chance of surviving outside the mother if born prematurely.

Agonists Chemicals that mimic the action of a particular neurotransmitter.

Agoraphobia A disorder involving anxiety about situations from which escape would be difficult or embarrassing or places where there might be no help if a panic attack occurred.

Algorithm A step-by-step procedure that is guaranteed to solve a problem.

All-or-none law States that neurons fire to generate an action potential only if stimulation reaches a minimum threshold.

Alpha waves Type of brain waves present when a person is very relaxed or meditating.

Alternate-forms reliability The ability of a test to produce the same results when two different versions of it are given to the same group of people.

Ambiguous language Language that can be understood in several ways.

Amplitude The height of a wave.

Amygdala A part of the limbic system of the brain that is involved in regulating aggression and emotions, particularly fear.

Animism The belief that inanimate objects are alive.

Anorexia nervosa A disorder characterized by refusal to maintain a body weight in the normal range, intense fear about gaining weight, and highly distorted body image.

Antagonists Chemicals that block the action of a particular neurotransmitter.

Anterograde amnesia An inability to remember events that occurred after a brain injury or traumatic event.

Antisocial personality disorder A disorder characterized by a lack of conscience and lack of respect for other people's rights, feelings, and needs, beginning by age fifteen.

Appraisal The process of evaluating an environmental challenge to determine whether resources are available for dealing with it.

Approach-approach conflict A conflict between two desirable alternatives.

Approach-avoidance conflict A conflict that arises when a situation has both positive and negative features.

Aptitude tests An assessment that predicts people's future ability to acquire skills or knowledge.

Archetypes Images or thoughts that have the same meaning for all human beings.

Assimilation The broadening of an existing schema to include new information.

Atherosclerosis Hardening of arteries because of cholesterol deposits.

Attachment The close bond between babies and their caregivers.

Attachment styles Types of attachment, which include secure attachment, anxious-ambivalent attachment, and avoidant attachment.

Attitudes Evaluations people make about objects, ideas, events, or other people.

Attributions Inferences people make about the causes of events and behavior.

Atypical antipsychotic drugs A new class of antipsychotic drugs that are effective for treating negative and positive symptoms of schizophrenia. They target the neurotransmitters serotonin and dopamine.

Auditory nerve A nerve that sends impulses from the ear to the brain.

Automatic thoughts Self-defeating judgments people make about themselves.

Autonomic nervous system The part of the peripheral nervous system connected to the heart, blood vessels, glands, and smooth muscles.

Availability heuristic A rule-of-thumb strategy in which people estimate probability based on how quickly they remember relevant instances of an event.

Avoidance-avoidance conflict A conflict that arises when a choice must be made between two undesirable alternatives.

Avoidant personality disorder A disorder involving social withdrawal, low self-esteem, and extreme sensitivity to being evaluated negatively.

Aversion therapy A therapy in which a stimulus that evokes an unpleasant response is paired with a stimulus that evokes a maladaptive behavior.

Axon A fiber that extends from a neuron and sends signals to other neurons.

B

Babbling A producton of sounds that resemble many different languages.

Basal metabolic rate The rate at which energy is used when a person is at complete rest.

Basilar membrane A membrane in the inner ear that runs along the length of the cochlea.

Behavior genetics The study of behavior and personality differences among people.

Behavior therapies Treatments involving complex conversations between therapists and clients that are aimed at directly influencing maladaptive behaviors through the use of learning principles.

Belief perseverance The process of rejecting evidence that refutes one's beliefs.

Benzodiazepines A class of antianxiety drugs. They are also called tranquilizers.

Beta waves The type of brain waves present when a person is awake and alert.

Bias The distortion of results by a variable that is not part of the hypothesis.

Big Five Five basic personality traits from which other traits are derived. They include neuroticism, extraversion, openness to experience, agreeableness, and conscientiousness.

Binocular cues Depth perception cues that require both eyes.

Biological rhythms Periodic physiological changes.

Biomedical therapies Treatments that involve efforts to directly alter biological functioning through medication, electric shocks, or surgery.

Biopsychosocial model of illness The idea that physical illness is the result of a complicated interaction among biological, psychological, and sociocultural factors.

Bipolar disorders Disorders in which people alternate between periods of depression and mania.

Blood-brain barrier A membrane that lets some substances from the blood into the brain but keeps out others.

Borderline personality disorder A disorder characterized by impulsive behavior and unstable relationships, emotions, and self-image.

Brain The main organ in the nervous system.

Brain waves Tracings that show the electrical activity of the brain.

Broca's area A part of the brain, in the left frontal lobe, that is involved in speech production.

Bulimia nervosa A disorder involving binge eating followed by compensatory behaviors such as vomiting, fasting, excessive exercise, or use of laxatives, diuretics, and other medications to control body weight.

Bystander effect The tendency of people to be less likely to offer help to someone who needs it if other people are also present.

C

Cannon-Bard theory The idea that the experience of emotion happens at the same time that physiological arousal happens.

Case study A research method in which an individual subject is studied in depth.

Castration anxiety The fear a male child has that his father will cut off his penis for desiring his mother.

Catatonic type A subtype of schizophrenia characterized by unnatural movement patterns such as rigid, unmoving posture or continual, purposeless movements, or by unnatural speech patterns such as absence of speech or parroting of other people's speech.

Catecholamines Hormones released by the adrenal medulla in response to stress.

Catharsis The release of tension that results when repressed thoughts or memories move into a patient's conscious mind.

Central nervous system The part of the nervous system that includes the brain and the spinal cord.

Centration The tendency to focus on one aspect of a problem and ignore other key aspects.

Cerebellum A part of the hindbrain that controls balance and coordination of movement.

Cerebrospinal fluid The fluid that cushions and nourishes the brain.

Cerebrum The largest part of the brain, involved in abstract thought and learning.

Chromosomes Thin strands of DNA that contain genes.

Chunking The process of combining small bits of information into bigger, familiar pieces.

Cilia Hair cells that are embedded in the basilar membrane of the ear.

Cingulotomy A surgical procedure that involves destruction of part of the frontal lobes. It is sometimes done to treat severe disorders that do not respond to other treatments.

Circadian rhythms Biological cycles that occur about every twenty-four hours.

Classical conditioning A type of learning in which a subject comes to respond to a neutral stimulus as he would to another stimulus by learning to associate the two stimuli. It can also be called respondent conditioning or Pavlovian conditioning.

Client-centered therapy A humanistic therapy, developed by Carl Rogers, that aims to help clients increase self-acceptance and personal growth by providing a supportive emotional environment.

Closure The tendency to interpret familiar, incomplete forms as complete by filling in gaps.

Cochlea A coiled tunnel in the inner ear that is filled with fluid.

Cognition Thinking. It involves mental activities such as understanding, problem solving, decision making, and creativity.

Cognitive appraisal The idea that people's experience of emotion depends on the way they appraise or evaluate the events around them.

Cognitive development The development of thinking capacity.

Cognitive dissonance An unpleasant state of tension that arises when a person has related cognitions that conflict with one another.

Cognitive schema A mental model of some aspect of the world.

Cognitive therapies Therapies aimed at identifying and changing maladaptive thinking patterns that can result in negative emotions and dysfunctional behavior.

Collective unconscious The part of our minds, according to Carl Jung, that contains universal memories of our common human past.

Color blindness A hereditary condition that makes people unable to distinguish between colors.

Commitment The intent to continue a romantic relationship even in the face of difficulties.

Community mental health movement A movement that advocates treating people with psychological problems in their own communities, providing outpatient treatment, and preventing psychological disorders.

Compassionate love Warmth, trust, and tolerance of a person with whom one is romantically involved.

Compensation According to Alfred Adler, the process of striving to get rid of normal feelings of inferiority.

Complexity The range of wavelengths in light.

Componential intelligence The ability assessed by intelligence tests.

Compulsions Repetitive behaviors that help to prevent or relieve anxiety.

Computerized tomography (CT) A method for studying the brain that involves taking x-rays of the brain from different angles.

Concept A mental category that groups similar objects, events, qualities, or actions.

Concordance rate The percentage of both people in a pair having a certain trait or disorder.

Conditioned response In classical and operant conditioning, a response that resembles an unconditioned response, achieved by pairing a conditioned stimulus with an unconditioned stimulus.

Conditioned stimulus In classical conditioning, a neutral stimulus that comes to evoke a response similar to an unconditioned response through pairing with an unconditioned stimulus.

Cones Photoreceptor cells in the retina that allow people to see in color.

Confabulation A phenomenon in which a person thinks he or she remembers something that did not really happen.

Confirmation bias The tendency to look for and accept evidence that supports what one wants to believe and to ignore or reject evidence that refutes those beliefs.

Conflict The experience of having two or more incompatible desires or motives.

Conformity The process of giving in to real or imagined pressure from a group.

Congruence According to Carl Rogers, the accurate match between self-concept and reality.

Conscious The part of the mind that contains all the information that a person is paying attention to at a particular time.

Consciousness The awareness people have of themselves and the environment around them.

Conservation The ability to recognize that measurable physical characteristics of objects can be the same even when objects look different.

Consolidation Transfer of information into long-term memory.

Contact comfort Comfort derived from physical closeness with a caregiver.

Contact hypothesis A hyposthesis stating that prejudice declines when people in an ingroup become more familiar with the customs, norms, food, music, and attitudes of people in an outgroup.

Content validity A test's ability to measure all the important aspects of the characteristic being measured.

Contextual intelligence The ability to function effectively in daily situations.

Continuity The tendency to perceive interrupted lines and patterns as being continuous by filling in gaps.

Continuous reinforcement A reinforcement schedule in which reinforcement happens every time a particular response occurs.

Control group A group of subjects in an experiment that receives the same treatment and is treated exactly like the experimental group, except with respect to the independent variable.

Convergence The turning inward of eyes when an object is viewed close up.

Convergent thinking A style of thinking in which a person narrows down a list of possibilities to arrive at a single right answer.

Conversion disorder A disorder characterized by medically unexplained symptoms that affect voluntary motor functioning or sensory functioning.

Coping Efforts to manage stress.

Cornea The transparent outer membrane of the eye.

Corpus callosum A band of fibers that divides the cerebrum into two halves.

Correlation coefficient A measurement that indicates the strength of the relationship between two variables. In a positive correlation, one variable increases as the other increases. In a negative correlation, one variable decreases as the other increases.

Correlational research method A research method that provides information about the relationship between variables. It is also called a descriptive research method.

Corticosteroids Hormones released by the adrenal cortex in response to stress.

Couples therapy A type of therapy in which a therapist helps couples identify and resolve conflicts.

Creativity The ability to generate novel, useful ideas.

Criterion validity A test's ability to predict another criterion of the characteristic being measured.

Crystallized intelligence Intelligence based on the knowledge and skills accumulated over the life span.

Culture-bound disorders Psychological disorders that are limited to specific cultural contexts.

D

Dark adaptation The process by which receptor cells become more sensitive to light.

Decay theory A theory stating that memory traces fade with time.

Decentration The ability to focus simultaneously on several aspects of a problem.

Decision-making The process of weighing alternatives and choosing among them.

Declarative memory The remembering of factual information. Declarative memory is usually considered explicit.

Deductive reasoning The process by which a particular conclusion is drawn from a set of general premises or statements.

Defense mechanisms Behaviors that protect people from anxiety.

Deindividuation The tendency of people in a large, arousing, anonymous group to lose inhibitions, sense of responsibility, and self-consciousness.

Deinstitutionalization The trend toward providing treatment through community-based outpatient clinics rather than inpatient hospitals.

Delta waves The type of brain waves present when a person is deeply asleep.

Delusions False beliefs that are held strongly despite contradictory evidence.

Dementia A condition characterized by several significant psychological deficits.

Dendrite A fiber that extends from a neuron. It received signals from other neurons and sends them toward the cell body.

Dendritic trees Highly branched fibers extending from neurons.

Denial A defense mechanism that involves refusing to acknowledge something that is obvious to others.

Dependent variable The variable that is observed in an experiment and that may be affected by manipulations of the independent variable.

Descriptive statistics Numbers that researchers use to describe their data so it can be organized and summarized.

Development The series of age-related changes that occurs over the course of a person's life span.

Developmental norms The median ages at which children develop specific behaviors and abilities.

Diabetes A condition caused by a deficiency of insulin.

Diagnosis The process of distinguishing among disorders.

Diagnostic and Statistical Manual of Mental Disorders (DSM) A reference book used by psychologists and psychiatrists to diagnose psychological disorders.

Dialectical reasoning A process of going back and forth between opposing points of view in order to come up with a satisfactory solution to a problem.

Dichromat **A person who is sensitive to only two of the three wavelengths of light.**

Difference threshold **The smallest difference in stimulation that is detectable 50 percent of the time. This threshold is also called the *just noticeable difference*, or *jnd*.**

Diffusion of responsibility **The tendency for an individual to feel less responsible in the presence of others because responsibility is distributed among all the people present.**

Discriminative stimulus **In operant conditioning, a cue that indicates the kind of consequence that's likely to occur after a response.**

Disease model of addiction **The idea that addiction is a disease that has to be medically treated.**

Disorganized type **A subtype of schizophrenia characterized by disorganized behavior, disorganized speech, and emotional flatness or inappropriateness.**

Displacement **A defense mechanism that involves transferring feelings about a person or event to someone or something else.**

Display rules **Norms that tell people whether, which, how, and when emotions should be displayed.**

Dissociative amnesia **A disorder characterized by an inability to remember extensive, important personal information, usually about something traumatic or painful.**

Dissociative disorders **Disorders characterized by disturbances in consciousness, memory, identity, and perception.**

Dissociative fugue **A disorder in which a person suddenly and unexpectedly leaves home, fails to remember the past, and becomes confused about his or her identity.**

Dissociative identity disorder **A disorder in which a person fails to remember important personal information and has two or more identities or personality states that control behavior. It is also called *multiple personality disorder*.**

Dissonance theory **A theory that proposes that people change their attitudes when they have attitudes that are inconsistent with one another.**

Distributed practice The practice of learning material in short sessions over a long period. It is also called the *spacing effect*.

Divergent thinking A style of thinking in which people's thoughts go off in different directions as they try to generate many different solutions to a problem.

Dopamine A neurotransmitter involved in voluntary movement, learning, memory, and emotion.

Double-blind A procedure in which neither the subjects nor the experimenter knows which subjects belong to the experimental and control groups.

Drive reduction theories of motivation Ideas that suggest people act in order to reduce needs and maintain a constant physiological state.

Drug therapy Treatment that involves the use of medications. It is also called *pharmacotherapy*.

Dysthymic disorder A disorder involving depressed mood on a majority of days for at least two years.

E

Eating disorders Disorders characterized by problematic eating patterns, extreme concerns about body weight, and inappropriate behaviors aimed at controlling body weight.

Echoic memory Auditory sensory memory.

Efferent nerves Bundles of axons that carry information from the central nervous system to muscles and sense organs.

Ego The component of the personality that manages the conflict among the id, the superego, and the constraints of the real world.

Egocentrism The inability to take someone else's point of view.

Elaboration A type of deep processing in which information being learned is associated with other meaningful material.

Elaboration likelihood model The idea that changes to attitudes tend to be longer lasting when people think about the content of persuasive messages they receive.

Electric stimulation of the brain An invasive method of studying the brain, in which an implanted electrode activates a particular brain structure.

Electrocardiograph (EKG) An instrument that records the activity of the heart.

Electroconvulsive therapy (ECT) A biomedical treatment that uses electrical shocks to treat severe depression.

Electroencephalograph (EEG) A device that records the overall electrical activity of the brain, via electrodes placed on the scalp.

Electromyograph (EMG) An instrument that records muscle activity.

Electrooculograph (EOG) An instrument that records eye movements.

Elimination by aspects The process of eliminating alternatives in a decision based on whether they do or do not possess aspects or attributes the decision maker has deemed necessary or desirable.

Embryo A ball of cells that develops during the embryonic stage.

Embryonic stage The period that begins two weeks after conception and ends two months after conception.

Emotion A complex, subjective experience that is accompanied by biological and behavioral changes.

Emotion work The process of acting out of an emotion that is not really felt.

Emotional intelligence An ability that helps people perceive, express, understand, and regulate emotions.

Empirically validated treatments Treatments that are shown by research to be more effective for a particular problem than a placebo or no treatment.

Empty nest The time in parents' lives when their children have grown up and moved away from home.

Encoding The process of putting information into memory.

Endocrine system A network of tissues that allows the body to communicate via hormones.

Endogenous biological rhythms Biological cycles that originate from inside the body rather than depend on cues from the environment.

Endorphins A group of neurotransmitters involved in pain relief, pleasure, and modulating the action of other neurotransmitters.

Episodic memory The remembering of personal facts.

Ethics A system of moral values.

Etiology The cause or origin of a disorder.

Evolution A change in the frequency of genes in a population.

Excitatory postsynaptic potential A positive change in voltage that occurs when a neurotransmitter binds to an excitatory receptor site.

Existential therapies Therapies aimed at helping clients find meaning in their lives.

Expected value The process of adding the value of a win times the probability of a win to the value of a loss times the probability of a loss in order to make a decision.

Experiential intelligence The ability to adapt to new situations and produce new ideas.

Experiment A research method that provides information about causal relationships between variables.

Experimental group A group of subjects in an experiment for whom the independent variable is manipulated.

Experimenter bias A source of error that arises when researchers' preferences or expectations influence the outcome of research.

Explicit attitudes Conscious beliefs that can guide decisions and behavior.

Explicit memory Conscious, intentional remembering of information.

Exposure therapies Therapies that aim to eliminate anxiety responses by having clients face real or imagined versions of feared stimuli.

Expressive language The ability to use language to communicate.

External attribution An inference that a person's behavior is due to situational factors. It is also called situational attribution.

External locus of control The tendency to believe that circumstances are not within one's control but rather are due to luck, fate, or other people.

Extinction In classical conditioning, the gradual weakening and disappearance of a conditioned response when a conditioned stimulus is not followed by an unconditioned stimulus. In operant conditioning, it's the gradual disappearance of a response after it stops being reinforced.

Extraneous variable A variable other than the independent variable that could affect the dependent variable. It is not part of the hypothesis.

Extrinsic motivation The motivation to act for external rewards.

Eye movement desensitization and reprocessing (EMDR) A type of exposure therapy in which clients move their eyes back and forth while recalling memories that are to be desensitized.

F

Facial-feedback hypothesis The idea that the brain uses feedback from facial muscles to recognize emotions that are being experienced.

Factor analysis A statistical procedure that clusters variables into dimensions depending on similarities among the variables.

Falsifiability The ability of a theory or hypothesis to be rejected.

Family studies Studies in which researchers examine trait similarities among members of a family to figure out whether that trait might be inherited.

Family therapy A type of therapy in which a therapist sees two or more members of a family at the same time.

Feature detectors Specialized neurons that are activated by specific features of the environment.

Fee for service An arrangement for health care in which people pay providers for health care services.

Feigned scarcity Implying that a product is in scarce supply, even when it is not, in order to increase demand for it.

Fetal alcohol syndrome A collection of symptoms that may be present in babies of alcoholic mothers who drank heavily in pregnancy.

Fetal stage The last stage of prenatal development, lasting from two months after conception until birth.

Figure What stands out when people organize visual information.

Fixation An inability to progress normally from one psychosexual stage of development into another.

Fixed-interval schedule A reinforcement schedule in which reinforcement happens after a set amount of time.

Fixed-ratio schedule A reinforcement schedule in which reinforcement happens after a set number of responses.

Flashbulb memories Vivid, detailed memories of important events.

Flooding A type of exposure therapy in which the client is exposed to a feared stimulus suddenly rather than gradually.

Flynn effect Phenomenon showing that people's performance on IQ tests has improved over time in industrialized countries.

Foot-in-the-door phenomenon The tendency to agree to a difficult request if one has first agreed to an easy request.

Forebrain The biggest and most complex part of the brain, which includes structures such as the thalamus, the hypothalamus, the limbic system, and the cerebrum.

Forgetting curve A graph that shows how quickly learned information is forgotten over time.

Fovea The center of the retina, where vision is sharpest.

Free association A psychoanalytic technique that involves having the client verbalize all thoughts that come to mind.

Frequency The number of times per second a sound wave cycles from the highest to the lowest point.

Frequency theory A theory explaining how people discriminate low-pitched sounds that have a frequency below 1000 Hz.

Frustration The experience of being thwarted in the process of achieving a goal.

Frustration-aggression hypothesis A hypothesis stating that aggression is always caused by frustration.

Functional fixedness The tendency to think only of an object's most common use in solving a problem.

Fundamental attribution error The tendency to attribute other people's behavior to internal factors such as personality traits, abilities, and feelings. It is also called *correspondence bias*.

G

GABA The main inhibitory neurotransmitter in the brain.

Galvanic skin response An increase in the skin's rate of electrical conductivity. It is also known as an *electrodermal response*.

Gambler's fallacy The false belief that a chance event is more likely if it hasn't happened recently.

Gate-control theory States that pain signals traveling from the body to the brain must go through a gate in the spinal cord.

Gender A learned distinction between masculinity and femininity.

Gender stereotypes Societal beliefs about the characteristics of males and females.

General adaptation syndrome The stress response of an organism, described by Hans Selye. The response has three stages: alarm, resistance, and exhaustion.

General intelligence factor (g) An ability that underlies all intelligent behavior, proposed by Charles Spearman.

Generalized anxiety disorder A disorder involving persistent and excessive anxiety or worry that lasts at least six months.

Generative The characteristic symbols of a language that can be combined to produce an infinite number of messages.

Genes Segments of DNA that function as hereditary units.

Germinal stage The two-week period after conception.

Gestalt psychology A German school of thought that studies how people organize visual information into patterns and forms.

Glial cells Cells that give structural support to neurons and nourish and insulate them.

Glucose A simple sugar that acts as an energy source for cells.

Glutamate The main excitatory neurotransmitter in the brain.

Grandiose delusion A belief centered around the idea that one is very important or famous.

Ground The background in which a figure stands when people organize visual information.

Group A social unit composed of two or more people who interact and depend on one another in some way.

Group cohesiveness The strength of the liking and commitment group members have toward one another and to the group.

Group polarization The tendency for a dominant point of view in a group to be strengthened to a more extreme position after a group discussion.

Groupthink The tendency of a close-knit group to emphasize consensus at the expense of critical thinking and rational decision making.

H

Hallucinations Sensory or perceptual experiences that happen without any external stimulus.

Hallucinogens Drugs that cause sensory and perceptual distortions.

Health psychology A branch of psychology that focuses on the relationship between psychosocial factors and the emergence, progression, and treatment of illness.

Heritability A mathematical estimate that indicates how much of a trait's variation in a population can be attributed to genetic factors.

Heuristic A general rule of thumb that may lead to, but doesn't guarantee, a correct solution to a problem.

Hierarchical classification The ability to classify according to more than one level.

Hierarchy of needs theory The idea, proposed by Abraham Maslow, that people are motivated by needs on four levels. Maslow believed people pay attention to higher needs only when lower needs are satisfied.

Higher-order conditioning In classical conditioning, the process by which a neutral stimulus comes to act as a conditioned stimulus by being paired with another stimulus that already evokes a conditioned response.

Hindbrain Portion of the brain consisting of the medulla, the pons, and the cerebellum.

Hindsight bias The tendency to interpret the past in a way that fits the present.

Hippocampus A part of the limbic system involved in memory.

Histogram or bar graph A plot that shows how data are distributed.

Histrionic personality A personality type characterized by a desire to be the center of attention and the tendency to be self-focused, excitable, highly open to suggestion, very emotional, and dramatic.

Histrionic personality disorder A disorder characterized by attention-seeking behavior and shallow emotions.

Homeostasis Maintenance of a state of physiological equilibrium in the body.

Hormones Chemicals that are produced in glands and released into the bloodstream, involved in regulating body functions.

Humanism A school of thought that encourages seeing people's lives as those people would see them.

Humanistic therapies Therapies aimed at helping people accept themselves and free themselves from unnecessary limitations.

Hypnosis A procedure in which suggestions are made to a person.

Hypochondriasis A disorder in which a person has constant fears of having a serious disease.

Hypothalamus A part of the forebrain that helps to control the pituitary gland, the autonomic nervous system, body temperature, and biological drives.

Hypothesis A testable prediction of what is going to happen given a certain set of conditions.

I

Iconic memory Visual sensory memory.

Id The component of the personality that contains instinctual energy.

Identity achievement A state in which a person commits to an identity after considering alternative possibilities.

Identity diffusion A state of confusion when a person lacks a clear sense of identity and hasn't yet begun exploring issues related to identity development.

Identity foreclosure A state in which a person has prematurely committed to values or roles prescribed by others.

Identity moratorium A state in which commitment to an identity is delayed while a person experiments with various roles and values.

Illusion A misinterpretation of a sensory stimulus.

Immune system The body's defense against harmful agents such as bacteria, viruses, and other foreign substances.

Implantation The process by which the embryo becomes embedded in the wall of the uterus.

Implicit attitudes Beliefs that are unconscious but that can still influence decisions and behavior.

Implicit memory Unconscious retention of information that affects thoughts and behavior.

Incentive An environmental stimulus that pulls people to act in a particular way.

Inclusive fitness The reproductive fitness of an individual organism plus any effect that the organism has on increasing reproductive fitness in related organisms.

Incongruence According to Carl Rogers and other humanistic therapists, a disparity between the self-concept and reality.

Independent variable The variable that is manipulated in an experiment.

GLOSSARY

Individual psychology Alfred Adler's school of thought, which maintains that the main motivations for human behavior are not sexual or aggressive urges but strivings for superiority.

Inductive reasoning The drawing of a general conclusion from certain premises or statements.

Inferential statistics Statistics used to determine the likelihood that a result is just due to chance.

Inferiority complex An exaggerated sense of inferiority.

Informational social influence An individual's tendency to conform because a group provides one with information.

Informed consent A subject's voluntary agreement to participate in a research study, given after he or she has learned enough about the study to make a knowledgeable decision to participate.

Infradian rhythms Biological cycles that take longer than twenty-four hours.

Ingroup A group to which one belongs.

Inhibitory postsynaptic potential A negative change in voltage that occurs when a neurotransmitter binds to an inhibitory receptor.

Innate abilities Abilities that are present from birth.

Insanity A legal term that refers to the mental inability to take responsibility for one's actions.

Insight therapies Treatments involving complex conversations between therapists and clients. The treatments aim to help clients understand the nature of their problems and the meaning of their behavior, thoughts, and feelings.

Insomnia A chronic problem with falling or staying asleep.

Instinctive drift The tendency for conditioning to be hindered by natural instincts.

Insulin A hormone secreted by the pancreas.

Integrative approach Therapy approaches that combine the ideas and techniques of several different schools of psychology.

Intelligence The capacity to acquire and apply knowledge. It includes the ability to benefit from past experience, act purposefully, solve problems, and adapt to new situations.

Intelligence quotient (IQ) A person's mental age divided by his or her chronological age and multiplied by 100.

Interference theory States that people forget information because of interference from other learned information.

Intermittent reinforcement A reinforcement schedule in which reinforcement happens only on some of the occasions a particular response occurs. It is also called *partial reinforcement.*

Internal attribution An inference that an event or a person's behavior is due to personal factors such as traits, abilities, or feelings. It is also called *dispositional attribution.*

Internal locus of control The tendency to believe that one has control over one's circumstances.

Interpersonal attraction Positive feelings about another person.

Interpretation A psychoanalytic technique that involves suggesting the hidden meanings of free associations, dreams, feelings, memories, and behavior to the client.

Interval schedule The schedule in which reinforcement happens after a particular time interval.

Intimacy The warm, close, caring aspect of a romantic relationship.

Intrinsic motivation The motivation to act for the sake of the activity alone.

Ions Positively and negatively charged atoms and molecules.

Iris A ring of muscle that surrounds the pupil in the eye.

Irreversibility The inability to mentally reverse an operation.

J

James-Lange theory The idea that people experience emotion because they perceive their bodies' physiological responses to external events.

Justification of effort The idea that if one works hard to reach a goal, one is likely to value that goal.

Just world hypothesis The tendency to believe that the world is fair and that people get what they deserve.

K

Kinesthesis The sense of the position and movement of body parts.

L

Laboratory observation An observational research method in which information about subjects is collected in a laboratory setting.

Language A system of symbols and rules used for meaningful communication.

Latent content The hidden meaning of a dream.

Lateralization The difference in specialization between the two hemispheres of the brain.

Law of effect A law proposed by Edward Thorndike stating that any behavior that has good consequences will tend to be repeated, and any behavior that has bad consequences will tend to be avoided.

Learned helplessness A tendency to give up passively in the face of unavoidable stressors.

Learning A change in behavior or knowledge that results from experience.

Learning model The idea that psychological disorders result from the reinforcement of abnormal behavior.

Learning model of addiction The idea that addiction is a way of coping with stress.

Lens Part of the eye behind the pupil and iris. It can adjust its shape to focus light from objects that are near or far away.

Leptin A hormone secreted by fat cells.

Lesioning studies An invasive method of studying the brain in which a specific, small area of the brain is destroyed.

Lie scales Statistics used to provide information about the likelihood that a subject is lying in a test.

Light A kind of electromagnetic radiation emitted by the sun, stars, fire, and lightbulbs.

Light adaptation The process by which receptor cells become less sensitive to light.

Light intensity The amount of light emitted or reflected by an object.

Limbic system A part of the forebrain involved in emotional experience and memory.

Linguistic relativity hypothesis A theory proposed by Benjamin Lee Whorf that claims that language determines the way people think.

Link method The process of associating items with one another in order to remember them.

Lithium A drug prescribed for treating bipolar disorders.

Lobotomy A surgical procedure that severs nerve tracts in the frontal lobe, formerly used to treat certain psychological disorders but now rarely performed.

Locus of control People's perception of whether or not they have control over circumstances in their lives.

Long-term memory A memory system that stores an unlimited amount of information permanently.

Long-term potentiation A lasting change at synapses that occurs when long-term memories form.

Lowball technique The act of making an attractive proposition and revealing its downsides only after a person has agreed to it.

Lucid dreams Dreams in which people are aware that they are dreaming.

M

Magnetic resonance imaging (MRI) A method for studying the brain that uses magnetic fields and radio waves to produce pictures of the brain.

Major depressive disorder A disorder diagnosed after at least one major depressive episode.

Major depressive episode A period of at least two weeks marked by sadness or irritability and loss of interest in activities. Other symptoms may include changed sleeping or eating patterns, low energy, feelings of worthlessness or guilt, difficulty concentrating, and recurrent thoughts about suicide.

Managed care An arrangement for health care in which an organization, such as a health maintenance organization, acts as an intermediary between a person seeking care and a treatment provider.

Manifest content The plot of a dream.

Massed practice The process of learning material over a short period; also called *cramming*.

Matching hypothesis The idea that people tend to pick partners who are about equal in level of attractiveness to themselves.

Maturation Genetically programmed growth and development.

Mean The arithmetic average of a set of scores.

Measures of central tendency The mean, median, and mode.

Median The middle score in a set when all scores are arranged in order from lowest to highest.

Medical model A way of describing and explaining psychological disorders as if they are diseases.

Meditation The practice of focusing attention.

Medulla A part of the hindbrain that controls essential functions that are not under conscious control, such as breathing.

Melatonin A hormone that regulates the sleep cycle.

Memory The capacity for storing and retrieving information.

Menarche A woman's first menstrual period.

Menopause The gradual, permanent cessation of menstruation.

Mental age The chronological age that typically corresponds to a particular level of performance. It is used as a measure of performance on intelligence tests.

Mental hospitals Medical institutions that specialize in providing treatment for psychological disorders.

Mental set A tendency to use only solutions that have worked in the past.

Mere exposure effect The tendency to like novel stimuli more if one encounters them repeatedly.

Metalinguistic awareness The capacity to think about how language is used.

Method of loci The process of imagining oneself physically in a familiar place in order to remember something.

Midbrain The part of the brain between the hindbrain and forebrain that is involved in locating events in space and that contains a dopamine-releasing system of neurons.

Midlife crisis A time of doubt and anxiety in middle adulthood.

Minnesota Multiphasic Personality Inventory (MMPI) A test developed to help clinical psychologists diagnose psychological disorders.

Misinformation effect The tendency for recollections of events to be distorted by information given after the event occurred.

Mnemonics Strategies for improving memory.

Mode The most frequently occurring score in a set of scores.

Monoamine oxidase inhibitors (MAOIs) A class of antidepressant drugs that increase the level of norepinephrine and serotonin.

Monocular cues Depth perception cues that require only one eye.

Monogenic traits Traits determined by a single gene.

Mood disorders Disorders characterized by marked disturbances in emotional state, which affect thinking, physical symptoms, social relationships, and behavior.

Moral reasoning The reasons and processes that cause people to think the way they do about right and wrong.

Morpheme The smallest meaningful unit in a language.

Motivated forgetting The idea that people forget things they don't want to remember; also called *psychogenic amnesia*.

Motivation An internal process that makes a person move toward a goal.

Motive An impulse that causes a person to act.

Motor development The increasing coordination of muscles that makes physical movements possible.

Muller-Lyer illusion Illusion in which two lines of the same length appear to be different lengths because of different diagonal lines attached to the end of each line.

Mutations Small changes in genes.

Myelin sheath The fatty coating around some axons that increases the speed of neural impulse transmission.

N

Name calling A strategy of labeling people in order to influence their or others' thinking.

Narcissistic personality disorder A disorder in which a person has an exaggerated sense of importance, a strong desire to be admired, and a lack of empathy.

Narcolepsy A tendency to fall asleep periodically during the day.

Narcotics Drugs that can relieve pain; also called *opiates*.

Narrative method The process of making up a story in order to remember something.

Naturalistic observation A method of collecting information about subjects in a natural setting without interfering with them in any way.

Negative correlation A relationship between two variables in which one variable increases as the other one decreases.

Negatively skewed distribution A data distribution with a few very low scores.

Negative punishment In operant conditioning, the removal of a stimulus after a response so that the response will be less likely to occur.

Negative reinforcement In operant conditioning, the removal of a stimulus after a response so that the response will be more likely to occur.

Negative symptoms Indicated by an absence or reduction of normal behavior.

NEO Personality Inventory A test that measures the Big Five traits: extraversion, openness to experience, agreeableness, conscientiousness, and neuroticism.

Nerves Bundles of axons extending from many neurons.

Nervous system A complex, highly coordinated network of tissues that communicate via electrochemical signals.

Neurons Nervous system cells that communicate via electrochemical signals.

Neurotransmitters Chemicals that are released from a neuron and activate another neuron.

Nocturnal emissions Signal of the onset of puberty for boys; also called *wet dreams*.

Norepinephrine A neurotransmitter involved in learning, memory, dreaming, awakening, emotion, and responses to stress.

Normal distribution A symmetrical bell-shaped curve that represents how characteristics such as IQ are distributed in a large population.

Normative social influence An individual's tendency to conform because of a need to be accepted or not rejected by a group.

Norms Data that provide information about how a person's test score compares with the scores of other test takers.

Nucleotides Biochemical units that make up DNA and genes.

O

Obedience Compliance with commands given by an authority figure.

Objective personality tests Tests that usually consist of self-report inventories. Commonly used objective tests include the MMPI-2, the 16PF, and the NEO Personality Inventory.

Objective test Generally a pencil-and-paper-type standardized test used to assess a psychological disorder.

Object permanence The ability to recognize that an object exists even when the object is not present and not perceived.

Object relations The relationships that people have with others, who are represented mentally as objects with certain attributes.

Observational learning A change in behavior or knowledge that happens by watching others. It can also be called *vicarious conditioning*.

Obsessions Persistent ideas, thoughts, impulses, or images that cause anxiety or distress.

Obsessive-compulsive disorder A disorder involving obsessions, compulsions, or both.

Occam's razor See *principle of parsimony*.

Oedipus complex In psychoanalytic theory, a male child's sexual desire for his mother and his hostility toward his father, whom he considers to be a rival for his mother's love.

Operant conditioning A type of learning in which responses come to be controlled by their consequences.

Operational definition A way of stating precisely how a variable will be measured.

Opponent process theory A theory of color vision that states that the visual system has receptors responding in opposite ways to wavelengths associated with three pairs of colors.

Optic disk The point in the retina at which the optic nerve leaves the eye. This point is also called the blind spot.

Optic nerve A bundle of ganglion cell axons that originate in the retina.

Optimism The tendency to expect positive outcomes.

Ossicles Three bones in the middle ear called the hammer, the anvil, and the stirrup.

Outgroup A group to which one does not belong.

Overlearning Continuing to practice material even after it is learned in order to increase retention.

Overcompensation According to Alfred Adler, the attempt to cover up a sense of inferiority by focusing on outward signs of superiority such as status, wealth, and power.

Overconfidence effect The tendency for people to be too certain that their beliefs, decisions, estimates, and accuracy of recall are correct.

P

Panic attack A period in which a person has uncomfortable and frightening physical and psychological symptoms, including heart palpitations, trembling, fear of dying, and a perceived loss of control.

Panic disorder A disorder characterized by recurrent, unexpected panic attacks.

Papillae Small bumps on the skin that hold taste buds, which in turn hold the taste receptors in the tongue and throat, on the inside of the cheeks, and on the roof of the mouth.

Paranoid type A subtype of schizophrenia characterized by marked delusions or hallucinations and relatively normal cognitive and emotional functioning.

Parasympathetic nervous system Part of the autonomic nervous system that keeps the body still and conserves energy. It is active during states of relaxation.

Parental investment The sum of resources spent in order to produce and raise offspring.

Partial reinforcement effect Phenomenon in which responses resist extinction because of partial or intermittent schedules of reinforcement.

Passionate love Sexual desire and tenderness for, and intense absorption in, a person with whom one is romantically involved.

Peg word method Process of remembering a rhyme that associates numbers with words and words with the items to be remembered.

Penis envy In psychoanalytic theory, a sense of discontent and resentment that Freud thought women experience, resulting from their wish for a penis.

Percentile score A score that indicates the percentage of people who achieved the same as or less than a particular score.

Perception Organization and interpretation of sensory information.

Perceptual constancy The ability to recognize that an object is the same even when it produces different images on the retina.

Perceptual set The readiness to see in a particular way that's based on expectations, experiences, emotions, and assumptions.

Perceptual speed The amount of time a person takes to accurately perceive and discriminate between stimuli.

Peripheral nervous system The part of the nervous system outside the brain and the spinal cord that includes the somatic nervous system and the autonomic nervous system.

Persecutory delusion A belief centered on the idea that one is being oppressed, pursued, or harassed.

Personality The collection of characteristic thoughts, feelings, and behaviors that make up a person.

Personality disorders Disorders characterized by stable patterns of experience and behavior that differ noticeably from patterns considered normal by a person's culture.

Personal unconscious An individual's unconscious, unique to him or her.

Person-centered theory A theory, proposed by Carl Rogers, stating that the self-concept is the most important feature of personality.

Person perception The process of forming impressions about other people.

Phi phenomenon An illusion of movement that arises when a series of images is presented very quickly one after another; also called *stroboscopic movement.*

Phoneme The smallest distinguishable unit in a language.

Phonemic encoding A way of encoding verbal information that emphasizes how words sound.

Photoreceptor Cells that are specialized to receive light stimuli.

Physical dependence Addiction based on a need to avoid withdrawal symptoms.

Pineal gland A gland that secretes melatonin.

Pinna The visible part of the ear.

Pituitary The master gland of the endocrine system, which regulates the function of many other glands.

Placebo effect The effect on a subject of receiving a fake drug or treatment. Expectations of improvement contribute to placebo effects.

Placenta The tissue that passes oxygen and nutrients from the mother's blood into the fetus and removes waste materials from the fetus.

Place theory Explains how people discriminate high-pitched sounds that have a frequency greater than 5000 Hz.

Pleasure principle The drive to achieve pleasure and avoid pain. It is the operating principle of the id.

Polygenic traits Traits influenced by several genes.

Polygraph or lie detector A device that detects changes in autonomic arousal.

Polygyny A mating system in which a single male mates with many females.

Pons A part of the hindbrain involved in sleeping, waking, and dreaming.

Population The collection of individuals from which a sample is drawn.

Positive correlation A relationship between two variables in which as one variable increases, the other does too.

Positively skewed distribution A data distribution with a few very high scores.

Positive punishment In operant conditioning, the presentation of a stimulus after a response so that the response will be less likely to occur.

Positive reinforcement In operant conditioning, the presentation of a stimulus after a response so that the response will be more likely to occur.

Positive symptoms Symptoms indicated by the presence of altered behaviors.

Positron emission tomography (PET) A method for studying the brain that involves injecting a radioactive substance, which collects in active brain areas.

Postsynaptic neuron At a synapse, the neuron that receives a neurotransmitter.

Postsynaptic potential The voltage change that occurs at a receptor site of a postsynaptic neuron when a neurotransmitter molecule links up with a receptor molecule.

Posthypnotic amnesia The phenomenon that occurs when a person who has been hypnotized and instructed to forget what happened during hypnosis accordingly claims not to remember what happened.

Post–traumatic stress disorder (PTSD) A disorder in which a person constantly re-experiences a traumatic event, avoids stimuli associated with the trauma, and shows symptoms of increased arousal.

Preconscious The part of the mind that contains information that is outside of a person's attention, which is not currently being attended to, but which is readily accessible if needed.

Prejudice A negative belief or feeling about a particular group of individuals.

Prenatal period The time between conception and birth.

Pressure A sense of being compelled to behave in a particular way because of expectations set by oneself or others.

Presynaptic neuron At a synapse, the neuron that releases a neurotransmitter.

Primary auditory cortex In the temporal lobe of the cerebrum, the brain part involved in processing auditory information.

Primary motor cortex In the frontal lobe of the cerebrum, the brain part involved in controlling muscle movement.

Primary process thinking Thinking that is irrational, illogical, and motivated by a desire of immediate gratification of impulses.

Primary punisher In operant conditioning, a consequence that is naturally unpleasant.

Primary reinforcer In operant conditioning, a consequence that is naturally satisfying.

Primary somatosensory cortex In the parietal lobe of the cerebrum, the brain part involved in handling touch-related information.

Primary visual cortex In the occipital lobe of the cerebrum, the brain part involved in handling visual information.

Priming The retrieval of a particular memory by activating information associated with that memory.

Principle of closure The Gestalt psychology principle that states that people tend to interpret familiar incomplete forms as complete by filling in gaps.

Principle of continuity The Gestalt psychology principle that states that people tend to perceive interrupted lines and patterns as continuous by filling in gaps.

Principle of parsimony The principle of applying the simplest possible explanation to any set of observations; also called *Occam's razor*.

Principle of proximity The Gestalt psychology principle that states that people tend to perceive objects as a group when they are close together.

Principle of similarity The Gestalt psychology principle that states that people tend to group similar objects together.

Principle of simplicity The Gestalt psychology principle that states that people tend to perceive forms as simple, symmetrical figures rather than as irregular ones.

Prison study A famous study done by Philip Zimbardo that showed the influence of roles.

Proactive interference The forgetting of new information because of previously learned information.

Problem solving The active effort people make to achieve a goal that cannot be easily attained.

Procedural memory Memory of how to do things. Procedural memory is usually considered implicit.

Prognosis A prediction about the probable course and outcome of a disorder.

Projection A defense mechanism that involves attributing one's own unacceptable thoughts or feelings to someone else.

Projective hypothesis The idea that people interpret ambiguous stimuli in ways that reveal their concerns, needs, conflicts, desires, and feelings.

Projective personality tests Tests that require subjects to respond to ambiguous stimuli, such as pictures and phrases, that can be interpreted in many different ways.

Projective test A test that requires psychologists to make judgments based on a subject's responses to ambiguous stimuli. It is used to assess a psychological disorder.

Prototype A typical example of a concept.

Proximity The tendency to perceive objects that lie close together as groups.

Psychoactive drugs Drugs that have effects on sensory experience, perception, mood, thinking, and behavior.

Psychoanalysis A technique developed by Sigmund Freud to treat mental disorders. It is also a theory of personality developed by Freud that focuses on unconscious forces, the importance of childhood experiences, and division of the psyche into the id, ego, and superego.

Psychodynamic model The idea that psychological disorders result from maladaptive defenses against unconscious conflicts.

Psychodynamic theories Theories based on the work of Sigmund Freud. These theories emphasize unconscious motives and desires and the importance of childhood experiences in shaping personality.

Psychological dependence Addiction based on cravings for a drug.

Psychological test An instrument that is used to collect information about personality traits, emotional states, aptitudes, interests, abilities, values, or behaviors.

Psychometric approach A method of understanding intelligence that emphasizes people's performance on standardized aptitude tests.

Psychophysics The study of the relationship between physical properties of stimuli and people's experience of the stimuli.

Psychotherapy The treatment of psychological problems through confidential verbal communications with a mental health professional.

Puberty The beginning of adolescence, marked by menarche in girls and the beginning of nocturnal emissions in boys.

Pubescence The two years before puberty.

Punishment The delivery of a consequence that decreases the likelihood that a response will occur.

Pupil An opening that lets light into the back of the eye.

Pure light Light of a single wavelength.

R

Random assignment A way of placing subjects into either an experimental or a control group such that subjects have an equal chance of being placed in either one group or the other.

Range The difference between the highest and lowest scores in a set of scores.

Rapid eye movement (REM) sleep A stage of deep sleep in which brain wave activity is similar to that in the waking state. It is also called paradoxical sleep.

REM rebound effect The tendency to spend more time in the REM stage of sleep after a period of REM sleep deprivation.

Rational-emotive therapy A type of cognitive-behavioral therapy, developed by Albert Ellis, that aims to identify catastrophic thinking and to change the irrational assumptions that underlie it.

Rationalization A defense mechanism that involves using incorrect but self-serving explanations to justify unacceptable behavior, thoughts, or feelings.

Ratio schedule A schedule in which reinforcement happens after a certain number of responses.

Reaction formation A defense mechanism that involves behaving in a way that is opposite to behavior, feelings, or thoughts that are considered unacceptable.

Reaction range The limits that heredity places on characteristics such as IQ.

Reaction time The amount of time a subject takes to respond to a stimulus.

Reality principle The awareness that gratification of impulses has to be delayed in order to accommodate the demands of the real world. It also acts as the operating principle of the ego.

Recall The process of remembering without any external cues.

Receptive language The ability to understand language.

Reciprocal determinism The process of interaction between a person's characteristics and the environment. This interaction results in personality.

Reciprocity norm An implicit rule in many societies that tells people they should return favors or gifts given to them.

Recognition The process of identifying learned information by using external cues.

Reflex An innate response to a stimulus.

Regression A defense mechanism that involves reverting to a more immature state of psychological development.

Regression toward the mean The tendency for extreme states to move toward the average when assessed a second time.

Rehearsal The process of practicing material in order to remember it.

Reinforcement The delivery of a consequence that increases the likelihood that a response will occur.

Reinforcement schedule The pattern in which reinforcement is given over time.

Relearning A method for measuring forgetting and retention, which involves assessing the amount of time it takes to memorize information a second time.

Reliability The ability of a test to produce the same result when administered at different times to the same group of people.

Replicability The ability of research to repeatedly yield the same results when done by different researchers.

Representativeness heuristic A rule-of-thumb strategy that estimates the probability of an event based on how typical that event is.

Representative sample A sample that corresponds to the population from which it is drawn in terms of age, sex, and other qualities on the variables being studied.

Repression A defense mechanism that involves keeping unpleasant thoughts, memories, and feelings shut up in the unconscious.

Reproductive advantage The outcome of a characteristic that helps an organism mate successfully and thus pass on its genes to the next generation.

Resistance A client's usually unconscious efforts to block the progress of treatment.

Response tendency A learned tendency to behave in a particular way.

Resting potential The slight negative charge inside an inactive neuron.

Resting state The period during which the inside of a neuron has a slightly higher concentration of negatively charged ions than the outside does. A neuron during this time is inactive.

Retention The proportion of learned information that is retained or remembered.

Reticular formation A structure that includes parts of the hindbrain and midbrain and that is involved in sleep, wakefulness, pain perception, breathing, and muscle reflexes.

Retina A thin layer of neural tissue in the back of the eye.

Retinal disparity The difference between the images picked up by the two eyes.

Retrieval The process of getting information out of memory.

Retrieval cues Stimuli that help to get information out of memory.

Retroactive interference Forgetting of old information because of newly learned information.

Retrograde amnesia An inability to remember events that occurred before a brain injury or traumatic event.

Reuptake The process by which neurotransmitter molecules return to presynaptic neurons.

Reversibility The ability to reverse actions mentally.

Reversible figure An ambiguous drawing that can be interpreted in more than one way.

Risky shift The tendency for a dominant, risky point of view in a group to be strengthened to an even riskier position after a group discussion.

Rods Photoreceptor cells in the retina that allow people to see in dim light.

Rorschach test A series of ten inkblots that subjects are asked to describe. Psychologists then use complex scoring systems to interpret the subjects' responses.

S

Sample A collection of subjects, drawn from a population, that a researcher studies.

Sampling bias A source of error that arises when the sample is not representative of the population that the researcher wants to study.

Scalloped response pattern The phenomenon in which responses are slow in the beginning of the interval and faster just before reinforcement happens. It occurs as a result of a fixed-interval schedule.

Schema A mental model of an object or event that includes knowledge about it as well as beliefs and expectations.

Schizoid personality disorder A disorder characterized by social withdrawal and restricted expression of emotions.

Schizophrenia A disorder involving a loss of contact with reality and symptoms that may include some of the following: hallucinations, delusions, disorganized speech or behavior, emotional flatness, social withdrawal, decreased richness of speech, and lack of motivation.

Scientific method   A standardized way of making observations, gathering data, forming theories, testing predictions, and interpreting results.

Secondary process thinking   Thinking that is logical and rational.

Secondary punisher   In operant conditioning, a consequence that is unpleasant because it has become associated with a primary punisher. It is also called a *conditioned punisher*.

Secondary reinforcer   In operant conditioning, a consequence that is satisfying because it has become associated with a primary reinforcer. It is also called a *conditioned reinforcer*.

Secondary sex characteristics   Sex-specific physical traits that are not essential to reproduction, such as breasts, widened hips, facial hair, and deepened voices.

Sedatives   Drugs that slow down the nervous system.

Selective attention   The ability to focus on some pieces of sensory information and ignore others.

Selective serotonin reuptake inhibitors (SSRIs)   A class of antidepressant drugs that increase the level of serotonin.

Self-actualization   The need to realize one's full potential. According to Maslow, this is human beings' highest need, which arises after the satisfaction of more basic needs.

Self-concept   According to Rogers, the most important feature of personality. The self-concept includes all the thoughts, feelings, and beliefs people have about themselves.

Self-effacing bias   The tendency of people in certain cultures to attribute their successes to situational factors rather than to personal attributes and to attribute their failures to lack of effort.

Self-efficacy   Confidence in one's ability to meet challenges effectively.

Self-help groups   Groups that are similar to therapy groups except that they do not have a therapist.

Self-report data   Information that people being surveyed give about themselves.

Self-report inventory   A paper-and-pen test that requires people to answer questions about their typical behavior.

Self-serving bias The tendency to attribute successes to internal factors and failures to situational factors.

Semantic encoding A way of encoding verbal information that emphasizes the meaning of words.

Semantic memory Remembering of general facts.

Semantic slanting A way of making statements so that they will evoke specific emotional responses.

Semicircular canals Three fluid-filled tubes that are the main structures in the vestibular system. They are located in the inner ear.

Sensation Occurs when physical energy from objects in the world or in the body stimulates the sense organs.

Sensory adaptation The decrease in sensitivity to an unchanging stimulus.

Sensory memory A memory system that stores incoming sensory information for an instant.

Separation anxiety The emotional distress babies show when separated from their caregivers.

Serotonin A neurotransmitter involved in sleep, wakefulness, appetite, aggression, impulsivity, sensory perception, temperature regulation, pain suppression, and mood.

Set point A genetically influenced determinant for body weight.

Sex A biological distinction between males and females.

Sexual script A set of implicit rules that allow a person to judge what sexual behavior is appropriate in a given situation.

Sexual selection Process in which females choose their mates based on certain characteristics that will then be passed on to their male offspring.

Shaping In operant conditioning, a procedure in which reinforcement is used to guide a response closer and closer to a desired response.

Short-term memory A memory system that stores a limited amount of information for a brief period.

Signal detection theory A theory used to predict when a weak signal will be detected.

Similarity The tendency to group similar objects together.

Simplicity The tendency to perceive forms as simple, symmetrical figures rather than as irregular ones.

Single-blind A procedure in which subjects don't know whether they are in an experimental or control group.

Sixteen Personality Factor Questionnaire (16PF) A test that assesses sixteen basic dimensions of personality.

Skinner box A device used to study operant conditioning.

Sleep apnea A condition in which a person stops breathing many times during a night's sleep.

Sleep spindles Short bursts of brain waves that occur during stage 2 sleep.

Smooth muscles Involuntary muscles that help organs such as the stomach and bladder carry out their functions.

Social clocks Social and cultural norms that indicate the typical ages at which people experience particular life events, behaviors, and issues.

Social desirability bias The tendency of some people to describe themselves in socially approved ways.

Social exchange theory A theory arguing that people help each other because they want to gain as much as possible while losing as little as possible.

Social facilitation The tendency for individuals to perform better in the presence of other people.

Social loafing The reduced effort people invest in a task when they are working with other people.

Social norms Societal rules about appropriate behavior.

Social phobia A disorder characterized by intense anxiety when exposed to certain kinds of social or performance situations.

Social responsibility norm A societal rule that tells people they should help others who need help even if doing so is costly.

Social roles Patterns of behavior that are considered appropriate for a person in a particular context.

Social schemas Mental models that represent and categorize social events and people.

Social skills training A behavioral therapy that aims to enhance a client's relationships with other people.

Social trap A situation in which one harms oneself and others by acting in one's self-interest.

Soma The central area of a neuron; also called the *cell body*.

Somatic nervous system The part of the peripheral nervous system that is connected to the skeletal muscles and sense organs.

Somatization disorder A disorder characterized by a wide variety of physical symptoms, such as pain and gastrointestinal, sexual, and pseudoneurological problems. The disorder begins before age thirty and continues for many years. It is also called *hysteria* or *Briquet's syndrome*.

Somatoform disorders Disorders characterized by real physical symptoms that cannot be fully explained by a medical condition, the effects of a drug, or another mental disorder.

Sound waves Changes in pressure generated by vibrating molecules.

Source amnesia Inaccurate recall of the origin of information in memory. It is also called *source misattribution* or *source monitoring error*.

Specific phobia A disorder in which a person feels intense anxiety when exposed to a particular object or situation.

Spinal cord Connects the brain to the rest of the body.

Spinal reflexes Automatic behaviors that require no input from the brain.

Split-brain surgery A surgical operation in which the corpus callosum is cut, separating the two hemispheres of the brain.

Spontaneous recovery In classical conditioning, the reappearance of an extinguished conditioned response.

Stable attribution An inference that an event or behavior is due to stable, unchanging factors.

Stage A period in development when people show typical behavior patterns and capacities.

Standard deviation A statistic that indicates the degree to which scores vary around the mean of a distribution.

Standardized tests Tests with uniform procedures for administration and scoring.

Standardization The use of uniform procedures when administering and scoring tests.

Standardization sample A large group of people that is representative of the entire population of potential test takers.

States Temporary behaviors or feelings.

Statistical significance The likelihood that a result was not due to chance.

Statistics The analysis and interpretation of numerical data.

Stereotypes Beliefs about people based on their membership in a particular group.

Stimulants Drugs that stimulate the central nervous system.

Stimulus discrimination In classical conditioning, the tendency *not* to have a conditioned response to a new stimulus that's similar to the original conditioned stimulus. In operant conditioning, it's the tendency for a response to happen only when a particular stimulus is present.

Stimulus generalization In classical conditioning, the tendency to respond to a new stimulus as if it's the original conditioned stimulus. In operant conditioning, it's the tendency to respond to a new stimulus as if it's the original discriminative stimulus.

Storage The process of maintaining information in memory.

Strange Situation An experiment devised for studying attachment behavior.

Stress The experience of being threatened by taxing circumstances. It also sometimes refers to circumstances that threaten well-being, to the response people have to threatening circumstances, or to the process of evaluating and coping with threatening circumstances.

Stressors Circumstances or events that are psychologically or physically demanding.

Structural encoding A way of encoding verbal information that emphasizes how words look.

Subject An individual person or animal that a researcher studies.

Subject bias Bias that results from the subject's expectations or the subject's changing of his or her behavior.

Subjective utility The process of making a decision by estimating the personal value of a decision's outcome.

Subjective well-being The perception people have about their happiness and satisfaction with life.

Sublimation A defense mechanism that involves channeling unacceptable thoughts and feelings into socially acceptable behavior.

Substance abuse According to the *DSM*, a maladaptive pattern of drug use that results in repeated negative consequences such as legal, social, work-related, or school-related problems.

Superego The moral component of the personality.

Suprachiasmatic nucleus The main biological clock regulating circadian rhythms of sleep in humans.

Survey A method of getting information about a specific behavior, experience, or event by means of interviews or questionnaires, using several participants.

Survival advantage The outcome of a characteristic that helps an organism to live long enough to reproduce and pass on its genes.

Symbol A sound, gesture, or written character that represents an object, action, event, or idea.

Symbolic thought The ability to represent objects in terms of mental symbols.

Sympathetic nervous system Part of the autonomic nervous system that prepares the body for action and expends energy.

Synapse The junction between the axon of one neuron and the cell body or dendrite of a neighboring neuron.

Synaptic cleft The gap between two cells at a synapse.

Synaptic vesicles Small sacs inside a neuron's terminal buttons, in which neurotransmitters are stored.

Syntax A system of rules that governs how words can be meaningfully arranged to form phrases and sentences.

Systematic densensitization A behavioral treatment that uses counterconditioning to decrease anxiety.

T

Tardive dyskinesia A serious side effect of antipsychotic drugs. It is usually a permanent condition, characterized by involuntary movements.

Telegraphic speech Speech that contains no articles or prepositions.

Temperament Innate personality features or dispositions.

Teratogen An agent such as a virus, a drug, or radiation that can cause deformities in an embryo or fetus.

Terminal buttons Bumps at the end of axons that release neurotransmitters.

Test-retest reliability The ability of a test to produce the same results when given to the same group of people at different times.

Thalamus The part of the brain through which almost all sensory information goes on its way to the cerebrum.

Thematic Apperception Test (TAT) A psychological test that requires people to make up stories about a set of ambiguous pictures. It is often used to measure the need for achievement.

Theory An explanation that organizes separate pieces of information in a coherent way.

Theory of natural selection A theory that explains the process of evolution. It states that inherited characteristics that give an organism a reproductive or survival advantage are passed on more often to future generations than other inherited characteristics.

Therapeutic window The amount of a drug that is required for an effect without toxicity.

Theta waves The type of brain waves present when a person is lightly asleep.

Timbre The particular quality of a sound.

Token economy A behavior modification program based on operant conditioning principles.

Tolerance The need over time for more and more of a drug to get the same effect.

Traits Characteristic behaviors and feelings that are consistent and long lasting.

Transcranial magnetic stimulation (TMS) A noninvasive procedure for treating severe depression that involves stimulation of the brain by means of a magnetic coil.

Transference The process by which clients relate to their psychoanalyst or therapist as they would to important figures in their past.

Transformation Making a series of changes to achieve a specific goal.

Trial and error Trying out different solutions until one works.

Triarchic theory of intelligence A theory proposed by Robert Sternberg that distinguishes among three aspects of intelligence.

Trichromatic theory A theory of color vision that states that there are three different types of cones in the retina, which are sensitive to light of three different wavelengths. It is also called the *Young-Helmholtz theory.*

Tricyclics A class of antidepressant drugs that increase the level of norepinephrine and serotonin.

Twin studies Studies in which researchers examine trait similarities between identical and fraternal twin pairs to figure out whether that trait might be inherited.

Two-factor theory The idea that people's experience of emotion depends on two factors: physiological arousal and the cognitive interpretation of that arousal. When people perceive physiological symptoms of arousal, they look for an environmental explanation of this arousal.

Type A personality A personality type characterized by competitiveness, impatience, time pressure, anger, and hostility.

Type B personality A personality type characterized by relaxed, patient, easygoing, amiable behavior.

U

Ultradian rhythms Biological cycles that occur more than once a day.

Unconditional positive regard A therapist quality that is considered crucial in client-centered therapy. It involves nonjudgmental acceptance of the client.

Unconditioned response A naturally occurring response that happens without previous conditioning.

Unconditioned stimulus A stimulus that evokes an innate response.

Unconscious The part of the mind that contains thoughts, feelings, desires, and memories of which people have no awareness but that can influence people's behavior.

Undifferentiated type A subtype of schizophrenia diagnosed if a patient does not meet criteria for paranoid, disorganized, or catatonic subtypes of schizophrenia.

Unstable attribution An inference that an event or behavior is due to unstable, temporary factors.

V

Validity The ability of a test to measure the characteristic it is supposed to measure.

Values Perceptions of what is important in life.

Variable An event, characteristic, behavior, or condition that researchers measure and study.

Variable-interval schedule A reinforcement schedule in which reinforcement happens after a particular average amount of time.

Variable-ratio schedule A reinforcement schedule in which reinforcement happens after a particular average number of responses.

Vestibular system The sensory system involved in balance.

Vulnerability-stress model The idea that individuals who have a biological vulnerability to a particular disorder will have the disorder only if certain environmental stressors are present.

W

Wavelength The distance between the peaks of waves.

Wernicke's area A part of the brain, in the left temporal lobe, that is involved in understanding language.

Withdrawal symptoms Symptoms such as sweating, nausea, or shakiness that occurs when drug usage ceases.

Womb envy In Karen Horney's view, the discontent and resentment that men experience because of their inability to bear children.

Working memory An active memory system that holds information while it's processed or examined.

Z

Zygote A cell that results from the combination of a sperm cell and an egg during conception.

Index

INDEX

INDEX

INDEX

478

INDEX

INDEX

environmental factors, 250–251, 260
genetic differences among individuals, 248–249
and habits, 250, 260
hormones, 250
and memory, 250, 260
and rich foods, availability of, 250, 260
set point, 248–249
and stress, 250, 260
and taste preferences, 250, 260
Huxley, Andrew, 54
Hypnosis, 131–132, 137, 440
Hypochondriasis, 328, 340, 440
Hypothalamus, 60, 65, 233, 249, 440
Hypothesis, 8, 440
Hysteria, 328

I

Iconic memory, 161, 441
Id, 269, 289, 349, 441
Identity achievement, 85, 89, 441
Identity diffusion, 85, 89, 441
Identity foreclosure, 85, 89, 441
Identity moratorium, 85, 89, 441
Identity vs. role confusion, 71–72, 88
Illusions, 108, 118, 441
  visual, 108–109
Immune system, and stress, 302, 307, 441
Implantation, 77, 441
Implicit attitudes, 388, 441
Implicit memory, 164, 175, 441
Implicit prejudice, 383
Impressions, 378–379
Incentives, 247, 258, 261, 441
Inclusive fitness, 40–41, 44, 441
Incongruence, 280, 355, 441
Independent variable, 16, 441
Individual psychology, 274–275, 290, 442

Inducing structure, 191, 205
Inductive reasoning, 193, 205, 442
Industrial-organizational psychologists, 4
Industry vs. inferiority stage of development, 71–72, 88
Inferential statistics, 25–26, 28, 442
Inferiority complex, 274, 442
Informational social influence, 402, 442
Informed consent, 20, 442
Infradian rhythms, 125, 136, 442
Ingroups, 383–384, 407, 442
Inhibitory postsynaptic potential (PSP), 442
Inhibitory PSP, 55, 64
Initiative vs. guilt, 71–72, 88
Innate abilities, 79, 240, 442
Innate needs, 248, 260
Inner ear, 112–113, 118
Insanity, 316, 338
Insight therapies, 348, 369
Insomnia, 129, 136, 442
Instinctive drift, 151, 154, 442
Insufficient coordination, 402, 409
Insulin, 63, 65, 250, 260, 442
Integrative approaches, to psychotherapy, 356, 442
Integrity vs. despair stage, 71–72, 88
Intelligence, 211–227, 443
  bodily-kinesthetic, 212
  componential, 213
  contextual, 213
  crystallized, 87, 89
  cultural and ethnic differences, 221–222
  defined, 212, 223
  emotional, 213, 223
  environmental influences, 221–222
  experiential, 213
  general intelligence factor (g), 212

heritability of, 219–221
interpersonal, 212
intrapersonal, 212
linguistic, 212
logical–mathematical, 212
musical, 212
nature, 212
psychometric approach to, 213, 456
spatial, 212
testing, 213–218
theories of, 212–213
triarchic theory of, 213
types of, 212
Intelligence quotient (IQ), 214–215, 223, 443
reaction range to, 219
Intelligence tests, 213–218, 223, 458
Binet-Simon scale, 214, 223
biological, 216
characteristics of, 217–218
critical views of, 218
and cultural bias, 217, 223
group intelligence tests, 216, 223
norms and percentile scores, 217–218
reliability, 218
standardization, 217, 223
standardization samples, 218
Stanford-Binet Intelligence Scale, 214, 223
types of, 214
validity, 218, 223
Wechsler Adult Intelligence Scale, 215, 223
Interference, 175, 443
Intermittent reinforcement, 147–148, 154, 443
Internal attribution, 385, 407, 443
Internal locus of control, 301, 443
Interpersonal attraction, 395, 443
Interpersonal factors, mood disorders, 324
Interpersonal intelligence, 212
Interposition, 106

Interpretation, 349–350, 369, 443
Interpretation of Dreams, The (Freud), 415
Interpreting data, 21–25
Interval schedule, 147–148, 443
Intimacy, 397, 408, 443
Intimacy vs. isolation stage of development, 71–72, 88
Intrapersonal intelligence, 212
Intrinsic motivation, 247, 260, 443
of creative people, 202, 206
Ions, 54, 443
IQ tests, *See* Intelligence tests
Iris, 97, 117, 443
Irrelevant information, focusing on, 195, 205
Irreversibility, 73–74, 443

J

James-Lange theory, 230–231, 240, 443
James, William, 230, 416
Jensen, Arthur, 221
Jet lag, 126
Job satisfaction, and happiness, 238, 241
Johnson, Virginia, 252, 260, 417
Jung, Carl, 273–274, 290, 416
Just noticeable difference (jnd), 94, 432
Just world hypothesis, 386–387, 407, 444
Justification of effort, 363, 392, 444

K

Kinesthesis, 115, 119, 444
Kinsey, Alfred, 251, 260, 416
Kinsey's sexual research, 251

Klein, Melanie, 275
Kohlberg, Lawrence, 70, 75–77, 88, 416–417

L

Laboratory observation, 13, 15, 27, 444
Lack of exercise, and disease, 304
Lange, Carl, 230, 416
Language, 204, 444
  ambiguous, 184
  babbling, 183
  biological influences on acquisition of, 185–186
  building blocks of, 182–183
  defined, 182
  development in children, 183
  environmental influences on acquisition of, 184–185
  generative, 182, 204
  metalinguistic awareness, 183
  morphemes, 182–183
  and nonhuman primates, 187–188, 205
  phonemes, 182
  structure of, 182–183
  symbols, 182
  syntax, 183
  telegraphic speech, 183
  theories of acquisition, 184–187, 204
  and Washoe the chimpanzee, 187
Language acquisition device (LAD), 185, 204
Latency stage, psychosexual development, 272–273
Latent content, 129, 136, 444
Lateral hypothalamus, 249, 260
Lateralization, 61, 65, 444
Law of effect, 145, 444
Lazarus, Richard, 232, 417
Learned helplessness, 323–324, 339, 444
Learned needs, 248, 260
Learning, 141–157, 444
  defined, 141

Learning factors, somatoform disorders, 329
Learning model, 315, 338, 444
Learning psychology, 2
Learning theory, attitudes, 391, 408
Left hemisphere, brain, 61, 65
Lens, 98, 117, 444
Leptin, 250, 260, 444
Lesioning, 58, 65, 445
Lewin, Kurt, 384, 417
Lie detector, 234–235, 240
Lie scales, 445
Light, 96, 117, 445
  adaptation to, 99
  complexity, 96
  ultraviolet, 97
  white, 97
Light adaptation, 99, 117, 445
Light and shadow, 106
Light intensity, 445
Limbic system, 60, 65, 232, 445
Linear perspective, 106
Linguistic intelligence, 212
Linguistic relativity hypothesis, 186, 204, 445
Link method, 170, 445
Lithium, 360, 371, 445
Lobotomy, 362, 371, 445
Location constancy, 108, 118
Loci, method of, 170, 447
Locus of control, 301, 445
Loftus, Elizabeth, 173, 417
Logical–mathematical intelligence, 212
Long-term memory, 162, 175, 445
Long-term potentiation, 171, 445
Lost memories, 163
Loudness, 111–112, 118
Lowball technique, 393, 408, 445
Low-calcium diet, and disease, 304
Low-fiber diets, and disease, 304

Murray, Charles, 221
Musical intelligence, 212
Mutations, 41, 44, 448
Myelin, role of, 54
Myelin sheath, 53, 64, 448

N

Name calling, 186–187, 204, 448
Narcissistic personality disorder,
   336, 342, 448
Narcolepsy, 129, 136, 448
Narcotics, 132–133, 135, 137,
   448
Nardil, 358
Narrative methods, 170, 448
Naturalistic observation, 8, 13,
   15, 27, 448
Natural selection, theory of, 39–
   40, 44
Nature intelligence, 212
Nearsightedness, 98
Needs:
   hierarchy of, 246–248
   types of, 248
Negative correlation, 11–12, 449
Negatively skewed distribution,
   24, 449
Negative punishment, 146, 153,
   449
Negative reinforcement, 145,
   153, 449
Negative symptoms, 449
Neo-Freudians, 273
NEO Personality Inventory, 286,
   291, 449
Nerves, 53, 449
Nervous system, 49, 64, 449
   central, 50–51
   peripheral, 51–52
Neural networks, 204
Neurons, 52–56, 64, 118, 449
   communication between, 54–56
Neuropsychologists, 4

Neuroticism, 267, 289
   and anxiety disorders, 321, 339
Neurotransmitters, 53, 56–57,
   64, 319, 449
   agonists, 57
   antagonists, 57
   and mood disorders, 323
   and schizophrenia, 333, 341
Nicotine, and receptors, 57
Nocturnal emissions, 84, 449
Nonconformity, of creative
   people, 202, 206
Nonhuman primates:
   and language, 187–188, 205
   skepticism about ape language, 188
   Washoe the chimpanzee, 187
Norepinephrine, 57, 63, 64, 235,
   323, 449
Normal distribution, 215, 223,
   449
Normative social influence, 402,
   449
Norms, 14, 217–218, 223, 449
   cultural, 39, 241, 331
   developmental, 79
   ethical, 27
   psychological tests, 217–218, 223
   reciprocity, 405
   social responsibility, 405, 409
Nucleotides, 34, 449

O

Obedience, 398–400, 409, 450
   factors that increase, 399–400
   Milgram's obedience study, 398–
   399
Objective personality tests, 285,
   291, 450
   Minnesota Multiphasic Personality
   Inventory (MMPI), 285–286, 291
   NEO Personality Inventory, 286,
   291
   Sixteen Personality Factor
   Questionnaire (16PF), 286, 291
Object permanence, 73, 450
Object relations, 290, 450

INDEX

INDEX

INDEX